THE

OBAMA

CONFESSION

Secret Fear. Secret Fury.

Andrew G. Hodges, M.D.

Village House Publishers

The Obama Confession
Secret Fear. Secret Fury.
Copyright © 2012 by Andrew G. Hodges, M.D.
All Rights Reserved

First Edition

Cover Design: Kim McKimmon (Bowe Creative Group)
www.bowecreativegroup.com
Interior Formatting: Ellen C. Maze, The Author's Mentor,
www.theauthorsmentor.com
Author Website: www.andrewghodges.com

Village House Publishers
Birmingham, AL
ISBN: 0-9617255-4-0
Also available in eBook publication

PRINTED IN THE UNITED STATES OF AMERICA

Dedication

To "the Laws of Nature, and of Nature's God."

The Declaration of Independence
United States of America
July 4, 1776

Also from Andrew G. Hodges

Jesus: An Interview Across Time
(A Psychiatrist Looks at His Humanity)

The Deeper Intelligence
(The Breakthrough to the Untapped Potential of Your Subconscious Mind)

A Mother Gone Bad
(The Hidden Confession of JonBenet's Killer)

Who Will Speak for JonBenet?
(A New Investigator Reads Between the Lines)

Into The Deep
(The Hidden Confession of Natalee's Killer)

Foreword

The year is 1994. I can envision Dr. Richard Halverson, esteemed chaplain of the United States Senate opening the august body of our elected senators with his usual eloquence in prayer—brief and profound. A gifted communicator, a man who was known throughout America as the distinguished pastor of Fourth Presbyterian Church in Washington, D.C. before becoming Senate chaplain— one reason he was carefully chosen to represent the Senate to invoke God's blessings daily. It was a long tradition—asking God the Overseer to continue to look out for America.

I'd met Dr. Halverson a few years before and was impressed with his thoughtfulness about another book I had written. He had sent several copies to friends. When I wrote a second book in 1994 I sent it to him and inquired if he might say an encouraging word about it. As a psychiatrist explaining an important new discovery about the workings of the mind, I thought he might encourage others to consider a new "outside the box" idea which had spiritual implications. I was somewhat shocked but thrilled by his comments. He had caught on to the new science of the mind—and then some.

He asked me if I would inscribe a copy of the book for President and Mrs. Clinton and a few senators, a task which I was glad to do. In fact, I later received thank-you notes from some of these powerful men and women whose respect for Halverson was apparent.

Here is what he had to say about my book which doubled as a message to President Clinton who Halverson knew desperately needed the knowledge.

> It is as if God planned this book for this crucial moment in time. Secularism, having ravaged our culture, is now exhausted. At a time when feelings often replace facts as a foundation for faith—as social/cultural order disintegrates and alienation fragments—as moral and spiritual anarchy threatens chaos, The Deeper Intelligence by Dr. Andrew Hodges brings us face to face with reality, transcendent and profoundly temporal. He addresses us with a healing message which is reconciling, restorative, and renewing.

Dr. Halverson had served as a counselor, both formally and informally, to many of our nation's leaders. From close up, he saw how our leaders think, detected their blind spots, and thus gained had a unique view of America and the direction in which it was heading

Obviously Dr. Halverson recognized how the unveiling of the human psyche's vastly superior deeper intelligence (which I now call the super intelligence) represented a tremendous advancement in knowledge about ourselves. A true paradigm shift. He was impressed by how it intuitively tried to guide us in wiser directions than our conscious minds ever did.

In particular he saw the failure of our cultural shift to a situational secular moral compass and grasped that the super intelligence discovery was a rediscovery of our founders' original moral compass in a fresh new way. He realized that—rather than being repressive—the moral code which underlies all civilizations is truly health-giving. That unlike our selfish surface minds, our subconscious possessed an inner genius motivated by a clear morality.

Think about it—Richard Halverson believed the discovery of the new "guiding" unconscious was cutting-edge knowledge which could be of value to the president of the United States as well as senators and congressmen. His message to them was the same which the super intelligence delivers to everyone: 'Gentlemen, we are in a whole new day and age of information which can benefit us all.'

The Deeper Intelligence had limited success, but it was a first step. New ways of thinking always must overcome difficulties.

Yet the knowledge that this super intelligence exists just below the surface of our conscious minds has slowly made its way in the world. The awareness of a "dazzling new unconscious" which reads situations in the blink of an eye has been popularized by a prominent author I mention in the book. And I developed a new forensic profiling approach based on listening to guilty perpetrators whose super intelligence insisted on confessing.

This attracted national attention in several major criminal cases and one national television host asked me if I could possibly read President Clinton's unconscious regarding the Monica Lewinsky scandal which had become front page news. When I studied a speech he had written, I found a key confession, so I did so.

Ironically, five years after Dr. Halverson had taken Bill Clinton a copy of my book, I would end up on national television reporting on the president's own super-intel messages explaining why he had lied to the American people and to himself over the Lewinsky affair. Unknowingly, he explained the deep pain that secretly drove him.

So now I come to another man who has been elected president, Barack Obama. Like Clinton, Obama has presented America with an unconscious super-intel confession of far greater magnitude. And he has revealed, like Clinton, that his misguided ways are secretly motivated by deep emotional pain.

In that light, when all is said and done, Dr. Halverson speaks posthumously in a very real way. I am certain he would say the same thing about this book; that God meant it for this day and age; that God reserved this breakthrough knowledge, revealed unconsciously by Obama's own hidden confession, to point America back to its true moral compass. (I am implying Dr. Halverson's endorsement of our deeper moral compass discovery not my views on Obama.)

Obama's revelations will shock you. They will challenge your imagination to realize that a man could become president under such circumstances. No matter how stunning, however, his revelations are all true. Like any man who has engaged in serious deception, Obama has a desperate need to confess. And the truth therein can certainly set us free.

Table of Contents

Introduction

In 2002, following a head injury after he suffered a concussion in a severe mugging, college dropout and party boy Jason Padgett suddenly became a mathematical genius of unbelievable proportions with talents unlike any other person in the world. With no interest or previous training in mathematics, Padgett suddenly began seeing patterns of mathematical formulae in the various shapes in nature all around him. As he describes it, "I see bits and pieces of the Pythagorean theorem everywhere. Every single little curve, every single little spiral, every tree is part of that equation." Possessing no prior art talent Jason suddenly began to draw intricate diagrams from what he saw in nature—perfect geometric shapes called "fractals"—but did not understand what he was drawing. He had to learn, after the fact, the mathematical equations—e.g., the Pythagorean theorem—reflected in his drawings. Today he is the only person in the world who can draw these "fractals" by hand instead of using a computer.

Jason's phenomenal ability prompted the curiosity of mathematicians and quantum physics experts from around the world. Research brain scans done in Finland reveal that Padgett's brain damage had caused his brain to overcompensate in areas that deal with math and mental imagery, regions of the brain most people cannot access. Officially he was then called an "acquired savant"–one scientist called him "superhuman." But really Padgett is an accidental genius who has tapped into the phenomenal potential in the human mind.

This story about the miraculous result of a head injury is really not a miracle per se; in fact it reveals that there is an inner genius—in all of us—far more brilliant than we might think. This is an area of the mind which I have researched clinically for the last 30 years.

The story also fits Barack Obama in some striking ways. Obama experienced a shocking unexpected event (a major emotional trauma) at a crucial point in his early development which caused him to tap into a deeper level of his mind and tell us his story in a creative unique way, 'between the lines.' In effect we can consider that Obama was stunned early in his life, and then suddenly his brilliant inner genius ends up speaking to America—albeit in code—as its president in the twenty-first century. For reasons I will explain in chapters to come, we can think of Obama overcompensating and using the right-brain part of his mind more to describe unconscious things.

Along these lines, Obama's story and his inner genius also remind me of a recent Meryl Streep interview on Fox News Channel's "Huckabee Show" regarding her movie role as Margaret Thatcher in Iron Lady. Streep commented how she had learned that Thatcher was a complex character—as we all are—which surprised her at first. Huckabee then observed how he appreciated Meryl Streep's creative efforts—which he called the 'right brain' artistic side of us. He noted personally that without the right-brain side of him— speaking of his creative musical inclinations—he would have been lost in his development.

Both observations link to Obama. He is a complex person with two striking sides to him and he will tell us all about it in a right-brain communication method. In a nutshell this inner genius, which I call the super intelligence, communicates always in a right-brain, symbolic language.

Obama will reveal that we all look at things in a deeper way. We are all much more familiar with this than we realize. We see secret communication between the lines, in hidden language patterns, all the time. Take the following common example.

Looking in the mirror

We've all had the experience of listening to someone going on and on about another person's shortcomings. They'll regale us with a litany of incidents supporting their conclusion. Then they walk away, and we think, You're talking about yourself without knowing it. In reality, we've heard them tell us their story. Freud called it 'projection.' Jesus put it more poetically: "Why do you see the speck that is in your brother's eye, but do not notice the log that is in your own eye?"

Obviously our friend talking about others was—at the moment—in total denial about himself, but he was simultaneously showing us the precise way around that denial. We need to understand why and how his stories are really about him. When our friend describes the negative consequences of his neighbor's bad behavior, he suggests that deep down, he recognizes the destructive effects of his own faults. Secretly, our friend's own "right brain" mind—his own inner genius—is symbolically, figuratively talking about himself when he consciously thinks he's only referring to his neighbor.

Keep this in mind as we explore Barack Obama's untold story—a story you've never heard before. We must understand that we all have a story to tell, and we always tell it—with our words and actions. Just like us, Barack Obama has told his own story repeatedly—not explicitly, but between the lines.

The first thing we will learn is that our own 'heart of hearts' is not what we think it is. We often hear someone say "in my heart of hearts," but they can't speak for it directly because of the natural tendency for denial. We really don't see our own heart of hearts as we think we do. Truth be told, our heart of hearts is deeper, more revealing and a far more powerful storyteller than our surface mind could ever be. It reveals the true passion and power in our lives. It speaks of the power of our role models—for good or bad—and what they built into us.

As we shall see, Barack Obama had emotionally powerful role models during his bitterly conflicted childhood, a childhood we can scarcely comprehend today without a deeper look. This book constitutes a different, deeper look at his intense and indelible life struggle.

We will listen to Obama's story as he unknowingly delivers it. We will listen to his hints and we'll use those hints to put Obama's story together. We will gradually see that for many years this man has been trying to tell his secret story to us, virtually every day, in a coded form.

It's safe to say you and I have never before heard a story like Barack Obama's, and it's safe to say Obama hasn't heard it either, even though he himself has been telling it—repeatedly.

Some of you will not want to hear Obama's true story. Many will stubbornly refuse to hear it; they will fight as hard as they can in resisting its truths, just as they dispute their own true life stories. But erstwhile brave readers will listen—and learn.

I urge you to open your mind as I unpack Obama's own words, as he tells us his true life story. For now, let's simply listen.

1

Obama Predicts His Assault on America

It was the middle of the night when the phone rang in the doctors' quarters in the hospital. As I roused myself from a deep sleep, I was momentarily disoriented—a familiar experience by then. I was an intern covering pediatrics and the charge nurse on the unit was calling to alert me to a "no code." A young patient had died. She needed me to officially pronounce the patient deceased and sign the death certificate. I would also meet with the family, something I had had to do more than once.

Shortly I entered the patient's room to find the emaciated body of a fourteen-year-old kid who looked even younger and who had finally succumbed to the ravages of acute leukemia. Since he'd finally failed to respond to any treatment, his family went home for the night knowing it was only a matter of time, but the end came—mercifully—sooner than expected. His great suffering was obvious. His arms were black and blue from multiple IVs, his skin pale beyond belief. He couldn't have weighed seventy-five pounds.

By the time I had finished documenting the event, the family—having been notified by a phone call from the nurse—had hastily gathered in the small room reserved for private meetings with doctors at such times. Opening the door, I immediately faced the mother and father sitting on a small sofa surrounded by eight or so family members—older siblings, aunts and uncles—who all knew why we were meeting. Reassuringly as possible, I told the parents, "Johnny passed away about 30 minutes ago. I know you've been through a lot, but now his suffering is over and he's in a better place." Seemingly undaunted by the news, the mother asked me if I would give Johnny something for his cough. I wondered if the words "passed away" had simply gone over her head. So I gently repeated myself, "I'm sorry, but Johnny just died thirty minutes ago." Without the slightest pause, the mother now urgently replied, "But doctor, are you going to give him something for his cough?" She simply could not face the loss of her son. It had overwhelmed her. At that point the family members assured me they would handle the problem, and I left having experienced one of the most shocking events in my life. A night I will never forget.

Looking back, the story made it clear that there are two types of people: **hearers and non-hearers**, seers and non-seers, those who face emotional trauma and those who don't—and nobody faces it perfectly. Emotional trauma leads to denial, the greater the trauma the more the denial. And in this mother's story we see the power of denial up close and personal. Let's be clear—it was denial of reality—a sad reality which failed to escape others in the room.

Shifting to America

America today is on the brink of a similar tragedy. Some people—like the mother living in massive denial—simply cannot face it, and instead they distract themselves with minor concerns. To those people America simply suffers a mild cough which can quickly be cured, while others plainly see America in dire straits, on the brink of real disaster, suffering a crisis that threatens our national life. It's a shocking story, unlike anything in our history.

Moving America's Secure Boundaries

America finds itself in a crisis which can be directly traced to President Barack Obama's drastic modifications of our nation's longstanding foundations of government. He has changed these fundamental stabilizers to suit himself, yet he and his supporters remain in massive denial of that reality.

The boundaries set by a president are much like those set by a parent. Strong boundaries create the firm frameworks that hold individuals, families, and nations together. Without those boundaries, individuals, families, and nations become weak and ineffectual. Attack the foundations and you destroy individuals, families, *and* nations. Powerful emotions can be expressed by actions—by changing fundamental boundaries— without saying a word. In fact, such actions can even *betray* our words as Obama often demonstrates by saying one thing and doing another.

For example, during the election year 2012, he announced he'd soon be approving permits for several nuclear power plants—the first such approvals in 30 years.[1] Yet the truth of the matter was that he had already canceled development in 2009 of the needed Yucca Mountain (Nevada) storage site for the radioactive waste from the power plants which meant the plants couldn't be built. All along he knew his promise of such plants and boosting America's energy production was an empty one.[2]

Many times we don't initially see the reality right in front of us—it takes time to break through to us. Although we know that someone's words can fool us, we remain too trusting. Even though, from the get-go, Obama was not the least bit subtle about changing things dramatically, millions of us refused to acknowledge the reality of his manipulations. Now, more than three years into his presidency, Obama has provided us a hearty dose of harsh reality, and Americans finally see what he has done. They grasp that Barack Hussein

---

1 Steven Mufson, "NRC approves construction of new nuclear power reactors in Georgia," http://www.washingtonpost.com/business/economy/nrc-approves-construction-of-new-nuclear-power-reactors-in-georgia/2012/02/09/gIQA36wv1Q_story.html accessed 15 April, 2012.
2 "Yucca Mountain nuclear waste repository," http://en.wikipedia.org/wiki/Yucca_Mountain_nuclear_waste_repository accessed April 15 , 2012.

Obama—supposedly our teacher-leader—has undercut America's fundamental foundations weakening our nation in numerous ways. But millions of other Americans continue in denial—and so does Obama.

"You Can't Handle the Truth."

There is a striking parallel between Obama's denial and the powerful denial demonstrated by a major character, an American military leader, in an award-winning movie. In the climactic scene of *A Few Good Men*, Jack Nicholson portrays self-righteous Marine Corps Colonel Nathan Jessep, commander of a military base at Cuba's Guantanamo Bay. Jessep had taken the witness stand to testify about an illegal harassment he had ordered of a weak soldier. That "Code Red" had led to the young soldier's death. When a trial lawyer, played by Tom Cruise, insists that he wants to hear the whole truth of the matter, Colonel Jessep, smugly pausing as only Nicholson can, glared at the counselor with utter contempt and finally spewed, "You can't handle the truth!"

But in the end it was Colonel Jessep, the military commander, who couldn't handle the truth. As his testimony concluded, he admitted that he had indeed ordered the illegal harassment—for the good of the country to weed out weak soldiers. Colonel Jessep couldn't see that his self-deception undermined core American values of protection and truth. Instead, he moved the boundary markers to suit himself. At that exact moment, certain he was doing the right thing, he secretly endorsed enormous destruction—the taking of a human life, and then he covered it up. Out of his love for power, blind to the meaning of his actions, blind to the reality that he relocated the boundaries, he rationalized his destructive behavior as love for America.

All the officers under his leadership had likewise followed him in denial—just as Obama supporters have joined in *his* denial.

Yet some citizens increasingly see past this destructive denial. Commentators and citizens are saying it one after the other: Obama is destroying America before our very eyes.

Never before have Americans realized how rapidly a president can unilaterally bring the United States to its knees. Obama is playing fast and loose with the rule of law as he imposes his radical agenda, willingly enabled by a sycophantic "yes-man" Congress (for two years, before the 2010 mid-terms restored some semblance of balance) and a continually doting mainstream media. Never in their worst nightmares could citizens have envisioned a president whom they experience as an enemy of this great nation, but, in essence, that's what he has become. Obama exerts his power over hundreds of millions of Americans, leaving them feeling overwhelmed, hoping they can somehow slow down the train wreck.

Doubt it not; this was what the Tea Party movement was all about—a reaction to Obama's "shock and awe" attack on America. And, for the record, the protest movement underscores the sad, blatant denial of the mainstream media to the reality of this increasingly out-of-control president. But African-American conservative columnist Thomas Sowell sees the president for who he is. Sowell speaks for many when he writes, "Barack Obama has brought more destruction upon this country in four years than any other event in the history of our nation, but it is just the beginning of what he and his comrades are capable of."[3]

Economically Out of Bounds

In decision after decision, this president has consistently disrupted America's secure economic boundaries—leading us to the brink of bankruptcy. He's radically raising the national debt, implementing multiple wasteful stimulus programs, creating a shockingly expensive health-care plan, and only postponing his plan to raise taxes short-term while Americans remain stung by recession and soaring unemployment. He's consistently increasing entitlements, inexorably edging America toward socialism (a record 44.5 million Americans are on Food Stamps as of March 2012)[4]. His administration has over-regulated business and has proposed increasing taxes on "the wealthy," a move which will surely hurt job creation, since it's successful Americans who own small businesses.

His energy policy—a vital part of a sound economy—seriously weakens America economically. Here he attacks our independence and ingenuity with excessive restrictions—preventing our drilling for oil and natural gas, refusing to approve the Keystone pipeline from Canada also creating thousands of jobs, and developing plans to cripple the coal industry. In short, he has erected an "off-limits" barrier around our strength: natural energy resources. The result forces more dependency on foreign oil which inevitably pushes gasoline costs higher. Just like Col. Jessep, Obama is manipulating the boundaries—with a resultant sapping of our national strength.

The cost in jobs is staggering. Obama's radical environmentalism (through the Interior Department) *"has put our employment potential in irons…this administration is pursuing unemployment, both in the Gulf and nationally,"* said Jim Adams, president of the Offshore Marine Service Administration.[5] Instead of real energy he offers us "green energy"—and "green" it is, untried and unreliable, mostly insignificant at this point. Obama also supports rapidly growing government unions which are bankrupting state economies. One observer commented, "Government unions are the backbone of the Obama dependency economy."[6]

3 Letter to editor quoting Sowell, *Knoxville News-Sentinel*, October, 17, 2011.
http://m.knoxnews.com/news/2011/oct/17/letter-occupy-example-obamas-america/
4 Huma Kahn, "Congress Mulls Cuts to Food Stamps Program Amid Record Number of Recipients,"
http://abcnews.go.com/blogs/politics/2011/05/congress-mulls-cuts-to-food-stamps-program-amid-record-number-of-recipients/ accessed April 15, 2012.
5 "Salazar's War on Jobs," *Human Events*, June 13, 2011, pp. 12-13.
6 Unattributed item in *The Morning Bell*, Heritage Foundation, February 16, 2011.

After America attempted to correct his radical economic plans in the 2010 mid-term elections by voting out many of his congressional supporters, Obama basically turned a deaf ear. After the people had spoken, he added a wasteful stimulus to his tax compromise bill. He extended expensive unemployment benefits to two years. Most strikingly the federal spending plans he presented to Congress in 2011 and 2012 each called for more than a $3 trillion budget, adding trillions to our river of red ink, in complete denial of our unsupportable national debt. Congress steadfastly refused to approve Obama's budgets.

Obama Intuitively Predicts His Economic Assault—and Others?
In his inaugural address of January 20, 2009 (which will be referred to herein as "ISp"), Obama prophetically describes—in an implied criticism of the prior administration —the exact behavior and consequences he will exhibit as president. We start with economics, "Our economy is badly weakened, a consequence of …irresponsibility on the part of some…our collective failure to make hard choices and prepare the nation for a new age. Homes have been lost; jobs shed; businesses shuttered. Our health care is too costly…And those of us who manage the public's dollars will be held to account to spend wisely, reform bad habits." (ISp)
In short, Obama sees the "speck [or fault] in the eye" of others while remaining in classic denial about the "log in his own eye"—good old projection. Indirectly he predicted the new age of destructive Obamanomics including costly Obamacare.
Another comment in the same speech reflects the identical denial and a secret picture of the Obama presidency, "The question we ask today is…whether our government…works…whether it helps families find jobs at a decent wage." (ISp) Unaware, he points precisely toward the predictable result of his own economic plans: widespread unemployment. He suggests that deep down he intuitively recognizes the exact effects of his destructiveness.

Out-of-Bounds Foreign Policy
Things are even more ominous on the world stage. With one ill-advised foreign-policy decision after another, Obama carelessly gambles with our nation's safety. He fails to ensure our most basic boundary—national security. In his inauguration speech, again alluding to the prior administration, he presents a classic denial and future picture of the Obama presidency: *"Each day brings further evidence that the ways we use energy strengthen our adversaries and threaten our planet."* Intuitively Obama alerts us that he will use his energy to continually strengthen our enemies and suggests that abundant evidence of that fact will surface—which indeed it has.
Astute observers see a character weakness in Obama—he fundamentally lacks something solid inside—which strengthens our enemies. Thomas Sowell observed Obama's constant waffling, especially in his tough talk over Iran,

tough talk but weak actions. Sowell commented, "The track record of Obama's pronouncements on a wide range of issues suggests that anything he says is *a message written in sand*, and easily blown away by the next political winds." A sandman president who writes in sand, nothing solid, nothing America can count on, as we should be able to count on from our president.[7] Keep this image of a "sandman" in mind.

Obama's delayed, half-hearted efforts to curtail Iran's nuclear weapons development during his presidency have been labeled "naive" and "mindless" by foreign-policy experts. Iran's nuclear initiative threatens Israel, the entire Middle East and indeed the whole world.[8] In March 2012 Israel Prime Minister Benjamin Netanyahu made plain his nation will not tolerate Iran's continual development of a nuclear bomb. Iran's expressed goal is the total annihilation of Israel. If and when Iran develops its bomb, Israel will surely launch a pre-emptive strike, which could easily escalate into a regional—or even worldwide—nuclear conflagration.

Despite his tough talk, Obama has allowed Iran's strength to increase. Privately he urged Netanyahu to shelve plans for military action. Instead of joining forces, Obama seems ready to let Israel go it alone. He made it harder for Israel to attack by committing again and again to lengthy open-ended negotiations with Iran—"giving peace another chance." He added, "I don't bluff," suggesting that is *precisely* what he is doing. *By the way, a key way of understanding Obama's true intentions is to simply read through his denials— here his true meaning is "I am bluffing."* In fact, Obama has a long history of pro-Palestinian favoritism.

After Obama's 2008 election two important authors (David Limbaugh in *Crimes Against Liberty: an Indictment Against President Barach Obama*, and Dinesh D'Souza in *The Roots of Obama's Rage*) emphatically underscored how Obama's policies and "blind spots" leave America vulnerable to an eventual nuclear attack. Yet even these two astute commentators can only go so far, lacking the ability to read Obama's deeper mind—as we shall see.

Obama completely ignored an opportunity to overthrow the radical Iranian regime by failing to support citizen protests in 2009—another example of how he's enabling Iran's strength. On the other hand, he freely encouraged civil unrest in Egypt—a risky move, potentially encouraging takeover by radical Muslims. In September 2011, Obama staff members met privately in Washington with members of the Society of the Muslim Brothers a.k.a. the Muslim Brotherhood.[9] Obama himself personally addressed Brotherhood members in Cairo in June 2009.[10]

---

7 Thomas Sowell, "Obama's Tough Talk on Iran May Be Too Late," *Birmingham News,* March 9, 2012,
8 Including former United Nations Ambassador John Bolton, "On the Record," Fox News Channel, August 6, 2010.
9 "Muslim Brotherhood Granted 'Direct Access' to Taxpayer's Stimulus Grants by Obama!," January 30, 2011, by Volubrjotr, http://politicalvelcraft.org.
10 David Ignatius, "Obama's Muslim Brotherhood Gamble," *The Korea Herald,* February 19, 2012.

The assassination of Osama bin Laden has taken the focus off Obama's misguided foreign policies only for the moment. After Navy Seals executed bin Laden on May 2, 2011, Obama showed his true colors by releasing vital "special ops" information about the secret mission to our enemies thus compromising future missions. Such behavior harkens back to the early days of Obama's administration when he discontinued enhanced-interrogation techniques (so-called 'water boarding' and other effective techniques) on terrorist prisoners. The CIA supported such interrogations because the information gathered greatly protected America after 9/11. But Obama remained unmoved—even after five former CIA directors, including Obama appointee Leon Panetta, recommended continuing the vital programs. The president's actions continue to undermine America's security.[11]

Obama's idea "to reduce [our] nuclear weapons to set a moral example for the rest of the world...is simply childish" and dangerously unrealistic, according to columnist Charles Krauthammer—with rogue nations such as Iran and North Korea enhancing their nuclear threat.[12] And Obama's handling of Islamic terrorism—refusing to even use the term even after several attacks by radicals on Americans—suggests massive denial. He also delayed sending more troops to Afghanistan, and then set time limits on its occupation while handicapping the military with limited rules of engagement. Obama's pattern of torpedoing our legitimate national security efforts continues—all while he seems, on the surface, to be a fairly vigorous Commander-in-Chief.

To make matters worse, Obama continually degrades America in speeches around the world, apologizing "for America's arrogance" and minimizing American Exceptionalism (the theory that the USA is unique and special in world political history—not without fault, certainly, but that we are special, given our unique founding, and against the backdrop of the history of other nations—for example, the failed experiment of Communism behind the Iron Curtain).

Another Arrogant Misstep

Our weakened foreign policy grew more troublesome when Obama's Defense Secretary Leon Panetta appeared before the Congressional Armed Services Committee in March 2012. He declared that he and the president planned to avoid asking Congress for approval of deploying military forces abroad—but instead look to international organizations such as the United Nations or NATO to lend "legal authority" to their actions. *"We would...come to the Congress and inform you and determine how best to approach this, whether or not we would want to get permission from the Congress—I think those are issues we would have to discuss."*[13]

---

11 Marc Thiessen, *Courting Disaster,* (Washington, DC: Regnery, 2011). pp. 11-15.
12 Charles Krauthammer, *Birmingham News*, November 27, 2010.
13 The American Spectator, March 12, 2012, http://spectator.org/archives/2012/03/12/leon-panetta-clueless-or-braze

Andrew G. Hodges, M.D.

In one fell swoop Obama had not only again completely ignored Congress in the crucial matter of foreign policy and war but handed over control of our military to the United Nations. Indirectly he raises the question, do we secretly have an international president already in office?

To continue the farce, Obama shortly ignored the needs of the rebels in Syria for support after Saudi Arabia, Turkey and France already had assisted them in various ways. He insisted that we couldn't act without the approval of the international community—translated, the U.N. Security Council where Russia and China possess a permanent veto and thus now control our foreign policy.[14] Speaking of strengthening our enemies and sabotaging America—how blatant must Obama's behavior become before we see his true intentions?

Moving Societal Boundaries: Favoritism

Obama issued another severe warning—again in his inaugural address—that favoritism will quickly lead to America's decline, "A nation cannot prosper long when it favors only the prosperous." Then he again demonstrates complete "log in his eye" denial with excessive favoritism, starting with the unions. He's blind to the true principle of the matter: favoritism of any group of people sends a great nation downhill. Yet we can see Obama's destructive class warfare taking shape, in stark opposition to the principle he consciously states.

More Favoritism—Overt Racism

Soon after he was inaugurated, Obama publicly criticized a white policeman for arresting a black Harvard professor, and apparently instructed his Attorney General not to prosecute Black Panther Party members for intimidating white voters at a Philadelphia polling place on Election Day 2008. Obama has appointed people with a history of race resentment and bias, such as Attorney General Eric Holder and Supreme Court Justice Sonja Sotomayor. These incidents vividly illustrate this president's race-based politics, a flaw even acknowledged by Democratic pollsters in a *Wall Street Journal* opinion piece.[15]

Moving the Rule-of-Law Boundary

Wherever we look, Obama demonstrates another major boundary violation—more disruption of America's foundation. His inaugural address *again* foreshadows the specific boundary he will attack next—in another caution to America. Here he repeatedly insisted on the pre-eminence of the rule of law and the Constitution, "Our Founding Fathers...drafted a charter to assure the rule of law and the rights of man...Those ideals still light the world."

Then Obama flippantly violates the rule of law in multiple milieus precisely for political expediency:

14 Charles Krauthammer, "Obama Administration Stands Idle on Syria," *Birmingham News*, April 28, 2012.
15 Patrick Caddell and Douglas Schoen, "Our Divisive President," *Wall Street Journal*, July 28, 2010. http://online.wsj.com/article/SB10001424052748703700904575391553798363586.html#articleTabs%3Darticle accessed May 20, 2012.

- ignoring the legal rights of stockholders in favor of unions in the General Motors and Chrysler fiascos;
- bypassing the Constitutional Appointments Clause and Senate Oversight by appointing multiple czars as ex officio cabinet members who shape U.S. policy;
- attacking America's constitutional foundation by rushing a massive 2,700-page health care bill through Congress, disallowing time for discussion;
- pushing through the same bill also violated the Constitution by forcing every citizen to buy health-care insurance or face a federal fine;
- refusing to enforce federal immigration law to the point of suing the state of Arizona for protecting their citizens from illegals;
- declaring portions of the Defense of Marriage Act unconstitutional— even though it was previously passed by an overwhelming majority in Congress.

Obama has also freely used "executive orders" to one-sidedly carry out his will. Familiar incidents include: recess appointments outside the rules of Congress; mandating free contraception be provided by insurance companies involving church-run schools (a likely constitutional violation); and in June of 2012 suddenly claiming "executive privilege" to protect White House communications with Attorney General Eric Holder at the peak of the ongoing Congressional investigation of a Holder cover-up in the "Fast and Furious" gun-running operation.

Obama has exchanged the American rule of law for the "Obama rule" which allows him to do whatever he wants, whenever he wants. No boundaries for him! Unconsciously, he dropped hints of such intentions in his inauguration speech: *"I want us to push the boundaries."* Clearly he has pushed every boundary he can get his hands on. He's only held back by opposing political leaders whom he immediately degrades as representatives of "the party of no." Or by these leaders themselves simply refusing to stand up to Obama's boundary destruction—a fact which will become much plainer in this book.

Extremely weak when it comes to abiding by healthy boundaries, Obama's relentlessly dominating personality is clear and focused when it comes to breaking boundaries. Interpersonally he knows no boundaries, doing as he pleases. He repeatedly forces his will on the American people over their protests with egregious displays of economic recklessness, crippling energy policies, expensive health care, favoritism, violating the law and creating national-security vulnerabilities, as we have seen. His inaugural address predicts this blind spot as well, "Recall that earlier generations faced down fascism and communism…They understood that our power alone cannot protect us, nor does it entitle us to do as we please. Instead, they knew that…our security emanates from the justness of our cause, the force of our example, the tempering qualities of humility and restraint.*" Lacking humility and restraint, Obama defines precisely how he—behaving like a fascist dictator—disrupts our security.

Fearless columnist Thomas Sowell recognizes Obama's fascist behavior explaining why "both pro-Obama and anti-Obama observers may be reluctant to see him as fascist." Mistakenly, many people today associate fascism with the political right when in fact Mussolini, the originator of fascism, and Hitler were initially embraced by the left. Sowell notes, "what socialism, fascism and other ideologies of the left have in common…(is the idea that) very wise people—like themselves—need to take decisions out of the hands of lesser people, like the rest of us, and impose…decisions by government fiat."[16]

Beyond The Tipping Point Of Trust

Indeed Obama brings us to the most basic and severe boundary violation of all for a president—he has broken the public's trust, refused to speak the truth and failed to match it by walking the talk. Already he has so blatantly violated multiple promises he made in his inauguration speech we must conclude that—in that inauguration speech—he was secretly confessing his intentions. Going through the particular promises, we find that he would violate each with one denial after another. Obama will increasingly demonstrate his true intentions through his frequent use of denial.

He described how his deception would reach the tipping point: "…those of us who manage the public's dollars will be held to account—to spend wisely, reform bad habits and do our business in the light of day—because only then can we restore the vital trust between a people and their government." While seemingly criticizing George Bush's spending, in reality Obama reflects another blind spot he predicted where his bad spending habits would greatly surpass those of the previous administration—deeply violating the citizens' trust.

Certainly Obama has a strong tendency toward fabrication and broken promises. Only a small sampling includes:

- Announcing immediately after being elected to the Senate in 2004 that he was too inexperienced to run for president when, in fact, he began campaigning within the year;
- Stated on his presidential campaign website that he'd never worked for ACORN in any capacity when in fact he was an active ACORN trainer;
- Impressive expert linguistic analysis by Jack Cashill suggests that Bill Ayers actually wrote Obama's book *Dreams from My Father* and another writer wrote Obama's second book *The Audacity of Hope*—both of which Obama claimed to have written himself;[17]
- Repeated broken promises including a pledge to provide transparent bipartisan discussion of his health-care bill. Obama's legislative partner, then House Speaker Nancy Pelosi, made sure all Obamacare meetings

16 Thomas Sowell, "Don't Call Obama a Socialist," *Birmingham News,* June 13, 2012.
17 Jack Cashill, *Deconstructing Obama* (New York: Threshold Editions, 2011), p.217.

were conducted behind doors closed to Republicans—and to many Democrat colleagues as well. While Obama's deceptive nature is without question, the media continually ignores it.

Obama's True Motivation

This brings us to Barack Obama's motivation—and his enormous blind spots regarding his behavior. Why does Obama attack America's foundations at every turn?

People blame Obama's behavior on his liberal leanings and plans to create a European-style socialist nation here by increasing the power of the state and redistributing wealth. Some blame the blind spots that result from these left-wing endeavors on his narcissism. David Limbaugh even labels it "malignant narcissism." In any case, it causes the president to misread the public's mandate. D'Souza spotted Obama's rage, attributing his motive to narcissistically fulfilling his father's anti-colonial mission. Yet while Limbaugh and D'Souza recognize Obama's danger, they join prominent conservative commentators, all of whom deny that he's intentionally malevolent.

Others also see him as ideologically driven—but more sinister. In his book, *The Manchurian President: Barack Obama's Ties to Communists, Socialists and Other Anti-American Extremists,* journalist Aaron Klein obsessively traces Obama's radical agenda to reshape America to a clear-cut plan long in the making. He notes that the adult Obama adopted subversive theorist Saul Alinsky's book, *Rules for Radicals,* which has been the playbook for leftist political activists since the 1960s. "Alinsky is generally considered the founder of the American movement of community organizing," Klein wrote, quoting a booklet by former sixties "radical-turned-conservative" David Horowitz, *Barack Obama's Rules for Revolution: The Alinsky Model.*[18]

Alinsky died in 1972, but Obama was clearly trained in the method by several of the man's devotees and later became an Alinsky trainer himself. Horowitz's painstakingly traces how Alinsky shaped Obama:

- urges "radicals should be political activists, undermine the system...take *power* from the Haves and give it to the Have-nots" –the radicals' most basic principle.
- a classic revolutionary "goal is *power* for the political vanguard."
- strategy: work within system, "accumulate... *power* to destroy"— "boring from within" like termites eating away at societal foundations.
- citing an SDS radical, "'issue is never the issue—[but] always the revolution...inner city, blacks or women is never the real cause...[the real cause is] the *accumulation of power* to make the revolution."[19]

18 Aaron Klein, *The Manchurian President: Barack Obama's Ties to Communists, Socialists and Other Anti-American Extremists,* (Washington, DC: WND Books, 2010), pp. 51-59.
19 David Horowitz, *Barack Obama's Rules for Revolution: The Alinsky Method,* (Sherman Oaks, Calif.: David Horowitz Freedom Center, 2009), pp. 5-9.

As to Obama's chief motivation, Horowitz minces no words. Obama is all about *power*—the one word at the heart of Alinsky's strategies. Tellingly, Alinsky's son, L. David Alinsky, praised Obama for applying his father's power principles to his 2008 presidential campaign. [20]

A brief bio on Alinsky born in Chicago in 1909 reveals that *his* primary mentor was Al Capone's enforcer Frank Nitti who took over the Chicago mob after Capone went to prison in 1931. As a young sociologist in the 1930s Alinsky blamed society for a criminal's problems—specifically he blamed the private ownership of property—and thus joined the mob's destructiveness in spirit. For Alinsky the problem was always outside the individual and he taught numerous followers to attack society, never accepting responsibility. [21] We will see how well this fits with Barack Obama's deepest needs.

But we must never forget at the heart of Alinsky's method is deception— and that at his core Obama remains a master of deception. He's a virtuoso at playing the media and bamboozling the people, particularly when the times are right for him—and without question he stepped into a perfect political storm as a presidential candidate. Shortly we will see how he came by his deceitfulness without realizing it, and what truly motivates him deep down, above all.

Obama's critics have concluded his ideology presents serious risks caused by blind spots and naiveté, but few critics have overtly stated that he is truly malevolent—intentionally dangerous. Of the above critics, Horowitz and Klein come closest to that conclusion. Also Phyllis Schlafly praised David Limbaugh's book in her newsletter noting his detailed, well-documented descriptions of Obama's *intentionally* destructive behavior.[22] She saw what Limbaugh did not see, or want to admit.[23]

Even though Obama hinted at his truly bad intentions toward our nation in his inauguration speech, now we can understand better what prompted those hints. To unearth those motivations, we must learn the secret of seeing through massive denial.

---

20 Klein, *Manchurian President,* p. 51.

21 Horowitz, *Barack Obama's Rules for Revolution*, p.13.

22 Of course, Obama himself remains in denial about the full extent of his intentionally destructive motivations but we can be sure he is consciously aware of significant deception. There is a famous phrase therapists use that applies here; we employ it to describe unconsciously intentional motives and actions: "accidentally on purpose." Later we will see how Obama's mind is secretly a master at describing such motives. Phyllis Schlafly, *The Phyllis Schlafly Report*, January 2011, p. 1.

23 Limbaugh continued to detail Obama's destructiveness: his war on the economy, the culture and values, and those who oppose his domination in his book, *The Great Destroyer: Barack Obama's War on the Republic*, (Washington, DC: Regnery, 2012).

2

The President Sings to America

At a January 19, 2012 fundraiser at Harlem's legendary Apollo Theater Barack Obama takes us straight to the matter of denial. On stage toward the end of the evening he gazes out at the appreciative audience and suddenly, spontaneously, he breaks into song! It had been a particularly musical occasion and the president's appearance followed several performers including soul singer the Rev. Al Green, whom Obama acknowledged. But the entertainers were expected to sing—Obama was only expected to speak.

Without warning, however, he delivered a surprisingly pleasing falsetto lyric, "I'mmm…sooo in love with you…"—the opening line from Green's 1972 hit "Let's Stay Together." Not believing their ears, the audience bursts into applause. After the ovation subsides, Obama takes it all in, then hesitantly glances toward his staff off stage right. Talking directly to them but also to America, he blurts out, *"Those guys didn't think I would do it. I told you I was going to do it."*

It was a festive night of musical memories punctuated by an unexpectedly melodious presidential performance followed by yet another moment of spontaneous banter. Not much to it, really—or was there?

His staff doubted he would sing even after he promised them he would. They were in denial. They couldn't handle the truth he presented. So he reminded them, "I told you I was going to do it."

They did not think a President of the United States would break into song on a public stage. They really didn't think he might do something spontaneous and unpredictable—take such a chance as singing when he was surrounded by gifted entertainers. He'd never risk looking foolish and out of place. He'd never allow himself to appear non-presidential.

And there was the subtle audacity of the matter, a sense of daring on Obama's part underscored by his tentative teasing glances first at the audience and then at his staff. Such teasing is, in and of itself, distinctly non-presidential. Still he implied that his "guys" should have thought through their denial and been prepared for something shocking.

Like everyone in high public office, Obama knows all his public comments are taped and widely propagated. As such, whenever he speaks he's indirectly addressing all Americans. If you don't think he was singing so all America would notice, think again. It fits him so well.

Consider that Obama is also unknowingly communicating a deeper message, admitting that he has done something unbelievable to our nation, something nobody would expect a president would do. By adding "I told you," he admits that he warned us that he was going to do it. Certainly, deep down, people are prone to confess.

The idea Obama did something inconceivable to America would come as no surprise to millions of Americans who've been shocked by his radical presidency. Citizens from all walks of life are also shocked that no one bothers to stand up to him.

Even so, Obama suggests America is in denial about who he really is—and so is he.

Keep two questions in mind: What has he done? and When and how did he tell us he was going to do it?

'I Am the Sandman'

After confirming his staff's denial with his side comment, he then says, "The sandman did not come out. Now don't worry, I can't sing like you, but I just wanted to show my appreciation."

Of course we have the surface message that Obama will not keep singing and thereby put his audience to sleep. But we immediately find the striking denial, "the sandman did not come out." Blatant denials often imply the exact opposite—especially following Obama's emphasis on overcoming denial—suggesting "the sandman *did* come out tonight"—indeed, he's saying "I *am* the sandman who came out on the stage tonight."

What could Obama possibly mean by "I am the sandman?" The vivid image initially suggests something soft and yielding, something lacking a solid foundation. There are other immediate possibilities, but in fact he leads in this very direction of weakness and something not real, not strong—something lacking in character—such as a president who would flippantly take a dare. Also "coming out tonight" suggests coming out with a secret. Is he advising us to look closely at his character and ask fundamental questions to unearth the secret?

Surely the character question also fits with telling Americans he has done something unimaginable, gotten elected president in spite of major character flaws.

We will return to the Apollo Theater incident for more valuable hints, but for now let's look more closely at his "sandman" image. Obama demonstrated two other denials—"don't [you] worry" and "I'm not going to sing," suggesting America *should* worry, and that "I *am* going to sing"—tell you about it. Following his clues ("I told you") we examine other public comments in which he previously began to define sandman for us. This is further evidence of Obama's secret confession.

17

Fathers' Day and the Sandman Father

We don't have to look far for a vivid connection to "sandman," which tells us this indeed represents a major clue to Obama's actual identity and his true intentions. He reveals a vital clue by blatantly pointing toward "sandman" while simultaneously denying it. Yet the denial reveals that we're looking at a tremendous revelation. As we will see from start to finish, "sandman" will fit him and his horrific story perfectly.

Certainly Obama remains a mystery to millions of people. Even his followers know little about him and his background. Just for openers, questions linger about his education, grades and medical history. More serious questions remain unanswered about his passport, foreign travels (to Pakistan, as one example), selective service registration and multiple social security numbers. For instance, he refuses to explain why his current social security number is from Connecticut, a state in which he has never resided. These unchallenged issues point to serious denial on the part of the media, but I digress.

We will see that Obama himself addresses the very questions the media will not. And he will take us on a far broader journey into his personal history, delving more deeply into these questions the media has failed to answer.

Obama Identifies the Sandman

In a Fathers' Day speech on June 15, 2008, Obama addressed the congregation of the Apostolic Church in Chicago. This wasn't just any Fathers' Day but one on which he was campaigning to be America's leader—the father of our nation. Obama delivered the speech virtually spontaneously, almost off the cuff, and—on such a personal day for him—he surely wrote it himself.

He opens with a striking story, a New Testament parable no less, "At the end of the Sermon on the Mount, Jesus closes by saying, "Whoever hears these words of mine, and does them, shall be likened to a wise man who built his house upon a rock: and the rain descended, and the floods came, and the winds blew, and beat upon that house, and it fell not, for it was founded upon a rock."[1]

Notice that Obama intentionally leaves out the second part of the parable about foolish builders erecting a house on a foundation of sand, but he refers to it extensively by implication—the centerpiece of his speech: "Now everyone who hears these sayings of mine and does not do them will be like a foolish man who built his house on sand: and the rains came, and the winds blew and beat on that house, and it fell. And great was its fall."[2]

We have the memorable story of two kinds of home builders: a wise one who builds on rock and a foolish one who builds on sand. Then comes the test.

---

1 Matthew 7: 24-25.
2 Mattthew 7: 26-27, NKJV. Immediately preceding this passage, Jesus insists his followers will be known by the fruit they bear and warns that many who call him "Lord" will not enter the kingdom of heaven because they hypocritically "practice lawlessness."

A violent storm challenges the foundation of both houses. The home built on rock stands while the home built on sand collapses.

Underscoring this parable on Fathers' Day, Obama depicts fathers as crucial builders of homes, men who structure their children's very foundations. And he particularly emphasizes a son's foundation. "Of all the rocks upon which we build our lives," Obama tells us, "we are reminded today…that family is the most important. And we are called to recognize and honor how critical every father is to that foundation."

Before long he links these comments to his absent father, thus confirming that he's unconsciously telling us his deeper story.

Foundation

Obama compares two types of fathers, the involved father who builds solid-rock foundations in his kids and the absent father who builds weak foundations for his children, foundations "made of sand." Yet Obama, by omitting the second part of the biblical parable, shows that he simply cannot bring himself to say the words 'sand foundation.' Why? For him, that phrase hits too close to home.

Obama immediately introduces human development—in particular father-son relationships on Fathers' Day no less—a day certain to stir him up. Shortly he discusses his own father, "I know what it means to have an absent father," which implies what it means to America that he had an absent father. His words strongly suggest that the parable could be titled "How Obama Sr. built Obama Jr." He was unconsciously pressured to tell us about that absent father, the foolish builder who left him with a worrisome foundation.

Obama makes repeated scathing references to absent fathers—selfish, unavailable, irresponsible, immature, and destructive. He underscores lost boys who have no father to show them how to be a man. He then describes how such absent fathers produce sons with "behavioral problems" which mirror their own. *In short, Obama tells us that he is the sandman son of a sandman father, a father who failed to build a solid foundation of character in him but instead left him with nothing but sand inside.* Obama in essence warns America that he would be like his father, lacking in integrity and prone to bad behavior which undermined the community. This according to the role model rule Obama so carefully establishes.

Now we have a partial answer. The reason why Obama would tell us through denial at the Apollo *he* was a sandman, a fictional man, a character in fairy tales who puts children to sleep by sprinkling sand in their eyes.

Go with the image. Obama first implies that he is a sandman president—not the real deal, a fantasy leader. The presidency is on loan to someone who badly needs it to cover up his pain of an absent father, a president lacking in internal strength. And he has tried to put America to sleep about what's he's up to.

Thomas Sowell's comment rings true: "anything [Obama] says is *a message written in sand."* And Obama himself has told us why: his absent father built him on sand. Sowell had unknowingly broken a key component of the Obama Code.

Hidden Guilt

Repeating the image of "sandman" when he's running for election in 2008 and re-election in 2012 suggests Obama's hidden guilt prompts secret confessions about his character deficits. Here we have further evidence that one of the things he has inflicted on America is to saddle our nation with a president who has a hole in his basic foundation as a person. In short, he knows he's lacking integrity, a dearth which could easily lead him to do incomprehensible things.

His 2012 re-election campaign has again triggered his hidden guilt. He suggests a secret confession that he has wronged America—"been bad"—in major ways and now must apologize as a candidate. The overwhelming guilt he feels forces him to admit he's not worthy of the office.

Just prior to his Apollo song, Obama said, "To know that Reverend Al Green was here," implying "know that the Big Reverend—God—is here tonight also!" Ever the teacher, Obama suggests that deep down he senses God looking over his shoulder at his misdeeds, even if he has consciously blocked out that reality—creating a further impetus to confess.

Obama consciously thinks he can have his way, do whatever he wants, and get away with it. He manipulates his moral compass to suit his immediate needs. But ever so carefully he reveals the striking truth: he has a deeper moral compass which will have its way with *him*. He cannot stop himself from confessing indirectly. Obama strongly suggests he has violated his deeper moral compass. Now we will see how in the world he could have two moral compasses.

The Science of the Super Intelligence

First I must tell you how we are able to discover with certainty the concealed messages Obama is communicating to America—which will explain his two moral compasses. In analyzing and interpreting Obama's remarks, as an experienced psychiatrist and forensic profiler I am utilizing a breathtaking new discovery in the science of the mind—the existence of our unconscious super intelligence.[3] A subliminal part of the human mind, the super intelligence quick-reads situations in the blink of an eye far more quickly than our surface mind does. It takes in everything. The world heard all about it in Malcolm Gladwell's

---

3 The super intelligence is an under-appreciated but immensely powerful part of the human psyche. I first explained this component of the human mind in my book *The Deeper Intelligence: the Breakthrough to the Untapped Potential of Your Unconscious Mind* (Nashville: Thomas Nelson Publishers, 1994). I have since renamed this phenomenal part of our being as the super intelligence which I expand upon it in Appendix A. I participated in validating the initial research establishing its existence.

best-selling book *Blink: The Power Of Thinking Without Thinking.*[4] This perceptive young author was so impressed with research findings, he called it the "dazzling new unconscious."

For example, Gladwell described how a fire chief used his super intelligence by instinctively quick-reading danger and ordering his men to clear a room where they were putting out a fire just moments before the floor fell into a ferocious hidden fire raging on the floor below. Elsewhere, he reported how three art experts accurately quick-read that a Greek-like statue supposedly from antiquity was a phony. They did that in a matter of minutes after other experts had, after a prolonged study, declared the object authentic. Gladwell demonstrated how their instincts surfaced after they unconsciously assessed the situation for the briefest of moments. He emphasized how accurate and helpful the quick-read mind can be.

Now understand that as his Fathers' Day speech constantly reflected, Obama's super-intel was *unconsciously quick-reading himself* and the reality of his missing father, in essence sizing up his father. He was asking, "Are you the real thing or not?"—and he saw that he was nothing but a sandman, an imposter for a father. He constantly realized his father represented "Danger—house on fire," meaning he had destroyed the family home—exactly as a horrific storm would level a house, particularly a house with no foundation. And inside Obama was sizing himself up, "just like my father built me—no foundation, nothing solid, nothing really but sand."

But obviously Obama wasn't just quick-reading what happened to him. He was also quick-speaking to us, telling us all about it in stories and images. *That was the huge step Gladwell missed*—not only does the new unconscious quick-read, but it also quick-speaks in its own unique language of story and images. It uses a symbolic language; we might think of the unconscious as speaking in a symbolic "right-brain" language while the conscious mind speaks in a literal "left-brain" language.[5] As Gladwell hinted, and as my work has validated, we are surely experiencing a revolutionary new age of the mind.

Obama's Super-Intel

And nobody demonstrates this new super-intel to the world better than Obama. *Ironically, Obama has no idea consciously that his quick-read, quick-tell mind is constantly revealing his story.* That's why, if you pay attention, Obama unveils his entire narrative over several major public communications as his super-intel continually speaks between the lines.

By far and away, this is the most brilliant part of Obama's mind—far brighter than his conscious mind—which will take us to his deepest motivations in the whisk of a broom. We can then see where they lead and how they play

---

4 Malcolm Gladwell, *Blink: The Power Of Thinking Without Thinking*, (New York: Back Bay Books, 2005).
5 By analogy we think of the left brain as literal—"just the facts"—and the right brain as symbolic and intuitive.

into, among other issues, his insatiable quest for power.

Obama's super-intel knows many things about him that his conscious mind continually denies. *This unique intelligence is extremely honest and understands that facing the truth is always best.* Obama demonstrates that often deep down, we are predisposed to confess the truth about our life choices and motivations—and that our surface minds are notoriously deceptive.

In a nutshell *at this crucial point in our history Obama's own super intelligence represents a phenomenal secret source inside the White House.* We thus have the ultimate inside source who has complete access to Obama's inner world and his most private thoughts. If anybody knows him—grasps his deeper motives, if anybody can see where they lead and how pained and destructive he is—it's this particular undercover source, who knows him best. We're talking about a mind bright beyond words—hundreds of times quicker than his conscious mind—an unimaginable "Deep Throat" insider who must communicate the truth. Brilliantly his super-intel speaks secretly in a vivid, rich, symbolic language of key narratives and images—all without his conscious mind having a clue.

This is where we are in understanding the human mind. Obama will make plain that his brilliant super-intel was secretly seeking someone trained in its language to reveal his true narrative, which is precisely where I come in. I am the expert language translator—the symbologist— educated in reading his deeper mind's symbolic language. Interpreting his words, stories and symbols, I am in effect the voice of Obama's super-intel; I speak for his own brilliant internal investigator. For years with therapy patients and forensic suspects I have been exposed to their super intelligence, which is always the smartest mind in the room—by far. Widespread public awareness of the super intelligence is still limited, which is typical of a new discovery of this magnitude. But the near-wildfire popularity of Gladwell's *Blink* is a testimony to the veracity of unconscious wisdom being something we use every day.

Just as new imaging techniques for the body have been developed in medicine, we now have a similar type of imaging breakthrough to the mind —a new way of using images from the super-intel to look deeper. Like an advanced MRI scan provides new information, Obama's unconscious mind does likewise but in both cases the messages must be interpreted by a professional, trained to read the images.

A full explanation of the discovery of the super intelligence including my participation appears in Appendix A. There I will explain how I moved from learning about the super intelligence in psychotherapy with patients and then applied the same listening skills to forensic profiling. More recently I've learned how to access the super intelligence of leaders, men and women charged with tremendous responsibility. In each environment a single person's brilliant unconscious guided me. 'The mind is the mind is the mind' wherever we go—whoever we are. But now, with the super-intel revealing so much more than we ever knew before, we will never look at our leaders the same way again. Thus armed, we are far more perceptive and communicative creatures than we ever imagined—and Obama will tell that story as well as anyone.

For now I will let Obama continue to unfold his story. I will report my findings as a reporter skilled in listening. In the end a psychiatrist trained in super intelligence work becomes a reporter and a teacher—following the lead of a particular person's all-seeing super-intel quick reading himself and the world around him.

Exactly like a good detective, you must pay close attention to small clues. That's often all you get at first. We must follow the trail of his thoughts. Pay particular attention to his spontaneous comments and speeches which he heavily influenced.[6] And be sure to read through his key denials.

Obama's Deep Pain

Between the lines Obama has verified that an extremely painful trauma constantly lives inside of him. It doesn't take much to reopen such a wound—"a hole" in himself created by his absent father. That's exactly what Obama later labeled it, "a hole," an emptiness within his inner self.[7] Right off he has revealed the motivations that have controlled him his entire life. At the same time, he remains consciously in denial about his personal pain.

One of the trickiest things about the mind to grasp is that we can see the world one way consciously, and our unconscious super-intel sees it, quick-reads it—in an entirely different way. We can believe two different things about ourselves at the same time. Talking about the pain of an absent father on Fathers' Day, Obama was in denial that he was referring to himself. Same thing at the Apollo. Consciously he believed he was an adored president surrounded by thousands of worshipful fans. Yet his super-intel was quick-reading his deep pain, picking up on the deeper story—as we shall see shortly.

Now with two clear levels to the mind in view we can also understand how Barack Obama has a superficial moral compass and a deeper, far wiser, moral compass.

Obama's Super-Intel Guides Us, Step-By-Step

Already Obama's super-intel has made it abundantly clear that we were on the right track in a new understanding of him, listening deeper. Obama's sandman story about the foolish builder on Fathers' Day took you *straight to his human development*—to how he was built by his absent father particularly into the type person he really is today. Unknown to his conscious mind, Obama laid out the secret story of his human development straight from inside his mind. He's a deeply wounded person—and deeply grieved about it, at that.

Again you'll find hints of that profound sadness in his Apollo Theater

---

6 Obama works closely with his speechwriters and in several key communications, given the context, he has essentially written every word. This will become clear.
7 Father's Day Speech 2008

appearance, which is just the tip of the enormous iceberg of his cold, hard grief. This grief has stayed with him continually over this three-and-a-half-year time span—just as it has been with him his entire life. Such a severely wounded person can be a very dangerous person in the end, and Obama is dangerous beyond belief. But we must be clear about what led to his danger, and about just how badly wounded he truly is.

Obama's Masking Smile

When we search for a few clues of Obama's grief on the night he spontaneously sang to his Apollo audience, they're hidden, but a little work uncovers them. The refrain from Al Green's song, "Let's Stay Together," highlights a theme of Obama's re-election campaign: "Let's, let's stay together. Loving you whether, whether/Times are good or bad, happy or sad." Looking back, Obama suggests that these clear treatments of grief in Al Green's song triggered his singing. The complete lyrics of the song's opening stanza read:

> "I'm, I'm so in love with you.
> Whatever you want to do is alright with me
> Cause you make me feel so brand new.
> And I want to spend my life with you.
>
> "...loving you forever is what I need.
> Let me be the one you come running to. I'll never be untrue.
> Let's, let's stay together. Loving you whether, whether times are good or bad, happy or sad.
>
> "...why somebody, why people break up...
> Oh, and turn around and make up
> I just can't seeeeee you'd never do that to me...
> Let's, let's stay together. Loving you whether, whether times are good or bad, happy or sad...."[8]

In the back of his mind, Obama suggests he's thinking of bad times, sad times—of people who are untrue and break up with you. He's fighting to keep his head above water, of finding some way of being brand new to voters—in a new world and not the old one of pain. Since pain triggers the need for love, he reiterates, "I'm in pain."

Obama suggests his deep pain is related to staying together and to crucial relationships in which he badly needed love, in which he needed some people to stick with him during bad times, during sad times—and they didn't. He implies someone pulled the rug out from underneath him—complete betrayal, a total breakup—and that left him with some sad, bad times of his own. Above all, Obama points to his absent sandman father who severely wounded him.

With his winning smile and charming, easygoing persona, Obama gives us

---

[8] Devin Dwyer, "Obama Sings Soul Tune in Harlem," http://abcnews.go.com/blogs/politics/2012/01/obama-sings-soul-tune-in-harlem.

24

no surface clue that he's fighting to keep himself together. But Al Green's words of pain remind us that you can't judge a book by its cover. People try their hardest to cover up their pain and that's what he's doing at that exact moment. Many performers and comedians have covered up personal pain by donning the mask of a permanent stage smile. Obama's no different.

Obama again suggests he has two beliefs about himself. First, he is a popular president on stage with his supporters singing his praises. Yet just below the surface of his mind he believes—he knows—that he is experiencing the strongest sadness, revisiting an underlying emotional trauma. Al Green's lyrics suggest this indeed is Obama's most primal song. Very subtly but plainly, Obama implies that he's still controlled by secret grief over his father, who totally betrayed him. In turn Obama unconsciously confesses again that he has done the same unthinkable thing—not kept America together as president. Secretly he counsels America, "[us] stay together," implying it would be best for our nation *not* to reelect him. His super-intel attempts to show our nation the light.

Sandman's Second Meaning

The super intelligence routinely utilizes symbology in its narratives. It will often take a crucial image and use it in a multitude of ways to further clarify its motivations. When Obama makes a comment like "the sandman came out tonight," in one key way that's his super-intel declaring its intention to speak, to say something for everyone in America to hear. In that statement, the super-intel identifies itself as "sandman," a word traditionally associated with sleep and its attendant dream-state, the unconscious. At night, our unconscious mind is fully alert and telling stories while our conscious mind is totally asleep.

But during the day, while we're consciously awake, our unconscious continues to function at an extremely high level. Our super-intel speaks while we're awake, telling stories using images with deeper meanings. Just as dreams are creative night stories from the unconscious—*symbolic messages*—which must be decoded to understand, so too these daytime communications must be decoded. In Obama's case, recall how we translated his Fathers' Day parable of the foolish builder to determine that it was secretly his destructive absent father.

We must realize that the conscious mind and the super-intel speak simultaneously. Consciously we speak literally while our unconscious speaks figuratively communicating extremely accurate symbolic messages.

Strikingly, Obama used "sandman" in two key ways. First he used it to describe his father (and then himself)—people who are destroyers, not builders, because they lack solid integrity. Second, Obama's super intelligence uses "sandman" to describe itself—the dazzling unconscious—the dazzling secret storyteller which in fact tells us the story of his destructive sandman father.

So how do we know when the super-intel speaks? We must listen for stories and images—Obama's parable on Fathers' Day and his rich "sandman" image with the story "he came out tonight." And there will always be a key issue that unlocks the story—*the trigger*. Obama was constantly quick-reading the pain that has plagued him ever since his father abandoned him (as we will see in multiple ways).

His response to that pain triggered an attack on America in retaliation for his unfair treatment as a child. He will repeat the same scenario over and over again. But to get to the depth of Obama's pain, to fully understand him, we have a ways to go.

A person's story always starts with the deepest of pain. Their response comes next—inevitably anger and frustration. Finally the pain erupts and is transferred onto others, the target, which invariably prompts hidden guilt. In telling the story of a person's pain, the super-intel carefully reads each individual component: the pain, the response (fury, in Obama's case), and the target, accompanied by ensuing guilt prompting the hidden confession. If we listen closely, we can see their super-intel focus on each separate element of an individual's story. *The real mark of the super intelligence is that it tells a consistent story—over and over again—to verify its message.*

'Dazzling' Unconscious

The super-intel is so profoundly perceptive, it's almost magical, just as Gladwell called it— "dazzling." The fact that we're carrying around this brilliant computer in the back of our minds that quick-reads situations so swiftly makes your head swim; what's more, this computer tells us all about itself. And Obama's "sandman" reference suggests "magic" with the mythical sandman sprinkling his magic sand. His super-intel made a brilliant choice with the image of "sandman." It simultaneously challenges and inspires, grabbing our attention in a dramatic fashion while emphasizing the underlying message.[9]

'Dreams from My Father'

Unconsciously Obama sticks with the image of "dreams," and guides us deeper into his story and to his memoir, his 1995 autobiography, *Dreams from My Father: A Story of Race and Inheritance.* Now that we understand that by "dreams" he means unconscious messages, we read the new title, *Unconscious Messages from My Father.* This fits all the hidden messages an absent father sends his son, which Obama has defined so powerfully. Thus we might consider an additional title, *Unconscious Messages from My Sandman Father—My Story.*

Obama's unconscious instructs us to search his book for important stories which will help us understand the major messages he received. He has hinted that we will find powerful narratives which take us deeper into the pain and central motivation in his life. He does not disappoint. Search for them."

---

9 As a point of comparison, think about 'body language.' Our unconscious can position our body to communicate symbolic messages, just as it can arrange words, stories, and images to communicate verbally in a special symbolic 'mind language' all its own.

Obama's Life Equation

Exploring Obama's *Dreams* book, we find that indeed his stories guide us step by step to grasp his enormous childhood pain and the extent of his rage. In a brief story, first Obama unconsciously advises us to fully examine his past—especially his role models.

In the Preface to *Dreams* he tells us, "as Faulkner reminds us, the past is never dead and buried—it isn't even buried...(this past, directly touches my own)."[10] He's actually saying, "My past is alive and well-reflected in who I am today." He's unconsciously advising us to search for it.[11]

Next he unfolds a brief narrative about his incomprehensible childhood suffering, suggesting that's where his emotional trauma started. He tells of the horribly neglected children he has seen in many places: in Jakarta when he was a child in Indonesia, in Nairobi, the capital of his father's country, and in Chicago's troubled inner-city—indirectly linking them to his own childhood and secretly implying how he experienced life early on.

Poignantly he writes,

> I know, I have seen, the desperation and disorder of the powerless; how it twists the lives of children on the streets of Jakarta or Nairobi in much the same way as it does the lives of children on Chicago's South Side, how narrow the path is for them between humiliation and untrammeled fury, how easily they slip into violence and despair.[12]

Obama implies that the key to ultimately understanding him is to focus not on power but on powerlessness. Humiliation, utter helplessness, total despair—these are the deep emotions which twisted his life, which shaped the future president—emotions people reflexively bury in the blink of an eye. He paints a deeper picture of his grief, just how great it was.

Does Obama's life story explain why he might be a perfect fit as a disciple of the radical Saul Alinsky, whose advice was to "bore from within" and secretly sabotage a nation? Indeed Obama's poignant description of severely emotionally wounded children leading to unspeakable rage—*crucially located at the very beginning of his story*—fits him hand-in-glove. Thus he strongly suggests this is indeed his life equation. Now he has suggested that two major emotions linger at his core: humiliating fear and payback anger. Obama himself locates in childhood the wounds that drive his "untrammeled fury." He takes us to the roots of his rage. He takes us from the deepest sense of powerlessness to rage, the perfect temporary sense of maximum power. His takes us from his painful victimization to the quick-fix of his political victory. As his story unfolds we will find striking confirmation.

---

10 Barack Obama, *Dreams From My Father: A Story of Race and Inheritance* (New York: Crown Publishers, 1995).
11 While Bill Ayers likely wrote Obama's two books for him, we can be sure Obama provided most of the stories—and it's the stories we will follow. Ayers also unconsciously would pick up on the truth about Obama and tell it. (Ayers' contribution to Obama's book will be addressed in a Chapter 7.)
12 *Dreams from My Father*, p. xi.

Glancing ahead in *Dreams from My Father*, we see Obama bring the entire matter of power closer to himself when he describes taking a major step while still in Jakarta from powerlessness to power. He writes of how his mother—who, as a 1960s era anti-establishment advocate, on the surface had great disdain for power—saw her greatest fear come true as his Indonesian stepfather taught Obama about self-defense and aggression, "Power was taking her son."[13] He was telling us that his deep helplessness and compensatory anger started long ago, when he was seven years old in Indonesia.

Note again Obama's strong emphasis on how quickly helplessness leads to the violence of "untrammeled fury." It is power gone far astray because of utter despair. We have seen time and again how Obama's own words confirm just how dangerous he is to America—unleashing his "untrammeled fury" upon our unsuspecting nation. Imagine the incredible risks posed by a sitting president suffering from such severe emotional pain.[14]

Powerlessness and Anger

As emphasized in his book, his life equation takes us back to his 2008 Fathers' Day parable which confirms the identical story. Here he described the deleterious effect of absent fathers on the home—he builds it on sand because he's not there, no builder at all—then he's also the raging storm that destroyed the home, the raging sandstorm. That's how Obama experienced him. How richly and poignantly he describes his pain.

He adds to this a prolonged explanation of absent fathers who destroy a son's foundation and instead build into that son the same destructive behavior as their own. The son becomes the raging storm. Unknowingly but unmistakably, Obama is describing himself.

Obama underscores his extreme anger, which points us to the real roots of his pain. He warns America that *he has taken the short step to fury and rage because of his pain.* He warned in his Fathers' Day speech that he will constantly attack the foundations of our society just as his father did. To see the father is to see the son. Indeed the sandman son came out at the Apollo Theater. Later we will examine specific attacks he later predicted, and we'll see how his super intelligence repeatedly tells us the same story in other key communications.

Dangerous Beyond Belief

Obama's hidden anger drives him. His own super-intel tells us. His danger is equivalent to his emotional suffering, and now he has established that his suffering is off the charts as utter humiliation and powerlessness overwhelmed

---

13 *Ibid*, p. 46.
14 For those who view childhood trauma as an old Freudian idea, the latest research on emotional trauma—far beyond Freud's analysis—demonstrates in a fresh new way the power of early emotional trauma as a central driving force in a person's life and how people unconsciously tell about it. See Robert Langs, *Freud on a Precipice*, (New York: Jason Aronson Publishers, 2009).

him. To allow us to understand his rage he had to tell us what caused it— and only he could do so.

Obama's plans to bring down America are more threatening than even his worst critics suspect. Obama is far from naive but filled with disguised rage carrying out a craftily planned *intentional* attack on America—albeit unconscious at times. Obama doesn't feel most of his extreme rage—but unconsciously he knows he has "unfinished business." Consciously, Obama has rationalized his decisions." Like Colonel Jessep in *A Few Good Men*, he doesn't really see how he is betraying America as its commander.

The Heart of Denial

As a psychiatrist, I understand how Obama's boatload of emotional pain propels him into massive denial of his motives and actions. Primal pain, the type that Obama experienced, creates a pattern of denial that leads to living outside the boundaries of common sense and natural law. In this case, it also leads to the extreme harm he inflicts on America.

Who in the political world can handle such raw truth about Obama, the truth that we're examining here? Surely we could create a lengthy who's-who list of media mavens, political activists and government officials—both elected and appointed, from both the right and from the left—who refuse under any circumstances to consider such potentially explosive self-revelations by Obama.

And then there's the denial which plagues Obama's supporters. They must overcome that blind hero-worship. Imagine the trauma of reality they would have to face—that the real Obama is a polar opposite of the idealized Obama. Look back at his 2008 campaign—he was hailed as hero, messiah, author, and orator. He was characterized as being above the pain of life, brilliant (and black to boot), a man who would solve all of America's problems and unify us as never before. Hope and change, a new day for America. But as his super-intel reveals, Obama was indeed bringing a fundamental change to our nation—by attacking America in ways that would make our country unrecognizable to its Founders.

Genial Nature Masks a Dangerous Man

As T.S. Eliot reminds us, "Human kind cannot bear very much reality,"[15] and the reality of Barack Obama is admittedly hard to take. Because Obama's surface personality is so pleasant and genial, it's doubly difficult.

At times some people recognize Obama's harmfulness. Columnist Thomas Sowell warned that if Obama is not defeated in 2012, "the fate of America—and of Western nations, including Israel—will be left in the hands of a man with a lifelong hostility toward Western values and Western interests. Obama is such a genial man that many people…cannot see him as a danger. *For every hundred people who can see his geniality, probably only a handful see the grave danger*

---

15 T. S. Eliot, *Four Quartets*

his warped policies and ruthless tactics pose to a whole way of life that has given…Americans unprecedented freedom and prosperity."[16]

Only Expert Education Reveals

Obama's super intelligence fully agrees with Sowell. Given his severe intentions and easygoing persona Obama unconsciously warns us of urgent danger if citizens fail to grasp his super-intel's revelations about the serious threat he represents to the country. Pay attention to his ominous images.

In the same Fathers' Day speech he insists, *"Education is everything to our children's future…We know the work and the studying and the level of education that requires."* Obama secretly pleads with America to choose cutting-edge knowledge, overcome denial, give up pride in previous knowledge and, as he puts it, whoever you are "get your butts back to the library"—be prepared to learn and keep learning. Clearly, super-intelligence education requires a whole new expertise. In his inauguration speech he stresses that we're now in a new day and age of education about the human mind and how it communicates, *"And we will transform our schools and colleges and universities to meet the demands of a new age."*

Again Obama warns us, *"new threats* [meaning, himself] *…demand even greater effort—greater understanding."*

The underlying message: America's future rides on the hard work of understanding his super intelligence and its quick-read take on him. It's the only source that fully understands his rage. It's the only way of getting past the cover of his book and seeing—quick-reading—what's inside. But then everyone can read a parable if they are open-minded to deeper meanings. Remember, Obama started his sandman story with a parable. Already we see that he can lead us within with his stories and images if we're willing to follow the trail.

Humility

Yet there's one thing required for the phenomenal new super-intel knowledge about Obama—humility. In his inauguration speech Obama's deeper self stresses this: *"Recall that earlier generations faced down fascism and communism not just with missiles…They understood that our power alone cannot protect us… that our power grows…our security emanates from the justness of our cause…the tempering qualities of humility and restraint."*

Although on a conscious level Obama almost certainly was criticizing the Bush administration (and other GOP presidents) of creating an arrogant foreign policy reliant on weapons, but in realty he was speaking about the need for humility. Unconsciously Obama knew that all the studying in the world wouldn't help you if you didn't have the deepest humility, the awareness of how much you don't know. In short you need *an open mind*—an image he will use over and over again.

---

16 Thomas Sowell, "'Super Tuesday' May Decide Fate of Civilization," *Birmingham News*, March 5, 2012.

When it comes to our engrained beliefs about the trustworthiness of the conscious mind, the virtue of humility is a rare commodity indeed! The conscious mind is all we can get in touch with immediately, and it's all too natural to put too much faith in that one lens. But that's what the breakthrough to the quick-read super intelligence was all about.

Imagine a brand new lens, a lens which we all possess. It's a very long stride, however, to the humility of this outside-the-box lens. Yet the step can be taken. It means humbly accepting the reality of our denial so that we can overcome it. The super intelligence simply reveals how denial is a fundamental part of or surface consciousness. It's why almost no one in America sees the 800-pound tiger in the room named Obama. Too many people—from White House sycophants to average citizens—cling to the comfort they feel when they see Obama as genial and pleasant personality, as Thomas Sowell so astutely observed. These people need humility because humility renounces comfort for truth, for reality—and it also renounces pride.

Denial and Belief

Obama really put his finger on it at the Apollo Theater—it all comes down to what you believe. And how easily we slip into denial when something seems the least bit hard to believe. As he said, *"These guys didn't believe* [that he would sing]." They were in denial—*"they didn't think."*

It is Obama the teacher who introduced belief and denial to show us what we must overcome in order to hear him. He also said, "think." And, for sure, what really counts is what you believe about words and the mind. It's all about how the mind thinks.

Naturally we all prefer to live in denial about the deeper meanings. After all, who can accurately discern hidden meanings? Obviously he was speaking literally, but who can say he was speaking figuratively? Well, his super intelligence can—and it validates its messages.

But if you don't believe the mind operates like that, then you can remain in denial. Belief comes from knowledge. Unbelief and denial stem from ignorance. Denial lets you sleepwalk through reality. Obama's sandman image at the Apollo speaks powerfully. He had successfully put much of America to sleep about who he really was, but now he was bringing the sandman out in the open to wake America up—secretly confessing what he had gotten away with, secretly admitting who he really was.

From Singing to Whispering

Just as Obama used a stage whisper that gave us a major clue when he sang to America, he whispered to the Russians two months later. He was thus whispering to America—and to the world—confessing his true nature, blatantly bringing his true self out into the open. On March 26, 2012, on a microphone inadvertently left open he was caught whispering to Russian Federation President Dmitry Medvedev during a conference. The closer Obama came to the

2012 election, the more his super-intel became desperate to confess. Do not think his super intelligence, which picks up on everything, didn't know about the open mic. Unknowingly his super-intel was whispering to America, "Forget the Russians, see who *I* am first." A whisper symbolizes deceit. "So listen to my whispered messages as I confirm the deceit."

For the record, Obama's super-intel loves to whisper a secret. He will use that very image at a crucial point in his inauguration speech when he'll whisper another huge secret to America. Now for what he got caught saying to the Russians. At the time he was talking to Dmitry Medvedev, a puppet on a string controlled by Russian Prime Minister Vladimir Putin. Obama said, "*On all these issues but* particularly missile defense, *this can be solved, but it's important for him* [Putin] *to give me space...This is my last election. After my election I will have more flexibility.*"

"Undeniably Obama keeps the truth from the American people. Obama was whispering to the Russians about our missile defense, informing them that he would deal with them when he had more space—that is after his anticipated re-election, when he could do what he really wanted without any consequences. Then he would be flexible—the sandman president lacking a backbone—and he guaranteed the Russians that he would solve their missile-defense problem with America. His deeper message was that he would be willing to give up our air *"space"* which is what protects us from the Russians.

But getting caught confessing that he intended to hand over our biggest defense, anti-missile protection, to Russia is nothing new. After all, he had already handed over the anti-missile defense of Eastern Europe—the Poles and the Czechs—and betrayed our friends. And that was after he had unilaterally agreed with the Russians against building it. This after he had also agreed to a new START treaty with Russia, stipulating that we wouldn't use our superior weaponry if they wouldn't use their weak, outdated weapons—hardly a fair deal, but there Obama goes again, sabotaging America when he thinks he can get away with it.

So Obama gets caught trying to give away the rest of the store. What did he use as a cover-up? He said that he was really trying to "reduce nuclear stockpiles" and "reduce reliance on nuclear weapons." It's as though he's actually saying, "Having agreed to give up the defense of America, now I want to give up any offensive weapons we could use to defend ourselves." Unconsciously he cannot stop confessing.

Consider one final unconscious message in his reference to "the last election." If we are conquered by Russia, the election of 2012 could indeed be the last election in our history.

With his secret whisper, Obama hands America a glaring clue on a silver platter. For an Alinsky clone, this is as good as it gets in a sound bite.

Columnist Charles Krauthammer called Obama's decision-making "unfathomable" but it's really not all that inscrutable.[17] Krauthammer just can't bring himself to say the obvious: Obama's anger has taken an anti-American bent. In his secret rage, this president is intent on wiping America off the face of the earth by setting us up for a nuclear attack.

The world has gone crazy in its relentless race to harness nuclear power—think Iran. Who is Iran's biggest enabler? Russia, the same nation which consistently obstructs sanctions on Iran and has facilitated completion of a major Iranian nuclear reactor in the Bushehr Province.

Obama's super-intel made a huge confession linking his betraying whisper to his re-election. His secret instructions to America: we need to "give him a lot of space," that is, send him packing. Do not re-elect him. America's future depends on it.

For the record, Obama said the same thing before about Russia. Remember, he used the image "missile'" in his inauguration speech in reference to the communists. His statement was, *"Recall that earlier generations faced down fascism and communism not* [just] *with missiles... They understood that our* [military] *power alone cannot protect us."* We have the super-intel confession that the day he took office Obama was thinking about facing the communists *without* missiles—secretly planning to take America down by giving them our missile defense. Think of the embedded image, "[this] generation face-down." To confirm the message, he unconsciously adds "understand then our power alone—all by itself in Russia's possession—cannot protect us." We simply cannot deny the two images—facing Russia (communists) not with missiles and America unprotected. He continues singing the same song, whispering the same secret. Indeed, to America this president is "untrammeled fury" personified.

Unrestrained 'Flexibility'

Recently Dick Morris, the former Bill Clinton advisor who knows presidents, assessed the possibility of a second term for Obama. It was a frightening interview.[18] Here is a summary of what Morris envisioned over four more years of an unrestrained "flexible" Obama:

> Total control of health care and the economy. Weakening America as much as feasibly possible. Rescind all oil drilling started under Bush that Obama takes credit for prior to the 2012 presidential election. Instead of using our energy advantages he increases the power of foreign terrorists. He then step by step hands our country over to foreigners. He signs the International Criminal Treaty which means he must get foreign approval before going to war—meaning Russia and China. (Sorry we can't fight you because you said so.) He'll go along with the Law of Sea Treaty and sign away royalties for ocean drilling for oil. Now for space: he will ban U. S. weapons in outer space eliminating anti-missile capability. In

17 Charles Krauthammer, "Obama's Flexibility Doctrine," *Birmingham News*, March 31, 2012, p. 7A.
18 "Hannity," Fox News Channel, March 26, 2012.

addition he will sign the global ban on small arms—in that way establish arms control in America.

After stripping America of all possible self-defense—then he will continue his economic war on America—first signing the Rights of Child treaty providing a legal basis for suing America for more foreign aid to further drain our coffers. Taxes will increase and entitlements [will also increase] to build a permanent government-dependent base.

In summary, as if Obama hadn't tried to destroy America before, he will now give it his best shot. Go back to Obama's whisper to Russia: "Then, America, I will have room...have space to be as anti-American as possible." Obama is counting on continued denial—there's nothing like it to hide one's true agenda.

3

Will We Heed George Washington's Warning?

Obama Confesses to Hijacking America

Obama's super intelligence speaks again through two key stories which stretch over fifteen years, revealing a consistent picture of his anger and displaced attack on America. They speak volumes.

In a 2007 church General Synod meeting, as a member of Jeremiah Wright's denomination, then-U.S. Senator Obama, at the time a presidential hopeful, commented that conservatives had "hijacked" the Christian faith—attacking them for their views on "abortion...school prayer and intelligent design."[1]

Yet we must appreciate the bigger picture. Appreciate his aggressive image, 'hijacking,' and what 'Christian faith' represents. Don't take it literally at first—read 'faith' as what Americans basically believe.

Symbolically 'Christian faith' is code for America's longstanding moral compass which was founded on principles of natural law—the 'laws of Nature and of Nature's God' as the Declaration states. In short, the "unalienable rights of life, liberty, and the pursuit of happiness." Most founders were explicitly Christian, believing these fundamental rights were God-given. These are the same principles George Washington (as a Christian) underscored at his inauguration, the first day our government was officially constituted on April 30, 1789 when he cautioned, "The propitious smiles of Heaven can never be expected on a nation *that disregards the eternal rules of order and right* which Heaven itself hath ordained."[2]

This 'do-right-by-others' natural law was referenced by the Reverend Martin Luther King Jr. in his April 16, 1963 *Letter From a Birmingham Jail,* in which he insisted that segregation violated the rights of African-Americans, rights that are part of the divine design. Did our founders really mean that all Americans, including blacks, had basic, fundamental, God-given rights? That was Dr. King's question—and America answered, 'Yes, indeed that is our moral compass—definite and written in stone.' King increased our awareness of our

---

1 Curtis Raye, "Christian Right 'hijacked' faith, says Obama,"
http://abcnews.go.com/blogs/politics/2007/06/christian-right/ accessed May 13, 2012.
2 Following his inauguration, Washington then led the first government, senators, representatives, cabinet members down the street to solemnly pray at St. Paul's Chapel, a small Christian church.

limited vision; he called us out on our collective blind spot.

In that light, understand Obama's broader meaning. At that very moment he degraded 'conservative' Christianity, Obama's super-intel suggests his confession, '*I have hijacked America's moral foundation. I have hijacked the rule of law—the same [natural] law that faced down slavery in the Civil War, and then segregation in the Civil Rights Era. Truth be told, I just glibly hijacked the most basic thing for which Dr. King stood.*' In one fell swoop Obama by fiat declares what the rules of human nature are—and aren't. Obama again appears as a disguised raging storm unconsciously attacking America's vital moral foundation.

A slew of questions arise: Was Obama secretly defining the most basic conflict in America today—our values conflict? Do natural laws of 'do right by others' actually exist in our minds as a deeper moral compass, or can we each make up our own values, as secular humanists suggest?

As our forefathers, such as Jefferson and later Dr. King agreed, deep down we are all guided by the same deeper moral compass. Does Barack Obama possess this same deeper moral compass? If so, his deeper values are far different than the values he consciously favors.

Hostage Takers

Briefly we find another striking image from Obama's mind along the same lines as "hijacking." On December 20, 2011 Obama commented that the '*Republicans are hostage-takers,*' portraying them as refusing to negotiate over the budget crisis. However, he was blatantly lying here—the Republicans privately had given him everything he wanted, as was later reported in the *Washington Post*. In short, when it came to integrity, the moral law, Obama was the real "hostage-taker" at that moment. Once again his super intelligence was describing his own actions. He was holding the truth hostage to his manipulative agenda.

Politics is one matter, overt lying and deception is another—as the *Post* underscored. For Obama this reflects an ongoing pattern.

Obama has confessed again that he has been hijacking America—holding America hostage—for the longest time due to his misguided anger, his unfinished business. Go back to his inauguration speech where he establishes the importance of our moral foundation: "Our Founding Fathers faced with perils we can scarcely imagine, *drafted a charter to assure the rule of law and the rights of man, a charter* expanded by the blood of generations. Those ideals still light the world, and we will not give them up for expedience' sake." But notice Obama's super-intel has carefully connected our founders, our charter and the rule of law to *two violent images*, 'perils we can scarcely imagine' and 'blood of generations.' It's another confession that secretly *he* is the peril threatening our rule of law. He also adds through a denial the idea of giving up the ideals to make sure we spot his confession.

His super-intel was foreshadowing his basic character as president. During his presidency he has so freely violated multiple laws that it's hard to keep count! But we keep this confession in mind, ever on the alert for more specific confessions from Obama that he has violated the rule of law in even more egregious violent ways—which we will find.

Remember, these images are straight from his deeper mind. His consistently violent imagery secretly reveals the overwhelming anger, a boiling rage which he tries hard to hide.

Audacity

Now go to Obama's second book. Notice how well his deceit and anger fit unconsciously with the title of this tome, *The Audacity of Hope: Reclaiming the American Dream.*

Following his mind's pattern, Obama points to dreams *and* to his unconscious super-intel confessing that, since he is audaciously hijacking the American dream, we must reclaim it. Unconsciously Obama suggests his real title, *Audacity—Hoping to Hijack the American Dream.* And he is instructing us that we'd better be prepared to fight if we really wanted to reclaim it. Secretly by confessing to his attack he was offering America hope—because if we don't know what we've lost, what he's covertly taking away Alinsky-style, then we will certainly be lost.

Now he again advises Americans to educate themselves about what he is doing—or the American dream will become history.

Religion

Notice the second major topic Obama more overtly introduced in his 'hijacking faith' comment and how central it is to his life and his presidency—religion.

Indeed Obama talks about leaders who use religion to destroy unity, people who are "driving us apart...too eager to exploit what divides us"—ironically, as Obama himself is doing at that exact moment. Here we are seeing the real Obama again through the lens of denial, the proverbial log in his eye. Read the symbolic message: he's talking about phony leaders who use religion to divide (matching his later comment when condescendingly he referred to bitter small-town Midwesterners "who cling to guns or religion").[3]

His super-intel introduces the idea of a religious imposter and thus a false religion --which leads us directly to the question, "Is Obama's stated religion false?"

Clearly he alluded to his personal religion. His super-intel suggests, "I have specifically hijacked the Christian faith." This combination invites an important question: Is he secretly a Muslim, trying to separate America from its Christian heritage? Privately, as a bitter man, does he cling to the Muslim religion of his

---

3 "Barack Obama: In Pennsylvania, people 'bitter, cling to guns, religion, anti-immigrant sentiment,' " http://cnbcfix.com/obama-cling-guns-religion.html accessed May 12, 2012.

youth? Surveys show that 50 percent of Americans believe that he does. Tellingly, Obama made a major slip-of-the-tongue, referring to "my Muslim faith" during a TV interview; the reporter, Democrat and former White House operative George Stephanopoulos, instantly pointed out the slip, suggesting the president amend his statement with "...my Christian faith," which Obama obediently did, mid-sentence. This ridiculous scene came off as the pre-scripted hoax that the question of Obama's true faith plainly is. Yet, through the wonders of denial, Obama, Stephanopoulos and the entire mainstream media passed it off as an innocent verbal slip-up.[4]

Unconsciously Obama was looking into the future and could see— predicting—how divisive a president he would be. Way back in 2007, his super-intel was warning America. He specifically addressed religion—long before anyone asked the question of whether he was a Muslim. Indeed *he* was the one who initially divided America over this issue. Was this a clue that as an undercover Muslim he intended on splitting America in a much deeper way regarding matters of faith?

Think for a moment how masterly being a Muslim would fit with an Alinsky-style attack of deceiving your enemies. Think of how his embrace of Islam would further express his 'untrammeled fury' toward America. Keeping such a secret would be a very real payoff for someone as angry as Obama.

Such a probability—that he's a closet Muslim—is of course ridiculed by the media because they are horrified by the possibility. Ridicule apart from reason is a tip-off, the cheapest of tactics and one of Alinsky's strategic staples. When you can't answer a question, when you're afraid of it, simply ridicule it and shout louder than your opponent.

The evidence so far from Obama's super-intel: he has clearly connected with Christianity the most violent of images—'hijacking someone's religious faith.' It certainly fits with Obama's insistence in a speech in Turkey that "America is not a Christian nation,"[5] suggesting an unconscious confession, 'because America is not guided by a Christian president.' Radical Islam would surely delight in such a president. The subterfuge adds another dimension to Obama's propensity for clandestine power grabs.

One more thing. If Obama happens to be a secret Muslim, his super intelligence will tell us in multiple ways. We have only scratched the surface in listening to his mind in a deeper more truthful way about this subject.

For good measure, after unconsciously confessing to hijacking America's natural law-based faith, Obama called for the nation to "rededicate ourselves to a new kind of politics—a politics of conscience." This would be a new kind of conscience—a deeper super-intel moral compass. He's informing us it has

---

4 George Stephanopoulos, "This Week," ABC, September 8, 2008. I suggest you view this interview to get its full import: http://youtu.be/SVn59TC2QqM accessed May 17, 2012.
5 "Obama to Turkey: We are not a Christian nation," "American Morning," CNN, Apr. 6, 2009
http://youtu.be/ni4X9Be-wwA accessed April 18, 2012.

everything to do with politics—especially his. *Once more he provides the key to the Obama Code—his separate super intelligence moral compass.* Obama shows us that indeed he has another wiser moral compass—that natural law truly lives inside of him as much as he tries to bypass it. This true compass will see America home, but only if we listen.

Obama's Hidden Rage, Way Back in 1991

A video was uncovered in 2012 of Obama as a senior law student at Harvard in 1991 introducing a radical black professor to a student protest gathering. Obama asked the gathered students to "Open your hearts and your minds to Professor Derrick Bell." Not long after Obama made that speech, Bell was interviewed in 1992 on PBS. The professor predicted that, for years to come, blacks and whites would never get along in America. Bell explained that his life goal was the same as a powerless black lady who pledged "to constantly harass white people."[6] Bell's writings promote an extremist hostility against white people.[7]

Obama is here unconsciously suggesting, 'Open your minds to who I really am.' Indeed his super-intel had opened his own deeper mind to reveal his anger and desire for revenge—and how he would use it to divide. Long before Obama became president, this was a brief snapshot of his development and a hidden confession that his problems didn't actually stem from being a victim of white racism. Obama was deeply wounded long before he reached Harvard.

Now Obama's super intelligence will tell us what he thinks about George Washington's warning to America.

President Washington's Warning

Before we explore Barack Obama's complete story we must remember the awesome responsibility we average citizens were charged with by none other than President George Washington, the father of our country.

In George Washington's farewell address we find echoes of Colonel Jessep's powerful line, "You can't handle the truth."

Washington told American citizens the plain, hard truth which other government officials couldn't handle. *Not one of the three branches of government is capable of holding itself accountable*, Washington said.[8] Instead, this Founding Father charged citizens with a permanent task—warning them that if they didn't hold government accountable, America would unquestionably decline. Notice that Washington did not assign major responsibility for this watchdog function to the media.

More than two centuries ago, Washington spotted a lesser version of Alinsky-like tendencies in government officials. Even early bureaucrats were

---

6 Derrick Bell, "Hannity," Fox News Channel, March 12, 2012.
7 Thomas Sowell, "The Fallout From Racial Quotas," *Birmingham News*, March 16, 2012, p. 11A.
8 J. Rufus Fears, "George Washington as Statesman," *The Wisdom of History*, Lecture 27, The Teaching Company, 2007.

power-hungry and glory-seeking politicians rather than faithful public servants. Over time, even the term "public servant" has progressively dropped from our vocabulary, and bureaucrats have become thoroughly "self-serving"—with Obama now taking it to an unheard-of level. Unfortunately, today "self-serving" means "special interests-serving"—the curse that haunts Washington, D.C. Today even the media, whom we have come to rely on for the watch-dog function since Watergate has followed suit by becoming self-absorbed, thoroughly politicized and bereft of journalistic integrity.

In essence, George Washington admonished citizens, "Use your power, people. Recognize you are the boss in America—not the Congress or the Supreme Court or even the president." How we have forgotten to heed his warning.

Washington's Instructions

Before we examine Obama's crucial childhood stories which paint a vivid picture of his chronological development, we must examine a story he related on the very day he became president. It's no coincidence that it's a story—at least on the surface—about George Washington, and it suggests the massive challenge Obama presents to American ideals. Remember, a story is a hallmark of the super intelligence speaking.

In his Inauguration Day speech in January 2009, Obama praised Washington's persevering spirit. The Revolutionary War hero overcame overwhelming odds when he led his troops across the Delaware River on a blustery December 26, 1776. The resulting victory at the Battle of Trenton revived America's war effort against the British and eventually delivered us to freedom. Obama recounted that story at the conclusion of his inaugural speech—one of the two most powerful positions in a speech (the other being the beginning):

> So let us mark this day with remembrance of who we are and how far we have traveled. In the year of America's birth, in the coldest of months, a small band of patriots huddled by dying campfires on the shores of an icy river. The capital was abandoned. The enemy was advancing. The snow was stained with blood. At a moment when the outcome of our revolution was most in doubt, the father of our nation ordered these words be read to the people:
>
> 'Let it be told to the future world ... that in the depth of winter, when nothing but hope and virtue could survive... that the city and the country, alarmed at one common danger, came forth to meet [it].'
>
> America, in the face of our common dangers, in this winter of our hardship, let us remember these timeless words. With hope and virtue, let us brave once more the icy currents, and endure what storms may come. Let it be said by our children's children that when we were tested, we refused to let this journey end, that we did not turn back, nor did we falter; and with eyes fixed on the horizon and God's grace upon us, we carried forth that great gift of freedom and delivered it safely to future generations. (Isp)

Hear the story—America is under a severe attack from a common enemy against seemingly impossible odds. The issue at stake is America's freedom. Greatly outmanned against a forceful enemy determined to revoke America's freedom, Washington called on citizens to unite around hope, faith and virtue. The primary virtue was the freedom of the individual—the inalienable right to life, liberty and the pursuit of happiness.

Then Obama makes a fascinating link: *we face a common battle and danger today—a huge test.* He challenges us to refuse to turn back, to not falter, to fix our eyes on God's grace and deliver "that great gift of freedom…safely to future generations." Was the *"common…danger"* Obama saw in America in reality himself? That is, was his super-intel confessing specifically to his secret sabotage of our nation? Did he tell us that story to bypass his denial and deliver to America a solemn warning of his ominous presidency, about to unfold? Was he warning us not to exchange our national security and our economic, societal, and media freedoms for oppression by Obama? Was he indirectly telling us that—supported by control of both houses of Congress and buoyed an ingratiating, enabling media—he recognized that we citizens were going to be greatly outmanned and outgunned?

Indeed Obama's super intelligence held up President Washington as a model of virtue, as the ideal leader and allowed Washington to speak for him because Obama already knew deep down exactly how he planned to mistreat America. He was using Washington as a proxy in the very city named for the first president, on the very day Obama would follow in his footsteps.

When he noted, "the father of our nation ordered these words be read to the people," Obama's super-intel suggests again he's unknowingly talking about himself, and he confirms this by actually reading Washington's words himself (not merely referring to them by a summary or distilling them down into a principle).

Notice, too, Obama makes a striking reference: "The capital was abandoned. The enemy was advancing." Here we are given another hint that Obama would figuratively abandon the office of president via his continual attacks on America's fundamental boundaries.

Already we can see the potential value in Obama's stories. He can't stop himself from seeing his faults in others and telling us about them. We get an inkling that if we pay attention Obama will confess to his misdeeds in his stories proving that deep down everyone knows the difference between right and wrong.

Now in the spirit of George Washington, we must begin holding the government accountable—starting with the President. Like Col. Jessep, we will discover who can and who can't handle the truth. We rest assured that the truth, whatever it is, will prevail, and that truth is stronger than untruth. The day we stop believing that is the day the music dies for America.

The Frightening Consequences

Barack Obama is a man on the move, always moving the boundary plumb lines that have historically secured and guided America. And he finagles these foundations on multiple fronts simultaneously. He does this all with a smile on his seemingly calm face while his insides churn, filled to the brim with denial. And the beat goes on as Obama leads our country on a stumbling, head-first decline.

Noted historian J. Rufus Fears tells us, *"Great nations fall because of bad decisions by individual leaders....Empires decline because of individual decisions by individual leaders."*[9] Dr. Fears makes plain the great difficulty presidents have managing success, how power leads to self-defeating hubris. Professor Fears thus advises us to pay attention to Obama's decisions. Later Obama will counsel us along the same lines, instructing us to monitor his behavior as well as his words.

Right before our very eyes we have a classic case of a leader making one bad decision after another. Millions of Americans see it, but millions don't. What will it take to open the eyes of the blind? Does America have to completely fall before its citizens realize the hour is late? Must we enable a leader making bad decisions and sit back and watch, helpless to do anything? As Obama's story unfolds, we learn we have a tremendous option, if we can only overcome our corporate—and personal—denial.

---

9 J. Rufus Fears, "Why We Study History," Lecture 1, *The Wisdom of History*, The Teaching Company, 2007.

4

The Unwanted Mistake

We begin where Obama's role models began with him—before he was conceived. Barack Hussein Obama was reportedly born on August 4, 1961, although no official "long-form" Hawaiian birth certificate has been publicly released by the state. Obama finally released a purported copy in April 2011, but significant questions remain as to its veracity. Legitimate citizenship or not, the sheer irony of a questionable birthplace befits all the secrets which surround him, from his entrance into the world stretching all the way to the present day.

Given his August 4th birth, he would have been conceived around November 1, 1960, just before his single mother, Ann Dunham, turned eighteen on November 29. In September of that year she met his father, Barack Obama Sr., in a Russian language class at the University of Hawaii when she was a seventeen-year-old freshman. Coincidentally, both were studying the language of America's greatest enemy in 1960. Who would ever believe this seemingly insignificant couple would produce a man elected president who himself would deal first-hand with Russia in 2009, nearly a half-century later?

Obama's very existence began in impulsivity, lack of planning and immediate gratification outside a committed relationship. In fact, there was a definite dose of denial and mutual self-deception involved. His mother hadn't planned on getting pregnant and was in denial about the possibility. The same went for his father—a foreigner on the prowl, a man who already had a separated African wife and family tucked away on another continent. But circumstances deceived them. In truth they fooled themselves.

While Dunham's unexpected pregnancy was not all that unusual for a young single college female, this definitely *was* an unusual set of parents. Both were bright students, and both emerged from a troubled backgrounds. A white atheist mother, an only child, originally from Kansas who had moved with her family—headed by a ne'er-do-well father—to Texas, Seattle, and finally Hawaii. Barack Obama Sr., also an atheist though a Muslim by birth, was apparently still married to his tribal wife. He had boundary problems, as did Ann Dunham, who had generally rejected middle-class societal values. These two were the early role models for Barack Jr.

Earliest Memory of Father

Obama opens his 1995 memoir, *Dreams from My Father,* by recalling the day, at age 21, he received news from his Aunt Jane in Nairobi, Kenya that his father had unexpectedly been killed in an auto accident there. Such a loss is the most significant event in a man's life, according to Freud (although Obama will reveal a far greater one—also death-related and linked to his father).

From the get-go, Obama told two crucial stories—his earliest memories of his father as related to him by his maternal grandfather, who was drinking whiskey at the time and reminiscing. He recalled the day Obama Sr. nearly threw a man off the Nuuanu Pali Lookout, on mountainous cliffs northeast of Honolulu. His father had first driven his mother and a friend up to the Pali Lookout site. "Your father was a terrible driver," Obama's mother would later tell him. "He'd end up on the left-hand side of the road, the way the British drive, and if you said something he'd just huff about silly American rules."[1] Obama's grandfather also mused that his father had probably been on the wrong side of the road the whole way there—both he and Obama's mother laughed it off at the time.

Right off we have a man who drives dangerously on the wrong side of the road, consequences be damned. Upon arriving at the Pali Lookout, Obama Sr. let a fellow African student, a sightseer, borrow his pipe. Promptly choking and coughing, the student accidentally dropped the pipe over the railing down the edge of the cliff. Obama's father grabbed the man and held him over the railing for refusing to retrieve his pipe, as a curious crowd gathered around them, and as Obama's mother begged him to stop. Eventually he let the terrified man go, acting as if nothing had happened, and suggested they go get a beer—telling Obama's now-angry mother that he had wanted to teach the man a lesson about respecting other people's property. Impulsive and life-threatening, oblivious to implications of his behavior, perpetually out of bounds and yet idealizing his behavior—this was Barack Jr.'s initial male role model.

Obama's reaction to his father's behavior was just as interesting. Following the lead of his father and grandfather, he also laughs it off: "I imagine myself looking up at my father, dark against the brilliant sun, the transgressor's arms flailing about as he's held aloft. A fearsome vision of justice."[2] Living in total denial of the cruelty and injustice, Obama vastly over-idealizes his father's behavior as "fearsome justice"—revealing an extraordinary capacity to distort reality. Obama must keep the secret of just how abusive and destructive his father could be. He was trained from an early age to ignore the violence of his father's behavior—at least on the surface. These stories all have the ring of authenticity. They substantiate the future president's obsession with his absent father, and serious concerns about grandfather Obama on the part of the entire family. The stories consistently portray Obama Sr. in an undeniably unfavorable

1 Barack Obama, *Dreams,* p. 6.
2 *Ibid,* p. 7.

44

light.

Later in Kenya, Obama Sr. became a severe alcoholic and repeatedly drove drunk. He caused several serious auto accidents, the first of which killed a man. In the second collision, he lost both legs. In November 1982, a third car crash in Nairobi took his life; he was only 46.

Henry Louis Gates Incident

Years later after having been elected President of the United States, Obama impulsively jumped into a fray between Harvard professor Louis Gates and the Cambridge Police Department. It's as though Obama held a white police officer over a cliff, blaming him for harassing this middle-class black professor who appeared to be breaking into an upscale home which turned out to be his own. Believing at first that he was teaching the police a lesson about respecting a black man and his property, Obama paid no mind to the silly American rules Gates had just violated with his erratic, disorderly conduct. Obama simply ignored the responsibility police had to enforce the law in this July 2009 encounter. Then, after causing a national incident and looking foolish making the mildest of apologies, Obama invited all parties to enjoy a beer on the White House lawn. He covered it all over with alcohol and a party, exactly as his father would've done.

Was Obama again alerting America about who he really was in *Dreams from My Father*? We may well wonder if these two introductory stories sum up Obama Sr.—there's no doubt Obama Jr. chooses to tell them for a reason. They communicate convincing messages about his father's fundamental identity and the major effect his father had on his son's life as a role model. We vividly see the result of Obama Sr.'s influence in the confrontational Gates incident that began on a porch in Cambridge and ended with a brew on the White House lawn (which the conservative media mocked as 'The Beer Summit').

Illegitimacy—'Obama the Mistake'

Obama Sr. and Dunham did not marry until February 2, 1961—and major questions exist if they married at all. As we will see, Obama Jr. has been reluctant to explore the matter. In his mind he was illegitimate and his parents never married. He never once mentions it directly, implying it was never discussed with him, although he alludes to it in a multitude of ways. Bearing the label of illegitimacy always has powerful effects on a person deep down, as Obama will clearly show us.

Obama strongly hints how he experienced illegitimacy's hidden repercussions. In his second book, *The Audacity of Hope: Thoughts on Reclaiming the American Dream*, Obama described

> ...a chronic restlessness, an inability to appreciate, no matter how well things are going, those blessings that are right in front of me. It's a *flaw that is endemic* to modern life I think—*endemic in the American character,* and one that is nowhere more evident than in

45

politics. Whether politics encourages the trait or simply attracts those who possess it is unclear. Someone once said that every man is trying to live up to his father's expectations or *make up for his father's mistakes,* and I suppose that may explain my particular malady as well as anything else.[3]

Unplanned pregnancies, particularly outside of marriage, are commonly known as "a mistake"—and Obama links this particular mistake directly to his father. Obama suggests one reason for his inability to appreciate blessings right in front of him was that his parents did not appreciate the blessing of having a child—that they took the whole matter of his conception so lightly that he felt completely unappreciated.

An unplanned pregnancy in a totally uncommitted relationship (with the father having a separated wife elsewhere) was not initially looked upon with the typical wonder of parents but with anxiety, uncertainty, and shock—possibly overt rejection. Subtly but powerfully, Obama's memoirs suggest his situation built into him *a core self-identity as one big mistake*, having an endemic character flaw—"unworthy of respect." Not an ideal way to enter the world. His basic need for maximum security which included his parents respecting him, wanting him from conception, bringing him into a secure stable home was violated by his illegitimacy—but he would suffer a far greater violation, as he will tell us shortly.

In this light, Obama implies another secret confession: that "politics attracts/attracted" Obama as a means to achieve dignity and respect, to prove himself worthy to his father. Achieving elected office first in Illinois, then in D.C. and ultimately achieving the White House would overcome the stigma of being "a mistake." And even more personally, becoming the most powerful leader in the world compensates for his obvious deep sense of helplessness, his childhood legacy. It even offers his parents a model of dignity which they lacked, a common pattern for a kid from a dysfunctional home.

Until recent decades, illegitimacy had a long history in American society of implying shame, wantonness and social stigma. That's why unexpected pregnancies are often 'rectified' as soon as possible with marriage. Wedlock quickly gives the couple and the expected child the security of marriage, including the self-esteem of dignity and respect.

Was he secretly speaking for numerous illegitimate children about their deep needs for maximum security? His entire book suggests the search for the father he never really had, and he repeatedly stresses that children need a mother and a father. Obama has a deeper moral compass that he secretly draws on, based on needs for security which he suggests are universal. Later, behaving presidentially, he will draw attention to the endemic flaw of illegitimacy in American society—suggesting it's from personal experience.

---

3 Barack Obama, *The Audacity of Hope: Thoughts on Reclaiming the American Dream,* (New York: Crown Publishers, 2006), p. 3.

Lending great credence to Obama's painful experience of illegitimacy, in a Fathers' Day speech in 2008 the president disparagingly referred to *African-American* fathers who "need to realize that responsibility does not end at conception ... who abandon their families, behaving like children instead of men." He bemoaned how "more than half of all black children live in single-parent households"—which means they are "more likely to have behavioral problems, or run away from home, or become *teenage parents themselves* [like his mother]. And the foundations of our community are weaker because of it."[4] With these words Obama suggests that his foundation as a person was greatly weakened by his illegitimacy—and it deeply haunted him and even predicted behavioral problems.

Certainly his illegitimacy would explain a chronic restlessness in Obama, an inability to appreciate how well things are going because he was shaped in an insecure environment where things were not going well at all. Deep in his bones, Obama still feels that shakiness.

'Obama: The Presidential Mistake?'

We also find him in *Dreams from My Father* mistakenly dating his parents' marriage back to 1960 instead of 1961, a 'mistake' that strongly hints that he wants to locate the marriage *before* his conception.[5] Possibly it's just a typographical error, but it's a date to which he would have been ultra-sensitive, suggesting the error was intentional. Thus we have Obama's first major secret—the powerful emotional effects of illegitimacy, which he kept from himself, locked away in his mind.

His "mistaken existence" would have led him to ponder—but not actually pose—several questions of his parents: *Why didn't you think enough of me to start me off within a legitimate family? Did you respect or love each other at all—or me? Did you realize how you were shaping me as a person—how helpless you made me feel?* Above all, Obama was concerned about his father's view of him: *Why was I not worthy of your respect?*

A brief look at Obama's presidency reflects a marked indifference to millions of Americans, frequently the vast majority—for instance, failing to provide economic security for the nation by fixing problems, not exacerbating them. Is he living out his fundamental identity— "I am a mistake"? Is he inflicting his own deep lack of security, in part stemming from his illegitimacy, on America? Is he reflecting a secret underlying self-image, becoming the president who was a mistake, by making mistakes right and left?

Was Abortion Considered?

But immediately we have an even more powerful issue and a whopper of a secret—*did either parent (or both) push for an abortion?* We would be surprised

---

4 Fathers' Day speech, June 14, 2008. See Appendix C.
5 Barack Obama, *Dreams,* p. 12.

if they didn't. Their relationship was replete with lack of a commitment. They had no religious prohibition against terminating a pregnancy. They were impulsive. Surely two strong-willed people in the early-1960s when abortion was considered a viable option would've at least mulled over the procedure, especially in free-spirited Hawaii—the first state to allow legal abortions.

Ann Dunham, the Kansas-born mother, seemingly had predilections toward abortion. Her high-school friends observed her comparative disdain for marriage. Education seemed more important to her than marriage and child-rearing, and she showed no affinity for children, refusing even to baby-sit. Her friends could not imagine her marrying and giving birth. She was varyingly described as a "novelty," "decidedly liberal...challenged the existence of God," an "intellectual rebel" with a beatnik sensibility. She preferred foreign films to American movies and often decried the "very dull Eisenhower-ness of our parents."[6]

One of her respites while growing up in a Seattle suburb had been a wing of Mercer Island High School called "anarchy alley" where a few professors taught "radical" courses.[7] Another classmate recalled, "Only once or twice was she teased [about her first name, Stanley, which she used in high school]. She had a sharp tongue, a deep wit, and she could kill. We all called her Stanley."[8]

Another motivation for an abortion came from her parents, who initially didn't want their eighteen-year-old pregnant daughter to marry Obama's black father. Eventually, she reports, they came around. They decided it was "the right thing to do."[9] Certainly they didn't want their only child burdened by single motherhood. They could have easily urged her to consider an abortion and continue college. They took time to decide "the right thing to do," implying the possibility they initially urged her to do the wrong thing and abort her pregnancy.

In his memoirs, Obama reflects, "...in the most sophisticated of Northern cities, the hostile stares, the whispers, *might have driven a woman in my mother's predicament into a back-alley abortion*" (p. 12). First Obama implies his mother was the one who most strongly considered an abortion, but the woman was driven to consider it by an apparent abandonment by the father. Driven to it by "hostile stares" also suggests that Obama's father, noted for his hostility, was angry over the pregnancy and urged an abortion. Obama further suggests a realization of his own potential abortion by depicting "sophisticated" parents—his bright parents in college—suggesting another hidden reference to the great family secret of his near-abortion.

---

6 Jonathan Martin, "Obama's mother known here as 'uncommon,' April 8, 2008,
http://seattletimes.nwsource.com/html/politics/2004334057_obama08m.html.
7 *Ibid.*
8 David Maraniss, "Though Obama Had to Leave to Find Himself, It Is Hawaii That Made His Rise Possible".
The Washington Post, August 22, 2008, http://www.washingtonpost.com/wp-dyn/content/article/2008/08/22/AR2008082201679_pf.html accessed May 20, 2012.
9 Barack Obama, *Dreams,* p. 125.

During the presidential campaign, Obama was asked when life begins. "That's above my pay grade," he famously replied, a rather flip retort that provides a quick window into Obama's core identity as "low grade, a mistake." His hidden pain was triggered by the question of when life begins, namely his life. He suggests that "higher grade" people above him—i.e., his parents—had struggled with that question and at first decided he indeed was simply a mistake, strongly considering aborting him. Acting as though they were of high value and he was of low value also suggests his view of them as arrogant and power-hungry.

Obama's flippant answer to this very serious question also implies that initially his parents did not answer the question affirmatively that life begins at conception, that the entire question as to his existence was up in the air—and in his mind, remains up in the air. His near-abortion (combined with his illegitimacy) left Obama's security forever up in the air and further explains his deep restlessness. His shallow answer to this question further implies that his parents have no answer for such potential cruelty. And the quick reference to a higher-up having the exclusive say-so about when life begins suggests a deeper moral compass which knows that God gives life at conception—something Obama will return to later as president.

We cannot imagine anyone discussing the possibility of his abortion directly with Obama personally—not ever. Yet if it was considered, we can be sure that he would've learned about it later—most kids eventually discover their family's most deeply hidden secrets. For example, he could easily have overheard a casual comment from his by-then-doting grandparents to his mother, saying, "Aren't you glad you never went through with that abortion?"

Imagine what such a possibility does to a child's mind. To think, your parents and your grandparents did not want you to live, in fact they wanted to destroy you! The burden would've been beyond comprehension—beyond despair. Total humiliation, absolute helplessness. Obama would certainly experience a new low. He'd see himself as not just a mistake but an insignificant mistake, his life truly a trifle in their eyes. He could almost hear his parents thinking, *If we get pregnant, we'll just get an abortion. He'll never really exist—we'll treat him that way. No attachment, no worries, just poof—get a minor medical procedure—and he'll be gone.*

Again imagine the questions in the back of Obama's mind: *How close did you really come to aborting me? Which one of you stood up for me? How important really was—is—my existence? Why would you considering taking my life from me?*

Lastly remember Obama's earliest memory of his father—driving recklessly and also threatening a man's life. Unquestionably, Obama would have quickly concluded his father had the potential to kill—and when he learned about a possible abortion, he would've seen himself as the one his father was holding by his legs, dangling him over the cliff before finally deciding to let him live. An abortion itself even suggests grabbing a fetus from the womb by the legs and jerking it out—a clear birth image linked to a doctor holding a newborn upside down. If you have any doubts about such thorough mental processing taking place in a young Obama, we will see how new research verifies indeed it does. Obama has had more than 50 years to go over such crucial questions in his mind.

Fast-Forward to 2012: Obama's 'Contra-Ception' Controversy

Let's look ahead at a related moment in Obama's life that provides a revealing snapshot of his underlying mindset and fixation on his pain. On February 9, 2012, he mandated that faith-based employers include birth control and other reproductive services in their health-care coverage. Specifically this applied to Catholic institutions where church leaders morally oppose artificial birth control and related services. They responded by insisting that Obama violated their constitutional right of freedom of religion.

Shortly afterwards Obama retreated in a fashion but just as dictatorially ordered the institutions' health insurance companies to provide free birth-control coverage—and in the end maintained his violation of religious freedom. Obama's extreme behavior first suggests that he was unconsciously reenacting on the Catholic Church a basic violation of his birth-related rights long ago. It all harkens back to his conception and near abortion. His preoccupation with birth control suggests that secretly and desperately he is ruled by deep "contra-ception" needs to prevent others from undergoing the pain of abortion.

From Obama's own thoughts we already find impressive evidence that we have unearthed his greatest childhood secret—near death by abortion. Thinking you are a mistake is one thing—but believing you nearly lost your life is another matter altogether. We must not overlook the simple fact—the idea of his being aborted originated in Obama's mind—and it precisely matched his own stories of his father's violence. He has painted a powerful picture of exactly where his deep sense of helplessness originated. And he has much more to say about this later.

Maternal Motivation for Abortion

Another subtle possible motivation for an abortion came from a buried trauma suffered by Obama's mother herself. During her senior year in high school, her friends lived in great fear of a nuclear bomb—"the Doomsday Clock seemed as close as it had ever been to boom" and a great "sense of malaise permeated the group. Why bother? The boom is going to happen."[10] Yet, as her friends noticed, Obama's mother demonstrated definite denial of the common concern. This left her vulnerable at her tender age to unconsciously reenact her own "near destruction" trauma on her child via near-abortion.

Such denial could help explain Ann Dunham's out-of-control behavior. The

---

10 David Maraniss, "Though Obama had to leave," p. 3.

summer before her senior year in high school she had run off to San Francisco with a boyfriend, a move which unsettled her parents. It was the first hint of her tendency to walk on the wild side. Soon after her move to free-wheeling Hawaii in the summer of 1960, she apparently became promiscuous. She frequented a pick-up bar alone in the red-light district—most likely Bill Lederer's Bar located at Two Hotel Street.[11] Her normally high academic performance slipped greatly, with a first semester grade point average of 1.35, approximately a D average. She was taking only two courses.

Such impulsive behavior can be partially explained by a common mentality in response to significant death-threats from a perceived imminent nuclear attack, "Tomorrow we die, so let's eat, drink and be merry today." Then throw in an unwanted sudden move to Hawaii, away from her friends. Even Ann Dunham's high school friend, Maxine Box, was surprised Dunham ended up pregnant her first year out of high school, recalling, "She felt she didn't need to date or marry or have children"—further suggesting a dramatic personality change for Dunham.[12]

First Meeting of Parents Revealing
The story of the parents' first date hints at his mother's and father's impulsive behavior. As Obama revealed in *Dreams*, his parents had agreed to meet in a park, having first met in a class which began September 26, 1960. His father was late arriving at the park as his mother describes, "It was a nice day, so I laid out on one of the benches, and before I knew it I had fallen asleep. Well, an hour later—an hour!—he shows up with a couple of his friends. I woke up and the three of them were standing over me." Obama's father comments to his friends, "See gentlemen, I told you she was a fine girl, and that she would wait for me."[13] Though this is a seemingly benign story, it contains strong symbolic suggestions which match Dunham's promiscuous behavior with him and likely with others. Obviously she slept with Obama Sr. shortly after meeting him and soon became pregnant around November 4.

This is their very first date and she is asleep, lying down on a bench, waiting for him—as Barack Sr. notes—she's doing what he wants. Symbolically, the story suggests she laid down—had sex—with him on their first date, just as he wanted. And not only was he late to their date, *she* was soon late with her period. The story appears authentic—both literally and symbolically.

She also likely slept with her father's older black friend, Frank Marshall Davis, by December 1960 as we will explore in Chapter 7 which focuses on Davis' role in the family. In *Dreams*, Obama Jr. himself later alluded to his

11 Jerome Corsi, "Does WND's Reporting Rule Out an Obama Kenyan Birth?," June 27, 2011, http://wnd.com/2011/06/316265/, accessed May 22, 2012.
12 Jerome Corsi, *Where's the Birth Certificate? The Case That Barack Obama Is Not Eligible to Be President,* (Washington DC: Regnery, 2011), p. 123.
13 Barack Obama, *Dreams,* p. 126.

mother's sexual attraction to black or dark-skinned men beginning at age 16 when she saw the stimulating film, *Black Orpheus*. Her early sexual awakening regarding black men was recreated before his very eyes years later when Obama attended a screening of the same film with her as an adult. He described witnessing her arousal, "fantasies that had been forbidden to a white middle-class girl from Kansas, the promise of another life: warm, sensual, exotic, different."[14] Indeed Ann Dunham always had an attraction for the different life and the different man.

For his part, Obama Sr. was obviously a man on the prowl. His sexual appetite was consistent with that of other male Kenyan students at the university, one of whom who left "two pregnant blondes."[15] In particular, as Obama Sr.'s Immigration and Naturalization Service files reveal, he was reprimanded by the foreign student advisor, Sumi McCabe, in the summer of 1960 for his promiscuous behavior—"running around with several girls since he first arrived [a year earlier]." She "cautioned him about his playboy ways." Obama Sr.. replied that "he would try to stay away from the girls."[16]

Parents' Wedding Date?

There was yet another complicating factor in Obama's early life. The humiliation of his illegitimacy and likely near-abortion would continue to grow as he faced the disturbing question: Did his parents ever actually get married? The wedding—supposedly a civil ceremony on February 2, 1961—had no known witnesses. No family members were present. There were no wedding pictures, no known marriage certificate, or engagement. There was also the questionable story that his mother had impulsively flown with his father to the nearby island of Maui to be married there.[17] Certainly that fits the mother's pattern—when in trouble, get out of Dodge on an airplane. And it fits with the lack of support for the marriage initially from her parents, and matches the divorce certificate in 1964 listing Maui as the place of marriage on February 2, 1961. However, thorough research has not turned up any public records of marriage.[18]

In the book Obama admits that the entire matter was so confusing and disturbing that he was afraid to explore it. First, he reports that his black father would not have made "my mother's engagement any easier to swallow" as if there were an engagement. He goes on,

> In fact how and when the marriage occurred remains a bit murky, a bill of particulars *I've never quite had the courage to explore.*

---

14 Barack Obama, *Dreams*, p. 124.
15 Jack Cashill, *Deconstructing Obama: The Life, Loves, and Letters of America's First Post-Modern President*, (New York: Threshold Editions, 2011) p. 253.
16 "Barack Hussein Obama Sr. Immigration File," http://www.scribd.com/doc/54015762/Barack-Hussein-Obama-Sr-Immigration-File p. 39, accessed May 18, 2012.
17 David Maraniss, "Though Obama had to leave," p.5.
18 Jerome Corsi, *Where's the Birth Certificate?* p. 125.

There's no record of a real wedding, a cake, a ring, a giving away of the bride. No families were in attendance; it's not even clear if the people back in Kansas were fully informed. Just a small civil ceremony, the justice of the peace. The whole thing seems so fragile in retrospect, so haphazard. And perhaps that's how my grandparents intended it to be, a trial would pass, just a matter of time, so long as they maintained a stiff upper lip, *and didn't do anything drastic.*[19]

Obama's reference to a murky marriage and his fear of exploring the matter with his mother and grandparents even as an adult suggests strongly he believed his parents never married. The first official declaration of their marriage that can be confirmed occurred in April 1961 was reflected in his father's immigration files (see below). It's possible Obama's parents took a prolonged time to decide what to do about their relationship following the pregnancy and never officially married.

Fragility Beyond Words
Secrets piled upon secrets for Obama about the supposed marriage and really the "whole thing"—the unexpected impulsive pregnancy, the questionable marriage, his parents' lack of commitment to each other, his grandparents disapproval of the relationship—and alluding again to abortion in the idea of his grandparents taking "drastic" actions.

He again implies that in the back of his mind he secretly knew about the chaos surrounding his birth but simply could not admit it and that, deep inside, he lives to this day with a fragile identity—one he's reluctant to explore. Clearly there were things his family did not want Obama to know, only heightening his fragile view of himself. Above all he would have developed a sense that all his primary nurturers at one point wanted to get rid of him—abort him—creating a sense that left him in constant danger, wondering whom could he ever trust?

Mixed-Race Problems
One issue surfaced repeatedly, providing answers why everyone treated him as so flawed. Shaky stories of the wedding and his grandparents' behavior would have spoken volumes to him, and he suggests how the story unfolded in his mind. His grandparents first urging his mother to do the wrong thing, demonstrating self-control to keep from taking "drastic action," and not notifying the relatives in Kansas about the wedding suggests no need for one because he wouldn't exist—all ideas implying his grandparents initially supported an abortion.

Later as an adult, he would speculate on his black father's first meeting with his grandparents when his mother invited her African classmate over for dinner. He viewed his mother grasping his father's hand beside her and his grandmother biting her lip, saying nothing. Later that night after Obama Sr. was

19 Barack Obama, *Dreams,* p. 22.

gone, Obama envisioned both grandparents commenting privately on how intelligent and dignified he was. Then Obama asks, "But would they let their daughter marry one?"[20] We can hear the follow-up question, "And would you want your daughter to have his child—a child of mixed race?" *Again Obama points to the development of a deep-seated idea first that he was nearly destroyed because of his black blood.* His grandparents' and mother's later denial of racism and avowed love for him aside, Obama would forever harbor deep in his mind this early close call and the idea his blackness was a problem to the people who raised him and supposedly loved him most.

Obama's Naturally Deceitful Core

Does Obama's political career and presidency secretly reflect his reaction to his own near-abortion and the initial views of his role models on terminating pregnancies? At the extreme far end of the political spectrum in supporting partial-birth abortions, Obama basically supports taking *the life of a baby who survived an abortion.* Also, Obama only got his healthcare bill passed by promising pro-life Representative Bart Stupak an executive order preventing the use of federal funds for abortion—which Obama knew was ultimately unenforceable. And indeed it was. This clearly misleading behavior shows Obama acting exactly how a child would react to near-abortion—having deceit built into his core. Does Obama's extreme position on abortion offer a further hint that he knows he was a near-abortion victim? Later, Obama will talk about damaged kids reenacting on others the trauma they experienced—his abortion policy strongly suggests he was a near victim.

In yet another way, Obama's frustrating inability to formulate pro-American foreign policy—failing to protect America and her allies—likely reflects how he felt unprotected by his parents and grandparents. Could he be placing America at risk of being "aborted"—attacked by a foreign power? Could he be carelessly treating America like an unwanted, flawed, mixed-race child of such little importance that he's ultimately unconcerned about its future?

But in the end, Obama wasn't aborted, and we wonder: Does he in his innermost being harbor an anti-abortion (i.e., pro-life) position? We will keep this important question in mind—coming back to it in the second half of this book. His super-intel will reveal that Obama is surprisingly divided about abortion.

Summary—Rosetta Stone in Place

We now have yet another major secret—disdain for his "mixed black blood"—on top of *the* major secret—near-abortion. Those two sources of shame stand on top of another secret—illegitimacy stemming from the parents' questionable marriage. Introduced by his key role models, these are all major issues which would shape his life. His humiliation explodes off the charts.

---

20 Barack Obama, *Dreams*, p. 18.

Shortly after birth he will have two more significant events in his life—the quick separation of his parents and his father's total abandonment—guaranteeing him another two tons of secrets, further magnifying his fragile world. At four weeks of age, Obama faced enough issues to keep him in therapy for years as an adult. But already he has admitted that would never happen—that he simply can't handle the painful powerful truths that came his way. On the surface he has covered up all the violence and humiliation directed at him.

But already we have uncovered plenty of evidence of precisely what Obama unconsciously told us we would find—tremendously deep unspeakable humiliation and utter helplessness. Now, following his instruction, we can take the short step of understanding that we Americans are now personally experiencing his secret rage—delivered just like the message was delivered to him by his role models, with a smile on their faces, as if their actions toward him were harmless. Indeed humiliation plus powerlessness equal untrammeled fury. Do the Obama emotional math—two plus two is four.

Obama repeatedly insists that the Rosetta stone for understanding him is to realize his early emotional pain. Without question that is the "permanent" lens through which he unconsciously sees the world—and we have only scratched the surface. His stories will provide many more of his unique views of the world, but now that we understand the deeper lens, we can understand what he sees. He paints rich pictures with his words, his stories. If we keep this dual lens—conscious and unconscious-- constantly in mind, we will see Barack Obama's mind as never before.

His repeated boundary violations are clearly attacks of unleashed fury on America making us feel his pain—his humiliation—as he brings a great nation down several notches. We can feel his helplessness as he imposes his will on our lives via destructive regulations and laws.

But we have more of his humiliation yet to explore before we can fully grasp the unrelenting rage which secretly controls him—and to finally learn then what to do about it, at his own super-intel's suggestion.

5

Obama's Mysterious Birth

As we continue to explore Obama's development chronologically, the issue of his birth and birthplace naturally surface. Before going further we must recognize the extreme resistance the mainstream media demonstrates about investigating the circumstances of his birth. Surprisingly, the conservative media has also failed to fully explore this crucial issue with a few exceptions.

Of course the media lacks knowledge about the super intelligence and how it communicates, which is why Obama unconsciously admonished them to educate themselves about this revealing, deeper part of the mind.

Obama's quick-read super intelligence can answer any question. We thus have an entirely new source for clarifying Obama's entire birth picture as we will see later.

Back to the Birth

Obama refused to produce a supposed long-form birth certificate for three years until suddenly releasing one on April 27, 2011 under dire circumstances (explored fully in Chapter 15). Until that moment, Americans increasingly believed Obama was foreign-born and questioned his eligibility as president for good reason (e.g., no viable birth certificate, spending millions preventing the official birth certificate release).

Yet the media not surprisingly accepted Obama's birth certificate at face value. Eventually the pressure increased when in March 2012 Sheriff Joe Arpaio of Arizona declared it to be a forgery following an extensive two-month investigation of Obama's online birth certificate. And still the media, other than a few conservative sources, refused to cover the story known on the Internet as "Forgerygate."

For the longest time Obama's presidential eligibility rested on two shreds of flimsy evidence (see below)—each open to manipulation. The media had built its "rock-solid" case supposedly proving that he was born in Hawaii on: (1) a short form "derivative" birth certificate known as a *Certification of Live Birth* or COLB, and (2) two identical birth announcements in Honolulu newspapers. We can throw in the fact that he was the Democratic presidential nominee when they made up their minds on this.

COLB

First the Certification of Life Birth (COLB) is issued by the Hawaii Department of Health (DOH) upon merely the testimony of a parent, grandparent or any known adult that a home birth has occurred—and simply states date of birth, parents, their address and sex of child. It could even be obtained by mail. The adult's testimony was never investigated. And a grandparent, for example, could register a foreign birth as a local birth easily obtaining a COLB reflecting a Hawaii birth. As late as 2008, the only requirement of the adult requesting a COLB was proof of Hawaii residence at the time of application.[1] The COLB is distinctly different from a long-form hospital-generated birth certificate—known as a *Certificate* of Live Birth---which lists the doctor and hospital.

In June, 2008 several "investigative" websites, claiming neutrality but obviously pro-Obama, released an Obama COLB on the Internet which they claimed to have gotten from Obama campaign spokesman Tommy Vietor. The document was never released to the public and only one website (factcheck.org) showed pictures of someone holding what they claimed was an accurate COLB copy. Importantly, they tried to mislead the public that this was Obama's actual birth certificate. And they completely ignored the fact that a COLB in no way addresses the conflict between "natural-born" and "native-born."[2] Furthermore, the Hawaii DOH never released a statement supporting any of the Internet COLBs as authentic. And several document examiners declared that the Internet COLB and pictures of it were fraudulent.[3] (An Obama supporter's attempt at validating the COLB backfired when he showed how to create a phony COLB online and claimed he could skillfully create phony birth certificates.)

The bottom line was that the COLB never proved the obvious—that Obama was born in Hawaii—because the entire matter rested on the testimony of the person who sought the COLB originally, possibly his grandparent. The fact that it alone was released as Obama's primary proof of citizenship—posted only on the Internet and not physically released for examination—demonstrates Obama's characteristic avoidance. Repeatedly hiding vital information about yourself blatantly says you have something major to hide.

There were other major problems which have gone ignored by the media. Most strikingly, Obama's birth registration number on his COLB was higher than the number on the birth certificates of two children, the Nordyke twins, born a day after him.[4]

---

1 Corsi, *Where's The Birth Certificate?* p. 74.
2 *Ibid*, p. 67.
3 *Ibid*, pp. 69-70.
4 "From A to Z: What's wrong with Obama's birth certificate? Examine for yourself mounting evidence that president's document isn't genuine," http://www.wnd.com/2011/05/296881/ accessed April 20, 2012.

Newspaper Birth Announcements

On August 13, 1961, when Obama was nine days of age, a birth announcement appeared in the *Honolulu Advertiser*. A day later, the identical announcement was published in the *Honolulu Star Bulletin*. Identical because both papers' got their information from the Hawaii DOH (*whose own source was again the person obtaining the COLB*). In effect we had one newspaper report of births with no attempt to verify the information from the DOH. Also, the hospitals did not report births to the newspapers. The address of Obama's parents, listed as 6085 Kalanianaole Highway (Honolulu), was actually the residence of his maternal grandparents which suggests they may have registered his birth with the DOH since proof of residence was required.

Democrat Party Certification of Eligibility

Strikingly, the Democratic National Committee (DNC) only certified him as constitutionally eligible to the one state that required it, Hawaii. House Speaker Nancy Pelosi, chairwoman of the Democratic National Convention, had signed the certification of nomination document declaring that Obama met constitutional requirements following the Democratic convention in August of 2008. The DNC had a separate letter and separate certificate of nomination for the other 49 states, intentionally omitting the constitutional eligibility phrase included in the Hawaii letter—strongly suggesting their uncertainty and avoidance. Most importantly, the DNC and specifically Pelosi refused to release any information as to how they determined Obama's eligibility. Most likely they simply accepted the COLB which the Obama campaign also presented on the web as the official birth certificate. On the other hand the Republican Party sent the same letter to all fifty states certifying McCain's constitutional eligibility.[5]

All in all, the previous evidence for establishing Obama's citizenship was really no evidence at all. The Internet COLB and the matching newspaper birth announcement established absolutely no proof of where or even when Obama was born. The DNC essentially did nothing.

The Media

At the time, totally lacking any real evidence, the media silently declared the investigation of Obama's eligibility issue officially over. Even today, they continued to degradingly label as "birthers" —a derogatory term suggesting far-out conspiracy theorists—anyone who questions the president's birthplace. As more and more Americans doubted his American birth, the more cynical and attacking the media became. A survey just prior to Obama's purported birth certificate release conducted by Public Policy Polling—a Democratic polling firm known for accuracy—had found 51 percent of GOP primary voters believed Obama was not born in the United States.

A prominent conservative columnist, George Will, demonstrated woefully

---

5 Corsi, *Where's The Birth Certificate?*, pp. 278-80.

Andrew G. Hodges, M.D.

inadequate research by ignorantly labeling the 51 percent "paranoid." He observed that Obama had spent the first six years of his life in Hawaii and completely failed to mention Obama lived in Seattle the first year-plus of his life.[6] Another conservative columnist, Debra Sanders, not only reacted with disbelief to the poll, she also stated, "Informed Americans understand Obama is American-born. Conspiracy theorists that suggest otherwise are too tortured to take seriously." She went on noting those who believe the 'birther' story "make Republicans look like rubes."[7]

With all due respect to Ms. Sanders, an otherwise fine commentator, we must consider another case of log-in-your-eye projection and that deep down she indeed realizes she's the one who's the rube. Resorting to name-calling, offering no support for her conclusion and the shallowest of investigations in a previous column (where her primary source referenced was the left-leaning factcheck.org website) weakens her analysis.

In reality, the media's flimsy investigation was—and is—an insult to millions of Americans, as Donald Trump noted in early 2011, when he called the birth issue "the potential scam of the century." Trump seems to be one of the only commentators around who has the guts to call a spade a spade; self-admittedly no sophisticate, he is not tempted to participate in the elites' conspiracy of silence. Many citizens had logically asked why Obama had spent millions avoiding the simple (and indeed it was) release of his actual, paper, physical long-form birth certificate, along with all his health and academic records. As an investigator in several fields—physician, psychiatrist, psychiatric researcher, and forensic profiler in major criminal investigations with a background in journalism—I know what a good investigation is.

This was never a careful investigation by the media—not by a long shot. And—let's face it—confronting a sitting president over a question of such magnitude is extremely uncomfortable even for experienced journalists. Unquestionably the media have failed in their responsibility to report Obama's failure to meet the presidential birthplace qualification.

Birth Questions
There were two concerns about Obama's citizenship and country of birth regarding presidential eligibility. First, concerned citizens raised the question of whether he was "natural-born" as required by the Constitution or "native-born" and therefore ineligible. *They did not question that Obama was born in Hawaii.* In a nutshell the distinction was whether or not Obama had one parent who was a legal U.S. citizen making him "natural-born." Certainly neither his father—a British subject and later a Kenyan citizen (when Kenya obtained its independence from the British Empire)—nor his 18-year-old mother met constitutional criteria to confer citizenship on Obama. His underage mother had

---

6 George Will, "The GOP's weirdness factor," March 6, 2011, *NY Post.*
7 Debra Sanders, "Birthers? Or simply don't like Obama?" February 17, 2011, *San Francisco Chronicle.*

not lived in the United States for the required five years after she was fourteen, which made Obama "native-born."

And if he were not born in the United States Obama would not be a citizen at all.

Obviously, many citizens were concerned he was foreign-born, with stories abounding about a Kenyan birth as many in Kenya claimed, including newspaper accounts, the Kenyan Congress, and a relative.

In this chapter (and part of the next) we will consider the question of where Obama was born as first a matter of human development reflecting family dynamics. In other words, the story of his life as it unfolds with place of birth being an important part. Naturally the "birther" issue surfaces. Understand at this point we are basically raising questions. We will examine an occasional super-intel message from Obama on the matter in this chapter and the next. Then in Chapters 11 through 14 his super intelligence will comment fully on the issue.

Who was Really Obama's Father?

Two important authors, Jerome Corsi and Jack Cashill, raise vital questions about the apparent lack of a warm relationship between Ann Dunham and Obama Sr. They reference friends of Obama Sr. who don't remember her or recall the two of them even dating. Certainly they remained unaware of any engagement or marriage.[8] The sole exception was Obama Sr.'s friend, Neil Abercrombie, the current governor of Hawaii, who many see as simply covering up for President Obama. The few surviving photographs of Obama Sr. socializing at the University of Hawaii fail to depict Ann Dunham.

Certainly, Obama's seemingly authentic story of his parents' first meeting strongly suggests casual sex early on between the two. It points to an unexpected pregnancy involving two promiscuous college students. There has been much speculation as to *whether Obama Sr. was even Jr.'s biological father*. Yet the undeniable fact is Ann Dunham became pregnant with a mixed-race child. The story of her quick sexual involvement with Obama Sr. fits with the timeline of Obama's birth on August 4, 1961, and points to Obama Sr. as the black father. Having met him in class on or after September 26, 1961, Dunham became pregnant around November 4th.

Mother 'Disappears'

After finishing her first semester in January 1961, Ann Dunham dropped out of college and seemingly out of sight until reappearing with Obama's birth in August. This has prompted much speculation (e.g. that she had gone to a home for unwed mothers, returning home with her child and a cursory marriage to Obama Sr.). Yet a likely explanation is that she was in shock, being suddenly pregnant at 18 by a black man from casual sex and unmarried, maybe unsure, for the moment, of who the father was, her wild child days suddenly coming to a

---

8 Corsi, *Where's the Birth Certificate*, p. 129. Cashill, *Deconstructing Obama,* p. 264.

screeching halt and time to pay the piper, her desperate days on the run as a primary coping style taken away, and possibly experiencing major morning sickness, typical of first-time mothers. In addition she lived at home and had to face her parents. All in all, Ann Dunham had a plateful of issues to cause her to take a semester off, including her academic drive already in decline.

Apparently as Ann Dunham surmised the father of her child was Obama Sr., and abortion became a real possibility, she discussed it with him, as we will continue to see. We have heard of the believable stories Stanley Dunham told about Obama Sr. (reckless driver, quick temper and life-threatening to others) which further suggest Obama Sr.'s negative impact with Ann's entire family.

Also, Barack Sr.'s friends admit, "to say we knew Obama (Sr.) well would be difficult," and that *"he was a private man,"* an academic hermit, holed up studying in his apartment. Yet they "wondered how he sustained himself outside of his focused…academic pursuits."[9] His friends apparently knew of no female relationship Obama Sr. had in Hawaii—obviously they were ignorant of his playboy ways which his INS (Immigration & Naturalization Services) supervisor had discovered. Yet the friends hinted at his need for a female. In fact, he typically always had a relationship with a woman going on, as the INS knew, just as he would later at Harvard. Such a secretive man could gradually have worked his way quietly into some sort of relationship with a woman carrying his child, and he would surely have met his prospective in-laws.

These same friends, who never saw him with Ann Dunham, obviously had no idea he had told INS that he was the father of Obama Jr. (We can be sure they had limited if any awareness of his dealings with the INS.) Certainly Obama Sr. would not dare mention he discussed an abortion with her. One friend, who claimed to know both Ann and Obama Sr. but never saw them together, did not even know Ann was pregnant.[10]

There would be plenty of reasons for Obama Sr. not telling his friends he was married—or that he was an expectant father. He did not want to stir up any issues regarding his sexual behavior and an unexpected pregnancy. By the time of their possible marriage on February 2, 1961, Ann Dunham had dropped out of school and was living with her parents eight miles away from campus. Obama Sr. also likely wanted to continue his playboy ways. Fidelity was never his strong suit. Not only a very private man, he was likely uncertain about the future of a marriage to a young white woman. He kept his own private apartment near campus, but one reason may have been his inordinate academic drive which could easily be complicated by living with his wife and her parents.

Various sources have described several scenarios suggesting Obama Sr. was not the father. One idea was that the marriage was a sham based on Obama

9 Corsi, *Where's the Birth Certificate?*, p. 130.
10 Jack Cashill, "Maraniss Bio Deepens Obama Birth Mystery," American Thinker, June22,2012.http://www.americanthinker.com/2012/06/maraniss_bio_deepens_obama_birth_mystery.html#ixz z1yXlJrHrI accessed June 22, 2012.

Sr.'s need for extension of his student visa. Obama Sr.'s INS immigration files, *in a memo dated 4/10/61,* reflect that his foreign student advisor Sumi McCabe had contacted INS expressing concern about Obama's recent marriage to Ann Dunham. McCabe feared possible bigamy since she knew about Sr.'s African wife. But Obama Sr. claimed he was divorced from her, which he reported occurs in tribal Kenya by a simple declaration. This was when McCabe mentioned she had confronted Obama Sr. previously in the fall of 1960 about his promiscuous playboy ways. She had also had noted how intelligent Obama Sr. was.[11]

Administrator Lyle H. Dahling who signed the INS memo recommended that Obama be closely questioned and that denial of his next student visa extension (in August, 1961) be considered on grounds of bigamy. He suggested if Obama Sr.'s new wife petitioned for the visa extension that the marriage then be investigated as to its legality. He was referring to the practice of foreign students using the "new American wife" ploy to guarantee continuation of their year-by-year visa extensions. [12]

On 8/31/61 Obama Sr. himself applied for a visa extension. Administrator Wood expressed no concerns over a bona-fide marriage or bigamy (as previously referenced). He simply noted Obama had reported the birth of his son—Barack Obama II—on August 4, 1961 *in Honolulu* and had plans for G26 graduate school in a year in the States. The administrator, oddly enough, expressed no concerns when Obama mentioned his wife was living apart from him with her parents and intended on going to the University of Washington that fall. The visa extension was approved, with Wood noting "no reason to deny" it. *The idea that a sham marriage had occurred based on Obama's need for a visa extension was put to rest.*

In reality, it never should have been raised as Obama's academic credentials were sterling. He would graduate in record time, completing four years in three, as a Phi Beta Kappa straight-A scholar who would be accepted to Harvard for graduate school. In addition, Obama Sr. was a celebrity of sorts— the University of Hawaii's first Kenyan foreign student whose picture had been in the paper with the university president.

Jerome Corsi implied that Obama truly was considering a "visa extension" scam on his April 10, 1961 visit to his student advisor. He observed that Obama Sr.'s failure to mention his marriage and his son on his visa extension form of August 31, 1961 meant that he had abandoned such a plan and had concluded he couldn't fool INS officials that he was married.[13] But Obama Sr. clearly acknowledged his wife and son on the same date to the immigration administrator (Wood), as mentioned above in the INS memo.

---

11 "Barack Hussein Obama Sr. Immigration File," http://www.scribd.com/doc/54015762/Barack-Hussein-Obama-Sr-Immigration-File accessed May 18, 2012.
12 *Ibid,* additional handwritten note dated 4/12/61 signed by administrator.
13 Jerome Corsi, "Documents Show Marriage of Obama's Parents a Sham," June 6. 2011, http://www.wnd.com/2011/06/308229/ .

Obama Claims Son

For his part on April 10, 1961, Obama Sr. reported spontaneously to his student advisor that he had married an American girl reportedly on Feb 2, 1961. This was the same advisor who had previously warned him about being a playboy. He reported his marriage to Dunham even though this caused the question of bigamy to be raised. Of course he was likely a bigamist, as his tribal wife Kezia claims to this day, bigamy being part of the Luo tribe's heritage. Obama Sr.'s own father had three wives.

Considering his motivations, we wonder if claiming a new wife made him look like a responsible husband and not the promiscuous playboy—but this could not have been a primary motivation. His INS files do not reveal his student advisor had stayed on his back about his disturbing sexual prowess which obviously continued with Ann Dunham—and then having impregnated her. But we have a much more powerful issue—the pregnant Ann Dunham now had leverage if it was his child. And he must have believed it—to the point he at least claimed to have married her. It would not have looked favorable on his record tainted by promiscuity (and infidelity) to have been accused of impregnating a vulnerable young 18-year-old American freshman coed—and not marrying her (or reporting he had).

We find continued evidence that Obama Sr. was indeed the father. (Already we have seen strong suggestions that she and Obama Sr. discussed abortion—and that early on he pushed her to obtain one. This crucial matter goes completely unaccounted for by those who support a view Obama Sr. was uninvolved with Ann Dunham.) His April 10, 1961 INS file memo noted that he had requested permission to work additional hours due to financial hardship. Permission was granted up to 25 hours per week. This indicates he had not suddenly received a sum of money in payment for serving as a stand-in father for Frank Marshall Davis—that's another theory we will explore further in Chapter 7.

In addition, suppose the INS had done some checking up on Obama (as they had done previously) after he announced his marriage to Ann Dunham? Imagine the risk Obama Sr. took if the INS had gotten wind of his standing in for another man as a proxy father for money. The 'pay the alleged father' scam would guarantee his sudden departure.

In summary we have much evidence on the table that Obama Sr. was Obama Jr.'s father—or thought he was. We will find significant psychological evidence Obama Jr. also acknowledged Obama Sr.'s paternity.

Apparent Denial of Son Mistaken

Again much has been made of Obama Sr.'s failure to mention his son on his visa extension form of August 31, 1961—implying he was *not* Obama Jr.'s father and had given up his pretense. But Obama Sr. had done nothing of the kind. As the INS memo on the same date established, Obama clearly acknowledged his wife and son to the immigration administrator (Wood).

Still, another powerful reason will emerge less than a year later at graduation explaining why Obama Sr. might have unconsciously left his son's name off the visa application. Others have also seen Obama Sr. mistakenly referring to his wife on the same form as "Ann S. Dunham" instead of the correct "Stanley Ann Dunham," reflecting a true lack of involvement with her and a sham marriage. Yet, Obama Sr. always referred to her as "Ann" according to Barack Jr.'s book *Dreams*—and Ann Dunham herself apparently dropped the "Stanley" in Hawaii signing her name as "S. Ann Dunham." Although it is interesting that, when listing Ann's name as his wife on his visa application form, Obama Sr. first crossed out another name obviously starting with "K," which hints at "Kezia," his African wife, a probable "slip of the pen" confession that he was a bigamist.[14]

After beginning Harvard in 1962, along the way Obama became involved with his eventual third wife, Ruth Nidesand. He was officially divorced from Ann Dunham in 1964.

INS files reflect that there were significant questions about Obama Sr.'s possible third marriage and his behavior. Investigator M.F. McKeon commented in his INS files dated June 9, 1964, "They [Harvard officials] weren't very impressed with him and asked us to hold up action on his application until they decided what action they could take in order to get rid of him. They were apparently having difficulty with his financial arrangements and couldn't seem to figure out how many wives he had."[15] (However, Obama never actually married Ruth until she came to Kenya after he left graduate school.) Harvard officials described Obama Sr. as a "slippery character," and university administrators eventually worked with the INS to have him returned to Kenya. Documents show that in July 1964 Obama Sr. was denied a student visa extension.

He had completed a master's degree in economics and was instructed to complete his Ph.D. Thesis in order to be considered for readmission. Obama later reported his thesis was stolen in Kenya and he never completed it. But he often claimed he had indeed earned a Harvard Ph.D. and called himself Dr. Obama.[16]

For the record Obama Sr. was uninvolved with all his various kids by all his wives. That was his style apart from brief moments such as we will see in Christmas 1971 when he visited Obama Jr. As Obama's half-brother Mark Ndesandjo told him later about their father, "He was dead to me even when he was still alive...showed no concern for his wife or children."[17] Yet deep down Obama Sr. was also very sensitive to rejection and his kids being taken from him—another aspect to this complex man which will surface later on.

---

14 "Barack Hussein Obama Sr. Immigration File."
15 *Ibid*, June 8, 1964, accessed May 18, 2012.
16 Sally H. Jacobs, *The Other Obama: The Bold and Reckless Life of President Obama's Father* (New York: Public Affairs, 2011) p. 168.
17 Obama, *Dreams*, p. 344.

Andrew G. Hodges, M.D.

Motivation for Obama Sr.'s 1971 Visit with Son

Before we explore the break-up of his short marriage to Ann Dunham, we skip ahead ten years to the time Obama Sr. made his only visit back to Hawaii—which constitute his son's only memories of him. He stayed more than a month with his in-laws who rented an apartment for him in the same building, passing the Christmas holiday there. Corsi and others have suggested Obama Sr.'s visit occurred simply to help facilitate Obama Jr.'s acceptance into the prestigious Punalou prep school. They contend that Obama Sr. was making *another sham appearance* as Jr.'s father, a lengthy trip from Kenya with all expenses paid by his former in-laws because Obama Sr. was broke. Yet Obama Jr. seemingly had already enrolled in the school earlier that fall. Obama Jr. convincingly told stories (in *Dreams*) that he had talked to his classmates about his father long before his father's visit. And he described a poignant moment of his father telling a story about Kenya to his fifth-grade class.

Things were not as simple, however, as a cursory visit by his father. Obama Jr. told the unflattering story in *Dreams* of how his father simply announced he was coming for Christmas, a visit his grandparents dreaded—his grandparents' stress giving it the partial ring of authenticity. If they paid for Sr.'s trip under these conditions it suggests he had some kind of leverage over them—yet simultaneously they had needs of their own for his trip while still dreading it. Their needs became quite clear. Upon reflection it appears Obama Jr. was not told the whole story about his father's visit.

Three black-and-white pictures of Obama Sr. exist from that visit. The first two were shot at the airport upon his arrival, one alone with Ann Dunham and one alone with his son. He is obviously comfortable with both, his arms on her shoulder and around his son. The third picture was taken on Christmas morning showing Ann Dunham dressed in her bathrobe and Barack Jr. each giving Obama Sr. a wrapped Christmas present—which strongly suggests a type of pose. Sr. is sitting and his crooked legs suggest injuries from a recent automobile wreck. Perhaps the pictures were posed to establish the "close" relationship of all three—not necessarily implying a sham father.

Very possibly the family wanted a picture of Obama with his father *in Hawaii* to authenticate his birth there if the need ever arose later which it obviously did. If the COLB was the only birth certification available such a picture might be helpful. Obama's use of these pictures when he became a public figure suggests he did so for this very purpose. The pictures suggest another strong possibility: there were no birth pictures of Obama Jr. *The family was getting the pictures which should have been taken 10 years earlier at his birth, yet they inadvertently revealed how obvious it was that the child's birth pictures were missing.*

Even more importantly, the family would want Obama Jr. to meet his father at least one time in his life that he could remember. Around age 10 would be a natural time a young boy starts to need a father more and Obama was settling into school in Hawaii and now had no step-father around. For his sake the family would want him to be validated by his father's attention and presence at least once—and they likely knew it would only be once just as turned out. The fact that a Kenyan visit to his father by Obama Jr. was never discussed suggests again under no circumstances would the family allow this---once more suggesting his father's custody rights and a Kenyan birth. Easily, Obama Jr. could have started to raise that possibility around 10, particularly since he had traveled to faraway Indonesia several times and lived there. But his grandparents by having Obama Sr. visit his son would satisfy that need.

Also there could have been questions regarding Lolo Soetero's adoption of Obama Jr. He had gone by the name of Barry Soetero for years. Obama Sr.'s presence in Hawaii could have cleared up paternity matters quickly regarding Obama Jr.

Obama Sr.'s poor health additionally could provide powerful motivation for young Barack's grandparents to pay for his trip. His reckless behavior— constant drunk driving—and injuries hinted that he was not long for this world, a sad fact which eventually proved true, and hastened the immediate need for a picture. Also the photo of his ex-wife, Ann Dunham, and son each giving him a Christmas present subtly suggests Obama Sr.'s trip was a present paid for by the maternal grandparents. In part this perhaps represented a bribe of sorts, maybe even a make-up gift for the two of them, for having left Obama Sr. immediately following his son's birth. (This story will unfold in the next chapter.)

On reflection, you might think the family would have preferred a picture of Obama Sr. giving his son a gift to show how much he missed him—for Obama Jr.'s sake. And in fact his father did bring him presents on arrival and departure, as Obama Jr. tells us later. We will have the opportunity for Obama's super-intel to elaborate on the matter when we explore his adult description in Chapter 7, as he looked back on his father's visit. His candid revelations will tell us much about his childhood trauma.

A major explosive event occurred, not surprisingly, during Obama Sr.'s stay. The visiting father disciplined his son for watching television instead of studying and accused his mother of spoiling him—clearly suggesting investment in his son and consistent with Sr.'s strong academic drive. The grandparents reacted to his strong hand, and Ann Dunham reportedly sided with Obama Sr. —a familiar family dynamic. Obama Sr.'s criticism of his son failing to do his homework also strongly suggests an unconscious confession that in abandoning his son he had failed to do the "home work" of a father—of being a stable father.[18] (Later, Obama Jr. as president will make the identical case for powerful unconscious guilt when a parent abandons a child—no matter how uncaring the parent appears on the surface.) Such guilt on Obama Sr.'s part implies he believed that Obama Jr. was his son. In a later chapter exploring the visit in

---

18 Obama, *Dreams*, p. 68.

detail we find numerous believable incidents suggesting Obama Sr. indeed was Barack Jr.'s father.

Other motivations for the visit include Obama Sr.'s recent serious car wreck, and never having seen his son past early infancy. If he was certain Obama Jr. was his son he would want to see him again—in part to undo his lack of parenting—and especially so if his son had been born in Kenya. Obama Sr. also would have known unconsciously that he wasn't especially long for this world because of his self-destructive drunk driving, and this might be his only chance to undo the emotional damage he knew he had inflicted on his son. (Barack Obama Sr. would die 11 short years later on November 24, 1982—never to visit America again.)

Obama Sr. was also recently divorced by his third wife, Ruth, who like Ann was also white, and he reportedly (in *Dreams)* wanted Ann Dunham to return with him along with Barack Jr. to Africa.[19] This would fit with his need to marry a white woman. And grief at Christmastime over his third wife Ruth having recently left him could have played into the matter. It had only been seven short years from his marriage to Ruth in Kenya on Christmas Eve 1964. Seven years was all Ruth could take—and Ann Dunham had lasted less than seven months "married" to him.

Maybe Obama Sr. understanding he had leverage over the Dunhams also wanted to visit Hawaii once more and see his old buddies—which he did a good bit of, on the visit. He could have basically told his in-laws and Ann Dunham that he would like to visit and they would have understood the implications of his power over them. This fits with the story that he announced to them he was coming. Conceivably his needs to visit and the Dunham's needs coincided. Imagine if a Kenyan birth occurred, the power that secret gave Obama Sr. to call the shots—at any point he could have gotten information to Obama Jr. about where he was really born. Perhaps he told him secretly on that visit—it would be a hard secret to keep from a son—particularly for someone as angry as Obama Sr.

But there was no knowledge of Obama Sr. and Ann Dunham living together at any point apart from Obama's descriptions in *Dreams from My Father*—seemingly supporting a lack of deep involvement between Obama's parents. Yet the fact that his in-laws dreaded his Christmas visit and the fact that he actually stayed with them in a nearby separate apartment suggest he had lived with them before and it hadn't worked out. Perhaps it was a trial run with the newly married couple living together off and on with Ann Dunham's parents during her pregnancy. And Obama Sr. with his inordinate academic drive could always escape back to his single-room apartment to study and simultaneously avoid a true one-to-one wedded relationship, ever the polygamist (either literally or symbolically). In Kenya Obama Sr. often went back and forth between his

---

19 *Ibid,* p. 126.

third wife Ruth and his first wife Kezia. The fact that Ann Dunham and Obama Sr. never clearly lived together as a married couple in Hawaii would not preclude Obama Sr.'s parentage of Obama Jr. All in all, Obama Sr.'s trip to Hawaii certainly suggested that he was emotionally involved both with Ann Dunham and his son, Barack Jr.—not a token visit by a sham father.

Then we have the notable exception of Obama Jr.'s Kenyan birth—another very real possibility. If he were born in Kenya, Ann Dunham and Obama Sr. would have been together there (a matter explored fully in Chapter 11). This would mean even if living apart most of the time in Hawaii, the couple had been working out a relationship that resulted in the mutual decision for their son to be born in Kenya. The idea that she would go to Kenya—nearly 9 months pregnant—without him to win over his family simply strains belief.

Reasons for African birth

This leads us to the major question: "Is there any way Obama could have been born in Africa? After all, it was his father's home country, the rumored place of his birth, and by far the most likely place of a foreign birth occurring. Of course the possibility, however distant at first, exists in a sea of unknowns. But why? What on earth would prompt such a desire on the part of his mother or father to take him so far away around the time of his birth?

We find some compelling reasons. His mother suggests her Midwestern Kansas roots took over and now she desperately wanted a husband, certainly a father for her child. Remember, too, this was 1961 and Ann Dunham was only six months removed from high school in Seattle where a single mother was not common and looked down upon. Perhaps she played the only card she could play, promising Obama Sr. that she would have his child in Africa. Even pledging to name a son after him may have reflected her willingness to embrace an African identity in exchange for Sr.'s continued involvement with her and her future son, perhaps feeling an African birth was possibly their last chance at making it as a couple. Unquestionably, such promises would prove to Obama Sr. he was the father of her child.

In addition, perhaps Ann's awareness of her husband's intention to eventually return to Africa inspired an idealized and very strong-willed, very desperate young woman to imagine she could raise her child in Africa. Obviously she would have discussed important political events with him, including Kenya's plans for independence. Perhaps she even envisioned the two of them as a team changing the political climate in Africa.

Ann Dunham also knew the tribal wife in Africa was not her husband's intellectual equal. And such a wife did not stop Obama Sr.'s third wife, Ruth, from following him to Africa and displacing his tribal wife in the hierarchy by having two children with him there. It wouldn't stop Ann Dunham either.

There are compelling reasons Barack Jr.'s mother could have gone to Africa in a desperate, idealistic, denial-filled state of mind as an 18-year-old mother, her judgment perhaps clouded by the hormonal swings of pregnancy.

Such a possibility is far from a stretch as Ann Dunham was motivated by similar ideals in her second marriage, moving to a foreign country halfway around the world. In 1967, she married Lolo Soetero—a dark-skinned foreign student—and moved to his country, Indonesia, and had his daughter (Maya Soetero) there. Dunham's second marriage suggests a striking parallel with her first, a repetition-compulsion. (People often resort to repetitive behaviors to undo traumas, as in, "This time I am going to get it right" and disprove all the pain and self-doubt that come with a failed relationship.)

In *Dreams* Obama Jr. suggests another reason his mother would go to Africa for his birth—a major way of declaring her independence from her parents. This was the identical reason Obama gave for her later marrying Lolo Soetero and moving to Indonesia, getting "beyond her parents' reach."

Surely something deep in Stanley Ann Dunham caused her to become involved with two foreigners. Some deep-seated desire to move faraway and live in a foreign land—just as she would return to live permanently in Indonesia even after her divorce from Lolo Soetero. This fact in and of itself suggests that she unconsciously selected Obama Sr. as the father of her child even amidst her promiscuity—and makes its own subtle case that he was Obama Jr.'s father.

Father's Wish for African Birth

Perhaps Obama Sr. was temporarily enamored with Ann Dunham's idealism. We can see his natural wish to have his child, particularly a son named for him, born in Africa reflected even ten years later in Hawaii during his only visit with his son—when Obama Sr. brings him gifts from "his continent."

Obama Sr. would have other reasons for promoting the African birth of his child. It would bond him to his child in a special way. Highly conflicted over having a mixed race child, he would have the strongest of reasons to want his child born in Africa—that would make his son blacker. And, after almost certainly urging an abortion, Obama Sr. was perhaps won over, too, by Ann Dunham's spunk in refusing that option, insisting she was keeping her child.

Other Indicators of African Birth

- Another factor also suggests an African birth—no birth photograph of baby Obama and his father. In 1961 a camera would not have been as readily available in Africa as Hawaii. If Obama were born in Hawaii with his mother naming him for his father, she would have wanted a photograph of the two together to comfort her child about having a father.
- While an expensive trip, Ann Dunham's parents might scrape the money together to insure the marriage of their only child, knowing she was returning and hoping that the trip would rid her of idealistic Kenyan fantasies—and give their grandson a 'permanent' father.
- The distinct possibility that no authentic Hawaiian birth certificate exists. If this is the case, a Kenyan birth becomes virtually an absolute

69

fact.

- Obama's Kenyan step-grandmother reported his birth there.
- Kenyan intelligence agents investigating Obama's possible Kenyan birth have reported that relevant files during the time Obama's birth appear to be missing.
- Celebration of President Obama's Kenyan birth in numerous Kenyan newspapers and by the Kenyan Congress.[20]
- INS flight records into Hawaii from foreign countries were completely missing for only one week—August 1 to August 7, 1961--from ten years' of microfilm records coincidentally around Obama's birth, as Sheriff Arpaio's investigators uncovered. [21]
- Ann Dunham would not risk an African trip and Kenyan birth if uncertain that she was having a mixed- race child.

Mother Leaves Father within Six Weeks of Birth

Another major clue of an African birth emerged shortly after Obama's birth. One of the brightest red flags in Obama's history was raised when his new, first-time mother abruptly left his father no later than six weeks after his birth—moving from Honolulu to Seattle. Inexplicably, neither the mainstream media nor most of the conservative media ever mentioned this critical blow to Obama's early human development.

A close look at this separation demonstrates its major implications for Obama personally—including the kind of leader he will become. Indeed his teenage mother was the one who suddenly pulled away from his father after birth. Years later, she would report that she was the one who sought a divorce and separation.[22] Normally, an inexperienced young mother needs significant help from her family with her first child. But, after living with her parents virtually her entire life, Ann Dunham booked a 2,680-mile flight for herself and her infant son from Hawaii to Seattle so she could enroll on September 19, 1961, for the fall semester at the University of Washington taking extension courses at the Seattle campus.[23]

Furthermore, Dunham enrolled as a "nonresident citizen," increasing her tuition and had the expense of room and board, whereas she had lived at home with her parents in Hawaii. Her move to Seattle appears to have been an urgent, desperate act. Records show she continued her studies at the University of Washington, eventually enrolling as a full-time student for the spring semester in April, 1962. (High school friends and a baby-sitter also verified Ann

---

20 Corsi, *Where's The Birth Certificate?*, p. 87.
21 Jerome Corsi, "Flight records missing for week of Obama's birth," March 23, 2012,
http://times247.com/articles/immigration-records-missing-for-week-of-obama-s-birth accessed May 28, 2012.
22 Obama, *Dreams from My Father*, p. 125
23 The University of Washington released a corrected transcript to WND showing her enrollment date corrected from 8/19/61 to 9/19/61 which matched the course catalogue. (See Corsi, *Where's the Birth Certificate?*, p. 120)

Dunham's stay in Seattle with her new mixed race child.)

Why, we wonder, would she wait in Seattle for over a year with no known visits home to Hawaii? Dunham would not return home until well after Obama Sr. left Honolulu for Boston immediately following his graduation on June 2, 1962. Already we have established that Obama Sr. was not a fill-in sham husband with her having agreed to get out of his hair right after the baby was born. The mother would have lived with her parents eight miles away from Obama Sr.—plenty far enough if he wanted no connection. Was she waiting until she was certain that the coast was clear, the pain of encountering her ex-husband just too great? She returned to the University of Hawaii, registering for the spring semester in April 1963 implying she would've preferred to have stayed there all along. So why did Ann Dunham suddenly go to Seattle within a month or so after Obama was born? Certainly she denied her newborn son contact with his father at a critical point in his life—implying that she had a good reason.

One real possibility seems obvious—some shocking event occurred around her son's birth, and his mother had to get away from his father immediately. The birth announcement address in the Hawaii newspapers showing the couple living with Obama's maternal grandparents suggests cover-up of the real story. Obama's father almost certainly never lived in the house at that time with his mother's departure only weeks away. The precipitous end of the tenuous marriage/relationship and the sudden departure with her son suggest the young mother felt inordinate fear and perilous vulnerability—her reaction tells us she was afraid of her husband's extreme behavior.

Did Obama Sr. Physically Abuse Dunham?

Spousal abuse is, unfortunately, a common occurrence—particularly in stressful circumstances such as when a young, interracial couple is dealing with an unplanned pregnancy. Clearly tension and rejection—the passion of racism—surrounded them. Given her husband's temperament, it's very possible that Dunham was threatened physically by him just before or soon after Obama's birth.

Dunham had repeatedly told stories about Obama Sr.'s perpetual and sudden capacity for violence. We know about Obama Sr.'s irresponsible driving which eventually cost him his life. He was later known to be a severe spouse and child-abuser as Obama's half-brother, Mark Ndesandjo, revealed in his 2009 book, *Nairobi to Shenzhen*. Ndesandjo's mother was a Jewish-American named Ruth Nidesand, Obama Sr.'s third wife.[24] Mark said he wrote the book in part to raise awareness of domestic violence: "My father beat my mother and my father

---

24 The similarity between Ruth Nidesand's maiden name and later name of Ruth Ndesandjo after leaving Obama Sr. is intriguing. "Ndesandjo" looks like an Africanization, for the sake of her sons. The two sons with Barack Obama, Sr., are Mark and David Ndesandjo; her third son, Joseph Ndesandjo, was born c.1980 from a subsequent marriage to a Tanzanian.

beat me, and you don't do that."[25] Clearly then a confirmed spouse abuser, the likelihood that Obama's father physically abused his mother is extremely high.

Several hints this was the case eventually emerge. First, we find a veiled suggestion in Obama's *Dreams* book in which his mother recalls Obama's only meeting with his father, *"He was probably a bit tough for a ten-year-old to take,"*[26] suggesting Obama Sr. had also been very tough and threatening for a 18-year-old wife to tolerate. Such near-truths often unknowingly communicate family secrets.

Yet Dunham could have weathered a "simple" hostile outburst by Obama Sr., however threatening, by leaving and continuing to live with her protective parents. She was not overtly seriously injured. Obama's father still had plans to graduate and would likely not have again risked his career with ongoing abusive behavior.

Suddenly removing Barack Jr. from contact with his father by moving to a distant place suggests his mother's primary motivation was concern for her son—specifically the possibility of losing him. This implies an intense vulnerability, a fear that his father had legal custody rights and even had threatened to take the son all to himself—*all of which points to a foreign birth. The mother's extreme behavior—moving far away—likely mirrors Barack Sr.'s ongoing threat to take her son far away to Africa 'where he belongs.'* By moving to Seattle, she would decrease Obama Sr.'s attachment to her son. She knew Obama Sr. could show up at any moment and take the child back to Africa. And she still had leverage over him: he could not protest such a move lest she inform the authorities of his abusive behavior.

Lastly, for the record, her sudden move to Seattle suggests a very tenuous bond with Obama Sr. and that the couple never actually married.

Maternal Grandmother's Story Suggests African Birth and Breakup

Another crucial story from Obama's autobiography hints at the explosive event which occurred in Kenya. His maternal grandmother, "Toot," feared if the couple ever moved to Kenya (a reported plan at one point) that "the Mau Maus" would kill her daughter and that Barack Sr. would keep the child there permanently.[27] A hint that the explosive event which set Obama's mother off indeed happened in Africa rather than Hawaii—and obviously far more likely to have occurred there around the time of delivery than in Honolulu. The story also locates the couple together in Africa—around an explosive event.

Under the conditions of an African birth, it is not hard to imagine Barrack Sr. exploding in a threatening rage directed at his wife. Surrounded by the conflicts of his tribal obligations, relatives perhaps pressuring him to renounce a

---

25 Keith B. Richburg, "Obama's half-brother goes public with new book," November 5, 2009 http://www.washingtonpost.com/wp-dyn/content/article/2009/11/04/AR2009110401214.html accessed June 7, 2012.
26 Obama, *Dreams,* p. 123.
27 Obama, *Dreams,* p. 126.

white outsider wife, uncertain about the relationship himself, he would have been sitting on a pressure cooker. His idealism and hers suddenly may have come to a tragic end. Maybe her husband frightened her by returning quickly to his domineering ways upon alighting on African soil, treating her as he treated women there—as second class citizens—and she realized the relationship would never make it. Then add to the mix his known alcohol abuse. Under such volatile conditions, things could have rapidly gone from bad to worse.

Imagine for the moment Obama's father experiencing his son being born in Africa and named for him. However ambivalent he had been about his son previously, now surrounded by his tribal people, it would be a particularly proud moment. Suppose then that his wife, now provoked, pulls away wanting to return home earlier, and he realizes the "marriage" is over. He can see the future plain as day: his wife returns to Hawaii with their new son, he moves on to graduate school a year later in the States and loses meaningful contact with his son forever. He just had a new son—his namesake—and now he'd turned around and lost him. That would not go down well for the dominant Obama Sr. It could easily have engendered threats to keep his son in Africa and have him raised by his people. It's also possible that Sr. even threatened to destroy her and his son in a fit of rage—"If I can't have him, nobody will." After all, he had once wanted to destroy him via abortion.

Such a scenario fits perfectly with the story of Toot's fear—precisely how family secrets emerge, hidden in key stories, if you can hear them. Obama's later emphasis in *Dreams* on humiliated children in Nairobi which he links indirectly to himself and to a 9/11 attack suggests that he knew the family secret that his father threatened him—again—specifically in Kenya as a newborn. Clearly Obama reflects the deep-seated belief his father hated him over his mixed-race blood.

In the face of such terror, Obama's mother would have quickly made arrangements to leave her husband as soon as possible. And she would have come to a sudden shocking realization—she had no legal rights to her son, now a full-fledged Kenyan and no American citizenship. There is nothing like a mother about to lose her newborn child to prompt sudden desperate action. Such circumstances of her son's African birth would have compelled her to take emergency action and quickly communicate with her family in Hawaii either by phone or telegram: to get a birth certificate—a COLB—along with a birth announcement in the newspaper as urgent first steps in establishing her child's American citizenship.[28]

Having attended high school in Seattle, Dunham would be well-positioned to have her family make arrangements to enroll her at the University of Washington. Another factor arises from the notable lack of a photograph of the newborn son with his father. That would now be the last thing on the face of the

---

28 Related scenarios occur not infrequently today. A Muslim man will marry an American woman, have their child in the U.S., and later return home to the Middle East where the mother then has no rights to the child.

earth his mother would want—unequivocal proof her son was born in Africa.

Parenthetically, some have hypothesized that Ann Dunham went to Kenya in an attempt to win over Obama Sr.'s family and ended up giving birth there. While possible, it doesn't fit the circumstances or the secret of Barrack Sr.'s violence revealed in the numerous narratives we have explored—and seems far-fetched. If Obama Jr. were born in Kenya, it is far more likely his father was present.

Jerome Corsi offers another explanation for Ann Dunham's sudden departure for Seattle—that she was heartbroken over Obama Sr. rejecting her—and wanted to get away. But there is no distinct evidence Obama Sr. rejected her and no evidence they were ever in love to begin with, as both were promiscuous, and it was a marriage of necessity. The sudden extended departure suggests a much more powerful situation which Corsi alluded to later—some type of severe estrangement associated with the birth of the baby.[29] The fact remains that Ann Dunham had no need to get away from a completely uninvolved Obama Sr. Yet if she were really afraid of him in a major way including fear for her child she had every reason to make a drastic move and make it quick, which she did.

Why Obama Sr. Claimed Son Born in Honolulu

Obama Sr.'s calm description on August 31, 1961 to the INS official that his wife and son were moving to Seattle suggests that he had regained his wits back in America. By choosing not to fight her move, Obama Sr. appears decidedly uninvolved in a tentative marriage. It also indicates that she had leverage over him, probably as a result of recent abuse she suffered at his hands. Ann Dunham could have easily explained that she simply wanted to get away to Seattle after an explosive outburst without tipping her hand that she feared Obama Sr.'s custody rights. Above all Obama Sr. feared losing his visa extension *which depended at that moment* on his keeping the peace at home with Ann Dunham. One phone call to the INS office that he had been abusive toward her or his son and he would have been on his way back to Kenya in short order.

Obviously Ann Dunham had told Obama Sr. she was moving to Seattle following an explosive outburst; in a real way she was the one rejecting him. Before his INS meeting on August 31, 1961, Dunham had surely elicited an agreement that Obama Sr. go along with the plan. Consider again Obama Sr.'s casual report, "Oh, by the way, my wife and I of six months just had a baby son named for me. And oh, by the way, they don't live with me—and on top of that are moving to Seattle for her to attend school there." Huh? But imagine him telling his INS administrator that he had taken his wife to Kenya where their son was born. It would raise fresh questions about bigamy, prompt a clear investigation of his marriage and establish his son was not American-born.

---

29 Jerome Corsi, "Does WND's Reporting Rule Out an Obama Kenyan Birth?," June 27, 2011. http://wnd.com/2011/06/316265/ accessed May 21, 2012.

74

Despite WorldNetDaily's report that Obama Sr. could not have traveled to Kenya during the summer of 1961 because he remained in Hawaii to attend classes and work[30] —those two obstacles are easily overcome. He could simply have taken off from work if Ann Dunham, 18 and pregnant, had pushed her family to pay for their trip to Africa. Before long, her parents would provide the money for another trip to Seattle and pay for her college tuition there. With his sterling academic record, Obama Sr. could have missed classes and taken early exams. And he had plenty of reasons to keep his trip secret, including not wanting his Kenyan political benefactor, Mboya, to find out about it. Kenyan Luo politician Tom Myboya was instrumental in eventually helping Obama Sr. obtain financial assistance to continue his education at the University of Hawaii after Sr.'s private funding ran out. Mboya helped him obtain grants from the African-American Students Foundation which had strong communist ties.[31]

The Long Flight Home with Newborn?

While it would be a long, difficult two-day flight home with her newborn son, a protective mother can do anything for her son when she has to. An experienced pilot also told me that such a mother would have received tremendous nurture and help with her child from stewardesses on the way back home. Certainly if Obama's young mother could travel a long distance by plane (Hawaii to Washington state) within a month of his birth, she could have done so when he was two weeks old. By then Obama Sr. could have calmed down and ridden right along with her.

Other Stories Confirm African Fiasco

- During her year or so stay in Seattle, Obama's mother told a friend that her husband's African family had complicated their marriage and had prompted Obama Sr. to return to Africa, but facts suggests this was a cover-up. She hints at a major complicating event in Africa regarding her husband which may have been precipitated by his family—and that *she* had to return *from* Africa. The story also locates Obama Sr. in Africa connected to marital problems with her.

- Ann Dunham also told another friend in Seattle that she would eventually return to Africa to live with her husband—yet another African-birth reference.

Lie That Father Left at Age Two

Keeping this great secret from Obama for years—that his mother had to move away from his father when he was at most six weeks old, far across an ocean—seems to confirm both an initially dangerous event and also implies that his father had legal rights over him, or so the mother feared.

---

30 Jerome R. Corsi, "Documents show marriage of Obama's parents a sham," June 6, 2011, http://www.wnd.com/2011/06/308229/ accessed May 28, 2012.
31 Corsi, *Where's the Birth Certificate?*, p. 133.

And the family wanted all this covered up to such an extent they created the fiction that, following his graduation, his father left him when the child was two. And Obama publicly adopted this party line for his entire life. Easily they could have told Obama that his father left following graduation when he was almost a year old—a natural explanation—but they were desperate to perpetuate the myth that "your father left you at two years old." It was imperative the family narrative extend the length of the father's stay to portray Barack Sr. as spending two full years with his son, implying he had carefully made a completely voluntary decision about leaving him. *This again suggests a tremendous need to disguise the fact that the child was hidden from his father for over a year in Seattle.*

Not only would his mother want to hide from Obama Jr. her fears that his absent father might have a legal claim over him but also that he had been born in Africa. If Obama found out about his African birth, there's no telling what he would do down the road during a turbulent adolescence. That fact alone could create a strong urge to be with his missing father—greatly intensified by an awareness his mother kept him away from father. And imagine the ensuing rage if Obama found out his almost unspeakable loss, his father pain, was worsened by his mother. Imagine the utter confusion it could cause. Under no circumstances could his mother reveal such secrets.

Obama lived for several years with the family myth that his father left when he was two years old. The myth was bolstered by his white maternal family continually telling positive stories about Obama Sr. His father supposedly wrote occasional letters to his son and his mother kept him informed about Obama's development. This suggests Dunham wished to remain in Obama Sr.'s good graces, constantly worried about custody issues. And they surely wanted Obama to remain blissfully ignorant of the terrible events associated with his birth. Obama's mother and grandparents built denial deep into his core, taught him not to explore his past, not to ask questions—which is one reason he was afraid to investigate matters surrounding his birth. From a very early age, denial and secrecy were a way of life.

The Pain of Father Abandonment

And then there was the raw pain of losing his father. Not only was Obama separated from his father by the tender age of six weeks, he actually saw his father only once in his life—ten long years later. The father's absence would forever haunt Obama, especially knowing that his father could have made efforts to see him but did not. In *Dreams*, Obama repeatedly refers to his absent father, first describing his musings as "a meditation on the absent parent" and "a record of a personal interior journey, a boy's search for his father."[32] Obama's Father's Day communications, 47 years later, make it clear that his search continues (as we will see in Chapter 8).

---

32 *Dreams from My Father*, p. xii and xvi.

Divorce in 1964

Separated from her husband immediately after her son's birth in August 1961, Ann Dunham did not seek a divorce until January 20, 1964, some two and a half years later. Even if a sham, the divorce decree would reinforce the father's lack of connection. This suggests she slowly eased her way into the divorce, not wanting to stir the waters with Obama, Sr. Such a plan does not exclude other reasons for seeking a divorce including her desire to help Lolo Soetero stay in America—thus proving to the INS for his sake that she was no longer married to Obama, Sr. and could eventually marry Lolo.[33] She also would want an official divorce to establish for her son Barack—and his future—that she had legitimately been married to Obama Sr.

Indonesian Stepfather and Obama's Possible Adoption

Perhaps his mother's relationship with Indonesian student Lolo Soetero was partially motivated by her lack of legal parental rights. Obama Jr. taking Lolo's name, registering as his step-son in school in Indonesia and possibly being adopted by him, would add another layer of protection from Obama, Sr. coming after his son.

Media's Denial of Human Relationships—and Child Custody Matters

Ever reticent to probe behind the red flags waving through Obama's life, the media has totally failed to examine the extreme parental conflicts in the boy's home. Let's face it, the marriage—such as it was—dissolved immediately after his birth, and then child-custody concerns naturally arose. This crucial turn of events represents but one of many red flags the media invariably ignore.

The media also remains blind to the power of the super intelligence, and that's a shame because it's a reliable repository of infinite inside information. Once more in Chapter 11 Obama's super-intel—the unquestioned source of truth on the subject—will weigh in fully on the actual facts of his birth.

---

33 Cashill, "Maraniss Bio."

6

Teen Obama Discovers a Startling Truth

As time progressed, secret questions about his missing father would arise in Obama's mind. Was his father present at his birth? Had his father ever actually seen him as a newborn? Did his father even care enough to make that much effort? If a picture is worth a thousand words, the fact that there's no picture of the father and his newborn baby boy together speaks volumes.

Always the question in the back of his mind, a question common to abandoned kids persisted—why had his father left him? Was it because Obama was flawed? Why doesn't he ever visit? Were those letters really from his father? Perhaps, he wondered, does my mother not want him to visit? He even may have wondered, "Am I really his son?" These are all natural questions and real possibilities in light of the facts: no photographs, a dubious marriage, and the sudden separation.

A Startling Discovery

Obama suggests he uncovered a key reason behind his parents' separation in a discovery he made regarding his father's graduation from the University of Hawaii in June 1962. Telling another detailed story about it suggests it was of great importance to him. As a teenager rummaging through his personal items Obama had come across an old newspaper interview with his father in the *Honolulu Star-Bulletin* about his graduation speech, "folded away among my birth certificate and old vaccination forms.[1]

First of all, the idea of Obama finding his birth certificate with a newspaper article seems contrived. Kids don't typically stumble upon birth certificates which are usually kept stored away in a special place. And the article "folded away" about his foreign father connected to his birth certificate suggests a secret hideaway regarding his birth certificate—that Obama himself was foreign-born. He also links the birth certificate with an "old vaccination form" suggesting a phony birth certificate story used to vaccinate him against any accusations of lacking American citizenship. Furthermore, the image of 'a speech' here suggests Obama is unconsciously announcing this for the world to hear. His rich symbolic images are impressive and together tell a cohesive story—again a hallmark of a super-intelligence confession. The fact that this casual reference to

---

1 Obama, *Dreams*, p. 26.

his birth certificate (very early in his *Dreams* book, reflecting the pressure to confess quickly) takes us straight to the central question of legal citizenship makes the brief story and set of images much more compelling.

Keep the picture of a folded piece of paper in mind, linked to his birth certificate, and the idea of mentioning a key issue at the beginning of *Dreams*. Later in Chapter 11 we'll see that Obama will come back to both indicators—he will use two powerful images at particularly crucial moments, one of which again happens to be at the beginning of his *Dreams* book. It will fit this brief story he has just "unfolded"—and will tell us more about the reality (or unreality) of his birth certificate.

In Chapter 7 a strong case will be made that Obama's friend Bill Ayers wrote much of the *Dreams* book, leading some to conclude that we are not always looking at Obama's images. However, Ayers would have known all about Obama's foreign citizenship (as will be clarified further in Chapter 15) and would have been equally prone to confess for Obama. Don't forget Obama provided the stories and most of the images himself. Thus the imagery speaks for itself.

Now back to his father who had delivered the speech as a representative of foreign students just before leaving Hawaii for graduate studies in Boston. Obama suggests that, by reading between the lines of his father's speech, he established why his father left him at two weeks of age—and he got the answer straight from his father's own mind.

First, Obama observed that his father left his mother and him entirely out of the speech, speculating that it was *intentional* because Obama Sr. was already anticipating his imminent "long departure" leaving them both behind to enroll that fall at Harvard. Obama suggests that unconsciously he already knew the powerful family secret—*as kids invariably do*—that mother had taken him to Seattle immediately after birth, which is confirmed by a lack of family graduation pictures. Such personal speculations as intentional neglect and connecting a "near-truth" story to the real one are how kids reveal they know the family secret.

Then Obama speculates further that his father's intentional neglect had led to *"a fight between his parents"*[2]—implying that he had knew his father had physically abused or threatened his mother. This was surely why his mother then moved to Seattle, taking the infant Obama away from his father. In addition, Obama offers another immediate explanation for his father not mentioning his mother or him in his speech—*he is striking back at her for leaving him, angry and abusive as ever. Also striking at her by abandoning, including not mentioning, her son.*

Still, several questions must have remained in Obama's mind. Why would his father became abusive toward his mother (which surely also would explain

---

2 Obama, *Dreams*, p. 27.

why his father continued to abandon him)? Obama implies that he is on the cusp of an answer to his father's motivation, which he then reveals.

Obama takes us to the heart of his father's speech—and an incredibly painful reality for Obama. As an ambassador for his continent, his father "mildly scolds the university for herding visiting students into dormitories and forcing them to attend programs designed to promote cultural understanding—a distraction from the practical training he seeks."[3] Remember, in Obama Sr. we have a man with great disdain—only somewhat disguised—for societal and interpersonal boundaries. Here he's rebuking the administration during his graduation comments. On a deeper level his father is likely revealing his problems with his "university wife" (and her parents) who forced him into a "cultural" marriage by appealing to him that 'in America you do the right thing and marry the woman you impregnate. And you especially allow the life you created to be born.' In the end, Obama Sr. didn't like that one bit and he had pushed hard for an abortion. He wanted to drive on whatever side of the road he wanted and certainly not have any "silly American laws (or culture)" tell him what to do. He would be especially bitter if Ann Dunham had then taken his Kenyan born son away from him—after he had gone to the trouble to enable a Kenyan birth. No wonder Obama Sr. acted as if he never had any relationship with the two of them for years.

Mixed-Race Trauma

His father's next comments take us to his deepest motives. Although he hasn't experienced any racial problems himself, he detects self-segregation and overt discrimination taking place between the various ethnic groups and expresses *wry amusement at the fact that "Caucasians in Hawaii are occasionally at the receiving end of prejudice."* First making plain he has not been a victim of racism in Hawaii, he suggests that he has self-segregated and discriminated against his white American wife in Hawaii himself by abusing her, letting her be on the receiving end—and deep down he enjoyed it.

Obama Sr.'s next comment about whites not willing to work together with other races suggests again he was unconsciously talking about himself. He certainly wasn't working with his wife, his most intimate representative of the white race. *Subtly but clearly his father introduced the entire matter of reverse black racism tied to violence toward whites.*

The teenage Obama would've certainly concluded un-consciously that his father abused his mother in a reverse racist fashion and relished it. And he'd done the same to him, deserting his son because he was half-white—not black enough. He and his mother were simply too white to deserve Sr.'s devotion. Years later in a Father's Day speech, Obama alluded to a home divided by race—appearing to confirm the painful secret of his confusing mixed-race identity and his father's mixed feelings about him.

---

3 Obama, *Dreams*, p. 26.

Immediately prior to mentioning his father's newspaper interview in *Dreams*, Obama suggested again he was unknowingly picking up on the real reason his father left—race.

> In the end I suppose that's what all the stories of my father were really about...a bright new world where differences of race...would instruct...A useful fiction, one that haunts me...no less than it haunted my family, evoking as it does some lost Eden that extends beyond childhood. There was only one problem: my father was missing. He had left paradise...their stories didn't tell me why he had left.[4]

First, he implies that he had indeed been instructed by his father's own story on the differences in race—between him, a mixed-race son, and his black African father. The real truth, he now knew but didn't want to know, was that his father left him over his mixed race—haunting Obama his entire life. His father was gone, leaving the son feeling as though he had just been cast out of the Garden of Eden by God because he was deeply defective—and indeed when you're that age, your father feels like God to you.

Obama implies that at his graduation, Obama Sr. was actually looking back at his wife having left him nine months earlier and unconsciously confessing what he had done to cause it. (Freud insisted people cannot keep their secrets—and the latest clinical research confirms that secrets spill out especially when people feel guilty and responsible.[5]) This was the perfect moment for a hidden confession. Obama Sr. was leaving Hawaii, leaving his former wife and son in "nearby" Seattle—all while knowing he would return to Africa in few short years. Even more deeply, Obama Sr. knew he had no true intentions—at least at the time—of being a real father to Obama. Since he had no idea if he would ever see his son again, this was the perfect time to tell him the story behind the breakup and to own up to what he had done—and why.

Without realizing it, Obama Sr. left clues about the truth in his graduation talk. And bright young Barry stumbled on those clues one day even though he didn't realize what he now understood unconsciously about his father leaving. That's why years later Barry put it in his book—so we could see what he couldn't. Between the lines, his father's confession—unburdening himself and his secret rage—points to significant involvement with Obama Jr. and his mother.

Despite his denial, Obama suggests that his father's graduation speech does much to explain his abandonment of the family. His father's explanation tied all his major mistreatments of Obama and his mother together: carelessly fathering him, inflicting a self-image on Obama that he was a mistake, then treating him poorly because of his white blood. First, he'd wanted to abort him, and then he abandoned him for good, as if his month-old son didn't even exist. In this way,

---

4 Obama, *Dreams,* pp. 25-26.
5 See Appendix A.

abandonment was like an ongoing abortion.

Obama paints a powerful picture of how he experienced yet another humiliating trauma—developing a deep sense that his mixed race had created a fatal flaw in him as far as his father was concerned, and what's worse, he was totally powerless to do anything about it. If this seems like a stretch, we need look no further than Obama's paternal grandfather, Hussein, whose name Obama carries. Receiving news that his son had married a white American wife, Hussein had written to Gramps, Obama's white grandfather, *"this long nasty letter saying he didn't approve of the marriage. He didn't want the Obama blood sullied by a white woman."*[6]

More on Obama Sr.'s Anger and Guilt

Jerome Corsi references a letter which Obama Sr. wrote to Tom Mboya, his Kenyan political benefactor, on May 29, 1962, immediately prior to his graduation—where he makes no reference to an American wife or child. Instead Obama Sr. asks Mboya to help his African wife in Nairobi, although he neglected to mention her by name or the fact that he had fathered a child with her (a sign of disrespect, in my opinion).[7] Upon his return to Kenya in 1965, Obama Sr. quickly displaced her with a new wife. Consider, too, Mboya likely would have disapproved of Obama Sr. having an American wife when he still had a Kenyan wife back home. He also makes a striking slip-of-the-pen, "I have been able to *cut on* [vs. "out"] at least two years for my B.A"—suggesting a hidden confession he has been cutting on somebody, namely his wife Ann and his son Barack Jr. (and his African wife). His image "cutting on" again suggests a confession he physically abused both wives.

Super-Intel Narrative of Kenyan Birth

On March 4, 2007, when Obama Jr. was a U.S. senator, he claimed in a speech in Selma, Alabama, that President Kennedy had brought his father to America in 1959 when JFK airlifted prominent Kenyan students to the United States. In fact Kennedy wasn't even president until 1961, but a Kennedy family foundation did provide funds for a second airlift of Kenyan students in 1960 following a meeting with Mboya at Hyannis Port, Massachusetts. In actuality Obama's father did not come to America on either the first or second airlift. President Obama was called out by a journalist for his distortions, but again Obama Jr. shows that he will resort to blatant deception when it fits his purpose. Fittingly, President Obama will later tell us that kids deceived by their fathers will repeat the identical deceptive behavior in their own lives.

But the most striking aspect of his Selma speech was the dialogue which Senator Obama invented. In his 1959 scenario, he quoted Kennedy advisors speaking with JFK in the White House: "You know we're battling communism.

---

6 Obama, *Dreams*, pp. 125-126.
7 Corsi, *Where's the Birth Certificate?* p. 136.

How are we going to win hearts and minds all across the world if right here in our own country, Jack, we're not observing the ideals set forth in our Constitution? We might be accused of being hypocrites."[8] Obama Jr. went on, "This young man, Barack Obama [Sr.], got one of those tickets and came over to this country."[9] Notice the blatant super-intel confession—that a "young Barack" came to this country as a foreign-born child from Kenya.

Amidst one fiction, Obama suggests another. By unconsciously linking a constitutional violation with his name, his deeper message is "This young man, Barack Obama Jr., is not planning to observe the Constitution because he's really from Kenya." With the 2008 presidency already on his mind, this was an early, though hidden, warning. The super-intel often confesses to secret deeds by having the person unknowingly link two ideas together which tell a deeper story.

And Obama again links himself to communists who are battled all over the world. He suggests he has usurped the Constitution like a dictatorial communist would, but he has done it covertly, Alinsky-style. Later he will make the same unconscious connection in his inauguration speech. Interestingly, too, Obama Sr. spoke at a "Mothers' Day Peace Rally" in 1962 along with Communist Party USA head Jack Hall.[10] He also wrote a policy paper espousing basic communist doctrines and siding with communist-allied leaders in Kenya.[11] Obama's adolescent mentor, Frank Marshall Davis, was also a known communist.[12]

Obama's Mixed-Race Conflict

Certainly it was intimidating for Obama to think he wasn't black enough for his father. Yet, it was a typical question that a mixed-race son in his circumstances would have raised, "Was I too white?" —kids invariably wonder what they did to cause a father to leave. And in *Dreams*, Obama described blacks themselves, privately reflecting on the self-esteem issues regarding the darkness of their skin with dark-skinned blacks resenting light-skinned blacks. He noted, "...perhaps you were unloved as a child... because you were too dark? Or too light?"[13] Obama's half-brother, Mark Ndesandjo, who strikingly resembles Obama physically, expressed an identical conflict over being a mixed-race child as a son of Obama Sr.'s third wife.[14]

In first describing his father, Obama noted how dark-skinned he was. "That my father looked nothing like the people around me—that he was black as pitch, my mother white as milk—barely registered in my mind."[15] Of course "nothing

---

8 Obama was alluding to segregation at the time in 1959 being a constitutional violation of blacks.
9 Corsi, *Where's the Birth Certificate?* p. 134.
10 Cashill, *Deconstructing Obama,* p. 260.
11 E. S. Atieno Odhiambo and David William Cohen, *The Risks of Knowledge* (Ohio University Press, 2004), p. 182.
12 Cashill, *Deconstructing Obama,* p. 273.
13 Obama, *Dreams,* p. 194.
14 Transcript, "Larry King Live," CNN, Nov. 7, 2009, http://transcripts.cnn.com/TRANSCRIPTS/0911/07/lkl.01.html .
15 Obama, *Dreams* , p. 10.

like the people around me" obviously would have included the light-skinned Obama himself. Notice that Obama's statement—that it "barely registered in my mind"—states exactly how a family secret is discovered. Consciously, it's barely noticed, but deep down all eyes can see it.

Given his repeated experience with his father's violence and learning that his father wanted to destroy him over his white blood, young Barry would have naturally developed a fear that his father might one day, in another fit of rage, do him in. Kids think like this—*He wanted to destroy me once, so why not again?*

Back to Abortion and Childhood PTSD

Obama presents several stories suggesting he had clearly learned that his father had wanted him aborted, a sad fact which he would naturally tie to his father's black racism. Clearly he understood his father was capable of extreme violence.

1. First, following the story about his father threateningly holding the man over the cliff by the legs, Obama *immediately puts himself in the man's place*, "I imagine myself looking up at my father, dark against the brilliant sun [emphasizing his father's color], the transgressor's arms flailing about as he's held aloft. A fearsome vision of justice." Obama again suggests an abortion image: a dangerous doctor holding a fetus by the legs, plainly linking it to race.

2. Early in *Dreams,* Obama tells of the terrorist attack of September 11, 2001, when "the world fractured." He then described how "his powers of empathy" cannot explain people *"who would murder innocents"*—another powerful abortion image suggesting his secret awareness of that fact, a near-trauma that had permanently fractured Obama's own world. (Later, to drive his point home, Obama will repeat the same idea about the abuse of "innocents" at a much bigger moment. We'll examine this in Chapter 16.)

He ties the 9/11 trauma to his past in two ways: *"What I do know is that history returned that day with a vengeance...as Faulkner reminds us, the past is never dead."* He admits the 9/11 attack on America stirred him up. He notes that the "bombs of Al Qaeda have marked, with eerie precision, some of the landscapes of my life—the...faces of Nairobi."[16] Here he's eerily and precisely connecting his abortion image to a face in Africa. Impressively, Obama compares his father's near-abortion of him to a terrorist attack—and implies again that he fears his father would one day return to finish the job.

Just for good measure, it is precisely at this point Obama talks about the powerless children he saw in Jakarta and Nairobi, indirectly linking them to his own childhood. Once more Obama underscores that the driving force in his life—his powerlessness and humiliation—occurred primarily at the hands of his father. Step by step, story by story, one striking abortion image after another— Obama makes a strong case that not only was his near-abortion his single greatest trauma, but also that he had personally unearthed this shameful family

16 *Ibid,* p. x.

secret.

Obama experienced a childhood post-traumatic stress disorder and, just as severely traumatized adults invariably see their world through the lens of their attack, that's exactly how he viewed his world. Such trauma lingers in the human psyche. Over and over again acute triggers re-activate the trauma like a recurring nightmare. To the vulnerable mind of a child, such trauma can be devastating. You never forget the day you were nearly aborted if you can see back that far, and Obama well demonstrates that kids can.

Obama provides another reason why he would've felt he was in constant danger from his father. His story of the 9/11 terrorist attack depicted a totally unexpected stealth attack—suggesting again that he feared one could re-occur at any moment. While such trauma of near-abortion may be difficult for many readers to consider, we must follow Obama's own mind, his stories—and they clearly indicate that his parents seriously considered abortion. Obama's consistent picture of his father's terrifying rage between the lines also leaves no doubt about who his father was in his mind.

Become Blacker to Survive

Obama would have an even more powerful motivation for becoming blacker. He believed that his father wanted to abort him because of his white blood, leading to the ultimate twist in his basic life code, "*if I can only be black enough I will survive my father's brutal wish to destroy me*"—convinced his very survival depended on it. Such a predicament would have propelled Obama to search for ways he could embrace black causes.

We see the same deeply engrained fear when Obama attends college and reads a book on Africa "to understand *what makes whites so afraid*." He also alludes to his deep "unnatural" fear of his white blood connected by classic denial to his black father in Africa.[17] Obama sets the stage for his desperate search for power and misplaced rage directed at "White America" as ways of proving his blackness. In characteristic denial, Obama again suggests this truth, "I reject a politics that is based solely on racial identity...or victimhood generally."[18] In fact, however, that's precisely what he does—day in and day out, both before and after he was elected president.

Groomed for Humiliation and Rage

We return to Obama's denial. First he denied the enormous harm directed at him by others, threats of which he became progressively aware albeit unconsciously, even while an engulfing rage grew in his heart, a rage he was also taught to deny. Anger surrounded him wherever he turned: his white grandparents' "disapproval" of his black father and, by extension, of him; his father's rage at his mother (much less him); and finally, his mother's reactive

17 *Ibid*, p. 103.
18 Obama, *Audacity of Hope*, p. 11.

anger at his father.

No wonder he went along with the family myth that 'We're all just a bunch of good guys who really get along.' That was an easier myth to swallow than the bitter pill of his father's likely blackmail lingering in the background, the threat that he could come for his son at any time.

As therapists say, denial is not just a river in Egypt, but it is indeed a river that runs through the center of Barack Obama. And the denial all started with his family whose shame and rage brought them all together, culminating in the birth of Barack Obama. Of course they had hoped by hiding the twisted drama of the events surrounding his birth that the child would suffer no ill effects. Instead at that very moment they taught him to deny the humiliation and rage they passed down to him—*so he could transfer that same pattern onto America*. They taught him to deny pain/humiliation received and pain/rage delivered. In the end they all had a hand in producing the man publicly perceived as the cool, detached Obama, the personification of the family myth. Of one myth producing another.

Continuing the Family Myth as Political Candidate

Obama provides abundant evidence of continued deception as an adult perpetuating the family myth regarding the timing of his father's abandonment. In *Dreams* his story of discovering his father's newspaper interview established that he knew as a teen that his father left the family for Harvard—before Obama was one. He describes with detailed precision exactly when his father arrived in Hawaii (1959) as the university's first African student and that he departed three years later (1962) upon graduating. We can be sure he learned consciously as an adult that his mother left his father when he was six weeks old. (This might also explain why his wife Michelle at a July 2008 college roundtable discussion commented that her husband's mother *"was very young and very single when she had him."* For all practical purposes Ann was a single mother from the get-go. And Obama himself would talk about being raised by a single parent.) Nevertheless again during his crucial Father's Day speech as a presidential candidate in 2008 Obama sticks with his "father left me at two" story—another warning as to what kind of president we were getting: one who would overtly distort the truth willy-nilly. Even after his election when the undeniable truth surfaced confirming that Ann Dunham left Obama Sr. immediately after his birth, Obama clung tenaciously to his original myth, unfazed by the truth.

7

The Family Code: A Deeper Look

To understand Obama we must further appreciate both sides of the family which produced him. The primary people who built him were themselves built by others. Striking patterns emerge; above all, patterns of humiliation and powerlessness abound.

THE FATHER

His father was a member of the Luo tribe in Kenya. Obama himself would later characterize them as tribal warriors.

Tribal Background

Barack Obama Sr. was born on June 18, 1936 and raised by a grandmother. Sarah Oqwel was the third wife of his father, Hussein Onyango Obama. His mother, Akumu, separated from Hussein and left him, with her children, in 1945. Obama Sr. clearly suffered an early parental abandonment which inevitably produces problems. On top of this he was severely physically abused by his father.[1] The severe self-destructive bent that resulted from his personal traumas would cause serious trouble for him throughout his life.

Because he grew up in Kenya, a colony then firmly under British control, Obama Sr. naturally developed a revolutionary point of view. His country, Kenya, would only gain its independence on Dec. 12, 1963, well into Obama Sr.'s adult years (he was 27). The overriding experience of African black man was that he was, while his native country dominated by white 'imperialists.' Despite having British citizenship, Obama Sr. would have been a second-class citizen under colonial control—overpowered and ridiculed. In a word, humiliated in the eyes of his people.

In certain ways this situation represented the opposite of the black man coming to white America. In Kenya, the foreigner had come in and taken over the country. In modern-day America, a black man could aspire to assimilate into the mainstream culture of the country. If he had higher education, this could help him significantly.

Obama Jr. would later report in his memoir that Obama Sr.'s father, Hussein Onyango Obama, had been imprisoned and tortured in a British colonial

---

1 Obama, *Dreams,* p. 418.

jail. Obama Jr. had been told this by Sarah Oqwel Obama, his grandmother, on a visit to Kenya as a young man following his father's death in 1982. (Perhaps Obama Jr. embellished this story later.) After discovering that his son, Barack Sr., had impregnated Ann Dunham, Hussein Onyango Obama wrote a letter to Stanley Dunham saying that he didn't want white blood contaminating the Obama family lineage.[2]

This gives us just a sense of how deep was Kenyan animosity toward the white British colonialists, and it explains why Obama Sr. would have such disdain for Obama Jr.'s white blood. No doubt, Obama Sr. the young man seethed with anger over the abject injustice of foreign occupation just as his father did.

Alcoholism

We can be sure the severe alcoholism which plagued Obama Sr. as an adult was a lifelong attempt to self-medicate, to ease his own pain. Similarly, his own desperate search for power was another means of assuaging his lingering feelings of rejection at the hands of the authoritative British occupiers.

Not in any way to excuse his choices, but life's circumstances had set up Obama Sr. to become the person who family members later described to Obama Jr. as an abusive husband, an alcoholic, and an embittered, damaged man who raged against the course of post-colonial Kenya days.[3] Sr. also carried horrific memories of pre-colonial days.

Rage and Abortion

Not only was Obama Sr. self-destructive, he was truly murderous. He repeatedly drove drunk, beat his wives and eventually killed a man in an auto accident. And he wanted to abort Obama Jr. And why not? Scarred by racism, this domineering playboy whose promiscuity already threatened his beloved academic career in Hawaii—why wouldn't such a man push strongly for the abortion of a baby conceived in a casual liaison? Its birth represented an enormous threat to Obama Sr.'s sense of racial identity—and his academic success.

Here is his first and only chance to really shine, shine in America and matriculate at Harvard preparing for a fruitful political career back in Kenya. Would such a man let a child with mixed-race blood come between him and his success? No, such a man would opt for the most convenient decision, one that was common in Kenya where tens of thousands of abortions are performed annually.

Despite his above-average intelligence, Obama Sr.'s self-sabotage continued at Harvard. He was eventually sent home by university officials because of this behavior. While in America, he had impregnated a white girl.

---

2 *Ibid*, p. 126. This was also another believable story pointing to Obama Sr. as the father.
3 *Ibid*, p. 344.

After the son was born he almost certainly alienated the young white girl with threatening behavior. Then he abandoned them with no contact, no claim on his son. At Harvard, he began dating another white woman, Ruth, who followed him to Kenya after he was deported. Bringing a white woman home to Kenya reflected dominance. Obama Sr. may not have said it, but his actions did, 'See whom I conquered! Here's someone I can overpower and control just as I—and our beloved country—were overpowered and controlled.'

Back in Africa, Obama Sr. extended his rage's reach to include his first wife and their children. The ugly emotional scenes became a regular soap opera as he frequently abused both families and wives. Our president's father was one abusive, power-hungry man. Nevertheless, he remained charming as ever—when he wanted to be.

Looking back, after Ann Dunham refused to abort her child, perhaps Obama Sr. consciously or *unconsciously* envisioned another possibility. Secretly he would revel in bringing a white woman home to Africa, pregnant with his child, and willing to have that mixed-blood child in Africa. He subtly suggests that he, in fact, enjoyed an African homecoming in 1961 with Ann Dunham and his soon-to-be-born son, Obama Jr. But Dunham and her baby were more like captive hostages than beloved family members. "See how I conquered," it was as though he was saying. "See whom I charmed. See the woman who bowed to me. See, she is a fine girl—she does exactly what I want." Such a thought exactly matches what he told her on their first date. How fulfilling for Obama Sr. to host the birth of a half-white, half-black son in Kenya! In 1961, inter-racial marriages were still shocking, and the ever-arrogant Obama Sr. likely enjoyed shocking Kenyan society. After all, the colony was where Obama Sr. and his family had suffered degrading institutional racism, as the white oppressors routinely dismissed the native blacks as inferior.

Maybe bringing Ann Dunham to Africa to have his child was also Obama Sr.'s way of standing up to his father, Hussein Obama, who had repeatedly threatened to have Obama Sr.'s student visa revoked if he went through with the marriage.[4] At the same time, Obama Sr. honored him by naming a son after him—Barack Hussein Obama, Jr. And once his father saw how his son had indeed 'conquered' the whites—maybe he too saw the joy of revenge in bringing back a white woman to give birth to his child in their beloved Kenya.

Political Rage

Regardless, however, of any satisfaction he gained by the Kenyan homecoming, rage continued to burn in Obama Sr.'s soul. He vociferously complained about the Kenyan government hierarchy which had undermined his career. He openly expressed anger at authorities for allowing the murder of his former sponsor, politician Tom Mboya, in 1969. More humiliation for Obama Sr. He would become especially enraged after imbibing at Nairobi nightspots.

---

4 *Ibid*, p. 126.

His nickname was "Mr. Double-Double," because that's how he ordered his Scotch.[5] How deep the pain: double-double scotch for double-double pain.

Rage to the Last Minute

Tragically but not surprisingly, Barack Obama Sr. ended his life in a single-car accident while driving drunk and alone. Many relatives later insisted it wasn't an accident but murder by his political enemies. The assassination scenario shifts the blame for his death onto unknown others, but the fact of his lifelong addiction cannot be disputed. Researcher Caroline Elkins, a Harvard historian and author of *Imperial Reckoning: The Untold Story of Britain's Gulag in Kenya*, reported that numerous reliable Kenyan sources depicted Obama, Sr. as a "serious, fall-down alcoholic." She also thought it was possible that, with Obama Jr. now president, relatives wanted to rewrite history. Elkins said, "Understandably, there are some Luos who have an interest in making Obama, Sr. out to be a perhaps more heroic and high-ranking figure than he ever was in real life."[6]

One way to look at it is to admit that Obama Sr. had been trying to kill himself in a car by driving drunk for years. He surely harbored deep yet secret guilt after devastating, in one way or the other, everyone he touched. Symbolically, his violent final ending well illustrates his self-sabotaging suicidal behavior—and self-atonement for having taken the life of another person in a car, nearly having taken the life of his son, and all those other people he had hurt.

Along the way, of course, he had tried to cover his pain with the big smile, the sophisticated international manner (cigarette and drink in hand), and the fraudulent doctorate from Harvard. But in the end a greater driving force—inside—prevailed.

THE MOTHER

We move now to the maternal side of the "equation" which produced Barack Obama. Then we grasp the family code which Stanley Dunham, along with his wife, established for their daughter Ann, resulting in her relationship with Obama Sr.

Stanley Dunham was initially destabilized by his womanizing father, a poor excuse for a family man, to say the least. Yet at age 8, Stanley's trauma traumatically deepened when his abused mother committed suicide—and he discovered the body. Shortly thereafter, Stanley was also abandoned by his father.

Now rejected and humiliated in multiple ways—and even more so without parents—he became an unpredictable, angry adolescent. Stanley was a poster child for Obama Jr.'s later Fathers' Day description of the angry, powerless son

5 David Remnick, "Was the President's Father Murdered?," *The New Yorker*, October 18, 2010, p. 27.
6 *Ibid.*

with no father to show him the way (nor even a mother). Sent away to be raised by his maternal grandparents (just as Obama Jr. would later be raised), Stanley's anger would have been off the charts. On top of that, he was carrying around an equal amount of guilt over his mother's suicide as kids invariably blame themselves for such events (*If I wasn't so bad, she wouldn't have done that*). And he would've suffered even more guilt for simultaneously being angry at his dead mother over her abandonment, which, after all hadn't been by accidental death or disease, but by her choice. Stanley covered all of this inner angst by becoming a boy on the move. After slugging his high-school principal, he dropped out of school before he was 18 and roamed the country womanizing and drinking, traveling around the Midwest by hopping boxcars.[7]

Eventually he returned home to small-town Kansas. Socially, Dunham was a loose cannon. His girlfriend's family discouraged Madelyn Payne from dating this ne'er-do-well, but of course that didn't stop her. In May 1940, when Stanley was 22, he married the smitten 17-year-old.[8]

Madelyn 'Toot' Payne Dunham

Impressed by Stanley's good looks and his reputation as a devil-may-care character, Toot Payne selected him as a husband despite the objections of her strict Methodist family. A rebel in her own way, she secretly married him on the night of her junior prom. It turned out to be a self-humiliating choice in many ways as Stanley wasn't much of a financial success. He moved his young wife and only child nomadically around the country where he often embarrassed her with loud behavior and off-color humor. Toot often had the better job and after they settled in Hawaii she became the main provider, further humiliating her husband, Stanley.

His resentment surfaced, leading to marital disputes which Obama Jr. witnessed living with them full-time during his later adolescence. Two tons of humiliation from his early life—often turned into scathing self-humiliation— haunted Stanley his entire life. But he had to find more outlets for his helplessness and at times took the short step from humiliation to anger, power, and humiliating others.

He cruelly humiliated his only child and daughter by naming her Stanley Ann, a male name which would cause her severe ridicule throughout childhood. The message was clear—her father had wanted a son—but most of all wanted her to be unwanted, degraded. Her name constantly reminded her that she was an unwanted child, just as her father had been. He had passed along to her his own deep humiliation and rejection. Naturally she, too, would become the secretly guilt-ridden child, blaming herself, the rejected "black sheep," which may explain her attraction to dark-skinned men. Eventually when it came her turn to carry out the secret family code, she passed it along to her son.

---

7 Cashill, *Deconstructing Obama,* p. 248.
8 Obama, *Dreams*, p. 14.

Stanley and Toot produced an only child, a young woman who Obama described in his memoir as sickly, a loner, cheerful but someone who would escape reality by burying her head in a book.[9] They produced a "fine girl" who would wait on Obama Sr.—submissive and infatuated with an older black man who would control and humiliate her. Thus her initial interpersonal pattern was to find a domineering, older, dark-skinned man.

Yet she would have the last word just as she eventually did with her controlling parents. She would leave both husbands, the fathers of her two children. She left Obama Jr. in the care of her parents while she returned to live in Indonesia with his half-sister. [10] Was this a final act of unconsciously humiliating her son, too? She was passing along the family code—and there's much more to this dynamic below.

Another Birth Theory

In his well-researched book, *Deconstructing Obama*, Jack Cashill helps clarify Obama's development and doggedly explores Obama's birth. He suggests that Obama Sr. was not Obama's father, instead offering two other potential fathers, thus implying that Obama Jr. was not foreign-born. First, he suggests Obama's mother was pregnant in May 1960—possibly by a black Seattle-based guitar player, Johnny Allen Hendricks who later changed his name slightly becoming the iconic Jimi Hendrix—which would explain her family's hasty move to Hawaii.

This far-out scenario means she was pregnant before leaving for Hawaii after her high-school graduation in spring 1961. Speculations even have her going to a home for unwed mothers on another island and returning to Honolulu with child, going through an arranged situation where Obama Sr. agrees to accept parental responsibility. Shortly, Ann Dunham supposedly returns to Seattle, pining for Hendrix.

But Ann Dunham's friends in Seattle later debunked this theory. As Cashill recognized, they verified that she had a new baby in August 1961, shortly after returning to Seattle for college that September.[11]

Three Photos

Yet Cashill quickly undermines his Hendrix theory when three nude photos, almost certainly of Obama's mother at age 18, surfaced in 2008 on the Internet. They were taken around Christmas 1960 in Hawaii, and they reveal that she was not yet overtly pregnant. Cashill makes plain the amateur photos were Obama's mother. As he describes, "The woman in the...photos looks not vaguely like the young Ann Dunham. She looks *stunningly* like her, right down to the long Dunham chin, the petite mouth, and the arched eyebrows. The timing is also perfect"—the jazz album cover seen on a table in one photo is the Stan

---

9 Obama, *Dreams,* p. 19.
10 *Ibid*, p. 75.
11 Cashill, *Deconstructing Obama,* p. 266.

Kenton LP, *Cuban Fire,* released in 1960, the year Dunham moved to Hawaii.[12] The photos also revealed a prominent tan line which matched exactly the shorts Ann Dunham gushed to friends about wearing to class.

Clearly they are not pictures of a bombshell pin-up model Marcy Moore—a cover story interpretation offered by a pro-Obama investigative Internet site. No wonder the media covered up such a story: imagine any president in our history having a mother who had posed for such pictures as a teenager.

Cashill speculates the photos were taken by Stanley Dunham's black friend Frank Marshall Davis, who later became a mentor to the future president. Davis, who was married to a white woman at the time, had a habit of enticing young white girls to pose unclothed for photographs. The pictures prompted a theory that Frank Marshall Davis was actually Obama Jr.'s father. Certainly the photos suggest the dynamics of Ann Dunham's relationship with the photographer and her family, offering valuable insights into her vulnerable and immature personality.

Cashill also believes "Pop," one of two poems Obama Jr. published under his own name in college, was actually written by Davis who was a sophisticated, experienced writer. Allegedly the poem suggests Davis was Obama Jr.'s father. Cashill maintains this is the hidden key which will truly deconstruct Obama. However the poem seemingly implies a different central message, as we will see shortly. Importantly, however, Cashill underscores the central issue in Obama's life *has to do with his father*.

Continuing his theory, Cashill sticks with the idea mentioned previously in Chapter 6 that Obama Sr. had no meaningful relationship with Ann Dunham. Cashill's proposal that the dictatorial Obama Sr. was a willing proxy for the real father, Davis, itself fails to hold psychological water. We have already established the numerous reasons Obama Sr. was the likely father. This includes the story of how his father pushed his mother strongly for an abortion—as Obama's super-intel spelled out (much more to come about this in Chapter 9). To miss his near-abortion is to miss the driving force in Obama's life. Pushing for an abortion was also not Frank Davis's style as will see below where he bragged about impregnating various women—but it fit the tempestuous Obama Sr. perfectly. And Cashill fails to account for the risk Obama Sr. took in announcing he was married and having a child to his INS officer in April 1961. He was already in trouble for possible infidelity to his African wife and now a possible bigamist.

Then we have the very real possibility of a Kenyan birth which Obama will clarify further himself beginning in Chapter 11—and the explosive incident which led Ann Dunham to move to far away Seattle once back in Hawaii. Again we must not overlook the centrality of a possible phony birth certificate which means the certainty of a Kenyan birth—and all that implies, including Obama

---

12 *Ibid*, p. 276.

Sr.'s involvement. Theorists who rest their case on Obama Sr.'s seeming non-involvement with Dunham leave too many matters unaccounted for which directly involve Obama Sr.—revealing a far more powerful believable story. (In addition they have not heard the real story from Obama himself—the new way of getting information from his super intelligence.)

Also Obama Sr.'s visit with Obama Jr. at age 10 in Hawaii, a visit completely ignored by Cashill, suggests that Obama Sr. is indeed the father. Accordingly, Cashill's suggested Occam's Razor test—that the simplest explanation is the most probable—points toward Obama Sr. as his father. And that is the truth that Barack Obama Sr. believed, strong enough to very possibly go to Kenya for his son's birth among other issues. However, Obama Sr. might not be Obama Jr.'s biological father in the final analysis. Davis is one other possibility. But it is not a simple matter—whichever man was Obama's father—as Obama will unconsciously tell us more about shortly.

Alleged Story Obama Born in Hawaii

While we are on the subject of Cashill and Obama's birth it is important to briefly digress because of Cashill's comments on supposed new information in June 2012 that "verified" Obama was born in Hawaii—much to the delight of the anti-birthers.[13] Cashill responded to author David Maraniss's new book *Barack Obama: The Story*,[14] where Maraniss reported in a single story based on one source that a woman claimed to be having lunch with an obstetrician in a Honolulu hospital just after Obama's birth there. Supposedly the doctor's comment was, "Stanley had a baby. Now that's something to write home about."[15] This was not the obstetrician who delivered Obama, but another doctor who had just heard about it through hospital scuttlebutt. The woman had been telling the story for years and as Cashill noted her memory from 50 years ago was all too good around one comment but provided no other circumstances. The idea that Obama's paternal grandfather was some hospital celebrity alone raises questions. Once more we have Cashill to the rescue. Now we come back to another new take on Obama's birth.

New Documentary Claims Obama's Father Frank Davis

A new documentary by Joel Gilbert basically makes the identical case Cashill did that Frank Davis was Obama's father, based primarily on physical similarities in pictures of Davis and Obama which are striking at times.[16] He, too, adds the nude photos of Ann Dunham as supportive evidence of sexual involvement with Davis. Gilbert makes extensive claims the film provides the

13 TV anchor Wolf Blitzer even commented about it on his CNN blog. Wolf Blitzer, "Blitzer's Blog: New details on Obama's Hawaii birth," June 18, 2012. http://situationroom.blogs.cnn.com/2012/06/18/blitzers-blog-new-details-on-obamas-hawaii-birth accessed June 19, 2012.
14 David Maraniss, *Barack Obama: The Story*, (New York: Simon and Schuster, 2012).
15 Cashill, "Maraniss Bio."
16 Joel Gilbert, *Dreams from My Real Father: A Story of Reds and Deception,* http://obamasrealfather.com/ accessed May 28, 2012.

first cohesive understanding of Obama's socialistic leanings—influenced by Davis.[17] *Of course, Davis could well have influenced Obama totally apart from paternity issues.* But Gilbert sets aside crucial issues of Obama's birthplace, the questionable birth certificate, Obama Sr.'s real involvement and most importantly doesn't comprehend that Obama Jr.'s super intelligence is unfolding a far deeper, more truthful story of his development. Simply because Obama Jr. resembles Frank Davis is not by any stretch of the imagination the entire story.

For the record Jack Cashill declares "that Obama strongly resembles the young Stanley Dunham. The likeness is powerful and undeniable." He adds that Stanley's brother Ralph noted the same thing that Obama "looks exactly like my brother, only he's dark."[18] (Looking definitely like his maternal grandfather would minimize Obama's similarities with Davis the uncertain father.) Other observers see the resemblance of Obama Sr. and Obama Jr., and between Obama Jr. and his half-brother Mark Ndesandjo whose mother was also white. Additionally, Obama Jr. shares other noticeable traits from Obama Sr.—his lanky frame, his distinctive strong voice, his charisma and big smile.

Finally, Obama's own super-intel—*which alone can truly deconstruct Obama*—will address the matter of Obama's father and his birthplace in Chapter 11 and beyond—and in one other story later in this chapter.

Real Author

Coming back to Jack Cashill, as a literary detective he made crucial discoveries about Obama Jr. and *his* claims to literary prowess. *Time* magazine had lauded Obama's 1995 memoir, *Dreams from My Father*, as "the best-written memoir ever produced by an American politician." Having also written a second book in 2006, *The Audacity of Hope*, Obama's intellect was acclaimed a vital part of his public persona. Cashill uncovered the startling reality that not only had Obama never demonstrated the literary skills apparent in both books—but that the style of *Dreams* uniquely fit Obama supporter William Ayers who is a fine writer.[19] The literary analyst also observed about *Audacity* that "there is no way Obama could have written the body of the book without substantial help." Cashill's choice for *Audacity* was Obama speechwriter Jon Favreau.[20]

Persuasively, Cashill made the case just months before the 2008 election that Obama had perpetuated a giant fraud on the American public—and soon discovered that neither the media nor the Republicans would inform the American people. And this even as a noted Obama biographer, David Remnick, observed that, if such a revelation were "believed...[by] enough voters, [it] could have been the end of [Obama's] candidacy." But of course not enough citizens were ever exposed to the truth of the matter.

---

17 Jerome Corsi, "Film: President's Father Not Barack Obama," *World Net Daily,* April 25, 2012.
http://www.wnd.com/2012/04/film-presidents-father-not-barack-obama/ accessed May 20, 2012
18 Cashill, *Deconstructing Obama,* p. 250.
19 *Ibid,* p. 138.
20 *Ibid,* p. 217.

Frank Davis and the Dunham Family Code

Cashill also focused on the chaotic relationship of Ann Dunham's family with Frank Marshall Davis—and opened the door to the Dunham family dynamics. The radical Davis fits in perfectly with the family code of humiliation Stanley Dunham had established for his wife and daughter. After the Dunhams moved to Hawaii in 1961, Stanley developed a close friendship with Davis, a bright, talented man who saw himself as an outcast. Stanley Dunham secretly viewed himself as an outcast as well.

But Davis was also perverse: a writer of smutty fiction and a participant in *ménage a trios* (group sex: a threesome) with a particular taste for sexually exploiting teenage girls. A self-admitted bisexual and adulterer, Davis proudly claimed to have impregnated three white women. The striking nude photos he apparently shot of an 18-year-old Ann Dunham in Hawaii in December 1960 suggest that it was her own father who further humiliated her by introducing her to Davis. Ann is depicted nearly naked except for stockings and high heels, surrounded by Christmas decorations and posed next to a table topped with the Stan Kenton album *Cuban Fire*—likely a signature symbol of Davis, the jazz lover, as photographer. The modern furniture suggests the setting is Davis' apartment. Ann is also wearing prominent makeup with dangling earrings, giving her a much older appearance. With her dark hair she matches the album cover suggesting she's Cuban—perhaps part of the ever-seductive photographer Davis's pitch to her.

Though her father enabled her to interact with Davis, Ann Dunham's own actions spoke clearly about her journey from humiliation to self-humiliation as she willingly desired sexual exploitation by a black man. In his fictional pornographic novel written under a pseudonym—with all stories supposedly drawn from his actual experiences—Davis' narrator has sex with a 13-year-old named Anne.[21] More revealing, Davis' character has sex with a white college girl called "Gloria" whose description closely fits Ann Dunham's. Gloria desires the black narrator to father her child, wanting "*to atone to Negro males individually*" because of *white guilt over racism*. (Of course, Davis could be alluding to the possibility that he was Obama Jr.'s father.)

Certainly Ann humiliated herself further with her promiscuity, sleeping with Obama Sr. almost immediately after meeting him—atoning to him first?—and likely slept with Davis in December 1960, as her photos suggest, when she was only four to six weeks pregnant with Obama Jr.

All three of the nude photos which survive center around a single large reading chair—she's kneeling on it, in it, and posed in front of it. *All three images imply that she's interacting with the invisible person/photographer in the chair, which suggests "father's chair."* In one picture she has a haunting, questioning look, as her eyes seek approval. All in all, she suggests a strong

---

21 Cashill, *Deconstructing Obama*, p. 277, concerning *Sex Rebel: Black*, a book Davis later admitted writing under a pseudonym, "Bob Greene."

"father hunger" wish to please the black father figure, Davis.

But there's an aggressive flip side to the photos. Her in-your-face nudity as an 18-year-old also matches Ann Dunham's typical, sometimes subtle confrontational demeanor—her way of overcoming her deep shame. Obama Jr.'s mother overtly passed down humiliation to her son—even with a nude picture of her humiliation (about which there is more to come).

Unspeakable Humiliation
So far we understand how Barack Obama got a triple barrel of humiliation: grandparents both sides, parents both sides and now we get just an inkling of how his rage originated in the deepest powerlessness. Later he will talk about the huge empty hole caused by his father's abandonment. We can be sure that at the bottom of that hole lies enough humiliation to sink a country. His unconscious motivation? Create an equal hole—in a nation, a people, the Constitution, the economy, and whatever else he can get his hands on. As president, he's passing along the family code.

And we're still not through, as he has significant helplessness yet to come. Most of all we are simply preparing to hear him tell us all about it in his adult life when his super-intel makes its appearance front and center in a crucial four-part saga that we'll examine beginning in the next chapter.

To Grandparents and then Indonesia (Obama: age 1½ to 10)
At 18 months of age, young Obama returned to Hawaii from Seattle with his mother and lived with his grandparents. He describes how his grandfather would embellish stories: his "...tendency to rewrite history to conform with the image he wished for himself."[22] Obama would become exactly like him, rewriting his own history to deny his deep humiliation caused by emotional trauma--particularly his father's rage over his white blood and also his near-abortion. Self-protectively Obama continually reversed the truth—characterizing white society as the enemy, due to his black blood. Again his grandfather's stories about Obama Sr.'s hostility are believable and suggest real involvement with Ann Dunham and her family.

He noted his grandparents' disguised racism, "...like most white Americans... *Blacks are there but not there...*", like his absent father treated him.[23] He was too black for his white grandparents and too white for his absent black father. In 1964, his mother obtained an official divorce decree. In 1967, Obama and his mother moved to Indonesia where his new step-father, Lolo Soetero, had gone ahead of them—and where Obama's great emotional pain would surface.

22 Obama, *Dreams*, p. 21.
23 *Ibid*, p. 18.

Indonesia

Arriving in Indonesia to live with his new father figure, Obama describes going into a panic over a horrific magazine picture of a black man who bleached his skin lighter—signifying a black man with white blood. Obama fictionalized this story in his memoir by borrowing it from another source, still his super intelligence selected it, which suggests the truth: his black father disapproved of Obama's mixed-race "bleached" skin.

Obama fully embraced his stepfather, Lolo Soetero—who quite possibly adopted Obama—taking Lolo's surname and attending a Muslim school. Yet a new fear of his biological father emerged now combined with his earlier ongoing terror that his father secretly wanted to destroy him—his "post traumatic near-abortion disorder." *His (age appropriate) unconscious competition with his father surfaced—the oedipal stage.*

Essentially Oedipus represents 'two's company but three's a crowd.' Here's the basic idea. A son's first 'girlfriend' is his mother—his first association with the opposite sex. Think of the phrase regarding parents having children: 'a girl for you' (the father) and a 'boy for me' (the mother). It implies the normal heterosexual male-female attraction—the same model heterosexual parents demonstrate to their kids. Sons naturally compete with their fathers—throw mother into the picture and you have a 'crowd of three.' Sons deep down despite their love and need for their father also want to dethrone him—and end up competing with father for mother's attention. A young child's primitive sexuality gets involved in these strivings. This leads to an underlying fear that the father will retaliate and you then have the hidden oedipal fear of the father. (Think about kings who have killed their sons fearing the son will dethrone them—an exaggerated version of such competition.) Eventually as the son grows up he realizes he must find his own 'girlfriend' –and the oedipal matter is resolved.

But the young son 'can't win' because there is another fear if he does so. In situations where the father is missing the young son experiences it as a 'See, I won out over dad' moment *unconsciously*—thinking he is omnipotent and he caused it. At the same time in his immature omnipotent state of mind he feels guilty for having 'conquered the father'—and feels he should be punished for the 'oedipal victory.' If the father is still alive, the son envisions the father returning at some point to take his 'pound of flesh.' And if the mother remarries, the young son experiences the stepfather as a stand-in father-figure in the same way, and the day of judgment has arrived. (A common derivative fear is 'if something good happens, something bad is soon to follow'—suggesting 'I must be punished.') Of course the young son loves his father and needs a father figure at the same time. We are not simple people—often 'of two minds' on a given matter.

In Obama's case the father-figure Lolo coming into the picture reminds him unconsciously of his biological father and momentarily increases his father fear.

He fears Lolo as a father figure will punish him for having had mother all to himself. Obama will go on to show us how he also was constantly looking over his shoulder thinking his biological father Obama Sr. also will return at any time.

Obama adds an important twist because of his mixed-race in this silent competition with Obama Sr. Recall Obama's father and grandfather had understandable resentments toward whites, specifically didn't want white blood contaminating their black blood. Obama himself then would have the 'contaminated white blood.' So Obama is programmed to look at this competitive matter with his father through the lens of race. Deep down with his father being absent Obama sees himself as victorious   having his white mother all to himself because of his own "white" blood, while his black father—despising Obama's "whiteness"—lost her. He reads the competition and rejection by his father through a racial lens and secretly concluded the parent's divorce was over race.

The point is, a missing father in the family creates special problems for the son. Obama brings to light this striking pattern with a doubly complicated version of race included which his stories reveal. Naturally, people deny such powerful competition exists in families—but not if they stop and think about it. Again all of this goes on subliminally but it can be very real inside the mind of the young son.[24]

In *Dreams*, Obama presents numerous competitive oedipal stories including repeated television dramas where the white man, not the black, always gets the girl—while the dangerous black man lurks in the shadows. Obama summed up the repressed terror of his black father in the back of his mind in another Jakarta story which he links specifically to his skin color—"There was a hidden enemy out there, one that could reach me without anyone's knowledge."[25]

Leaving Jakarta at age 10, Obama's worldview had taken shape: white society victimizes blacks. This covered up his greater unconscious terror of his black father's rage over Obama's white blood—complicated now by his competitive victory over winning his mother. Leaving step-father Lolo would reinforce Obama's secret oedipal victory over yet another father, while greatly enhancing his "father terror."

Earlier during a poignant moment when Lolo was describing his years in the Indonesian military, the young Obama after noticing numerous scars on Lolo's calves spontaneously asked him if he had ever seen a man killed—subtly pointing to his "father terror." Lolo responded, "Yes."

Obama wants to know, "Why was he killed?"

---

24 I have extensively studied the difficulties men can have with handling success. In therapy, this "victory fear" often emerges in men who have lost a father in their development. Other similar men who are successful have learned to sublimate their fear of winning to 'my father would be proud of me.' A strong case can be made that Obama, like Bill Clinton who also lost his father early, has serious problems handling success.
25 Obama, *Dreams*, p 51.

Lolo tells him, "Because he was weak…Men take advantage of weakness in other men. *They're just like countries in that way. The strong man takes the weak man's land.* He makes the weak man work in his fields. If the weak man's wife is pretty, the strong man will take her." (A powerful oedipal image—two men competing over one woman with Lolo much stronger than Obama.) Lolo asks Obama, "Which one would you rather be?"

Obama remains silent, and then Lolo counsels, "Better to be strong. If you can't be strong, be clever and make peace with someone who's strong. But it's always better to be strong yourself. Always."[26]

Lolo had described to Obama's mother his own severe humiliation during the terrifying war Indonesia had fought with the Dutch for independence when he was a boy. All in a single day, Soetero learned not only that the Dutch army has set his home on fire, but also that his father and oldest brother had been killed in battle. Vividly, he recalled the family fleeing to the countryside, his mother selling her jewelry piecemeal so that the family had food. (While reported later that Obama fictionalized this story about the Dutch killing Lolo's family nevertheless it tells us how Obama unconsciously sees the world. How he constantly sees the home in danger of attack by a powerful outside source. This idea remains core to his psyche.)

Later Lolo served in the Indonesian army. Obama noticed the scars on Lolo's legs from leeches that got in his army boots where they ate away his flesh. Over and over Obama describes holes in people. His stepfather Lolo also drowned all his troubles in alcohol—just as Obama's father had done.

At the same time losing Lolo deepened the huge hole in him caused by his missing father as Obama described years later on Fathers' Day, "I came to understand… the hole a man leaves when he abandons his…children is one that no government can fill."

Beggar Leper

Years later as a presidential candidate in 2008, Obama's recollections of Jakarta surfaced in *Newsweek* magazine, "He didn't know what to make of the leper who came to his door, who had a hole where his nose was supposed to be and made a discomfiting 'whistling sound' as he asked for food." The Newsweek story of his life in Indonesia continues with more striking images,

> He had to learn to deal with street beggars *of all types.* Obama's big-hearted mother gave easily. His Indonesian stepfather, an unsentimental man with a more practical view of the world, counseled the boy that *the demands of the needy have no end;* it was best to be strong because [again] 'men take advantage of weakness in other men.'[27]

---

26 *Ibid*, pp. 40-41.
27 Jeffrey Bartholet, Jessica Ramirez, Richard Wolffe, "When Barry Became Barack," *Newsweek*, March 22, 2008, pp. 25-32.

Again we find a story of needy people—of all types—who have incessant needs with "no end" who will try and take advantage of weakness in other people, such as his own mother. A fore-shadowing of Obama's public policy demands fueled by his deep needs—which will soon eat a hole in the American economy and our nation's other crucial foundations. He's a president taking advantage of a nation's soft spot, a weakness. Obama's super-intel remains a vivid symbolic communicator. If we pay attention to his images and stories, they will take us all the way down to his deepest pain.

In Jakarta the powerful forces of humiliation and powerlessness again came together at this crucial developmental time. No wonder Obama links Jakarta with overwhelming pain. Here he also began his lifelong compensatory search for power, reflected in his stepfather boxing with him, teaching him to fight. Despairingly, his mother noted, "Power was taking her son."[28]

Race Reigns (Obama Age 10-18)

Returning to America for good, Obama goes through customs at age 10. He carries his passport and a wooden mask given to him upon leaving Indonesia. Upon seeing his grandparents, Obama impulsively covered his face with the mask, swaying his head "in an odd little dance," prompting a customs official to ask, "Are you an American?" By including this story in his book, unconsciously Obama introduces the crucial question everyone wants to know. Arriving from a foreign country, Obama's behavior—dancing with the mask—suggests the answer: *he has a secret African tribal identity.* He was born in Africa. By age 10, he would unconsciously know the great family secret.

Immediately he focuses on his *"grandparents'* racism,"—and how much *"they* had changed." In one striking incident his grandmother is frightened by an unusually aggressive black panhandler. Obama immediately sees her reaction as racist and feels it sting "like a fist in my stomach." This incident triggered his own real fear of a black man's aggression toward a half-white person, i.e. his father's toward him.

Punahou School: Racism Preoccupation

Obama enrolled in the Punahou School, a prestigious Hawaiian prep school he attended from fifth grade through high school. Obama saw himself as lower class vs. the wealthy whites who were in the majority at the school. His life shaped by deep humiliation, he describes ongoing ridicule.

Alluding to competitive oedipal issues—Obama recalls that he was humiliated, mocked about a black girl being his girlfriend—and asked whether his African father was a cannibal. Obama then makes up a story to his classmates about his father being a prince and future king. Subtly, he suggests his African birth by mentioning his own plans to return one day to his home and eventually succeed his father—although he would have to wait on his father

---

28 *Ibid*, p 46.

eliminating competitors for his throne, another oedipal suggestion. As he explained, "it's sort of complicated...the tribe is full of warriors. *The men in our tribe all want to be chief*, so my father has to settle these feuds before I can come."[29] Obama had revealed such competition with his father was clearly on his mind.

Throughout prep school, Obama continues to focus on white racism— describing a black friend who sees everything as racist (as did his mentor, Davis). He recalls a coach humiliating him, asking him jokingly if his dark skin rubs off: another hint of Obama's terror of being too white. His ever-present view of "white racism" continually protected him from his deepest terror of his father's black racism—the deep belief his father would return at any moment to destroy him as his story about his competitive African father also suggests. Jack Cashill and others question Obama's racial suffering but Obama's stories reflect deep-seated racial conflicts of a surprising nature: primarily deep-seated fear of black racism toward his white blood.

Only Visit with Father

Obama only met his father once who visited Hawaii for a month after Obama had returned there from Indonesia at age 10—providing valuable clues about their relationship. Subtle pictures of aggression linked to racial conflicts permeate Obama's account. The immediate context: his mother has just returned from Indonesia, reminding Obama of his competitive (oedipal) victory. In the back of his mind he is acutely aware of his father's previous abandonment, particularly his wish to abort him—which now merges with his other major fear: dangerous oedipal competition with father.

We continue with "Oedipus" upon Obama meeting his father and consider subtle pictures of aggression from Obama's point of view. His father is injured, thin as a rail, using a cane, his eyes yellow from malaria. His "grandmother verbally *spars with his father*" whose presence "had summoned the spirit of earlier times," as if "Dr. King had never been shot...and war" were temporary setbacks. Obama suggests a past event that mentally, in his secret competitive role, he has battled his now-damaged father, injured him and, in effect, killed the black leader (Dr. King death reference) by winning the mother.

Then Obama presents the flip side—fear of his father's competitive payback revenge suggested by his father's three gifts of wooden figures: a lion, an elephant and an ebony man in tribal dress.[30] The message: "I am a dangerous, dominant black tribal warrior who never forgets [like the elephant]," subtly introducing skin color difference. Later, his father *humiliates* his son yet again for being "spoiled by his grandparents," i.e., favored by his mother. His grandparents label his father a "bully"—another competitive oedipal reference. Unconsciously, we can be sure Obama recalls the familiar story of his father

---

29 Obama, *Dreams*, p. 63.
30 *Ibid*, p. 66.

holding a man over a cliff by his legs linking the man to himself, and implying an abortion image.

The visit with his father also contains suggestions of Obama's African birth: (1) concern his lies about Africa to his classmates and his father being exposed; (2) his father's gift to Obama of African music "from his son's continent"—and the two of them dancing arm-in-arm to the music, reminiscent of Obama's tribal dance in customs; (3) thoughts of taking over as tribal king in Africa; (4) he and his father seeing a "remodeled hospital" where he was supposedly born suggests a remodeled story, that he was actually with his father in Africa at his birth.

Here and Gone

An overview of Obama Sr.'s only visit with his son at Christmastime 1971 gives us another perspective. It started and ended in a flash.

We now have the charming visit. Big smiles all around at the airport. Endearingly, his arm wrapped his son and his "ex-wife" in separate photos. The perfect long-lost father and former spouse now back in town—with gifts for his son upon their first meeting in 10 years.

They immediately follow up with another photo shoot on Christmas morning, this time of Obama Sr. with his son and Ann Dunham presenting him with gifts. How glad they are to have him in town. Reminiscent perhaps of how they both presented him with the gifts of their presence in Kenya at his son's birth. How well they had served his secret purposes then.

And he did love his son, his namesake, on some level—though Obama Jr. still felt afraid of him during the trip.[31] There were other tender moments during the visit, but then the inevitable confrontation with Ann Dunham's parents exploded. Shortly after, Obama Sr. is off to Kenya—with Obama the son never to see his father again. And from what the son says, never to hear his voice again. Obama Jr. never mentions a phone call from him—he does mention a call from relatives in Kenya, but never his father. All in all, his father's visit and follow-up behavior ended on a similar note of humiliation. It was all over before it started—and when he left again, Sr. ripped a fresh hole in young Obama.

Finally at the time of Obama, Sr.'s death 11 short years later, a month before Christmas Eve —Obama Jr. wrote, "my father remained a myth to me, both more and less than a man."[32] The Mystery Father—who paid his son The Mystery Visit, who produced The Mystery President—and as Obama will show us over and over again, in many ways, 'Like father, like son.'

Revisiting Frank Davis—Obama's Father?

We return to Frank Marshall Davis and the possibility he was the biological father of Obama. Jack Cashill believes two poems Obama released as a 19-year-

---

31 *Ibid*, p. 63.
32 *Ibid*, p. 5.

old Occidental College student appear to shed great light on the matter.[33] According to literary scholar Cashill, the first poem, "Pop," was sophisticated and likely written by Davis—far beyond Obama's abilities. By contrast the second poem "Underground" sounds to Cashill "as if it were written by another, lesser poet"—the 19-year-old Obama—and he calls it "a silly adolescent ode to apes that eat figs" in underwater grottoes.[34]

Acknowledging that both poems are obscure and require subjective decrypting, Cashill points out that the primary evidence for Davis as father resides in the title, "Pop."[35] (He explains that if it were about Obama's grandfather he would have entitled it 'Gramps.') The poem centers around an older man interacting with a young man, telling the boy a long joke. Eventually in frustration the boy holds a mirror in front of the older man, demanding answers. At that point the man opens up, "Makes me smell his smell, coming/From me," and then "Stands, shouts, and asks/For a hug." Cashill decodes this as Obama asking Davis, "Pop," to acknowledge his paternity, which Davis does.[36] All in all, not much evidence to go on.

Yet Cashill mentions that a therapist blogger—whom he believed had the most insight on the poem—noticed the imagery in "Pop" as more suggestive of sexual abuse of Obama by Davis.[37] From my take, Obama's poem "Underground" also contains sexual imagery suggesting that he is answering that question. However, that discussion is for another day. But if Obama was sexually abused by Davis we can scarcely imagine how much more abuse and humiliation it would heap upon young Barack—and how that would further feed his reactive fury.

For now *we have a much more revealing story of Obama and Davis* which does allow for far more accurate decoding—given our knowledge the super-intel speaks in detailed stories. First some background on Stanley Dunham and Davis.

Obama's grandfather unconsciously selected Frank Marshall Davis as Obama's black mentor for powerfully destructive reasons. His grandfather had told Obama about Davis' notoriety as a writer—showing him Davis's work "anthologized in a book of black poetry." Starting at age 11-12, Gramps would take Obama over to Davis's house where the two men would drink together while Davis read poetry. Obama describes, "As the night wore on, the two of them would solicit my help in composing *dirty limericks.*"[38] Stanley Dunham thus exposed Obama intentionally to Davis who was obviously behaving inappropriately in a sexual way around a much younger person. This to say Dunham knew all about Davis's sexual proclivities we can be sure.

---

33 Cashill, *Deconstructing Obama*, p. 280. The poems were published in the spring 1981 edition of Occidental College's literary magazine, *Feast.*
34 *Ibid*, p. 279.
35 *Ibid*, p. 278
36 *Ibid*, p. 279.
37 *Ibid*, p. 283.
38 Obama, *Dreams*, pp. 76-77.

To add fuel to the fire Obama reports his grandfather not infrequently took him to black bars in the red-light district of Honolulu, urging him to keep the visits secret from his grandmother. As the only white in the place his grandfather would drink whiskey while Obama would have a coke, his legs dangling from the high bar stool while he blew bubbles into his drink and looked at the pornographic art on the wall. Sometimes he and Gramps played pool there, as Obama recalls, "the excitement I felt...the enticement of darkness and the click of the cue ball." At the same time he observed that, like his grandfather, the people were all there where nobody would judge them—only Obama could see it didn't work. He sensed that "most of the people in the bar were not there out of choice...Our presence there felt forced." Eventually Obama "knew with the unerring instincts of a child that he [his grandfather] was wrong" and he became the adult in the room and in junior high school begged off from going to the bars.[39] Thus we have Gramps exposing his grandson repeatedly to a highly charged sexual environment.

At one point as a teenager, upset over an incident involving his grandmother's fear of blacks, Obama visited Davis by himself for counsel. Frank poured Obama several shots of the whiskey he was drinking. First Frank depicted having grown up near Wichita, Kansas like his white grandfather that if they had passed on the street Davis would have had to "step off the sidewalk to give [him] room." He then tells Obama a story related to him by Stanley Dunham about a black (girl) whom his grandparents had once hired years before to look after their young daughter Ann, Obama's mother. This black "became a regular part of the family." Davis goes on to tell Obama how his grandfather didn't know about humiliation as some Hawaiians and blacks did who have "seen... their mothers desecrated." He describes Obama's grandfather as being totally unaware about such humiliation—connecting him to being asleep in Davis's own chair—oblivious also to the fact that "blacks have a reason to hate [whites]." He goes on to inform Obama that Toot was right to be scared of blacks. At one point Davis also told Obama that his grandfather "doesn't know me, any more than that [black] who looked after your mother"—indirectly connecting himself to the person who came into his grandparents' home.[40]

In a nutshell Davis suggests he desecrated Obama's own mother—had sex with her—again introducing the prominent chair in the nude pictures. He unconsciously suggests to Obama he did so for racial reasons: that was his way of taking revenge, having power over a young vulnerable white girl. Davis also appears to be telling Obama that he very well could be his father, that 'he is a part of Obama's family.'

At a deeper level, Obama's super-intel picked up on the message and he described Davis falling asleep in his chair. Poignantly, he adds after the revelation, *"The earth shook under my feet, ready to crack open at any moment.*

39 *Ibid*, pp. 77-78.
40 *Ibid*, pp. 90-91.

I stopped, trying to steady myself, and knew for the first time that I was utterly alone."[41] Not only was Obama caught between two racial worlds, he now had to face the shocking possibility that Frank might be his father—and surely had abused his mother sexually. Is it any wonder that his world was about to come apart and swallow him up?

What Frank Davis missed was that Gramps was atoning for his own guilt—that he did know "what it feels like to" have his mother desecrated. He likely offered his daughter up to Davis to make up for his awful burdensome guilt over his mother's suicide, a way of atoning—to a black man. It would fit with Frank's story in his porno novel of the young white girl "Gloria" allowing him to impregnate her--in a passed-down atonement. For Stanley Dunham it really wasn't about sex or race, but about guilt and dysfunctional atonement.

All in all, Obama and his mother were products of a disturbing, highly sexualized, chaotic environment—hugely dysfunctional ways of handling emotional trauma—above which he attempts to rise. On top of that, he now wasn't sure who his father was. (Still there's more of the story to come on who really is Obama's father. For sure it was a black man.)

College Years

After high school, Obama initially attended Occidental College in the Eagle Rock neighborhood of Los Angeles. He increasingly kept secrets as others had done to him for years: his registration name, his grades, most of his associations. Withholding secrets gives him leverage on his journey from powerlessness to power. He may have lived in a dormitory for foreign students. In his junior year Obama transferred to Columbia in New York where few remember him. Obama reports a trip to Pakistan with a foreign student when American passports would not allow entry. Desperately hiding something, today's Obama refuses to release academic, medical or passport records. His reticence in such matters strongly hints at crucial citizenship concerns. Also, while he should have first been issued a Social Security number in Hawaii, his current Social Security number is from Connecticut, where he has no known connections. That strange fact raises major questions, including the question of its legality, but with the media protecting him, no one dares raise them.

Father's Death and Obama's Dream

At age 22, a year after his father's sudden death, Obama reports a dream: he's on a bus journey where an old white man suddenly becomes a black girl and a lady with a secret appears. Next Obama visits his father in jail because a judge refused to release him. The two embrace. For the first time his father declares his love for Obama and soon becomes sad, asking his son to leave. Obama awakens sobbing, declaring himself his father's "jailer, judge, and

---

41 *Ibid*, p. 91.

son."[42] He suggests competition and especially rage—a secret wish to eternally punish his father for abusing him, hinting again at his father's wish to abort him and hatred of his son's white blood. Obama deep down believes his father deserves a permanent jail sentence. Once again we must not miss his anger—he wants to jail the man who hurt him just as he was hurt, severely so.

Community Organizer and on to Harvard Law

Despite his secrecy a picture of Obama emerged along the way. As his college friend John Drew at Occidental observed Obama viewed himself as "part of an intelligent, radical vanguard that was leading the way towards this revolution and towards this new society."[43] He was an elitist with a secretly radical mission early on. On his journey Jack Cashill perceived Obama as a master at attracting and using powerful people.[44] We must keep this trait ever before us.

At age 24 Obama becomes a community organizer in Chicago through a $25,000 grant from the Woods Fund. Later in 1999 William Ayers serves as president of the board which Obama eventually joins himself as a Congressman.[45] (Ayers and Obama continually claim little interaction with each other.)

Obama's community organizer job spelled out means 'How do I use these people to further my political career?'—'How do I continue to shape my radical agenda and where do I go from here?' He was following the instructions Alinsky laid out in his manual *Rules For Radicals* that the community organizer had one central driving force: to build a mass power base for the ultimate purpose solely of revolution.[46] Establishing his roots in Chicago, Obama continues to learn all about inside politics at its finest.

He will adopt a subversive, deceitful mentality just as others deceived him. Predictably he would seek those groups out—deeply committed to the Alinsky strategy of deceit—an "underground" network of socialistic saboteurs as later affiliations suggest: anti-American, anti-capitalist, anti-rule of law, anti-Constitution, pro-Palestinian, anti-Jewish.

On the surface he was a benign community organizer—but secretly he was an Alinsky clone. He heads toward following Alinsky's "boring from within" advice by entering Harvard Law School. No grades were ever released, no proof of college graduation surfaced—all negative templates proving favoritism. Early on, Obama embraced the "first black" role. He became the first black editor of the Harvard Law Review. He also supported a radical black law professor Derrick Bell who espouses racism. After Harvard the focus of Obama's political activities was building ACORN, the largest radical organization in the United

---

42 Obama, *Dreams*, p. 129.
43 Cashill, *Deconstructing Obama*, p. 224
44 *Ibid*, p. 275.
45 http://www.thenation.com/article/obama-under-weather accessed May 21, 2012.
46 Saul Alinsky, *Rules for Radicals*, (New York: Random House, 1971) p.8.

States until he became a full-time legislator in 1996.[47] Also after Harvard if not earlier, he associates with radical anti-Americans Bill Ayers and the Rev. Jeremiah Wright—a minister with strong Muslim sympathies. Wright for example has had the Nation of Islam leader Louis Farrakhan as a guest speaker in his church and featured him on the cover of the church magazine. Admittedly he does not push Muslims to renounce their faith before joining his Christian church.[48]

Along the way people noticed two traits about Obama—he was entitled and easily bored. Raised to believe he was extraordinarily special, Obama quickly moves up the ladder from community organizer to civil rights law to the state senate to U.S. Congressman and then senator. His closest aide Valerie Jarret said, "He's been bored to death his whole life. He's just too talented to do what ordinary people do."[49]

'Bored' suggests he was not really interested in doing the job as much as he was using people to get to the next level of power. Obama reflects he's the man on the way up. The perpetual campaigner (the job he does best of all), self-centered, eloquent speaker, dapper but like he said empty as the house of sand which is his foundation. Built on nothing solid, he builds nothing solid—ever on the move but you can't go beyond the presidency. You have to stop and be evaluated.

Not only did Obama use people when problems arose with supporters he would throw them under the bus as he did with Ayers and Jeremiah Wright. Obama distanced himself from both during the 2008 campaign when they became problematic to him. A former Chicago supporter said, "I think he's arrogant, self-absorbed....He walked away from his friends.[50]

At the same time all along the way he tries to keep secret who he is and what he's really about. Clearly identified with radical forces in America he still attempts to appear mainstream. His book *Audacity* could be summed up on the one hand 'I believe this' and on the other hand 'I believe that.'[51]

Upon election to the U.S. Senate, he's playing hard-ball Chicago politics, and he becomes the most radical leftist senator in Congress: an anti-military, pro-abortion extremist. Deceitfully, he 'writes' two books—but Ayers was the actual author of *Dreams* and another writer of *Audacity*. More secrets follow—financing of his presidential campaign from the likes of George Soros and significant foreign (Muslim?) money.[52] He considered himself continually entitled to favoritism and rejected efforts to measure his accountability. In fact,

---

47 Horowitz, *Barrack Obama's Rules for Revolution*, p. 14.
48 Ed Klein, *The Amateur: Barack Obama in The White House,* (Washington, DC: Regnery, 2012).
49 Cashill, *Deconstructing Obama*, p. 224.
50 *Ibid*, p. 225.
51 *Ibid*, p. 222
52 Among others, the author cites the case of two Palestinian brothers from the Rafah refugee camp in Gaza who donated *$33,000* to Obama's 2008 campaign. Pamela Geller, "Obama's Foreign Donors: The media averts its eyes," American Thinker, August 14, 2008,
http://americanthinker.com/2008/08/obamas_donor_contributions_sil.html accessed May 28, 2012.

he refused to be accountable about how he came into this world by never releasing records, including his original birth certificate (if one exists) until a crisis three years into his presidency prompted him to suddenly produce an 'authentic long-form birth certificate' on the Internet—about which there are many questions except the media's. Deceit is a major part of his rage—as he was deceived.

The Ayers-Dohrn Connection

In March 2012 in conjunction with Arizona Sheriff Joe Arpaio's investigation of Obama's birth certificate, a new witness was uncovered who revealed an important connection between Obama and William Ayers. A retired Chicago mailman, Allen Hulton, had delivered mail to William Ayers' parents for more than 20 years. He recalled how in the late 1980s and early 1990s Mary Ayers, the mother, boasted of providing financial help for college to a particular black "foreign" student. She was highly enthusiastic about this student. Around the same time, Hulton met the student in front of the Ayers' home. Hulton is convinced that "foreign" student was Barack Obama, and was particularly struck by Obama's boast. The student had gone out of his way to speak to Hulton and excitedly informed the postman that he was going to be president one day. Distinctly Hulton recalls it was as if it were a done deal—"although you hadn't gone to work yet."[53]

The boastful behavior sounds so characteristic of the self-centered Obama. But the boasts on the part of both Obama and Mary Ayers point to an unconscious confession: that back then they both knew they were proposing to break the constitutional requirement prohibiting foreign-born candidates from running for president. *Boasts are often secret confessions* (secretly, wrongdoers want to get caught). In short, we have a foreign college student already intent on becoming president who was being financed by the Ayers family. Clearly the entire group including Obama had a plan, and they had money. It would be a drop in the bucket to help Obama through law school at Harvard. And his radical political agenda would fit hand-in-glove with the destructive anti-American William Ayers. Now it all comes together how and why Obama's political campaign started in 1995 in the home of William Ayers and Bernadine Dohrn, how Ayers came to write Obama's books and his motivation for doing so.

Secretly Bill Ayers must have been downright delighted to take part in this plan. The former Weather Underground activist had found a way of continuing his attacks on America: the perfect future president who, like Ayers, would thumb his nose at America's most precious foundation, the Constitution. This time Ayers couldn't go to jail for bombing a government building, but true to his word, he would do it all over again. Ayers and Obama—both intent on secretly

---

53 Jerome Corsi, "Mailman Discouraged from Telling Obama Story," March 25, 2012, http://www.wnd.com/2012/03/mailman-discouraged-from-telling-obama-story/ accessed June 1, 2012.

attacking America—were blood brothers. And still are.

We are reminded how Obama distanced himself from Ayers during his 2008 presidential campaign, dismissing him with the wave of a hand—with the lap-dog media following Obama's lead. And of course the media never reported anything about the Chicago mailman who came forward in 2012. But when deceit comes home to roost, deceit extracts a price.

Now another new witness has also surfaced, and he has far more to say than the Chicago mailman. Obama's super-intel will tell us a story every bit equivalent to the byline, "Why Sheriff's Obama Probe Could be Biggest Scandal in American History."[54] In a crucial four-part saga, Obama's super intelligence probe will take us far deeper into the narrative. So deep that it will advise Americans how to finally overcome this pressing constitutional crisis.

---

54 Jeff Kuhnert, "Why Sheriff's Obama Probe Could be Biggest Scandal in American History," *Washington Times*, March 24, 2012.

8

Father Abandonment

On two of the most important days in the life of Barack Obama—Fathers' Day and his Inauguration Day—this ambitious politician made several stunning confessions. Doubt it not. Without even realizing it, he tells us all we need to know about his truest motivations. On those two days, his super intelligence addresses America and the world, graphically revealing his deepest drives and dynamics. Here his super intelligence speaks unimpeded.

Obama's most honest moral compass offers us an inside look at a president, a close-up view which we've never before seen. He adds a personal letter to his daughters on both days, underscoring his hidden confession in a four-part super-intel saga: two speeches and two letters. His exceedingly brilliant unconscious mind cuts to the chase by condensing his secret story into these four communications. We will see how he confirms and elaborates on his secret story from one communication to another.

The following abbreviations will be used for attribution:

> FD1: Fathers' Day speech (June 2008)
> FD2: Fathers' Day letter (June 2009)
> ISp: Inauguration speech (January 2009)
> ILtr: Inauguration letter (January 2009)

All professional politicians employ speechwriters, of course, but on these four occasions Obama—an obsessive micro-manager—would have written or arranged every single word. His Fathers' Day speech touches on deeply personal issues as do the two personal letters to his daughters, and his Inauguration Day address was certainly his most important speech to date.

Beyond that, his super intelligence will reveal striking concise repetitive messages, informing us without question that Obama himself essentially wrote every single word.Before we get started, I suggest you turn to Appendix B and E now, and read through Obama's Fathers' Day speech (FD1) and his Father's Day letter (FD2) the next year; neither are long and they will help you as I analyze different portions.

Father's Day 2008: Barack Obama's Autobiography in One Story

We revisit Obama's story of where it all began with his sandman father.

Let's take a closer look at Obama's Fathers' Day speech delivered on June 15, 2008, at the Apostolic Church in Chicago. Remember that by mid-June, Obama's campaign for the presidency was already in high gear as he sought to become the new father of our nation. He delivered the speech almost entirely extemporaneously, an approach which gives the super intelligence free reign to communicate loudly and clearly.

He opens with a compelling story—a New Testament parable, no less— which indicates his super intelligence is in overdrive. Narrative remains the super-intel's unique language. A parable itself implies deeper messages, reinforcing the idea that Obama's stories are parables about him, messages from his deeper intelligence. If you understand this parable, he suggests, you'll understand the situations which shaped his very identity.

He begins, "At the end of the Sermon on the Mount, Jesus closes by saying, *'Whoever hears these words of mine, and does them, shall be likened to a wise man who built his house upon a rock: and the rain descended, and the floods came, and the winds blew, and beat upon that house, and it fell not, for it was founded upon a rock'"* (Matthew 7: 24-25).

He intentionally leaves out the second part of the parable about home builders who foolishly build on a foundation of sand, but indirectly he refers to it: *"Now everyone who hears these sayings of mine and does not do them will be like a foolish man who built his house on sand: and the rains came, and the winds blew and beat on that house, and it fell. And great was its fall."* (Matthew 7: 26-27, NKJV).[1]

The tale of the two home-builders is one of the best-known biblical stories. When a fierce storm attacks the foundation of both houses, the home built on rock stands but the home built on sand is washed away. While the gospel writer tells this story to teach an important concept about the foundations of faith, Obama finds the story remarkably relevant to his own life experience.

Obama thus characterizes fathers as builders of homes, and the best homes are constructed upon the strength, the rock, of the family. While fathers are charged with building a strong foundation for the entire family, Obama specifically emphasizes how important it is for a father to tend to a *son's* foundation —as he will go on to extensively talk about fathers and sons. And then he links these comments to his absent father, thus confirming that he's unconsciously telling us his own deeper story. Once again Obama underscores, "Of all the rocks upon which we build our lives we are reminded today... called to recognize and honor how critical every father is to that foundation."

---

1 Immediately preceding this passage, Jesus insists his followers will be known by the fruit they bear and warns that many who call him "Lord" will not enter the kingdom of heaven because they hypocritically "practice lawlessness."

Andrew G. Hodges, M.D.

'Hear My Deeper Words'

> Of all the rocks upon which we build our lives, we are **reminded today** that family is the most important. And we are **called to recognize** and honor how critical every father is to that foundation. They are teachers and coaches. They are mentors and role models. They are examples of success and the men who constantly push us toward it. (FD1)

He surrounds his story with crucial unconscious message markers, phrases or images implying communication which the super-intel uses to alert the listener that important information either immediately precedes or follows. In this case the message markers are "reminded today" and "called to recognize," heralding his unconscious instructions to America, alerting us to recognize that he's revealing his hidden autobiography.

In this light, consider the scriptural declaration, *'Whoever hears these words of mine...shall be likened to a wise man.'* For openers we have the most important message marker in this speech, "hear these words of mine"—truly the byword of his four-part personal saga. Obama suggests we should pay particularly close attention to his words, implying "think super intelligence words," words on two levels, words having two meanings. Literal words from the surface mind, deeper symbolic words from the super intelligence. Basically he informs us that when we understand multi-level communication, we listen like a wise man and we can hear messages emanating from our deepest and truest wisdom.[2]

Obama quotes Scripture (itself a powerful symbolic message marker apart from its words) as if to mark his own words with the message 'this is the absolute truth about my personal life.' His super intelligence speaks with phenomenal authority and wants to give these deeper words the authority they deserve. From the very beginning, Obama puts everything on the table in the message "words." Wise Americans, shrewd listeners, will read his deeper words.

His super-intel reveals its great teaching wisdom:

- Specifically referencing words in a parable—words with double meanings—where the immediate goal is to read the deeper messages. His basic message: if you can read parables, you can read my secret communications.

- Emphasizing the importance of deeper words in the most prominent place—the introduction of his first speech.

Obama will also use "word" itself as a particularly key word at crucial places in his four-part communicative saga. All in all, Obama makes the case that everything comes down to how you hear words. We can only hear his super intelligence with these deeper, symbolic words. Basically Obama challenges citizens to listen more deeply. If they remain focused simply on his surface

---

2 The super intelligence hidden away in the unconscious is also called *"the deep wisdom center"* of the mind, reflecting its superior assessment on virtually every situation. See Appendix A.

113

words, then they will miss out on his secret story, his confession and the list of harmful plans he has in store for our once-great nation. Fortunately, his super-intel is so wise and morally pure that it also explains the way to reclaim his own honor and restore America. His initial message is listen carefully: Go slowly, read more deeply.

Follow-up Story

Here at Apostolic, you are blessed to worship in a house that has been founded on the rock of Jesus Christ [our Lord and Savior]. **But it is also built on another rock, another foundation—and that rock is Bishop Arthur Brazier...on this Fathers' Day,** it must make him proud to know that **the man now charged with keeping its foundation strong** is his son and your new pastor. (FD1)

To further validate his personal message, Obama immediately follows up his parable with a similar story about the robust and resilient pastor of the Apostolic Church—the "rock," the "foundation"—on which a church (a home) was built. He elaborates how this rock of a pastor also built a solid son who will succeed him, "the man now charged with keeping [the church's] foundation strong."

There are two types of fathers, Obama reminds us. Involved fathers build solid foundations for his children and absent fathers who build foundations "made of sand." Yet Obama simply cannot speak the phrase "sand foundation." Why? It's as if that sand would bury him. *He knows he's the son of a sandman.*

His Story: *'What it Means to Me to Have an Absent Father'*

I know what it means to have an absent father, although my circumstances weren't as tough as they are for many young people today. Even though my father left us when I was two years old, and I only knew him from the letters he wrote and the stories that my family told, I was luckier than most.(FD1)

What better day than Fathers' Day for Obama to discuss the dynamics of the father-son relationship? "I know what it means to have an absent father," he said. And he builds his entire speech on that quick and candid admission, one which shows Obama Jr. for what he really is. He's the son of a man who abandoned his responsibilities and abandoned his son, leaving the child defenseless in the face of life's inevitable storms and strife. The foolish builder who left him with a weak foundation.

As his story unfolds, Obama establishes a fundamental rule of fatherhood: only fathers with strong foundations can build strong foundations in their sons. You can't build what you don't know. Unconsciously Obama's super-intel clearly compares him with the pastor's son: how a strong son was built rock-solid by a strong father who was present, versus how he himself was built by an absent father on a shaky foundation of sand.

114

The Question

Obama's stories have raised the exact questions Americans should want answered in order to know about this inexperienced stranger who ran for president. Even without those answers, however, millions of voters were simply caught up in the false charisma of the moment.

The crucial issue before him—and before America in 2008—was: What kind of president would he make? Remember, the super intelligence will be pointedly straightforward. Rest assured Obama's deeper mind will answer in great detail every major question about him. What are his true intentions for America? Running for president, Obama unconsciously wants America to know all about the real candidate, warts and all—and secretly he wants to know himself. Don't be misled by his surface concern with America's fathers. Obama's super-intel is continually talking about *him*.

Super Intelligence Education

Obama draws attention to the crucial role of the super intelligence—primarily here by his emphasis on education. One key comment jumps out at us, *"education is everything to our children's future."* Before Obama's super-intel provides a wealth of utterly unique information about him, it first points toward its very existence and extraordinary abilities.

We find other vital educational references: "we need… more outstanding teachers… more after-school programs for our children" [read, citizens]; "the opportunity to go to some of the best schools in the country." Read, "Pay attention America, my super-intel is an outstanding teacher—you are in the best school about me in the country—if you work hard and do extra work." We will see just how good a teacher Obama's unconscious truly is.

> We should expand programs … **help them learn** how to care for themselves… programs that have helped increase…readiness for school. (FD1)

To demonstrate, Obama tells us "We should expand programs…and help them learn" (FD1) suggesting 'expand—stretch—your mind so that you can learn' to understand his deeper messages. Above all he stresses, "Learn," informing us he's trying to help us learn all about his super-intel. This is the only way to truly care for and protect ourselves against his untoward intentions as we discover his unconscious confession. To increase our awareness and make us ready for his super intelligence school, he continues with educational references and what new learning demands.

> We know that education is everything to our children's future…We know the work and the studying and the level of education that requires….To really compete, they need to graduate high school… need to graduate college, and they probably need a graduate degree too. An eighth-grade education doesn't cut it today. Let's give them a handshake and tell them to get their butts back in the

> library! It's up to us – as fathers....to instill this ethic of excellence
> in our children. (FD1)

He advises us, "We know the work and the studying and the level of education that it requires," his super-intel implying that to comprehend its messages requires paying close attention and studying another level of communication. "To really compete," Obama goes on, "they need to graduate high school, and then they need to graduate college, and they probably need a graduate degree too. An eighth-grade education doesn't cut it today. Let's give them a handshake and tell them to get their butts back in the library!"

Mentioning "graduate" three times Obama repeats the message, "Think grad work." He's implying, "Everybody you've got something new to learn. Think about a higher level of consciousness—in a nutshell think about the super intelligence everyone possesses." Like a good teacher, he unconsciously encourages everyone—gives them a symbolic handshake—reminding them that everyone can learn how to listen to the super-intel, 'just take it one step at a time like you did earlier in your education.' "Graduate" also contains the message that we should never stop learning, that we should persist and complete the job of understanding his super intelligence. Then we can protect our nation.

In his Fathers' Day letter the next year he subtly repeats the message mentioning fathers who work "that extra shift so their kids can go to college." (FD2) But he's talking to regular people implying if you pay attention to the 'extra' message, do the work of looking deeper you'll see my secret messages, the story within the story. Knowing that there are capable people who can catch on Obama stresses the urgency of understanding his deeper messages. Here he warns that America's future depends on "education"—new knowledge about his unconscious messages. *His warning that America's future is up in the air suggests that indeed he presents a huge threat to America.*

Quickly and unmistakably Obama has introduced the single-most important issue for a future president—*character*. Again he invites several fundamental questions:

- What kind of person was his father? Since his father was the supposed critical rock "upon which we build our lives," did he have a rock-solid foundation or one of "sand"?
- What kind of foundation did his father build in him?
- In short, did we elect a president of great character?

Obama has answered the implied question—"How important is my human development in forming my character?"—by highlighting a crucial story about fathers building sons, sons who become leaders on Fathers' Day no less. For the record, it's a question the media never asked. Before we hear Obama answer that character question in far greater detail, we must first appreciate a related and equally crucial question he raises.

What Type of Nation-Builder?

On the heels of his opening parable, Obama elaborates about the strong pastor and father—"a rock"—who also builds a community foundation on solid ground to withstand the storm of a chaotic community. The Apostolic Church's crime-ridden neighborhood overflows with homeless, uneducated people, often controlled by drug-dealers. But "because of his work and his ministry," Obama noted, "there are more graduates and fewer gang members…surrounding this church." (FD1)

He implied that this weak community was run by weak people built on sand. Indirectly but plainly he links the story of community leaders to himself. It centers on a change of office, a new leader—the pastor's son—charged with keeping the church and its foundation strong, a situation which mirrored Obama's own ongoing ascendancy to the presidency. Now, as a son built by his father, he raises a second question. Will he be the community leader, the national leader, the rock on which America can depend? Later, he refers to the identical matter in his Inauguration Day speech, "To those leaders around the globe who seek to sow conflict…Know that your *people will judge you on what you can build, not what you destroy*." (ISp)

After introducing the two most important issues for a potential president, character and leadership, Obama hints at a dark autobiographical truth. His father's absence built him into a chaotic, angry person.

Obama's 48th Year without his Father

Obama adds further confirmation that his Fathers' Day stories have to do with him. He praises the rock of a father figure, the pastor who spent 48 years building his church home and his son. At this point Obama was a month from entering his 48th year on this earth, and for 48 years his father had been absent, and his absence itself had a profound effect on Obama Jr. When he talks about this pastor father's pride about his son becoming pastor, surely on Fathers' Day above all others, in the back of his mind Obama must have reflected on how proud *his* father would have been of him now that he was just a step away from winning the White House. Finally he might become an honor to his father and not a disgrace.

Obama praises the rock-solid pastor for being "the reason this house has stood tall for half a century." Yet because of his absent father, Obama was never able to stand tall, to stand up for things like a leader should. You stand on rock. But you sink on sand. From the get-go, Obama suggests he will fail as president.

Too Many Missing Fathers

Almost immediately after telling us fathers "are the rocks upon which we build our lives"—notice the personal "we" and "I"—Obama emphasizes the failure of absent fathers: "But if *we* are honest with ourselves, *we'll* admit that what too many fathers also are missing—missing from too many lives and too many homes. They have abandoned their responsibilities, acting like boys instead of men. And the foundations of our families are weaker because of it. You and I know how true this is in the African-American community." (FD1)

Message Markers, Built-In Guides

Notice the phrases, "if we are honest," "we'll admit," and "know how true this is." As noted earlier, the super intelligence tags messages with communication references—here repeating the image of "honesty" and "the truth is." These might be considered truth tags or truth markers. Such key *message markers*—as we will call them—remind us to pay very close attention to what follows, in this case the deeper message is "I am about to tell you the *real* truth." The fact that so many message markers are in connecting sentences particularly suggests the central message is important.

Here we also have a second type "message tag"—a personal marker "I" and "we." Combining these two markers, Obama is telling us that whatever crucial subject follows has to do personally with him. Just as he did in the very beginning, "Whoever hears these words of *mine.*"

Another common type of message marker Obama uses is an education marker, a reference to institutions such as universities, schools, technology—red flags implying that, "I'm about to teach you about something important." Already we have seen him include such markers in a key story about his super-intel's efforts to help us learn its new communication method.

'All About Me'

In conjunction with message markers Obama unconsciously uses vivid stories with key phrases and key locations to emphasize his secret narrative. We glance ahead briefly at a unique place--the close of his Father's Day speech which was the first of four major personal communications—to understand a special message about his hidden confession that unfolds before us. He notes a time, *"When I was a young man, I thought life was all about me"*—reiterating that this entire speech from start to finish is all about his life, from the time he was young child. His key phrase gives us the overriding title of his four part saga, "All About Me." He suggests that he is unfolding first the impact of his missing father on him and then what kind of father/leader he will be to America. Now we continue with a new appreciation of his story.

Missing Father Leaves a Hole

Obama paints one of the most powerful pictures imaginable of how an absent father affects his children—he leaves behind a hole in their hearts, a flaw in their very foundation. As he said, "Too many fathers are AWOL, MIA...There's a hole in your heart if you don't have a male figure in the home that can guide you...lead you...set a good example." (FD1)[3] Again look at his images, "MIA"—missing in action—and "hole." These depict the absent father,

---

3 Some transcripts of this speech accidentally omitted this reference.

who should provide a manly "warrior" identity for a son, but the father wasn't there, causing the son's significant loss of strength and lack of manly energy.

A year later, on the next Fathers' Day, (2009) in his letter to his daughters Obama specifically described his father wound and the hole left in him: "I came to understand the importance of fatherhood through its absence…in my life…I came to understand that the hole a man leaves when he abandons his responsibility to his children is one that no government can fill." (FD2)

Think about Obama's initial story, his parable right out of the box. The foundation of a home built on sand leaves a lot of holes. A sink hole can appear at any moment particularly during a storm. Unquestionably Obama warns America, "See if I can stand up in a crisis."

Missing Manhood

Also in the 2009 letter Obama adds another dimension to his father's absence in a vivid story about fatherless Chicago youngsters, "I would often walk through the streets of Chicago's South Side and see boys [without fathers] marked by that same absence." Obama was "marked" all right—scarred deeply. Remember that word, "marked," because he will use it again in an unbelievably brutal story describing his father.

He went on, "(boys) without supervision or direction or anyone to help them as… [they] struggled to grow into a man…I identified." (FD2) That's another subtle reminder that this is his story. Looking at those boys would tear him up. They reminded him that he himself was a lost, inner-city fatherless kid lacking a male role model. He was looking in a mirror—experiencing an intimidating flashback which grew stronger and stronger with every passing year.

Obama desperately missed his father showing him how to be a man. When his father left, he took much of Obama's manhood with him. That was the hole his father left in him, his sense of what it was to be a man. Two years in a row on Fathers' Day, Obama painted vivid pictures of the extensive damage an absent father inflicts on his kids—confirming just how badly he was wounded.

Disrespected, Ignored

Too painful to really see (or feel) what he had experienced, Obama just kept talking about other kids' absent fathers, "our young boys see—when you are ignoring or mistreating your wife…see when you are inconsiderate at home; or when you are distant; or when you are thinking only of yourself." Kids see everything their father is—or isn't. Obama didn't stop there: "[that's] why we pass on the values of empathy and kindness to our children by living them. We need to show our kids that you're not strong by putting other people down." (FD1)

Obama compared the absent father to the involved father who worked hard, treated others with respect, contributed to his home/community, was involved on a daily basis with school and athletics, and financially supported the family. All

119

those things the absent father wasn't. The absent father mistreated the family, ignored them, showed them no empathy and put them down. He disrespected the community and tore down its foundation—the home. This disillusioned, disrespectable man, this was the father Obama knew—like the back of his hand.

Later, reflecting just how out of touch he will be as president, Obama eerily notes, "The second thing we need to do as fathers is pass along the value of empathy to our children. Not sympathy, but empathy...to look at the world through their eyes. Sometimes it's so easy to...forget about our obligations to one another. There's a culture in our society that says remembering these obligations is somehow soft—that we can't show weakness, and so therefore we can't show kindness."(FD1)

Here Obama reveals a major secret—his distorted sense of manhood. To carry out our obligations to one another, to show kindness, means you are weak and soft. We can hear Obama processing his father's neglectful emotional abuse, "Oh, that's how you show you're a man." It's as though Obama's putting the best spin possible on total abandonment and his father's insensitivity to his child's most basic needs. It's as though Obama's saying, "See? My father was really a tough man. He really did love me after all. He was just showing me how to be a man."

Yet eerily Obama also unconsciously confesses to Alinsky's powerful influence on him precisely here—"a culture in our society that says remembering...obligations is soft...can't show weakness." That was the exact culture Alinsky was attempting to build—all about power. His manual would instruct idealists who wanted to show kindness that they were 'cowards for not wanting power...power is good.'[4] And how well that idea fit with Obama's needs to somehow find a manhood to overcome his sand foundation—this explains why he was so vulnerable to Alinsky's control.

Amazingly Obama's super-intel had to answer the specific question of how much influence Alinsky had over him—which Obama had all along attempted to consciously minimize. He did so appropriately on Fathers' Day—but in the end Alinsky, the surrogate father, truly was another absent father to Obama. Deep down Obama knew such ruthless power strivings meant he couldn't show kindness like he really wanted to, just as he did with his daughters. Upon reflection Alinsky brought Obama sadness, contributing to Obama's deep-seated grief. Offering him a "rebel" as Alinsky identified himself instead of a father.[5]

In the end Obama's self-protective, misguided seeking of power was just another denial of how badly he was abused by his biological father. And a denial about his lack of empathy for the American people—he continually leads the country in directions which hurt the people.

---

4 Horowitz, *Obama's Rules*, p. 13.
5 *Ibid*, p. 3.

Denial of Abandonment's Effect; Four Absent Fathers

To appreciate Obama's unfolding story we must understand the depth of his denial. How he consciously cannot handle the truth about himself. Even as he shows us the way around denial—through his stories—he has no conscious idea his super intelligence is giving away all his secrets.

Despite setting up the undeniable equation that an absent father means a sand foundation, the deepest hole imaginable in you, loss of your manhood, no internal guide, Obama cannot allow the word "sand" to cross his lips. It's simply too painful to admit. At times he resorts to overt denial. While insisting that "my circumstances weren't as tough" as other kids without fathers, in the same breath he admitted, "I know what it means to have an absent father" (FD1)—followed by blatant criticism of absent fathers.

As previously noted, *one of the best methods to understanding his super-intel messages is to **read straight through** his frequent denials.* When he says something like "My circumstances weren't as tough" as other kids,' he's actually saying the exact opposite. He did, in fact, have it as tough as other kids did, far tougher than anyone can imagine.

While noting how lucky he was to have had wonderful grandparents helping his mother, he nonetheless makes plain that he pined for his father. "I still felt the weight of his absence throughout my childhood." He continues with, "still I know the toll it took on my mother...I know the toll it took on me"—repeating "toll" twice for emphasis. The meter is still running on that toll and we can believe that his grandfather and surrogate father, Stanley Dunham, also took a toll on him when he hand-picked the shadowy Frank Marshall Davis as Obama's black mentor. These surrogate fathers—Stanley and Davis—were as absent in their own way as was Obama's biological father, and then throw Alinsky into the mix. Now we understand that whenever Obama speaks of his absent father, he unconsciously speaks of all four absent fathers in his life—but with major emphasis on by far Obama Sr.

Denial When Father Left

We get another glimpse of Obama's denial when he tells us, "Even though my father left us when I was two years old and I only knew him from the letters he wrote and the stories that my family told, I was luckier than most." (FD1) Actually his father left when he was two *weeks* old—a fact so hurtful it explains why Obama clung to the myth that he was two *years* old when he father left. In truth, Obama saw his father in person once in his life for two weeks at age ten. One brief visit and scattered letters perfectly captures the absent father, doubly underscoring the typical denial of a son seriously wounded by abandonment. We must not forget that denial is unconscious—that Obama consciously believes his pain was minimal.

In his autobiographical *Dreams,* Obama unknowingly described the severity of his emotional abuse at the hands of his father. He defined sufferings of abandoned kids as "unimaginable." Emotional pain leads to the mask of denial, the greater the pain the more impenetrable the mask. From beginning to end, his saga becomes a high-powered lens through which we can see through his denial. Instead, he desperately pleads with the American people to face the truths which he cannot.

Two Letters, Two Speeches

Notice that Obama specifically tells us, "My father left...I knew him mainly from the letters he wrote." Obama provides a huge clue and tremendous super-intelligent guidance by implying *"know me from the letters and speeches I personally delivered to America—the two letters to my daughters and the two speeches* (Fathers' Day and Inauguration Day) *connected to them on the same important two days."*

With the powerful message marker "knew [know] him," Obama unconsciously confirms that these personal communications are the key to understanding his hidden confession and deepest drives. Underscoring the importance of personal letters from his father in his personal speech, he links the two types of communication. Importantly, he repeats the identical message in his Fathers' Day letter a year later (which we'll examine in more detail in Chapter 11), providing further evidence his super intelligence is telling a secret story.

Absent Father Profile—Poverty, Hunger, and Prison

Obama continually invokes the keyword "poverty," often connecting it to his absent father. With his words, he paints a picture of a pervasive poverty instilled in him, that father wound, that "hole" inside him. "Children who grow up without a father," he said, are "more likely to live in poverty and commit crime... twenty times more likely to end up in prison." He repeatedly makes note of the money problems of single mothers, including his own: "I know the toll that being a single parent took on my mother—how she struggled at times to the pay bills; to give us the things that other kids had..." (FD1) The struggle to pay the toll remains ever-present—pay the toll or you can't cross the bridge; you can't go anywhere in your life's journey toward maturity and becoming a person of character because you're really broken deep down and full of holes.

The lack of money was scary enough in itself, but Obama suffered a worse kind of poverty—being "father poor" with no "father bread" at all in the house. He hints that the hole his father left was a special prison all its own. He implies that he grew up on "prison bread" devoid of father nurture, a junk food meal which inevitably left him emotionally hungry. That emotional hole in him could not be filled and he went to bed "father hungry" every night. And he still goes to bed hungry—that hole never goes away.

So great was his need he could not stop talking about it even *in his inaugural address*—one striking section overflowed with his father-deprivation issues, "To the people of poor nations, we pledge," (ISp) that is, *to the people from father-poor families—I pledge.* The word "pledge" is one of those passionate message markers presaging a high-priority message. On this deeper level, look what follows—all the issues linked with his father leaving: "...pledge to nourish starved bodies and feed hungry minds." (ISp) First the fear of literal starvation, "starved bodies"—a very tangible fear when you see your single mother struggling to put food on the table. In your mind the father, the one person between you and starvation, is failing in his role as provider. Obama constantly felt his father's empty seat at the head of the table.

Obama's extreme father hunger was a craving for love, something we humans need as badly as food. Notice *"feed hungry minds"*—describing his desperate father hunger. He virtually shouts, *I am still starving for a real father.* His history of father hunger has led Obama to frequently bow to male foreign leaders—just one of the results of his desperate need to fill that hole in his heart.

Notice the entire phrase, "no longer afford indifference to suffering outside our borders" suggesting Obama's particular situation with his father faraway in Africa all those years. Surely the young Obama would have wondered innumerable times, "Why don't you send for me?" "Why don't you come visit me?" Obama Sr. only visited his son once in his life.

Needy

> **We need** to help all the mothers out there who are raising these kids by themselves...So many of these women are doing a heroic job, but **they need** support. **They need** another parent. **Their children need** another parent. That's what keeps their foundation strong. It's what keeps the foundation of our country strong. (FD1)

Looking back at his Fathers' Day speech briefly we clearly see Obama's deep-seated father need in his repeated references to "needy" people left behind in single-parent homes. Note the personal reference, *"We* **need** to help...mothers...raising these kids by themselves...they **need** support. They **need** another parent." Notice who comes next. "Their children **need** another parent." (FD1) Need, need, need, need—four times—a huge "shout out" of just how great was his father need. It's the central story of his life, literally everywhere we turn in his four-part serial.

Everyone who has had a father knows the power of his voice, the impact his words can have. But Barack Obama never had that experience. His family related them to him, occasional letters, and a two-week visit actually hearing that voice in person—a miniscule drop in the bucket of "father's words."

Five months after his inauguration, in the Fathers' Day letter to his daughters, Obama tells us all about it as he discusses other kids' absent fathers. He admonishes aloof fathers: "[We need to] step out of our own heads and tune in. We need to turn off the television and start talking with our kids and listening to them, and understanding what's going on in their lives. We need to set limits and expectations." (FD2) Read Obama's repetitive "we need" as "I needed." Here Obama confesses that he desperately needed his father to step out of own head, desperately needed his father's words—to talk to him, set limits and inspire expectations. He needed to hear words to believe in and words that believed in him. But all Obama had was total silence—his father's missing voice, missing words. No words to obey, no words to set boundaries, no words of expectations, no words of understanding. Instead of a legacy of warmth and understanding, Obama's sandman father left his son with nothing but a silent deep hole in his core which cried out in its own way.

Excessive Television Appearances

Notice Obama's words, starting with the personal "we." "*We* need to turn off the television and start ...listening ...and understanding ...set limits..." (FD2) Now read the message "we need" as "I need" to cut off television and set limits. Here we can see one place where Obama's lack of limits reflects the lack of self-control that resulted from his absent father. Recall a frequent complaint about Obama from his critics, "Words, words, words—doesn't this guy ever stop talking on television?" It seems no president has ever talked so incessantly or sought such constant TV appearances.

Another oft-heard complaint is that he's too often is in his own head, not listening to the citizens, that he's oblivious to their needs. Two brief examples: he attempted to force his health-care bill down the throats of Americans. He failed to address the needs of people on the Gulf Coast after the horrific oil spill of 2010. Unconsciously Obama had predicted this very behavior—his super-intel knowing full well he would repeat his insensitive father's behavior on a new victim, the USA. Obama will go on to predict he'll repeat his missing father's behavior by failing to set limits for himself and become completely out of control as a president.

Also his instruction, "we need to turn off television" was a message to millions of misguided supporters who were seduced by his campaign television appearances. Unquestionably television played a major role in his election. Obama had all the natural ingredients of an entertainer—trim, sharp dresser, good looking, mesmerizing orator, nice looking family—creating a charismatic "Tulip Mania" moment.[6] Obama counsels citizens to ignore that false facade, and instead see his real nature. And he instructs them to "start listening...and understanding," suggesting they learn to understand his super intelligence confession to them in his four-part saga.

Disguised Grief and Guilt

Continuing in his Fathers' Day letter Obama acknowledges his own absence as a father due to his career. He recalls his poignant grief over his father loss, "(father) a million miles away...missing moments of my...lives [father's life]...that...never get back...a loss I will never fully accept." He adds that he "lost count of all the times, over the years, when demands took [my

---

6 "Tulip mania" is an investor's description of uncontrolled stock market purchases—stemming from a historical event when the price of tulips skyrocketed in uncontrolled buying, only to shortly thereafter collapse.

father]...from the duties of fatherhood...plenty of days of struggle and heartache." (FD2)

Undoubtedly he must have "lost count of all the times" his heart had ached for his father, moments he would "never get back," his father in truth thousands of miles away, representing "a loss... (he) will never accept."

Looking back, we see similar clues about Obama's abandonment at the beginning of his Fathers' Day speech: "It's good to be home on this Fathers' Day [with my girls]." Obama suggests that it is good to finally have a home on Fathers' Day because his entire life he never had a home with a father, a sad fact of which he's painfully reminded on this special day.

Notice the matching theme in the second part of his opening sentence, "it's an honor to spend some time with all of you today in the house of our Lord" (FD1)—the idea of being honored by spending time in a house with the head of that household, "our Lord." And, of course, for a small kid the "Lord" is first "his dad"—further suggesting when Obama's lord, his father, spent no time with him he felt dishonored, totally unimportant.[7]

'My Highest Goal'

In this brief story in the same speech, which we can call 'My Highest Goal,' Obama brings us to the crucial matter of his basic foundation—the type man he really is. Obama's greatest desire—to break the curse of abandonment in his daughters' lives, and build in them a "rock" foundation reveals just how badly his missing father weakened his foundation. "So I resolved many years ago that it was my obligation to break the cycle—that if I could be anything in life, I would be a good father to my girls; that if I could give them anything, I would give them that rock—that foundation—on which to build their lives. And that would be the greatest gift I could offer." (FD1)

Obama emphasizes over and over the words "if," "could" and "would," as in, "*if* I could be anything in life, I *would* be a good father to my girls... *if* I *could* give them anything, I *would* give them that rock —that foundation—on which to build their lives. And that *would* be the greatest gift I *could* offer." He strongly suggests that he has not yet fulfilled his greatest wish, that his plans have not come to fruition, but they could possibly one day.

The gift of rock and not sand—the gift from his father he himself longed for, in vain—this gift he would try to offer his daughters. His primary duty in life is now to break the cycle of sand foundations—yet the fact that such a cycle exists proves he is not at all free from his absent father, the missing builder. Obama clearly confesses that indeed he has been cursed with a shaky basic foundation—no foundation at all, really. He's a man lacking internal strength. Hardly the kind of man we should have 'hired' for our next president, but that's what happened in 2008.

---

7 As a forensic profiler I have learned to pay attention to first and last sentences or first and last stories which can be especially important. Obama demonstrates both.

9

A Victim of Violence

Now with Obama's super intelligence in high gear and speaking plainly, we can understand with absolute certainty his life's equation described in *Dreams*, as he says: "I know, I have seen, the desperation and disorder of the powerless; how it twists the lives of [such] children….[the] humiliation…how narrow the path is for them [between humiliation and untrammeled fury]."[1] Note the familiar message marker, "I know"—this is his super-intel's guarantee that it accurately paints an up-close-and-personal portrait, including "the desperation and disorder of the powerless" and the "humiliation." The Lone Ranger president has just pulled off his mask. Beneath it, he tells us, lurks utter desperation and loss of dignity—leading to a deeply disorganized self.

We glimpsed the powerlessness and humiliation caused by his rudderless family. But now he takes us to his deepest loss of dignity at the hands of his own father's violence.

Poverty Means Violence

At the outset of his Fathers' Day speech, Obama described the violence in poverty, poverty which leads to severe suffering—"the fierce winds and heavy rains of violence and poverty; joblessness and hopelessness… homeless… chaos." (FD1) It's an early portrait of his missing father who rained down poverty on his son in a hundred different ways. No father, no rock, no money. His father was jobless in more ways than one. He certainly didn't do his job as a father, leaving Obama "home-poor" without a real home, yearning for a home with a head of the household. Obama Sr. simply left his son to struggle alone against the chaos of a disjointed and dysfunctional single-parent family. Although Ann Dunham gamely endeavored to establish a home for her son, she could do nothing to dispel the underlying sense that his father had, in essence, sabotaged their home.

As with "fierce winds and heavy rains," Obama frequently uses harsh meteorological images to paint an animated picture of his father's destructiveness.

---

1 Obama, *Dreams*, pp. x-xi.

Storm Erodes the Home's Foundation

Stormy weather also swirled at the center of the parable about the two home builders. We note that in the second part of the story which Obama left out, "a foolish man who built his house on sand: and the rains came, and the winds blew and beat on that house, and it fell. And great was its fall" (Matthew 7: 26-27, NKJV). That house was Obama Jr. and great was the destruction to his personal foundation because his father had built him on the sand of his father's own weaknesses.

In Obama Jr.'s internalization of the parable, the sorry builder—his absent father—simultaneously becomes the violent storm itself, the fierce winds that beat upon Obama's house destroying his foundation. This storm comes down on you with descending rains that overwhelms you in floods, knocks you down with furious winds, and beats upon you until nothing is left. Like a level-4 hurricane demolishing a home, this storm completely devastates a person. In a word, Obama's father destroyed him—which is exactly how kids often describe the way they feel when they lose a father.

Look again at his follow-up story of the pastor who while building his church faced "fierce winds and heavy rains of violence…gang members," suggesting that Obama experienced his stormy father as a ferocious gangster willfully attacking him.

In his Inauguration Day speech another storm story surfaces: "[Yet] every so often, the oath is taken amidst gathering clouds and raging storms." Amidst a crisis—that familiar idea—to remind us of Obama's ongoing inner crisis. Indeed he lives constantly with the bad weather that was his father, this time upgraded to a "raging storm." Pure raw anger. "Hurricane Obama."

At that moment, standing on the podium facing the Chief Justice, his hand on a Bible, his father's rage was alive and well, ever-present in the back of Obama's mind. Notice "the oath *is* taken," present tense. It's as though he's saying, "I swear my father ripped a huge hole in me, and that wound's as fresh as the day it first happened."

> It is the kindness to take in a stranger when the levees break; the selflessness of workers who would rather cut their hours than see a friend lose their job which sees us through our darkest hours. (ISp)

Obama continues describing storms in several brief stories of homes being destroyed and abandoned, tragedies which he links to *"our darkest hours"*—personally connecting them to himself.

First, he speaks of taking "in a stranger when the levees break"—yet another picture of storms that destroy everything in their paths including the family home. He suggests vivid images of family members near drowning, fighting to stay afloat, washed out into the water. The storm casting people—strangers now homeless—on the mercy of the world. The scenario perfectly matched the storm story he told in the opening of his self-portrait, the parable about the fierce winds destroying the foolish builder's house. We can feel Obama's pain from utter abandonment—his father treating him like a total stranger.

Another word-picture of similar devastation follows, describing a "firefighter's courage to storm a stairway filled with smoke." You can feel the panic—house on fire, family members trapped, smoke burning their lungs and eyes, smoke so thick they can't see to escape, virtually certain they are going to die. As the house nears collapse, the fireman risks his life to get to them. The firefighter must storm the smoke storm—yet another storm, yet another home destroyed. If they escape, the home will be gone for sure. This time he pictures his father as the ferocious fire and suggests his mother was the firefighter who fought to save him—and barely got him out alive.

Child's Fate Hangs on Parental Nurture

"It is the firefighter's courage to storm a stairway filled with smoke, but also **a parent's willingness to nurture a child,** that decides our fate." (ISp)

Obama next tells us about a crisis involving a parent and a child. He continues with part-three of his "darkest hours" with, "It is...a parent's willingness to nurture a child that finally decides our fate." But notice the way Obama weaves in the idea that a child could be in danger because of a lack of nurture. Thus he also implies the opposite possibility however seemingly inhuman—a parent's unwillingness to nurture a child would certainly decide that child's fate. *Upon reflection, this is a shocking and unusual image.*

What kind of parent would have to think over that decision? Obama's message: first he is trying to tell us that his father destroyed him both when he left and even prior to that. At the same time he suggests his mother's nurture allowed him to survive.

Notice how the threatening images progress, starting with an individual person in danger from attacks on the home—to a child in danger because of a parent's failure to nurture. That's what Obama suggests he felt inside—as if his father just stood there watching him go hungry without offering him so much as a breadcrumb. Can a person get any lower? Obama said later that absent fathers don't count for much—"...life doesn't count for much unless you're willing to do your small part to leave our children—all of our children—a better world." (FD1)

But the haunting thought of a parent unwilling to nurture a child prompts another possibility—abortion—a very real possibility Obama alluded to in a previous story. We have a striking description of abortion, an intentional decision not only to avoid nurturing a child but to actually destroy the child.

Once again, with the super intelligence leading the way with its symbolic stories and images, we find a plethora of communications confirming that parental neglect shaped his entire life.

Obama Whispers a Secret

> To the people of poor nations, we pledge to work alongside you to make your farms flourish and let clean waters flow; to nourish starved bodies and feed hungry minds. And to those nations like ours that enjoy relative plenty, we say we can no longer afford indifference to suffering outside our borders; nor can we consume the world's resources without regard to effect. For the world has changed, and we must change with it.
>
> As we consider the road that unfolds before us, we remember with humble gratitude those brave Americans who, at this very hour, patrol far-off deserts and distant mountains. **They have something to tell us** today, just as the fallen heroes who lie in Arlington **whisper through the ages.** We honor them not only because they are guardians of our liberty, but because they embody the spirit of service; a willingness to find meaning in something greater than themselves. (Isp)

People whisper their secrets. Obama's astute super intelligence uses "whisper" once in his four-part story as a message marker pointing to two deep secrets. We must pay particular attention to what comes before and after "whisper." He had repeatedly told us about his tremendous father hunger with images of poor nations, starved bodies, hungry minds, and his father's indifference to suffering. He then depicts brave soldiers on patrol "who have something to tell us" and dead soldiers who "whisper through the ages." He suggests that the first secret is his near-abortion—that *he* was the nearly dead, starved soldier who barely survived his father's attack. And he further confirms the message after mentioning "whisper" with his three crisis stories back-to-back, alluding to his near abortion along with his father destroying the home.

But there's another huge secret he's also whispering to us. Keep that second secret in mind—we will come back to it in Chapter 13. Now Obama starts to shout about the overwhelming trauma of his near-abortion that he has just whispered to America. Consciously he has tried to hide this never-ending emotional experience which has wreaked havoc on him and America but his super-intel continues to reveal the extraordinary power it exerts over him.

Left in Grave Danger

> But now, my life revolves around my two little girls. And what I think about is what **kind of world** I'm leaving them. Are they living in a county where there's a huge gap between a few who are wealthy and a whole bunch of people who are struggling every day? Are they living in a county that is still **divided by race**? A country where, because they're girls, they **don't have as much opportunity** as boys do? Are they living in a country where we are **hated around the world** because we don't cooperate effectively with other nations? Are they living in a world that is in grave danger because of what we've done to its climate? (FD1)

Reflecting back toward the end of the Fathers' Day speech, Obama's super-intel tells a brief story of the "kind of world leaving [my daughters]" which clearly alludes to "the kind of world my father left me when he went away." He points to specific unconscious ideas he had about why his father left, all presented as questions typically asked by abandoned kids. First Obama depicts himself as a dedicated father whose entire life revolves around his daughters—suggesting that in his own early life he faced the exact opposite. His father could have cared less about him. His father's plans didn't include him—the unplanned one.

Now substitute, "home" for "country" in the four matching questions that follow and the picture is clearer. First, are they living in a home with a "huge gap" between the few wealthy and "a whole bunch of people who are struggling every day?" This question suggests that Obama believed his father ("the few") left to live in comfort, keeping his money to himself, while he and his mother ("bunch of people") struggled financially every day. Next, "Are they living in a home that is still divided by race?"—implies a logical belief that racial problems ended the marriage. Then he asks if an un-favored child (such as a girl instead of a boy) is denied an opportunity, suggesting his father nearly denied him the opportunity of life itself.

Obama unconsciously repeats the same story we considered when looking at his early development. Namely that his father had racial problems with his mother and wanted her to abort him, fulfilling Obama Jr.'s paternal grandfather's desire that the Obama lineage not be contaminated by white blood.

His idea of America being "hated around the world" for not cooperating suggests that his African father on the other side of the world would eternally hate him. On the heels of "whispering" a secret and "a parent being unwilling to nurture a child to the point of death," Obama suggests even more strongly that his father pushed for an abortion, hating him because of his unplanned existence. Looking back, his description of a home being destroyed and his becoming "a stranger when the levees break," suggests a prominent image of an abortion: a pregnant woman's water first breaking, flooding out of her, her uterine home no longer holding him and now her fetus and future son being a stranger to her.

His next idea adds significant weight to that belief. Was he living in a home where he was in grave danger because of what he had done to its climate? Obama implies he had developed a deep sense of ever-present danger and blamed himself simply for existing. We can be virtually certain that he had picked up on the fact that abortion had been a serious consideration. The world had thus forever become a totally unsafe place for him. This powerful unconscious super-intelligent reality could have easily led Obama to conclude—to feel—that his father might one day return to finish the job. This may sound extreme, but that's exactly how severely wounded children think.

'Slaughtering Innocents'

The number of escalating violence references in Obama's four-part serial is overwhelming, all pointing to the likelihood he knew his parents had considered aborting his life.

Having labeled absent fathers as childish, "acting like boys instead of men," he portrays one immature kid killing another kid—"hearts stopped in the middle of the night with the sound of a gunshot" (FD1). Killing here equates to abortion. His violent images become more and more ominous with an even more powerful picture of complete devastation—a hate-filled enemy launching a nuclear attack, "with... former foes, we will work tirelessly to lessen the nuclear threat." (ISp) This is yet another photo for the family album—his father 'going nuclear,' wanting to destroy him.

This dovetails with his most specific violent images pointing to abortion, "those who seek to advance their aims by inducing terror and slaughtering innocents." We cannot imagine a more accurate picture of abortion than *"slaughtering innocents"*—so brutal that Obama's super intelligence invokes a powerful anti-abortion slogan. How well it matches the cruel image of *a parent unwilling to nurture a child*. And how well it matches his earlier description of *"murdering innocents"* which he linked to his deep humiliation as a child—his basic life equation that we established in Chapter 2 which constantly controls him. The super intelligence uses the most powerful and most blatant images to get its most crucial messages across, once again verifying the message by repeating the images as we see Obama continually refer to the destruction of innocent children over a 20-year time span.

Briefly we fast-forward to the end of this Inauguration Day speech for another specific abortion image, "This is the source of our confidence—the knowledge that God calls on us to shape an *uncertain destiny*." (Isp) Continuing to follow Obama's sequential thought patterns,[2] we see him sum up in a single phrase the dangers inflicted on him, "perils we can scarcely imagine." Here he contends that we have no idea how bad it was for him as a child. "Unimaginable perils" is his personal summary of his life story.

Following the Thread

Obama's absent father haunts his son's everyday existence. Looking back two short paragraphs in his inaugural address, after the crisis stories suggesting his near-abortion, Obama references his father for the first of two times in this speech. Coincidental? Hardly. The brilliant super intelligence masterfully weaves together the otherwise hidden story. By introducing his father and the issue of his father's birth first Obama between the lines takes us back to his own birth/conception and reveals how his father treated him. Unconsciously, amidst all his abortion images he must establish for all the world to see how his father urged his destruction.

Later in the same speech Obama introduces his father when he discusses "why a man whose father less than 60 years ago might not have been served at a

---

2 I have named such thought patterns "thoughtprints," a concept that is a hallmark of the forensic profiling method I developed, "Thoughtprint Decoding," which utilizes a suspect's own super intelligence.

local restaurant can now stand before you to take a most sacred oath." But follow the big ideas: When he says "a man...might not have been served...can now stand before you to take a most sacred oath," he's reiterating that, as a child, he wasn't served by his father. It's as though he's saying, "I swear my father did not serve me less than 60 years ago when I was a child" or "I swear I was that completely neglected un-nurtured child who was nearly aborted."[3]

Constant Inner Crisis

Obama has suggested that unconsciously he was living in a mental state "of grave danger" and of being hated—in a constant state of crisis, in a constant state of terror.

We've reviewed three home-based disaster stories—a flood, a fire, and severe child neglect. Recall that he opened his Fathers' Day speech with stories of two crises linked to his absent father, the raging storm that destroyed his very foundation. And as he opened his inaugural address Obama suggested that he was still living with the ravages of a raging storm, the indelible memory of his destructive, absent father.

He refers to "crisis" numerous other times in the same speech including, "We are in midst of crisis...homes have been lost." Translation: "I am constantly in the midst of a crisis in my mind, a crisis of homelessness in all its forms." He has continually pointed to one perpetual crisis of abandonment—an ever-present fear of total aloneness, losing everything and everybody, including his own life. He's like a shell-shocked soldier living with post-traumatic stress disorder and suffering constant flashbacks of the hellish conflict he has somehow survived.

'My Fragile Psyche'

Another incident reveals Obama's fragile mental state. He recalls being asked a question during the campaign at a Wisconsin town hall meeting for which he was totally unprepared: "What does life mean to you?" This existential query caught him so completely off guard that he stammered for a while before regaining his balance. Clearly the question struck his vulnerable core, revealing his fragile psyche. No wonder he's so dependent on Teleprompters to protect him from such moments.

Then unconsciously he shows us what was behind his coming apart. Regaining his wits, he tells the Wisconsin audience a story about parent-child relationships—how his life revolves around his daughters, hinting that their childhood is quite unlike his own neglected youth. He suggests that the question "What does life mean to you?" triggered that 'forever moment' a millimeter below the surface, the trauma he described on Fathers' Day recalling when his father abandoned him—went missing from his life for good.

---

3 Note Obama's vivid message marker—"sacred oath"—on his oath he is telling us the truth about his severe pain.

Then we hear the questions he has been asking his father for years, "Does life, my life, mean anything? And, most of all, does it mean anything to you, Dad?" Of course he gets the same shocking answer over and over, a negative reaction that for half a century now has been keeping Obama perpetually unstable: "No." Who can ever be prepared for that answer? In the back of his mind, he hears that same answer day after day after day.

Narcissism—Another View

Obama's eventual answer to the Wisconsin question speaks volumes, "When I was a young man, I thought life was all about me. How do I make my way in the world, and how do I become successful?"

By mentioning he "thought life was all about me," he reminds us that he has been labeled a narcissistic personality by observers such as Dr. Sam Vaknin, the author of *Malignant Self Love: Narcissism Revisited.* But we must remember that narcissism is often simply the self-protective facade a person adopts when they're all alone. Narcissism fills that hole inside yourself when your father isn't around—as Obama himself has instructed us so well.

Teleprompter President

Many describe Obama as "Joe Cool," coming across as unflappable and confident. Combined with his trim appearance in expensive suits, his speaking ability, and capable intellect, he seems unlikely to harbor self-esteem problems. If anything—known for his self-centeredness, even admitting to the narcissistic tendency himself—Obama appears to incline toward egotism.

But you can never judge a book by its cover. Obama carefully hides his self-esteem issues. Having heard his story thus far, we must wonder how he has retained even a remnant of authentic self-esteem. People so easily forget narcissism is a huge cover. But his lack of confidence shows up—i.e. his dependence on Tele-prompters—and he often sabotages himself with bad judgment, directing abuse at himself even in "little ways," such as smoking heavily.

Two Patriots

It was no accident that Obama saves his most powerful story—depicting another "crisis"—for the end of his inaugural address. It was the most important story for the most important speech in his life. Intuitively he chose this tale *for several reasons—the first to reveal how brutal were his childhood's "unimaginable perils."*

Note how cleverly and quickly his mind links this story to the beginning of his life—a strongly implied birth marker. The story starts, "[let us] mark this day with remembrance...who we are...how far we have traveled...in the year of [America's] birth." But with that thinly disguised reference to his own birth, he's telling us how far he has come, what he has overcome.

133

Consciously it's a story of America's great journey, but unconsciously it recounts his own journey as told by his super intelligence. Right off he repeats the idea that indeed he was "marked"—scarred at birth, wounded—matching his earlier comment about inner city kids marked by father loss.

Now his final story starts with the day his father totally left him, the day he was scarred for life.[4] Feel exactly what that moment felt like inside Obama. His brilliant intuitive mind remembers everything. We let his images speak for themselves.[5]

It was: "in the coldest of months…a small band of patriots [my mother and I]…huddled by dying campfires, shores of an icy river." Here was the small band of two [patriots] fighting for the home/homeland, his mother and himself fighting for survival. They were cold, cold, barely warm, barely alive, clinging to each other—on the shores of that icy river, his heartless father. His father is also the winter storm, the blizzard which had cast them out of the home. "The capital was abandoned"—the head of the household had left us. "The enemy was advancing"—his father who surely hated him in Obama's mind—was moving in to destroy them. Notice how plain he makes it, "…snow stained with blood…outcome most in doubt…the father"—here he was innocent as the driven snow now stained, marked by his own blood and blood kin, growing colder by the minute, filled with doubt, doubting whether he would even survive, alluding to his "white-stained blood' in his father's eyes.

But he's not through yet.

"Let it be told to the future world…that in the depth of winter, when nothing but hope and virtue could survive…that the city and the country, alarmed at one common danger, came forth to meet [it]." He's telling the world the rest of his story, also set in the absolute depth of winter when nothing but hope—and virtue—could survive. His mother's caring gave Obama, the hope to overcome their "one common danger"—his father—who had tried to destroy them, tried to destroy his son. Together they met that challenge. His mother had clung to her virtue. "…brave once more the icy currents, and endure what storms may come"—they had braved the icy current of his father who had tried to sweep them away, they had endured his father—the Obama Storm.

"Let it be said by…children"—Hear Obama, he's speaking for himself as a child the day he was nearly aborted "…that when we were tested, we refused to let this journey end, that we did not turn back, nor did we falter"—he and his mother had refused to give in "…and with…God's grace upon us, we carried forth that great gift of freedom and delivered it safely"—in the end the one thing his father did not take from him was his life, his freedom to make his way as best he could.

---

4 Note the "message marker'—"Mark with remembrance" highlighting that what he is about to say has extreme importance.
5 Obviously he's talking about the day he had matured enough so that his deeper mind could go back and process it.

Finally, Obama has prepared us as best he could to handle the most shocking story in America's history. He has told us all about the "unimaginable perils" he faced hinting that his response to such awful experiences will be equally unimaginable. Tit for tat. Be prepared—the truth never comes easy.

10

The Abused Obama Responds

We have gazed through a powerful super-intel lens to magnify Barack Obama's "unimaginable" pain, particularly the wounds suffered at the hands of his father. His brilliant unconscious mind has shown us the violent assault his father delivered without so much raising a hand to him—quiet, devastating, crippling violence in the form of abandonment. This leads us to a question. Apart from his grief, guilt and terror, how did Obama respond to such massive insults? Through the same secret lens we can now see how he responded. We can see the other side of Obama, the shadow side. Now his super-intel will quick-read his response—be prepared. We will listen to all his stories and images as now describing himself.

The Son Responds

First he makes it unequivocally clear that he did indeed respond to the trauma of his separation. Recall that Obama succinctly describes humiliated kids who take that short step to "violence and untrammeled fury, how easily they slip into violence and despair." Establishing his intense humiliation, Obama reveals how quickly his powerlessness turned to rage and "untrammeled fury." Obama himself took that short step, hinting also that we need only to take one short step to understand that rage. In *Dreams* Obama warns us he is uncontrollably angry. Furious. He implies the "eye for an eye" rule—the degree of humiliation he suffered determines the degree of rage, and he describes his rage as "unimaginable." Yet America lives in denial about just how furious he is. Even those who realize his destructiveness deny it. If he is that wracked with rage—and he is—it means his supporters and the media live in "unimaginable" denial.

Author Dinesh D'Souza reported Obama's overwhelming anger in his book, *The Roots of Obama's Rage*. D'Souza assumed the anger originated with his father's rage at unjust British colonials in Kenya. But that's only the surface rage. Obama's anger is directed first and foremost at his absent father, not the colonial figures which the father reviled. We got just a whiff of it when, after his thin idealization of his father, he called him the absent father, childish, and irresponsible. He characterized him as someone who didn't count for much and obsessively detailed his faults in both Father's Day communications.

Reenactments

From the get-go, Obama defines the basic reaction of a severely traumatized kid—it is to reenact his pain on others, to abuse others just as he was abused. It's called transference of abuse. Psychological studies show that more than one-third of abused children later abuse members of their own family. Cutting-edge clinical work with the super intelligence demonstrates that such reenactments are far more common and far deeper than even therapists have realized.

Reenactments—transference of abuse—are the most common way victims attempt to make others feel their pain, temporarily ridding themselves of it as a way of avoiding the helplessness of a victim, expressing extraordinary "payback" revenge. There's a deep, abiding sense that somebody should pay for wronging you. Because the absent father is never around to pay, such victims attack others. Everybody knows people who were traumatized in early life, people who carry heavy emotional baggage and have major unfinished business. Obama is one of them—times ten.

Break Cycle

Obama describes his ongoing transference of abuse in several striking ways beginning with a vicious behavioral cycle. He mentions that he's trying *to break the cycle* of abandonment with his own daughters. So great was his pain it became his deep passion. "If I could be anything in life I would be a good father to my girls...I would give them that rock—that foundation—on which to build their lives." (FD1)

But unconsciously Obama points out how he repeats the abandonment cycle by inflicting his pain on America—instead of on the father who wasn't around anymore. In his most striking picture of reenactment he speaks about "...leaders... who seek to sow conflict, or blame their society's ills on the West." (ISp) In other words, leaders like himself who take out their pain on America, who blame America. Translation: Obama will reenact his deeply personal pain—"his ills"—on the United States. His unconscious super-intel cannot be any plainer. It's as clear as his behavior was when he went all over the world "blaming" America whenever he addressed foreign audiences.

To reiterate his rage, he adds vivid images of these leaders who sow conflict. They're destroyers, not builders, and he portrays them raising a clenched fist against America, demonstrating the extent of his own pent-up anger. Immediately before this he spoke of "those who seek to advance their aims by inducing terror and slaughtering innocents," noting that "old hatreds shall someday pass." This implies that, for him, the old hatreds have yet to pass. He further suggests that he's reenacting his rage—payback revenge—from the time he was a figuratively "slaughtered innocent."

Emotional Picture of Obama's Reenactment and Rage

Immediately after the powerful opening of his Inauguration Day speech, Obama makes a second major announcement. He tells us,

"On this day, we come to proclaim an end to the petty grievances and false promises, the recriminations and worn-out dogmas, that for far too long have strangled our politics...We remain a young nation, but in the words of Scripture, the time has come to set aside childish things." (Isp) But reading through his denials we find a thinly-disguised unconscious message in which he paints a vivid picture of an emotional reenactment, "On this day, [I] proclaim... petty grievances and false promises, the recriminations and worn-out dogmas, that for far too long have strangled [my] politics"—read "strangled me personally." He asserts that he intends to inflict on America all the grief, broken promises, criticism and cover-up lies which have choked the life out of him. He links it to his painful youth, "We [read, I] remain young."

Furthermore, he knows he's wrong: "in the words of Scripture, the time has come to set aside childish things." Again, Obama uses *"words"* to remind us of deeper meaning, here "words of Scripture"— as powerful a message marker as possible, in essence linking his wrongful behavior to natural laws of God. Unconsciously he confesses, "I swear on the Bible that I'm telling you how I'm taking revenge on America." His entire speech unfolds his confession and prediction of just how severely he will take out his own "petty grievances" on America. By "petty" he unconsciously means "small" and even "childish." It may be his own personal unfinished business, but it's in no way small, inconsequential or harmless.

Try as he might to break the cycle of his father's curse by simply proclaiming an end to it, he can't. The mind simply doesn't work that way. Of course, the conscious mind lives off denial and if ever anyone was addicted to denial it is Barack Obama. Denial is his drug. He needs it desperately in order to survive mentally.

He wants to get over his pain but can't. He wants to be a better president than he will be and tells us why. He describes being frozen in his trauma as well as anyone could. He is what we clinicians call "fixated." He suffers pain that has stunted his emotional growth. He secretly tells us and tells himself that he's not emotionally grown-up yet. That he needs to "set aside childish things"—his childhood experiences—but you can't simply wish away the pain of severe abuse. It's deep, unremitting, everlasting pain that rips a fresh hole in you daily. You don't waltz around unforgettable pain by simply wanting to.

More importantly, we can read his statement in a deeper way. He tells America in advance—"get ready to proclaim an end to what I am about to do." Between the lines of this speech Obama reveals precisely how he plans to strangle America's political culture by taking partisan politics to an entirely new level. Despite his conscious rhetoric about "hope and change," Obama warns us that his presidency will inflict the *same horrific division and cracks in our*

138

framework which existed in his early home life. It won't be pretty, he says—and that's exactly how it turned out.

Now look at his proclamation immediately prior, "On this day, we gather because we have chosen hope over fear, unity of purpose over conflict and discord." Reading through his denials we find the same unconscious message, "On this day, we gather because we have chosen...fear...conflict and discord." We know fear rules Obama's life, and we're experiencing his revenge on America, revenge won by creating discord.

Like Father, Like Son: Anger Expressed in Behavior

Obama describes his reenactments—repeating his father's treatment of him on others—in yet another way. He establishes the undeniable "role model rule," how he'll express his rage exactly as his father did—in his *behavior*—even providing the statistics, "Children who grow up without a father are five times more likely to...live in poverty and commit crime...more likely to drop out of schools and end up in prison. They are more likely to have behavioral problems..." (FD1)

To make sure we get the picture, Obama repeats himself about how and what his father built into him. He tells us how he secretly "watched" his absent father moment by moment, memorizing his exact behavior: "But our young boys and girls *see that. They see* when you are ignoring or mistreating your wife. *They see* when you are inconsiderate at home; or when you are distant; or when you are thinking only of yourself. And so it's no surprise when we see that behavior in our schools or on our streets." (FD1)

Obama saw the temper, the rage all wrapped up in his father's behavior. Although it was disguised behind a smile, although it was explained away by a myth spun by his mother and grandparents, the rage was buried deep in his unconscious. There the constant ache, the relentless insult was alive and well. And then he copied it. He did exactly as his father taught him to do—and covered up his fury just as his father tried to do.

A year later on Fathers' Day—beginning with the message marker "we need to realize" that children model their parents' angry behavior—he underscores the unconscious message, "Don't be surprised at my behavior. Understand the anger behind it."

Prediction: Obama Will Attack America's Basic Foundations

In Chapter 2 we speculated about Obama's unconscious warnings to America about the dangers of his impending presidency. Now, with a clear awareness that his super intelligence is confessing to us, we zero in for a more detailed look at his unconscious admissions.

First Obama has told us *how* he would express his rage through his behavior—often through presidential decisions and policies. Next he identifies specifically *where* he will direct his disguised attacks on America. The same place his absent father lashed out—the foundation of the family, the community and the country. Note his progression. First fathers attack the family foundation—"too many fathers also are...missing from too many...homes...And the foundations of our families are weaker because of it." (FD1)

Then he shifts to community foundations: "You...know how true this is in the African-American community... children who grow up without a father... more likely to live in poverty and commit crime... drop out of schools... more likely to end up in prison...more likely to have behavioral problems... And the foundations of our community are weaker because of it." (FD1)

Then, speaking of single mothers bearing the entire load, Obama said, "children need another parent...It's what keeps the foundation of our country strong." (FD1)

Obama's emotional mathematics are easy to follow. As the son of an absent father he will manifest behavioral problems as president. As his absent father attacked basic foundations, so will Obama attack the very foundations of America.

'Obama Jr.' Storm Descends Upon America

Now, let's look at the specific foundations Obama has predicted he will attack—and to what extent he'll carry out that battle plan.

We follow the simple equation Obama has unconsciously shared with us: see the father, see the son. Now we continue to apply the identical stories describing his father's abusive behavior to Obama's behavior. Obama's images have two sides: first in describing what was done to him as the victim and then how he got even, reenacted his pain on his own victim—our nation.

These powerful stories express the full extent of his rage.

Remember his initial parable about the storm that demolished the poorly built little house sitting on sand, waiting to collapse. To appreciate his anger we must appreciate his pain. Obama had applied the parable to his father's devastating attack on the son's very foundation as a person. He was a small house wiped out by one gigantic wave, with nothing but sand left in its place. And Obama heard the command that was built into him, 'Now go ye and do likewise.' And he did—to America's foundations.

Early on he implies that he aims to destroy as much of America's house— our nation—that he can. He has taken dead aim upon all the foundations that make us strong. Indeed, he will be The Absent Father of our nation—the absent president—but like his absent father he will make his presence felt by the power of his absence, by all the foundations he can destroy by abandoning them.

Attack on Economic Foundations

Obama points initially to an economic attack. To confirm the message in his second story about another storm that surrounds the strong church, he describes "the fierce winds and heavy rains of violence and poverty, [joblessness] and hopelessness," and then he refers to the homeless.

This is a clear reference to the deep sense of poverty which controls him. It also fuels his rage just as it did the gang members surrounding the church. Obama's imagery hints that a "gangster-type" rage will emerge in him matching his "untrammeled fury."

Consider the homeless. When you lose your home, you lose everything. It is painfully obvious that Obama has hurt millions of Americans with his economic policies. Thousands of Americans have, in fact, lost their homes in the implosion of the housing market and failure of banks.

If you want to know what it really felt like, just ask a person who lost his home. A person who had done everything in his power to own his own home, stretched a bit to get it, worked extra hours to keep it until his job was gone, his wife working as well, and suddenly—WHOOSH!—the rug was pulled out from underneath them. Their home isn't worth what they paid for it, and they can no longer afford it. They can't weather the storm because there's no reserve left. Their dreams are washed away. They're now walking around with a "Lost Home" sign around their necks weighing them down with the shame that goes with it. That was Obama's gift of rage to his neighbor, making sure his neighbor shared his pain whether he wanted to or not.

Though Obama may not have personally ignited this economic fire, when he served in Congress he fanned its flames by supporting devastating policies. Then the blaze roared with intensity when, as president, he doused it with gasoline.

As for joblessness to accompany homelessness, ask the good people of Louisiana and along the Gulf Coast. There Obama inflicted more "joblessness" on people already bashed economically. There he ignored the crippling effect of the Gulf oil spill and doubled the damage by banning further ocean drilling while funding Brazil's offshore oil explorations. He did all that unilaterally, callously ignoring the pleas of Louisiana Governor Bobby Jindal who begged him to preserve American jobs by lifting the ban. All the while Obama rubbed salt into their wounds by giving their jobs away to Brazilians. Beyond that Obama refused to approve the Keystone Pipeline, which would have brought oil from Canada and created 20,000 jobs—as always, he rationalized his economic growth-dousing actions as necessary for "environmental reasons." The ironic thing about Obama killing the Keystone pipeline was that our government wouldn't have had to even pay for building the pipeline, it just had to approve the plan, since it would cross our national border with Canada; private funds from Canada would have paid for its construction, estimated at $5.2 billion. And Obama will continue to eliminate American jobs at every turn—as much as he can possibly get away with. Too many remain in denial about his intentional attacks on America.

By his behavior, he has issued an ominous weather alert: Storm Obama descends upon America. At the outset of his inaugural address, Obama's words predicted his behavior, "Our economy is badly weakened, a consequence of greed and irresponsibility on the part of some." Now his confession is crystal clear. It's as though he's saying, "I will irresponsibly weaken an already weakened economy because of my 'greed'—my greedy irresponsible need for payback."

Statistics bear out his behavior: higher unemployment, huge increases in the national debt, driven specifically by excessive entitlement spending, the business community strangled with regulations and radical environmentalism on the rise, in the guise of the EPA. Immediately after he took office, he wasted a nearly trillion-dollar stimulus plan on his friends on Wall Street and in the unions. The 'shovel-ready jobs' never materialized—a deception that Obama himself later admitted, shamelessly putting a joking spin on it. Losing your job is hardly a laughing matter, yet Obama tries to cover up his guilt with the cloak of humor.[1] In November 2011 the Congressional Budget Office revealed Obama's stimulus bill had—in the long run—no real ability to offset unemployment.

Unconsciously, Obama had no real intention of truly reviving the economy. His preoccupation with taking care of friends by returning political favors guaranteed America's long-lingering economic stagnation.

Three More Crises Illustrate His Attacks

We continue to review Obama's images to explore his role as the perpetrator, the one who reenacts the pain which was once inflicted on him. He is saying to us, "Without understanding my powerful "right-brain" stories and images you will never grasp the anger that controls me." Recall that Obama presented three brief crisis stories—all depicting violent attacks on foundations—in his inaugural address. Two of them involve total destruction of homes.

First, he talks about taking "in a stranger when the levees break"— a flood and yet another storm image—which wears away the home's foundation. Vividly, Obama portrays his overflowing rage directed at America's foundations. "Flood" is such an apt image. Indeed Americans feel flooded by Obama from a thousand different directions. Almost every week he presents another economic roadblock: wanting to raise taxes, throwing more entitlement money out the window, wasteful spending on solar energy with guaranteed political kickbacks, raising the debt--again, buying car companies, establishing a wasteful gas guzzler buyback program ("Cash for Clunkers"), blocking economic development if it involves non-union employees (such as when the NLRB attempted to block Boeing's new Dreamliner plant in N. Charleston, SC, which Obama later withdrew under fire and after Boeing made concessions to

---

1 "Obama Jokes: 'Shovel-Ready Was Not As Shovel-Ready As We Expected,'"http://www.realclearpolitics.com/video/2011/06/13/obama_jokes_shovel-ready_was_not_as_shovel-ready_as_we_expected.html accessed April 24, 2012.

the unions back in Seattle), and on and on. If we just step back we see how accurate his confession was at the Apollo Theater that he would do unbelievably aggressive things to America.

In his next story, a fire attacks the foundation of a home, a blaze so consuming its flames crawl upstairs—more economic damage for starters. In a quiet blue streak of rage, Obama has set fire to America's economy. Soon he'll make specific reference to living upstairs in the White House while alluding to another foundational attack on our nation. The bottom line: Pay attention to his repeated "upstairs" images which suggest he'll attack America from within while occupying the White House.

Even now, after hurricane storms, floods, and devastating fires, Obama still has more anger to tell us about. In the last of his three crisis stories he alludes horrifically to a parent unwilling to nurture a child, much like a president unwilling to encourage his country to flourish. Clearly his economic policy fails to nurture America, which remains mired in a precarious recovery from a debilitating recession. During the week of September 6, 2011, Neil Bortz commented on his syndicated radio talk show that Obama's policies amounted to *"economic terrorism."* Along identical lines, Libertarian political commentator Wayne Allen Root stated, "Obama is *economically murdering millions of Americans."*[2] Coincidentally Root was a classmate of Obama at Columbia, yet—along with many other Obama college classmates—Root retains no memory of Obama. Was the future president operating undercover even then? Certainly he's trying to operate undercover now with his *war on the economy*—but his secret is impossible to hide except from his blind supporters.

Obama's vivid imagery continues—"Those who seek to advance their aims by inducing terror and slaughtering innocents" (ISp)—reflects his prediction of the economic attack which he has since carried out. Indeed many innocent Americans have been financially slaughtered, leaving them extremely frightened about their future. How well *'slaughtering innocents and inducing terror'* describes Obama's childhood—and now the transference of his pain upon Americans.

'Kind of World He's Leaving' Stories

His stories illustrate Obama's secret attack on the U.S. economy. Obama refers to the "kind of world I am leaving my daughters," a phrase implying a deeper concept, "the kind of world my father left me when he went away." Now we see the "reenactment" version where he reflects his father's rage. He presents a series of questions—each one relating to a different foundation of America— suggesting the kind of country "I am leaving the citizens" in the wake of his destructive presidency.

Again Obama confesses that his economic policies will create a whole

---

2 "Bill Cunningham: I'm a Great American," WERC radio, Birmingham, Alabama, October 22, 2011.

generation of people who must struggle daily for their very existence, just as he struggled to grasp his own existence in the face of his father's abandonment. As president, he has clearly favored the few made wealthy by his choices, e.g. the unions. His auto bailout illegally benefited organized labor over stockholders (and especially bondholders, who by law are supposed to be paid before any stockholders or creditors). The only reason he bailed out GM was because of the unions. Obama usurped the federal government's Troubled Asset Relief program (TARP) program to benefit his friends and campaign contributors. TARP purchased assets from financial institutions to strengthen America's financial sector, but since Obama took office, a disproportionate amount of TARP money has gone to unions such as the United Auto Workers, AFL/CIO, the Teamsters and SEIU (Service Employees International Union, the group Obama cut his teeth on in Chicago during his community organizer days before politics) and to 'fat cats' like Affiliated Managers Group, Inc., (AMG) a global asset management company. And of course money went to ACORN, the radical community organizer group which Obama helped build.[3]

Envy Fuels Attack on Economic Foundations

In his question—"What kind of country am I leaving America?"—Obama raises the specter of "a country where... [some kids] don't have as much opportunity as" others. (FD1) Unconsciously Obama cites another motive for attacking our economic foundation: envy, stemming from what he missed out on—his deep-down deprivation. Immediately prior to this question he alluded to America as a country favoring the rich with "a big gap between the rich and the poor." The word "gap" clearly refers to the huge hole his father left in him. It's no wonder we see class warfare at the heart of his presidency. For instance in his September 2011 Job Acts speech, he incessantly talked about how the rich "should pay their fair share." Through his denial that "This is not about class *warfare*," he revealed that, in fact, that's *exactly* what it was, by using yet another violent image—war.

Attack Via Entitlements

Another economic attack reveals how short the step is between deprivation to demanding entitlements. After warning us in his inaugural address that favoritism was the surest way to America's decline, he promptly inflicts it on as many of us as possible. Shockingly, in the final year Obama's watch, 2012, more than 50% of all federal spending will be entitlements. Obama increased entitlements in the federal budget significantly and it's growing.[4] During the GOP primary race, Republican presidential candidate Newt Gingrich

3 Kevin Mooney, "ACORN got $53 million in federal funds since 94, now eligible for up to $8 billion more," http://washingtonexaminer.com/opinion/special-reports/2009/05/acorn-got-53-million-federal-funds-94-now-eligible-8-billion-more accessed June 7, 2012.
4 "More than Half of All Federal Spending Will Be on Entitlement Programs in 2012," http://www.heritage.org/federalbudget/budget-entitlement-programs accessed June 7, 2012.

commented that he wanted to become history's most successful paycheck president, unlike Obama, whom he said is history's most successful food stamps president (a humorous quip which captured Obama's spending problems).[5] Entitlement programs unquestionably create the biggest threat to the future solvency of the U.S. budget. See them for what they are—an unmitigated attack on a nation already swimming in debt.

Unconsciously Obama even warned us about his planned entitlement, "Obamacare." He noted, "Our health care is too costly…indicators of crisis, subject to data and statistics." Deep down he understood that Obamacare represented another assault, pushing us further toward an economic crisis.

Joe the Plumber

Regarding his economic plan, let's reconsider Obama's comment to Joe the Plumber, "(By increasing your taxes) I don't want to take away your success."[6] Reading straight through his denial, that is *precisely* what Obama wants to do to Joe—and to the rest of America. Take your success, take your money—"take" is Obama's byword. He's truly a president 'on the take,' albeit legally. In a spontaneous moment the Alinsky-inspired byword *"take from the have's* (to give to the have not's)" came pouring out of Obama. Frightening.

Recall that Obama poignantly described how his absent father took the life out of him. It was as if his father just stood there watching him go hungry while offering him not as much as a breadcrumb, allowing the son to starve to death in terms of father hunger. Now he transfers that onto America—threatening our most basic needs by taking from us, spending our money wastefully, figuratively starving America—as cruel, cold and indifferent as his father.

Personal Indulgence: Entitlements for Barack and Michelle

Briefly we see another way Obama attempts to cover the pain in his unending sense of personal entitlement. We think of his self-indulgent 2009 "date night" trip with Michelle to New York and back for dinner and a Broadway play at considerable costs to taxpayers—the *Washington Times* estimated it cost a quarter-million dollars,[7] and the foreign press estimated higher, at more than $1 million overall[8] (the White House refused to disclose the actual cost, blaming it on the Secret Service's insistence on providing security). That 'date night,' just three months into Obama's term, was a symbolic display and a brief glance at how Obama really operates. Three years

5 "Gingrich: Obama 'food Stamps' President," January 6, 2012, http://youtu.be/VXcyX8blbu0 accessed June 7, 2012.
6 Natalie Gewargis, "'Spread the Wealth'?" http://abcnews.go.com/blogs/politics/2008/10/spread-the-weal/ Accessed April 15, 2012.
7 "CURL: The cost of a NYC weekend," June 1, 2009, http://www.washingtontimes.com/news/2009/jun/01/curl-cost-nyc-weekend/ accessed June 7, 2012.
8 Warner Todd Huston, "Foreign Press Assails Obama's Expensive 'Date Night,' U.S. Press Not So Much," http://newsbusters.org/blogs/warner-todd-huston/2009/06/02/foreign-press-assails-obamas-expensive-date-night-u-s-press-not-#ixzz1x8CDibqE accessed June 7, 2012.

later, partying continues unabated at the White House at a shameless pace of frequency.[9] His days are usually filled with photo ops, speeches that are in reality thinly-veiled reelection campaign efforts, and frequent golf outings.[10]

Then we have First Lady Michelle Obama who too often reflects her husband's endless sense of personal entitlement. One striking example comes to mind of her June 21-21, 2011 what amounted to a thinly-disguised vacation trip to South Africa and Botswana—accompanied by her extended family and staff. They flew on a military aircraft. What stands out first was the effort to conceal the indulgence—instead of the transparent, above-board policy her husband promised America. As it turns out, the passenger manifests include the Obama's two daughters, Malia and Sasha, who are listed as "Senior Staff." Also on the list were list Mrs. Obama's mother, Marian Robinson, and niece and nephew, Leslie and Avery Robinson, as well Mrs. Obama's makeup artist and hair stylist, Carl Ray and Johnny Wright.

While Michelle Obama had several meetings and speaking opportunities, the trip included visits to museums and historical sites. The family enjoyed a private safari at a South African game reserve. Judicial Watch concluded the trip was as much an opportunity for an Obama family African safari as it was for government business. Judicial Watch, an organization that monitors government accountability, had to file suit to get the particulars on the trip; it turns out to have cost taxpayers more than $424,000.[11] The watchdog organization president Tom Fitton stated, "This junket wasted tax dollars and the resources of our overextended military. No wonder we had to sue to pry loose this information."[12]

In the end Obama is pulling of a quiet heist in broad daylight. In reality, all this taking is just another word for aggression, anger and rage. And Obama wants more of America's money. His Jobs Act proposal would put the economy in further peril by increasing America's debt by $450 billion.[13]

But, as always, Obama unconsciously confesses. In his inaugural address he tells us that American economy's "power to generate wealth...is unmatched." Again we see his target—America's great success—and the secret envy that drives his attack. He then cautions us that "without a watchful eye, the market [read the market manager, Obama] can spin out of control—and that a nation

---

9 Keith Koffler, "At the Obama White House, the Party Never Stops," February 22, 2012, http://whitehousedossier.com/2012/02/22/obama-white-house-party-stops accessed May 20, 2012.
10 Kevin Dewhurst, "Says Barack Obama has played over 90 rounds of golf as president," April 4, 2012, http://www.politifact.com/texas/statements/2012/apr/04/david-dewhurst/david-dewhurst-says-barack-obama-has-played-over-9/ accessed June 7, 2012.
11 Paul Bedard, "Michelle Obama's Africa Trip Cost More Than $424,000," U.S. News & World Report, October 4, 2011, http://usnews.com/news/blogs/washington-whispers/2011/10/04/michelle-obamas-africa-vacation-cost-more-than-432142 accessed May 20, 2012.
12 "Judicial Watch Obtains Documents Detailing the Cost to Taxpayers for Michelle Obama's Family Trip to Africa," October 4, 2011, http://www.judicialwatch.org/press-room/press-releases/judicial-watch-obtains-documents-detailing-the-cost-to-taxpayers-for-michelle-obama-s-family-trip-to-africa/ accessed May 20, 2012.
13 Whit Johnson, "Even Democrats skeptical of Obama's jobs act," October 3, 2011, http://cbsnews.com/stories/2011/09/17/eveningnews/main20107801.shtml

cannot prosper long when it favors only the prosperous." How perfectly this fits Obama's out-of-control favoritism of certain groups who prosper from his directing money their way: the unions, entitlement programs and green energy government loan guarantees to firms that repeatedly declare bankruptcy (e.g., the Solyndra debacle, which pulled the plug after receiving $528 million in federal loan guarantees, leaving taxpayers holding the bag).[14] Translation: "I am destroying our nation's prosperity."

Then reading through Obama's crucial denial, we find "*the question before us: whether the market* [market maker, Obama] is *a force for good or ill.*" (ISp) Having established that he's carrying out a plan to destroy America's prosperity, Obama's super-intel emphasizes that he's inflicting ill will on America. That exactly matches his comment, "leaders who blame their society's *ills* on the West." (ISp) And in a subtle twist in his 2012 presidential campaign Obama goes around the country blaming Congress—'the West'-- for his economic woes because they won't pass more of his extravagant bills.

Foreign Policy

Now turning to America's most crucial foundation—national security—we hear Obama's super-intel speak about foreign policy. Many of his stories about attacks on foundations—storms or floods or out-of-control criminal gangs—also apply to foreign policy. A storm devastates *everything* in its path. We find vivid stories of destruction specifically linked to our nation's security.

In his implied "kind of world I am leaving America" story he asks another question, "Are they [we] living a world that is in grave danger because of what we've [I've] done to its climate?" Obama again speaks figuratively, and the translation shouts at you. He confesses that his foreign-policy decisions will leave America in "grave danger." How grave?

His own images, his own super intelligence spells it out, "with... former foes, we will work tirelessly to lessen the nuclear threat." Hear him emphasize that point in his own words. He cites the possibility of complete devastation and death—a hate-filled enemy delivering a nuclear attack. Obama unconsciously suggests the potential of the "untrammeled fury" within him: great enough to allow a nuclear attack.

We ask one basic question. Has Obama's behavior increased the possibility of a nuclear threat against America and the world? We can answer the question in one word—Iran. Despite all his rhetoric Obama continues to enable Iran's nuclear build-up. He has simply not been tough enough with that rogue nation. In fact, while he supported protestors around the Middle East during the "Arab Spring" of 2011, recall he completely failed to support Iranian protestors who attempted to overthrow Mahmoud Ahmadinejad's corrupt regime. In the end, that Arab Spring created tremendous uncertainly and a significantly increased

---

14 "Solyndra," May 31, 2012, http://topics.nytimes.com/top/news/business/companies/solyndra/index.html accessed June 7, 2012.

radical Muslim threat.

Recall two astute observers, D'Souza and David Limbaugh, each viewed Obama's decisions as increasing the risk of nuclear proliferation. Additionally, columnist Thomas Sowell repeatedly warns that America could be destroyed by a nuclear attack. How easily we take national security for granted. Obama experienced the emotional equivalent of a nuclear attack at the hands of his father in the form his near death and total destruction of his home, and now he threatens the world because of his payback fury.

In addition to Iran, almost everywhere we turn, we see Obama weakening our nation's security. Dean Reuter, co-author of *Confronting Terror* (with John Yoo), noted that Obama plans to return to the feeble foreign policies of Bill Clinton who evinced a decidedly weak diplomacy, a convoluted approach that ultimately led to 9/11. Obama supports civilian trials for captured terrorists, trials conducted in public, trials which would expose our security secrets and undermine valuable interrogation.

Former United Nations U.S. Ambassador John Bolton has courageously protested numerous Obama attacks on our national security. The president slashed $400 billion from the military budget at a time when increasing dangers threaten us around the world, Bolton points out. **Obama is the first post-World War II president who failed to list national security his highest priority.** On his watch he ignores not only Iran but North Korea, two rogue nations aggressively pursuing nuclear weapons. He concedes military strength to Russia through treaty renegotiations. He continually victimizes Israel. "As our most anti-Israel president to date, bar none," Bolton says, "Obama fundamentally misunderstands the nature of security threats to Israel in the Middle East."[15] What Bolton cannot see is that, deep down, Obama understands full well his continual attacks on America and has been unconsciously confessing to that fact.

And Obama has *completely* mishandled the last stages of the Iraq war. After that country's warring factions—Sunnis, Shiites and Kurds—eventually united to conquer subversive militia forces in response to the Bush surge, Obama refused for three years to sign the agreement completing the unification. Then, when things began to fall apart, Obama declared the U.S. will essentially pull out of Iraq totally leaving a token force of 3,000 soldiers—when his military advisors recommended 30,000 to 40,000, similar to U.S. troop strength in Germany and South Korea. In effect, Obama significantly risks undoing all the progress made in Iraq.[16]

Do not be misled by Obama's foreign-policy 'successes' in eliminating leaders of Al-Qaeda either by special ops missions or drone attacks. These missions were also championed by staff members including CIA director Leon Panetta and the Pentagon—and were in the works long before Obama was president. Think what a perfect cover such dramatic headline-grabbing events

---

15 John Bolton, *Human Events*, August 8, 2011, pp 12-13.
16 Charles Krauthammer, "Who lost Iraq?" *Washington Post*, November 3, 2011.

provide for Obama—making him appear tough on the world stage when the exact opposite is true. In addition, figures such as Osama bin Laden represent evil foreign father figures to Obama, providing him an opportunity to displace the enormous fury he had for his own foreign father.

Would Obama intentionally inflict such national security risks on our nation? Not consciously. But unconsciously *he would do it in a heartbeat.* Remember the "90-10 percent" rule—the often-quoted idea that 'We only tap 10% of the potential of our minds.' Obama's unconscious therefore controls 90 percent of his motivation. Obama's shadow side can brilliantly plan devious attacks far more efficiently than his conscious "10 percent" mind. He can deal under the table faster than any Las Vegas croupier.

"Hatred for America"

We return to Obama's story about the "kind of world I am leaving America" in which he poses another question, "Are [we] living in a country where we are hated—around the world because we don't cooperate effectively with other nations?" (FD1) Obama has now indisputably used the very words *"hate America."* His unconscious confession poses the real question, "Do Americans live in a country where Obama secretly hates them as he refuses to cooperate and truly protect America, continuing his disguised attacks?" Recall his previous references to "old hatreds" which control people—Obama introducing the very word "hate." Remember, too, his life equation: utter powerlessness and humiliation prompting the short step to "violence and untrammeled fury"—another way of describing hate.

We might also ask, "Does Obama secretly represent another part of the world that hates us because they view us as morally uncooperative? Is he a secret Muslim, either in truth or in spirit? Certainly he has behaved like a hateful Muslim toward America. Actions speak louder than words.

Hard to Conceive

It's hard to believe we're actually witnessing such rage directed at our country from its elected leader, but commentators all around us can't help but notice it. Floyd Brown, president of the Western Center for Journalism, minced no words regarding Obama's plan reflected in much of his staff, whose "main goal is to destroy the USA and make a one-world government."[17]

Syndicated radio talk-show host Rush Limbaugh commented on July 25, 2011, "It distresses me to see what has happened to this country and to know it need not have happened, to know that has happened because of policies implemented by someone who—I don't care—is either clueless or is himself a saboteur." Of course Rush is not yet trained how to hear Obama's super-intel

---

17 Floyd Brown, "Do Recent Scandals Expose Obama's Leadership Weakness?," April 19, 2012. http://www.westernjournalism.com/gop-sen-scandals-expose-obama-leadership-weakness accessed May 15, 2012.

language, but he's sharp enough to see Obama's destructiveness—and brave enough to describe it.

And millions of citizens are repeating the word-of-mouth message: Obama is ruining the America we've known and loved right before our eyes. But denial, ever present common, keeps our collective eyes closed to the full truth. Obama tells us his pain was unimaginable, which means his rage is unimaginable—and unimaginable to everyone—even his opponents, even the citizens he hurts. We simply cannot handle the full extent of his anger, and only the super intelligence can accurately describe it for us.

We are not consciously prepared to accept such truth, the whole truth. As Emily Dickinson so well described, "The truth must dazzle gradually or every man be blind."[18] Like a bloody accident along the road, we can only glance at it to begin to take it in—but glance we must. That describes in a nutshell why the unconscious mind uses powerful stories and images, to first give us a glance, to let us return at our own pace to the real story behind the images.

Indeed the evidence surrounds us of Obama's combined attack on our national security and our economic well-being. How much more can he get away with until America fully recognizes that we have a secret saboteur in the White House?

Millions of people and commentators allude to it, but to truly see it, warts and all, is altogether another story. Yet, even in the face of a massive threat to our nation, the mainstream media remains in the depths of denial.

Once again the image of "saboteur" fits strikingly with Alinsky's central tactic of deception, gaining power for power's sake at all costs. Alinsky was a very angry man and he encouraged that in Obama, his disciple.

Societal Foundations: Race Relations

We come now to another major foundation of our nation—our character, our values as a culture. In that light, Obama asks another revealing question in his story about "country I am leaving America"—"Are we living in a country still divided by race?" He introduces the subject of race for good reason: it is tied up with his core issues.

When it comes to race in America, Obama has demonstrated extremely divisive behavior at definitive moments. Most emblematic remains his endorsement of the two members of the New Black Panthers dressed in black combat garb carrying billy clubs at a Philadelphia polling place in the 2008 presidential elections, where they intimidated white voters. Through his surrogate voice, Attorney General Eric Holder, Obama refused to prosecute them, although former civil rights activist attorney Bartle Bull called the Panthers' behavior "the most blatant form of voter intimidation I've ever

---

18 Emily Dickinson, "Tell all the truth," http://www.poemhunter.com/poem/tell-all-the-truth accessed May 20, 2012.

seen."[19] Then over a four month period in 2009 black street gangs—spewing hate speech and class envy—ran wild in Denver, harassing whites.[20] The same behavior was repeated two years later in Philadelphia. When Michael Nutter, the black mayor of Philadelphia, confronted the racist gangs in no uncertain terms, "you have damaged your own race," Obama uttered not a word.[21] Yet in 2009, without knowing the facts at all, Obama had rushed to publicly aid one black man, a Harvard professor, in the Cambridge police incident.

In March 2012, when black teenager Trayvon Martin was tragically shot and killed by a Hispanic (George Zimmerman) involved in a neighborhood watch, it instantly became a national story, with veteran race-baiters Al Sharpton and Jesse Jackson issuing very public inflammatory statements. Obama immediately declared that "If I had a son, he would look like Treyvon." While Obama stated that the situation needed to be clarified, we have a black president essentially calling the young victim his son—an extremely powerful symbolic message. Now George Zimmerman (who claimed he was acting in self-defense) had in effect killed the president's son. And the black community responded by doubling up unsubstantiated charges of racism. The New Black Panthers (having received Obama and Holder's virtual endorsement as the racial haters of choice) even went so far as to put out a bounty on Zimmerman's head. Obama had severely inflamed racial tension once again, instead of being the true voice of reason. He also enabled the Black Panthers once more to flaunt the rule of law.

A new book exposes just how extensively Obama encourages the racial divide in America. *Injustice: Exposing the Racial Agenda of the Obama Justice Department,* by J. Christian Adams, a former attorney in the Department of Justice. Adams handled the New Black Panthers case regarding voter intimidation and anticipated a just sentence of punishment after the court awarded a default judgment in the case, since the defendants didn't show at the hearings. But Eric Holder essentially had instructed the Justice Department not to sentence the convicted Black Panthers because it was payback time for whites, and that, 'voter intimidation laws were not written to defend whites' civil rights.' Adams also later commented about Obama's Treyvon Martin remarks, "No president in our history would inject himself into a criminal matter using racial code like Obama did."

Adams described how Eric Holder, with his long history of racial grievances, has been given free reign by Obama—who aided and abetted such distortions of justice by stuffing the DOJ with numerous radical lawyers once

19 John Fund, "Holder's Black Panther Stonewall," *Wall Street Journal*, August 20, 2009, http://online.wsj.com/article/SB10001424052970203550604574361071968458430.html accessed May 1, 2012.
20 Alan Gathright, December 4, 2009, 7NEWS, ABC-TV, Denver, www.thedenverchannel.com/news/21868721/detail.html accessed May 1, 2012.
21 Dave Boyer, "Philadelphia mayor talks tough to black teenagers after 'flash mobs,'" *The Washington Times*, August 8, 2011, http://www.washingtontimes.com/news/2011/aug/8/mayor-talks-tough-to-black-teens-after-flash-mobs accessed May 1, 2012.

Obama took over the presidency.[22]

The Justice Department has become a proxy for Obama's hidden racism and another weapon in his arsenal which he utilizes to undermine America. Obama's own words confess to such behavior. In his inaugural address, he harkens back to America's history of racism: "We have tasted the bitter swill of civil war and segregation," followed shortly by *"old hatreds* shall someday pass," suggesting his own underlying resentment lives deep inside. As part of his reenactment, he has increased racial and political divides, just as his own home was divided.

And once more we must not miss that this is a core strategy of Saul Alinsky who strongly encouraged black racialists as he developed a coalition of radicals—including liberals, social justice activists and even communists. Following Dr. King's death Alinsky used racial unrest in communities to pressure corporations "to hire more blacks, a form of racial extortion that became a standard of the civil right movement."[23]

Race Symbolic of Deeper Issue

Once more we must understand "race" for Obama is highly symbolic; it's a potential powder keg. It represents the perfect weapon for him to express his deep anger stemming from his pain—secretly retaliating constantly against the true source of his rage: his attacking father. His goal is to attack back—and "race" provides the blinding cover for "boring from within," Alinsky-style. Truly it remains difficult to see past the disguise with "race" being such a loaded issue enabling him to quadruple its freight without anyone noticing.

Angry Role Models Reinforced Racial Anger

Looking back at Obama's life we find key figures who have sanctioned and modeled his violent behavior—disguised in his actions. We must not forget about his early surrogate father figure, Frank Marshall Davis, who was personally selected by Obama's white grandfather. Davis was an avowed communist with a profound hatred for America even as Obama reflected when Davis warned him about college, "they'll train you so good, you'll start believing what they tell you about equal opportunity and the American way and all that s____....Until you want to actually start running things and they'll let you know...that you're an ____ just the same."[24] Clearly Obama followed Davis' angry lead—ironically after he started running things as president.

And it was a mean-spirited thing for his grandfather to do, to let such a man shape his grandson's life. Stanley Dunham would have known all about Davis' anger. Somewhere in his vulnerable mixed-race identity Obama would have experienced his grandfather's choice--of such a significant destructive black role model--as an angry putdown of Obama's own blackness. It's no wonder that

---

22 J. Christian Adams, "Fox and Friends," Fox News Channel, March 28, 2012.
23 Horowitz, *Obama's Rules for Revolution*, pp. 6-7.
24 Obama, *Dreams*, p. 97.

Obama later lashed out at his maternal grandmother, labeling her a "typical white person." That attack was in part meant for his neglectful grandfather, the one who had sent him to Frank Davis.

Obama's Friends Act Out His Anger

Later he selected friends both as role models and people who would act out his anger to continue his transference of abuse. There was Weather Underground co-founder William Ayers who tried to bomb a federal building, who avoided jail on a technicality (and later stated that he regretted he hadn't done more to harm America). Ayers' wife, Bernadette Dorn, likewise attacked America in identical ways as a hippie anti-American radical involved in bombings. And we must not forget Obama's U.S.-hating minister Jeremiah Wright damning America from the pulpit. All these folks only fueled the fire of Obama's hatred.

Hate for America is a strong concept but look at Obama's friend Bill Ayers' unmitigated hatred, and again we consider his father's hate for his unintended progeny, his mixed-race son. It's really no surprise that such a severe father wound would prompt hate, a rage equivalent to his childhood devastation. Repeating the idea several times and in multiple stories, Obama tells us, "It's going to be bad, America. I will wound you as deeply as I was wounded."

'Never Let a Good Crisis Go to Waste'

We've established beyond a shadow of doubt that his early life was one tremendous crisis after another when his very existence was in doubt from the get-go. He experienced an internal world of one ongoing perpetual "unimaginable" peril. "Crisis" does not do justice to what he went through and how his mind became fixated on the danger he faced. But the word "crisis" remains the best one to describe what he's about: creating a crisis for the chief target of his reenactment—the United States.

Obama's presidency began with his chief of staff, Rahm Emanuel, telling his boss, "Never let a good crisis go to waste." On the surface Emanuel was referring to the economic "crisis" Obama had inherited, giving him free reign to aggressively begin his disguised attack on America. But Obama would not "waste" his own personal crisis state, and came at our nation in every conceivable way—constantly reenacting his pain on a largely unsuspecting America. And indeed he has.

A Warning from the Super Intelligence: The Key to Understanding Obama

Obama's super intelligence tells us more about him than we could have hoped for in our wildest dreams, far beyond the analysis of any commentator. But first his super-intel must establish its crucial role. Since Obama's super intelligence alone provides such unique information about him it first informs us, in all four communications, of its very existence and extraordinary abilities. It reveals its vital role: to look clearly into the future and lay out precisely the kind of president Obama will be.

His super-intel then issues a warning: America's very future, it says, depends on hearing its messages. His deeper mind announces that Obama is so deceptive and so self-deceptive that—without understanding this hidden spy within his own mind—Americans will never fully comprehend the danger he represents.

First we jump ahead to his inaugural address as he tells us how important his secret informer—his own super intelligence—is to America. He underscores that, speaking between the lines, his super intelligence is "The Key" to understanding him. His super intelligence repeatedly describes itself in striking images to establish its existence: (1) using technology (unconscious intelligence is a "new technology") to protect our nation's health and harness the weather (the storm known as Obama—a favorite self-image); (2) using "new instruments" for "new challenges" to restore science (suggesting the new science of unconscious intelligence); (3) using the inventive mind, the most powerful part of the mind—the deeper mind out of which inventions come— along with the creative super intelligence story-telling language.

In summary, Obama's super intelligence informs us, "I" am a new technology, a new instrument, and the brilliant inventive mind introducing a new science which alone can see the world in crucial new ways—see new possibilities and realities.

America's Crucial 'Weatherman'

How appropriate and ironic that this president becomes the man who because of his position most popularly introduces the science of unconscious intelligence to the world, a science which has been waiting for centuries to be discovered. Such a discovery deserves a "grand introduction." Unconsciously Obama recognizes the truth—that the super intelligence has not yet been appropriately recognized broadly by the public or professionals, that indeed it presents information by using a scientific method.[25] His deeper mind also communicates that Obama's "big plans for America" will require a major restoration.

Obama's super-intel warns us that, without this new scientific way of looking more deeply and hearing him deconstruct the dangerous challenge he represents, he will continue to run over us, storming his way across America. He will use this very image, this very "thoughtprint" (as I call it in forensic work) — "storm"—to show how the super intelligence presents its evidence. Basically, Obama unconsciously confesses, "Without hearing my super intelligence—the 'secret weatherman'—you will never know I am the perfect storm, America's secret enemy."

Think for a moment about Obama's perfect cover: He's a charming and articulate man, the first black president who poses as a visionary unifier, a

---

25 Research in psychotherapy and forensic profiling has made the case that the super intelligence communicates in a scientifically predictable way. (See Appendix A)

heroic character right out of a Hollywood script. Under those circumstances, he cannot be challenged. Dutifully, the mainstream media has obeyed, but his super intelligence—tough as nails—insists that the secret storm, Hurricane Obama, must be abated to protect America from its devastation.

Danger If Overlook Super Intelligence: Trust but Verify

Recall the admonition given to us by President Reagan, concerning arms-reduction talks with the USSR: "Trust but verify." We first trust that Obama's super intelligence is present and accounted for, as it is in every human being, quick-reading its way through life—then we verify. To verify its message, the super intelligence endlessly repeats itself, just as Obama has demonstrated. And he's not through yet.

Obama has secretly warned America. While he severely attacks America surreptitiously, on another level he simultaneously attempts to rescue America, hoping people will catch on. Deep down he wants us to know what he is really about so that we can confront him. Imagine such a turn of events—a president confessing to his misdeeds so that he can finally walk the righteous path. It's as if Obama's deeper self asks America to become the father who cares enough to discipline him—the father he never had. Will we as a country rise to his challenge to be such a father?

11

Pre-Inauguration Letter

Bad News for Daughters: 'Dad's an Illegal President'

Author's note: On a website I established before the 2008 election I posted several articles about my concern over an Obama presidency, and presented an early brief analysis of him.[1] Then, as now, I was listening for his super intelligence communication for guidance. It is obvious that I was not concerned at the time over the matter of his citizenship. I was not then a 'birther' because the matter had not fully come into the limelight and I had never explored what his super intelligence might have to say about his citizenship. Finally, it dawned on me around 2010 that I could "ask his super intelligence"—to see if he commented on the matter unconsciously. To my utter surprise he did so extensively. But I let his great unconscious mind lead the way. That story unfolds here: basically we have Obama's super-intel responding to the question: Are you a legal citizen or not?

It was one of the biggest days of his life—his Inauguration Day, January 20, 2009. For Barack Hussein Obama Jr. that day shares equal billing with Fathers' Day. On both of those days, Obama stressed their personal significance with a speech and a letter to his daughters. On January 18, 2009, two days before being sworn in as president, Obama wrote the first personal letter to his daughters, Sasha and Malia.[2] His timing is no accident. I suggest you stop reading at this point and turn to Appendix C to read this letter; then come back.

Prior to his inauguration *Parade* magazine asked the president "to get personal and tell us what you want for your children." In agreeing to do so, Obama actually "gets personal" with America. Given his unceasing unconscious confession of his planned attack on our nation's foundation, we can expect more startling revelations here. But what will he emphasize?

We have one last great foundation of America—the U.S. Constitution. It is absolutely unique in world political history and forms the vital backbone of our unique nation. From the beginning, however, many observers have expressed concern that Obama violated the Constitution by running for president because they believed he was an illegal candidate lacking American citizenship.

---

1 http://www.americasstrugglewithsuccess.com
2 Barack Obama, "'We Need Fathers To Step Up,'" *Parade,* January 18, 2009.

Let's recall two instructions Obama issued at the 2010 National Prayer Breakfast. Whenever people get around God, we should note, confessions seem to spill out as a matter of course. But first we must read through his two blatant denials, *"...you can question my policies without questioning my faith, or, for that matter, my citizenship,"* he said, delivering a distinctly unconscious message that we should do both. As we examine the 2009 letter to his daughters, we will keep in mind the questionable legality of his presidency. It's an issue the media refuses to explore and one which we have yet to fully address.

Obama's payback anger directed at the nation remains our central focus. An illegal presidency would reflect another attack on America, an overt and offensive affront to our Constitution—our most basic foundation. Given the enormous anger he will direct at America and at the rule of law, his fraudulent ascendancy to the White House shouldn't be a surprise—but again "The Rage" in all its disguised forms is our main issue, not simply the legality of his presidency.

If in fact Obama has bypassed the Constitution, we would anticipate a confession. Unconsciously he would be telling us that he's the biggest 'birther' of them all. And we can be certain that—reacting to his unconscious impulse—he would address this crucial issue even while the media and the Congress assiduously avoided it. Despite the efforts of those persuasive enablers, he later felt compelled to produce a purported birth certificate because questions about his eligibility, questions from Americans of all backgrounds, continued to plague him—even at this key moment of his career.

With his guilt running high because of his secret dishonest intentions toward our great nation, the pre-inauguration letter to his children vividly reflects his inner turmoil. We must also remember his key *secret* instruction in his Fathers' Day speech: that we would really know him from his letters and stories, the same way he knew his father.

Campaign Mistake—Feeding Children

"I know that you've both had a lot of fun these last two years on the campaign trail, going to picnics and parades and state fairs, eating all sorts of junk food your mother and I probably shouldn't have let you have." (ILtr) Again Obama opens with a brief and striking story, as his super intelligence is engaged in full splendor. Right off, his story concerns his campaign and a regretful action—indulging his daughters with "all sorts of junk food." He suggests a blatant confession, "America, for two years I've been feeding you 'political junk food' on the campaign," implying his presidency is junk—not authentic, not the real thing. In short, using a vivid image of a sham, his super intelligence strongly suggests he's an illegal president.

Next, the striking phrase, "I shouldn't have let you" suggests "I shouldn't have let *me* go this far." In truth, he's even more strongly suggesting, "*We* shouldn't have let me go this far," pointing to the complicity of his wife—the mother of his daughters—in usurping the presidency.

157

Michelle Prone to Confession

And he makes another suggestion—that we should examine his wife's speeches to see if she confesses. During the campaign, Michelle made an infamous comment regarding her true disdain for America: "For the first time in my adult lifetime, I'm really proud of my country, and not just because Barack has done well, but because I think people are hungry for change."[3] Her super intelligence connects "for the first time" to "pride in America" –a common phrase symbolic of being an American citizen. The symbolic message, "I am a new American citizen." Her super intelligence implies, "My husband is not an American, and my behavior is anti-American for supporting him." Reading through her denial "not because Barack has done well," tells us precisely that her statement was motivated by the strong possibility Obama could indeed do well, i.e., become president. By using the exact imagery as Obama, "people are hungry [for a change]"—she hints of gorging herself on the junk food of his illegal candidacy, starving for the fame and wealth his election would bring her. (Unconsciously she suggests another prophetic meaning: by the time he is through his first term, America will be hungry for a change. In the face of multiple persistent national problems, Obama's job approval rating of 33% on June 21, 2012 implies America is indeed starving for a change.)

Making Up for Father Abuse

> But I also know that it hasn't always been easy for you and Mom, and that as excited as you both are about that new puppy, it doesn't make up for all the time we've been apart. I know how much I've missed these past two years, and today I want to tell you [a little more about why I decided to take our family on this journey]. (ILtr)

Right out of the box Obama confesses one motive for his improperly seizing the nation's leadership: "It hasn't always been easy…it doesn't make up for all the time…been apart. I know how much I missed these past…years." Obama again implies that his presidency *represents a "make up" to him*— another entitlement to fill that withering emptiness that sears inside him moment by moment. He can still feel exactly how much he missed when his father abandoned him. And again he reminds us that this desperate attempt to fill that hole "doesn't" work and that he sees the presidency "as a new puppy" for his excited "inner child" that still aches regardless of his new prize. And he suggests that as president he will treat America like a dog and be an absent president in numerous ways transferring his father's abusive behavior.

'I want to tell you'—Obama Must Confess

I want to tell you a little more about why I decided to take our family on this journey. (ILtr)

Then we see the message marker, "I want to tell you," followed by "why I decided to take our [American] family on this journey." Translation: this letter

---

3 Jake Tapper, "Political Punch," ABC News, February 18, 2008.

contains the hidden confession and story that America has been "taken," that he will take America on quite a trip—that he is illegally taking America for a ride. *Obama provides the code to his keyword "journey"—translated "his presidency"—which he will repeat.* Following this marker, we should expect a story which further explains his deeper motives.

Obama's unconscious voice impressively continues to confess his ineligibility as president. We should expect strong linkages between his seemingly different ideas which, when woven together, continue to tell a cohesive story, a strong confession. His comment ends with "take family on...journey," suggesting that he should leave office—a message we'll keep in mind for matches.

All About *Me*

> When I was a young man, I thought life was all about me—about how I'd make my way in the world, become successful, and get the things I want. (ILtr)

So why did he run when he knew he was ineligible to pursue the presidency? Obama admits his selfish motives, "When I was a young man, I thought life was all about me—about how I'd make my way in the world, become successful and get the things I want." In essence, he's admitting this journey *now* is "all about me," all about "my way," about how I "get the things I want" and "become successful." He's defining just how selfish his illegal presidency truly is: it's all about him!

Again he ties his political aspirations to "when I was a young man"—that is, when he was a young *child*. His super intelligence is reminding us about the early pain that drives him. "All about me" suggests the typical way severely wounded kids attempt to repair—and how he will run the country. Nine times a desperate Obama uses the phrase "I want" in this letter.

'Don't Count My Votes'

> But then the two of you came into my world with all your curiosity and mischief and those smiles that never fail to fill my heart and light up my day. And suddenly, all my big plans for myself didn't seem so important anymore. I soon found that the greatest joy in my life was the joy I saw in yours. And I realized that my own life wouldn't count for much unless I was able to ensure that you had every opportunity for happiness and fulfillment in yours. (ILtr)

In another brief story, Obama provides two more impressive images—"mischief" and his "life... [would] not count." Translation: Obama tells us that his election reflected his "mischief" and that he is *the missing chief.* He would not count the votes he got because his life as president did not count—even stronger images of his illegal presidency. He continues his confession by perfectly placing the word "count"—the bottom line in any election—here as "*not* count."

Then Obama's super intelligence instructs us, "came [come] into my world with all your curiosity"—that is "investigate me—my inner world and unconscious communication." When he uses the phrase "light up my day," it implies shining the light of his super intelligence at this exact moment on his day, Inauguration Day, two days hence. He suggests that we thoroughly investigate his "mischief"—and that we'll find proof to verify his lack of citizenship and other bad deeds.

In, "my heart—light up my day" Obama further implies that citizens should examine his heart, bring his life into the sunlight of full disclosure. Unconsciously Obama confronts the failure of both the media and Congress to actually investigate him.

Then he references the birth of both daughters—coming into the world— right before the advice to investigate him. With this "birth marker" he suggests specifically that we should closely probe *when* and *where* he was born.

Smiles That Fail

In mentioning a father's great joy in a child, Obama poignantly suggests his own pain, "smiles that…fail to fill my heart and light up my day"—his father's smile that was never there. Years of dark days replaced what should have been years of sincere smiles. Obama admits this pain still propels him toward uncontrollable self-centeredness, the entitlement mindset that led to his presidential candidacy regardless of his foreign birth.

In *Dreams From My Father*, Obama confesses that his own great smile is often simply a huge mask, just as his father's was. In *Dreams*, Obama recalls entering America from Indonesia to permanently live with his grandparents when he was 10 years old. Coming through customs he suddenly put on a large wooden mask—suggesting the foreigner with the mask. He's the foreigner who would wear a false face as president.

Obama introduced the word "light"—a message marker synonymous with the super intelligence, another entreaty to citizens to listen to his unconscious messages. He describes the magic effect of children: their curiosity, their mischief, their smiles that fill your heart and light up your day providing a parent's greatest joy.

But the sad reality is that his father never appreciated his son. Obama Sr. thought it was all about himself and missed all the magic and joy that his namesake could have given him. Obama Jr.'s very words about his daughters— "…then the two of you came into my world"—reflect how Obama never came into his father's world *and* how close Obama came to never entering the world at all because of his father's desire to abort him.

In The End—Why I Ran

And I realized that my own life wouldn't count for much unless I was able to ensure that you had every opportunity for happiness and fulfillment in yours. In the end, girls, that's why I ran for President: because of what I want for you and for every child in this nation. (ILtr)

Andrew G. Hodges, M.D.

Obama closes this story: "In the end, girls, that's why I ran for President." First he desperately ran for the presidency as an illegal candidate because of "what I want"—"what every child wants"—what we already know that the deeply wounded child in him didn't get, the "opportunity for happiness." His absent father had left him to rot forever in a bottomless hole filled with unhappiness.

We also find a succinct self-instruction as he continues to confess. "The end, girls" indicates that he really desires the end of the charade, and that he should resign as president. Those are truly the *words of contrition he longs to say* to his daughters. Only then can he be their authentic rock of integrity.

Another meaning he is conveying here is dire despair: "This is the end, girls...." Again he implies horrific fear of his father who constantly made him feel like it was "The End" for Obama—a striking picture of abortion. All along he has told us he sought the power of the presidency to overcome the helplessness of his near destruction.

Center of Letter—Confession

Clearly, the epicenter of this letter contains Obama's secret confession that he is an illegal president. Deep down, that was his main purpose in writing it—and precisely where we would expect to find it. He has been lying to all Americans, but lying to his daughters bothers him in a more personal way because he desires so strongly to be a beacon of integrity for them—to be everything his father wasn't.

For now we continue to listen to the rest of the story in his letter to his daughters, as he admits that he treated the Constitution like a rag doll, to be carelessly tossed aside.

The Key to Confession

I want all our children [citizens] to go to schools worthy of their potential, schools that challenge them, inspire them, and instill in them a sense of wonder about the world around them. I want them to have the chance to go to college—even if their parents aren't rich.

And I want them to get good jobs: jobs that pay well and give them benefits like health care, jobs that let them spend time with their own kids and retire with dignity. (ILtr)

We find repeated educational message markers (first "schools [with] worthy potential" and "go to college") suggesting the messages: "Get the highest education possible about me from my brilliant super intelligence."

In that light Obama then becomes obsessed with "jobs"—each description conveying the job he is not doing. He implies, "I want them to get a president who will do a good job, a president that pays off for America and will take good care of them by producing a healthy nation—a president who spends quality time with his 'own' citizens." Adding that one word, "own," conveys his confession that American citizens are not really 'his' citizens to govern.

Finally Obama adds, "retire with dignity"—precisely what he, as an ineligible president, should do: retire. The only way he could be an effective role model to citizens and to his daughters would be to admit his error and resign. Such a move, he tells himself, could be done with the dignity the office deserves.

We Must Investigate the Boundaries to Discover Truth

> I want us to push the boundaries of discovery so that you'll live to see new technologies and inventions that improve our lives and make our planet cleaner and safer. And I want us to push our own human boundaries to reach beyond.... (lltr)

First we find the embedded message repeated twice, "I want...to push the boundaries" in which Obama confesses he pushed the legal boundaries aside to become president. He also cannot wait to "push the boundaries" of America in numerous ways. As president, he quickly pushed boundaries in his drastic policies such as sinking the nation far deeper into debt. He is a presidential boundary-breaker of the first order, as he has repeatedly demonstrated. Likewise he instructs the American people: "push the boundaries of discovery, as in "Investigate my presidential eligibility thoroughly, and you will discover that I'm out of bounds and have overreached." His unconscious is once more painting a beautiful picture of the super intelligence, instructing us to use it.

Boundary is a vital keyword, a definitive method of measuring. Boundaries reflect who we are and how we know who we are—how we can know who Obama is or isn't. Obama leads us to one central question, "Is he within constitutional boundaries, legally qualified to be president? He answers definitively, "No!"

Dividing races, regions, and religions

> And I want us to push our own human boundaries to reach beyond the divides of race and region, gender and religion that keep us from seeing the best in each other. (ILtr)

Obama wants to "push our human boundaries beyond" where they now stand. He secretly suggests once more (as we saw in Chapter 10) that he plans to encourage the divisive forces presently at play in America, to essentially drive the American people as a whole further apart. A division, after all, is a clear boundary. The subliminal message is that he's a divider, and he specifically plans to worsen the divisions of race, region, gender and religion—inspiring animosity instead of harmony. He refuses to see the best in his critics. He discourages Americans from seeing the best in each other. He suggests that he will be "The Great Divider," exactly as his father was.

Very early his behavior as president clearly matches this warning of dividing Americans.

- He has become a polarizing figure, far from the unifier he had pledged during the campaign to be.

162

- Regarding "race," first on his list of divisions, we've already seen his reverse racism in the Cambridge Police incident, giving the Black Panthers a 'pass' on their voter intimidation conviction, and calling his grandmother a "typical white person."

- During his 2008 campaign at a $35,800-per-plate San Francisco fundraiser, Obama mocked Americans in rural areas where people "...get bitter, they cling to guns or religion or antipathy to people who aren't like them or anti-immigrant sentiment...."[4] Not only did he try and divide America over gun ownership rights, religion and immigration he subtly confessed to being 'a person not like these Americans—an immigrant.' A truly striking image and confession: Obama the immigrant. Obama again suggests his secret bitterness causes him to cling to his anti-guns, anti-Christian and anti-American sentiment.

- In the above comment on "immigration" Obama unconsciously revealed his secret plan to use the subject of his legal claims to the presidency to divide the nation into 'birthers' and 'non-birthers.' He knew no one would hold him accountable over his citizenship—already having powerful Democrat Party support and understanding the weak media's reluctance to confront a black candidate.

- He reinvented America's religious history saying, "America is no longer a Christian nation. We are a nation of Christians, Muslims and Jews...and non-believers," moving Jews down in priority from their historical "Judeo-Christian" status. He continually puts down Jews/Israel while elevating Muslims—which is even more egregious, since he said this in a speech in Egypt.

- Also in "I want to push the boundaries...of region," we find the embedded suggestion that he stretched the geographical qualification for president all the way to Africa.

- In America, he enflamed a gender conflict over the issue of abortion with his controversial speech at Notre Dame University, which is officially pro-life. The school's administration was roundly criticized for inviting the president to speak there, and for not canceling his invitation after Catholic bishops applied pressure in advance of the speech. As a central 2012 campaign strategy he has emphasized the Republican Party's supposed "War on Women."

War and Citizenship

> Sometimes we have to send our young men and women into war and other dangerous situations to protect our country—but when we do, I want to make sure that it is only for a very good reason, that we try our best to settle our differences with others peacefully, and that we do everything possible to keep our servicemen and women safe.

---

4 James Joyner, "Obama on Guns, God, and Hate in Rural America," http://www.outsidethebeltway.com/obama_on_guns_god_and_hate_in_rural_america/ accessed April 26, 2012.

> And I want every child to understand that the blessings these brave
> Americans fight for are not free—that with the great privilege of
> being a citizen of this nation comes great responsibility. (ILtr)

Connecting two major concepts—war and citizenship—Obama suggests a crucial turn in his hidden confession by linking key ideas. He mentions war and other dangerous situations where we have to send in our armed forces, specifically when differences of opinion cannot be settled peacefully. Next he links such battles to citizenship, reminding us that at times Americans must fight for the privilege of citizenship. Now we put his sequential story together.

After the continual build-up in which he confesses to an illegal presidency, Obama unconsciously picks this precise time to introduce the idea that "citizenship is not free." By implication, he puts the question of his own citizenship boldly on the table. Wracked by hidden guilt, his super intelligence realizes he must come clean. He then reminds his own wounded child and all citizens: "I want every child to understand the blessing of citizenship is not free"—underscoring his point with the message marker "understand." Obama suggests the blatant confession, "I took the privilege of being a citizen for free— I could not pay the price, since I didn't actually qualify."

In essence he again raises the burning question for all Americans, "Have I, Barack Obama, simply taken American citizenship illegally, by my own will?" He implies that American citizenship is such a great privilege that the question of his citizenship requires a thorough investigation. He recommends that Americans must be brave and fight for the ideal of authentic citizenship as we did in 1776. Yet Obama also makes plain how delicately this issue must be handled. He knows full well that an exploration of his African birth could provoke nationwide race riots.

The Danger

Obama contrasts two narratives, two different stories: The unselfish Patriot Narrative and the selfish narrative—the story of someone who would try and claim American citizenship for free, illegally, hinting at the great divide within himself, the personal conflict around his illegal presidency. His peaceful side knows he should resign, settle the matter non-violently. The other side of Obama suggests he would fight any legal challenge to his presidency even if it meant promoting racial tensions necessitating the activation of the National Guard. He tells this shocking story with crucial links: (1) pushing the boundaries leading to divisive dangerous conflicts particularly racial and regional, (2) escalating into violence, and (3) necessitating troops sent into that war.

This is only his second major reference to violence in this letter where his primary intent was to confess to his illegality. Several commentators believe such riots would occur if the Obama presidency is ever seriously challenged.

Surely we can empathize with the tremendous pain black communities would experience if Obama had to step down. Here a "heroic black" has for the first time received the highest honor in the land, and suddenly their great symbol of acceptance and equality is challenged because he's not who he says he is. His reputation would be in shambles.

But a clear examination of his citizenship would positively answer the question, "Are all Americans—black and white—going to live by the Constitution?" In his following comment, referring to marches for freedom, Obama informs us exactly how Dr. King would answer that question: It must be a "color-blind" decision, not a decision blinded by color.

Declaration of Independence—Important or Not?
> That was the lesson your grandmother tried to teach me when I was your age, reading me the opening lines of the Declaration of Independence and telling me about the men and women who marched for equality because they believed those words put to paper two centuries ago should mean something. (ILtr)

After stressing the high cost of American citizenship and highlighting that "citizenship is not free," Obama moves to the legal basis of citizenship in the most personal of ways. He then references the Declaration of Independence connected to two negative messages suggesting (1) his grandmother "tried to teach him," but he failed to learn, (2) that "those words should mean something" revealing they don't to some people—namely him—and that he treated them as meaningless "words on paper." The two ideas fit perfectly: he didn't learn and didn't believe.

His super intelligence doubly underscores its communication with the amazing message markers "lesson" and "tried to teach," suggesting "Here is the hidden lesson I'm trying to teach America." Then we find the almost blatant message, "reading me—the opening lines of the Declaration of Independence." Translation: "You can read exactly who I am there." The message marker "telling me" suggests "telling *on* me," which immediately follows, confirming the instruction.

Following his guidance we turn to the opening lines of the Declaration of Independence.
1. "When… it becomes **necessary for one people to dissolve the political bands which have connected them with another**…they should declare the causes which impel them to the separation."
2. "We hold these truths to be self-evident, that all men…are endowed by their Creator with certain unalienable Rights, that among these are Life, Liberty and the pursuit of Happiness…"
3. "…to secure these rights, Governments…*deriving their just powers from the consent of the governed*…**whenever any Form of Government becomes destructive of these ends**, it is the Right of the People to alter or to abolish it, and to institute new Government."
4. "…**when a long train of abuses and usurpations**, pursuing invariably the same Object evinces a design to reduce them under absolute

Despotism, it is their right, it is their duty, to throw off such Government."

5. **"He has refused his Assent to Laws,** the most wholesome and necessary for the public good."

The opening lines of the Declaration (point #1 above) contain Obama's directive that the people must dissolve their political connections to him. Unconsciously Obama confesses (in point #3) that he has not derived his presidential power from the people—"the consent of the governed"—but by deception and that his illegal presidency disregards the rights, life and liberty of the people (point #2). In a nutshell, "he has refused his assent to Laws"—to presidential requirements of the Constitution (point #5). He predicts that this will be the first of "a long train of abuses and usurpations," that his presidency will reflect a pattern of "despotism"—and indeed it has.

We find the undeniable confession that he is a law-breaker who must be removed from office by Americans who cherish the Constitution. Fittingly in the Declaration of Independence itself Obama has shown us a striking picture of himself--the foreign usurper (just like King George III of England, against whom the Declaration was directed) who should be removed from office. His super intelligence has used our most sacred document to make a powerful confession—one of the most impressive in a long line of them.

His all-wise super intelligence gives a final instruction. Mentioning "men and women who marched for equality because they believed," he insists, "You must believe my unconscious confession that I am an illegal president, and believe so strongly that you will march on Washington for justice."

With the 2012 election just around the corner, momentum for citizens to march is unlikely to build—even though millions of Americans believe Obama is foreign-born. Still the president's super intelligence implies that a metaphoric "march" on the ballet boxes could manifest in November, so voters can right the wrong which was perpetrated by Obama in 2008.

Improve America or 'Our Union Falls'

She helped me understand that America is great not because it is perfect but because it can always be made better—and that the unfinished work of perfecting our union falls to each of us. It's a charge we pass on to our children, coming closer with each new generation to what we know America should be." (ILtr)

The convincing sequence of his main ideas offers impressive evidence of Obama's unconscious admission he is a foreigner. First he directly references the Constitution ("perfecting our union") with its opening lines, "We the People of the United States, in Order to form a more perfect Union."

With the phrase "helped me understand...America," Obama unconsciously confesses that he is helping us understand what he's doing to America. He then alludes to damaging our nation: "America is not...perfect, and "America can be

166

made better." How should great correction take place?

We have "unfinished work of perfecting our union," again the message that citizens must do the work of removing an inauthentic president, an "unfinished work" lacking the legal qualifications for president. Additionally he suggests unless we carry out that unfinished work, America falls.

Finally he implies in "a charge we pass on to our children [citizens] coming closer...what we know America should be." Again he urges citizens to draw close and pass on his presidency to a legal president—then we can have back the America we know.

Obama Reprimands Himself—Three Ways
1. Right wrongs
> I hope both of you will take up that work, righting the wrongs that you see and working to give others the chances you've had. (ILtr)

Obama talks about "righting wrongs," underscored by the message marker, "you see." What his unconscious is really saying is, "See the wrong I've done"—become president by deception. His guilt remains paramount. His deeper moral compass continues to guide telling him again to "Right the wrong you've done. Give a legitimate candidate the opportunity to be president." A message he cannot hear.

2. Give something back
> Not just because you have an obligation to give something back to this country that has given our family so much—although you do have that obligation. But because you have an obligation to yourself. Because it is only when you hitch your wagon to something larger than yourself that you will realize your true potential. (ILtr)

He reveals how heavily guilt weighs upon him as a result of his ill-gotten gain. With the phrase "you have an obligation to give something back to this country," his confession becomes as overt as the unconscious can be. He specifically stresses *the country* "that has given our family so much." Unmistakably he's confessing, "I've been *given* the magnificent presidency— not earned it—and I have a tremendous obligation to return this office to the nation. It is America's presidency, not mine." In this light, his ethical super intelligence has one final familiar recommendation for him: "hitch your wagon"—as in, "leave town voluntarily."

3. Grow up—face limits
> These are the things I want for you—to grow up in a world with no limits on your dreams and no achievements beyond your [my] reach, and to grow into compassionate, committed women who will help build that world [instead of tear it down]. (ILtr)

Obama continues with the perfect sequel to "give the presidency back to the country." Again he paints a vivid picture of lacking citizenship as his images become stronger and stronger. He suggests the embedded, thinly-disguised

167

confession, "I want to…grow up" and face reality: that there are "limits on [my] dreams" and "achievements beyond [my] reach." This reflects his childish decision to run for president. He reveals how his denial tells the truth because there were achievements beyond his reach and constitutional limits on his dreams.

I Want the Same Chance

> And I want every child to have the same chances to learn and dream and grow and thrive that you girls have. (ILtr)

Once more we find the same understandable childish wish still alive in Obama. He wants the "same chances"—"to learn… dream… grow… and thrive" which others had, which he didn't get in his lost childhood. He had no personal navigator like a full-time father would have been. In that light, Obama justifies his great illegal act: "I want…to have the same chances…[my] dream." With that omnipresent ache to fulfill his dream, tortured by the hole that burns deep inside and so lacking the nurture—the chance—he needed, he aggressively took his own chance.

"Chances" also suggests America took its chances on him as president. The American citizenry elevated a completely average Chicago politician to the nation's top job. Giddy voters made Obama the first black president despite a decided lack of background checks. The American electorate threw wisdom out the window and put into office a deeply insecure and immature individual. The voters instead selected the most inexperienced and weakest president in our long history. In so doing, Americans rolled the dice on the future of the greatest country in the world.

Over and over, deeper and deeper, Obama tells us why he chose to become an illegal president. And we are getting his story, warts and all. Again he poses the question to us all: "Who can handle the sordid, painful, self-deceptive truth of Barack Obama Jr.?"

Obama's Great Adventure

> That's why I've taken our family on this great adventure. (ILtr)

Having explained the pain and rage that drives him, Obama confesses again that with his presidency he's "taken" the nation—"taken America for a ride." Here he repeats the identical image of "taking" the family at the beginning of his letter—in a way setting it off with these two bookends, informing us the letter really reflects one cohesive confession: his illegal presidency.

Obama predicts that his deceptive presidency will be "one great adventure"—an unbelievably chaotic experience with people in way over their heads. He took America on an adventure, all right, on a roller-coaster ride of disruptive changes and a house of mirrors where he masqueraded as a legitimate leader.

168

Humor—the New Life in the White House

I am so proud of both of you. I love you more than you can ever know. And I am grateful every day for your patience, poise, grace, and humor as we prepare to start our new life together in the White House. Love, Dad (ILtr)

We must not overlook Obama's moving apology to Sasha and Malia in which he recognizes that he needs their patience and grace, their forgiveness because of his flawed role as a deceiver of the highest order.

In "humor… prepares… start… new life…in the White House" he suggests the confession, "America, as an illegal president the joke is on you, a really bad joke. You've got 'new life in the White House' you never imagined. Perfectly placed at the conclusion of his letter, we find another matching embedded recommendation, "new life…in the White House." That is, "America must get a new legal president who can really bring life to the job."

"Love, Dad" suggests a "cruel joke" like the one played on him by his father also suggested by "humor… prepare… start… new life"—giving him life and then immediately wanting to take it away with an abortion. The ugly joke took Obama on a lifelong journey of uncertainty and, in turn, Obama played a similar joke on his kids—he wasn't a real president, just as his father wasn't a real father, and he cannot give them a rock-solid foundation of integrity as he promises. And the joke was on America, too: he wasn't the real father of our nation because he simply didn't qualify, constitutionally, for the job opening.

With this revealing letter to his daughters, Obama has set the stage for his Inauguration Day speech where we will find a matching confession of his ineligibility.

Two Other Journeys, Two Key Confessions

Before moving to that speech we need to appreciate two other vital ways Obama has been unconsciously trying to tell America about his illegal journey to the presidency. At the very beginning of *Dreams from My Father*, immediately after the title page, Obama has a single one-sentence quote on a page unto itself (from the Scriptures no less). Supposedly, this introductory quote captures the essence of his book—and indeed it does, but in a far deeper way than Obama consciously envisioned. Once again his super intelligence controls his confession as he states, *"For we are strangers before them, and sojourners, as were all our fathers"* (1 Chronicles 29:15).

His super-intel message declares that he indeed is a "stranger"—a foreigner—president standing before the people. He takes us back to his long sojourn across the ocean from Kenya where his foreign father was. Plain and simple, Obama finds another way of telling us, "I am a foreigner just like my father." In selecting this verse from the book of Chronicles Obama further implies that in multiple key communications (that book, his crucial four-part saga under examination here, and other places) he is an unconscious chronicler of this story; in fact here he's swearing on the Bible it is true. Once again he

169

locates this secret confession at the central most crucial place in his book—his very first words. His plan all along for years had been to run illegally for president. In his inaugural address Obama will continue his image of a sojourner to make sure we get the super intelligence picture.

Obama chronicles his same confession in a controversial dramatic decision on June 15, 2012 when by executive order he granted temporary amnesty to approximately 800,000 illegal young immigrants, aged 30 and under. They had journeyed to America illegally with their illegal parents but have adjusted to America society so well that Obama declared: "They are Americans in their heart, in their minds, in every single way but one: on paper."[5] Again they were really citizens *except for a piece of paper*. Once again Obama paints a perfect picture of himself: he had come to America illegally but his parents (mother and grandparents) covered up his lack of citizenship; in fact by now he is so Americanized that all he is missing as a legal citizen is "a piece of paper."

The missing piece of paper so necessary for citizenship blatantly spotlights the key issue surrounding his presidency: Does he have a legal birth certificate or not? We have a memorable super intelligence confession uttered so prominently Obama wants to make sure we don't miss this one. Yet again Obama highlights his excessive sense of entitlement to the presidency: 'Hey guys, remember—a legal birth certificate is only a piece of paper,' a rationale which also tells us why he would, in the same 'you-owe-me-one' mode, produce a phony online birth certificate without batting an eye.

Just for good measure, Obama had earlier announced in 2010 and 2011 that he would never impose such an executive order because it was completely illegal—outside the Constitution and the laws of Congress.[6] His 2012 actions thus declared yet another aspect to chronicle, "See, once more I have violated the Constitution with my illegal presidency." While he had a political purpose to gain the Hispanic vote before the election, don't miss his overwhelming crippling guilt. He simply had to illegally allow more illegals into America so he could declare "It's the right thing to do," attempting to ease his conscience. Heavy lies an illegal presidential crown. On top of it all, his amnesty plan 'for the children' was guaranteed to cause administrative and cultural chaos, and yet another tell-tale sign of Obama's Alinsky-style presidency—always on the attack.

5 "Remarks by the President on Immigration," *TheCriticalPost-Chicago*, June 15, 2012 http://thecritical-post.com/blog/2012/06/president-obamas-speech-at-press-conference-about-amnesty-for-illlegal-aliens-at-white-house-15-june-2012-transcript-text-tcpchicago/ accessed June 23, 2012.
6 Charles Krauthammer, "Obama's Utter Lawlessness," *The Birmingham News*, June 23, 2012.

12

The Speech: Stunning Confession and Strongest Warning

I suggest you turn now to Appendix D and read the entire speech Obama gave at his inauguration, to gain a sense of the totality of his message. Then come back.

> I stand here today humbled by the task before us, grateful for the trust you have bestowed, mindful of the sacrifices borne by our ancestors. I thank President Bush for his service to our nation, as well as the generosity and cooperation he has shown throughout this transition.
>
> Forty-four Americans have now taken the presidential oath. The words have been spoken during rising tides of prosperity and the still waters of peace. Yet, every so often, the oath is taken amidst gathering clouds and raging storms. At these moments, America has carried on not simply because of the skill or vision of those in high office, but because We the People have remained faithful to the ideals of our forebears, and true to our founding documents.
>
> So it has been. So it must be with this generation of Americans.
> -Inauguration Address, January 20, 2009 (ISp)

Standing on the platform at the West Front of the U.S. Capitol in Washington, D.C., facing a crowd of a million listeners at the National Mall with many millions more around the world watching on television, Obama begins, "I stand here today." Pay close attention—he will refer to "today" over and over.

How does he "stand?" He has just stood before millions of American citizens with his hand on the same Bible used by Abraham Lincoln having just taken the presidential oath administered by the Chief Justice of the Supreme Court—the final step in his deceptive plan. It was an act he had anticipated for years, the moment frozen in his mind forever. His prompt use of the word "stand" suggests "standing." Where does he stand in relation to the Bible, the law, and the American people? More importantly, where does he stand as president—in reality or fantasy, illegal or legal?

In his speech on Fathers' Day 2008 we heard him confess his intentions.

Now God enters the picture again. Taking an oath as a false president in front of the deity—even while looking the American people right in the eye—would take him beyond the pale unconsciously, and we should expect a striking confession filled with violent images. Obama will not disappoint. In his first two words he introduced the crucial issue of truth. He will proceed to tell us where he really stands. In fact, his entire speech addresses that issue.

His very next word "humbled"—and the complete message "I stand here today humbled"—suggests this is the most humbling day of his life and, for his super intelligence, the most humiliating day of his life. If he's an illegal president, 'humiliating' is a precise description. He has broken a powerful trust, as his next phrase suggests, "grateful for the trust you have bestowed"—he knows trust goes with the job. Later, he will describe leaders who break the public's trust.

Obama's phraseology is revealing: first "humbled by the task before us" suggests he's humiliated by what he has done and what he intends to do, specifically humbling America. He will soon enumerate the steps he will take to bring down the country—of course disguising his intentions. Being an illegal president is quite a start, but not the end by a long shot. Throughout his inaugural address, he unconsciously confesses his betrayal of America. Imagine the great Inauguration Day of a president of the United States—in fact the first black president. Such a day would normally be the single greatest day in a person's life, yet here Obama stands having pulled off one of the most devious political ploys in history. He will later refer to "our darkest hours"—and indeed this is his and America's darkest hour. We have never before had a president so deliberately disregard the law. And we have never before had a president who unconsciously, yet clearly, confesses to it.

His next phrase reveals the result of breaking America's trust, "mindful of the sacrifices borne by our ancestors." First he has alluded to the patriotism undergirding the birth of our nation—informing us that his story-telling super intelligence is fully engaged. At the end of his speech—providing a pair of matching bookends—he will return to this narrative with a distinct reference to our country's origins. It's his way of saying, "Americans, never forget who you are."

Now he tells us exactly what he did to America's proud history.

As an illegal president he asks citizens to bear the sacrifices of his actions. His behavior would cause a "mind full of sacrifices"—indeed sacrifice would be very much on his mind—because he knows he's sacrificing the trust of the people and sacrificing the Constitution, both of which had likewise demanded sacrifices of our ancestors.

His super intelligence's increasingly blatant confession of his ineligibility begins as expected early in his speech. Impressively, he introduces a *birth-marker* in the first sentence— "sacrifices borne [by our ancestors]," suggesting three matching messages: (1) his "foreign" presidency has just sacrificed our ancestors' heritage; (2) "sacrifices birth"—ignoring the birth requirement of the Constitution; (3) "borne" (virtually identical to "born," orally) alludes again to "birth" suggesting the crucial question: Where was he born? In his initial sentence Obama himself has introduced the issues of birth and integrity.

Humbled by the 'Ask'

Here's an example of how creative the super intelligence can be: we find the word "ask" within the word "task"—which fits the situation perfectly. "Ask" introduces the idea of a hidden question which Obama proposes to all of America, hinting that our first task is hear his embedded question that leads to his confession. Think of the word game 'Charades,' which utilizes "sounds like" words to identify famous songs, etc.; the super-intel works like that—it has an oral component. Thus we read, "I stand here today humbled by the *'ask'* before us...[in light of] the trust you have bestowed, mindful of the sacrifices borne by our [citizens today and our] ancestors." Humbled by the "ask"—the question— before us: Have you, Barack Hussein Obama, sacrificed the trust of American citizens along with the foundational efforts of our ancestors? His repeated question implies the answer—yes.

Grateful for Trust

Obama's confession will also bear out that, unconsciously, his moral compass is "grateful for...trust," grateful for the opportunity to confess, because the other side of Obama wants to be everything his father wasn't. He actually *wants* to be upstanding, reliable, and honorable. Just as strongly, however, another side of him wants to attack America. Which side will prevail? So far, the scheming, narcissistic politician has won out over the side that wants to make it right, that wants to confess and live a life of integrity. Later in his speech, Obama speaks of those who need to "do our business in the light of day" and "restore the vital trust between a people and their government." Unconsciously, he tells us, he's referring to himself.

We continue to watch Obama's tremendous inner battle play out. As much as his deception offends, we must be open enough to appreciate his innate moral compass. In the end he attempts to lead America through his failures, revealing an admiration of natural law completely in tune with the Declaration of Independence. That deep morality exists in everyone—no matter how hard, how self-deceitfully, they attempt to deny it. In his own way Obama will call America back to its deepest roots. We continue to decode his message—his stories, images and ideas from his freely speaking super intelligence.

Transition from a President Who Serves—and a False Oath

I thank President Bush for his service to our nation, as well as the generosity and cooperation he has shown throughout this transition. (Isp)

"Service to our nation" calls to mind the armed forces of which President George W. Bush had been a member (his Texas Air National Guard service); eventually he became its commander-in-chief. It rekindles memories of military battles fought by all four service branches to win and preserve our freedom—the cooperation, generosity and unity they demonstrated. He holds up an ideal—above all "serve America." Yet, Obama immediately implies he has already transitioned (a major keyword) and will continue to transition away from the expected service of a president. Instead, he'll adopt a selfish and uncooperative role.

Specifically he describes the country making a transition to a different type of president—a non-citizen—much less become commander-in-chief. In his speech Obama will confess how he has secretly transitioned away from 'service to nation' to 'sabotaging our nation' exactly as his mentor, community agitator Saul Alinsky, instructed. Shortly, Obama will return to the keyword "serve" in the second of two crucial stories about his father. Remember, his super intelligence carefully chooses every single word.

"Forty-four Americans have now taken the presidential oath. The words have been spoken during rising tides of prosperity and the still waters of peace. Yet, every so often, the oath is taken amidst gathering clouds and raging storms." (Isp) On the heels of his announced transition to a new type of president—a taker, not a server—Obama returns to the presidential oath twice in rapid succession, revealing just how intensely it preyed upon his mind. First he links the oath to the crucial citizenship issue, "Forty-four *Americans* have taken presidential oath." Bingo! *Obama again—obsessively—places the issue of his eligibility squarely on the table*. Is he legally the 44th American president, or have we only had 43? Insisting he is American raises a further question. Has he arrogantly presumed citizenship? Underscoring the specific number of presidents further suggests the instruction "count, and count carefully." Having continually confessed to his deception invites the reading, "Forty-four Americans—an overt untruth—means 'I have at this exact moment taken—stolen—the presidential oath and presidency.'" Sentence by sentence, phrase by phrase, image by image, Obama's confession spills out of him.

In fact, his assertion that 44 men have taken the oath happens to be a mistake. There have been 44 different presidencies, but one man, Grover Cleveland, served two of those terms, the 22nd and 24th presidencies. Even if you count Obama, 43 men—not 44—have taken the oath and only 42 Americans. His historical inaccuracy points to another subtle confession that the legality of his presidency is "way off." *Twice in the first three sentences* Obama has strikingly alluded to the citizenship matter—this time even more clearly and here he surrounds it with the word "oath," the most crucial message marker in his entire speech.

Unique Conditions of Obama Oath

The words have been spoken during rising tides of prosperity and the still waters of peace. Yet, every so often, the oath is taken amidst gathering clouds and raging storms. (ISp)

When he says *"The words* have been spoken" Obama suggests we should pay close attention to his words, implying "think super intelligence" which points to words on two levels, words that have two meanings. Go slowly. Read more deeply. He has just falsely spoken a sacred oath, and the words echo in his mind. First Obama tells us a president can speak the words—the oath—during "rising tides of prosperity and still waters of peace"—but not in his case. Establishing that America is mired in a crisis, he implies his presidency will lower our boat of prosperity, will storm against our peace.

Following with "every so often," implying never before like this, he tells us "the oath is taken amidst gathering clouds and raging storms." He's really saying, "I unconsciously swear that I am indeed a raging storm which has just descended on the presidency." Gathering clouds suggest a "cloudy presidency" covered in darkness exactly like the dark hole inside him. Similarly, he'll try to cover up the illegality of his presidency with clouds of obfuscation, avoidance and legal maneuverings.

Also identifying his hidden motive—the overwhelming anger eating away inside him—he confesses his intention to bring a dark cloud over the country while Americans witness a chaotic, secretly violent president. His ominous weather images perfectly mirror the identical images—thoughtprints—"heavy rains and fierce winds," the devastating storm that destroys foundations of homes in his 2008 Fathers' Day speech.

Roberts and Obama Fumble the Oath

Even more ominous, now we hear his implied confession, "America, today I have directly attacked your most basic foundation, the U.S. Constitution." As it happened, Obama incorrectly recited the presidential oath, *misplacing the word "faithfully."* Obama stated "...execute the office of president *faithfully.*" Justice Roberts quickly realized that he had initially recited the word "faithfully" out of order, and he corrected himself. Nevertheless, Obama persisted in the error—suggesting yet another unconscious confession that he was not faithful to the oath/Constitution. Obama's unconscious chose the one key word ("faithfully") to communicate, "Error, error—I am not a loyal president!" I suggest readers watch C-SPAN's video record of the ceremony to fully appreciate the various stumblings of both Roberts and Obama at http://youtu.be/VjnygQ02aW4.

To take it a step further, I suggest that Justice Roberts' own super intelligence had picked up on the illegality of Obama's presidency, and that Roberts made his slip-up to offer Obama a public test of his assumed faithfulness to America. Would Obama go with the error, or would he go with the correct way, which Roberts restated after his initial fumble? Obama's super intelligence answered: "I am an erroneous—unfaithful—president." Never underestimate the ability of the quick-read unconscious to craft such brilliant plans—and respond.

Due to those missteps, Roberts later administered the oath privately a second time, being uncertain of the strict legality of a botched oath the first time. During the discussion that followed, Obama joked about repeating the ceremony—because **"we decided it was so much fun."**[1] In other words, "It's so much fun to play games with America and the oath. Don't think I took it seriously." It was another confession, another disguised form of rage. Again the joke is on America—matching the conclusion of his pre-inauguration letter.

So It Must Be—The Constitution

At these moments, America has carried on not simply because of the skill or vision of those in high office, but because We the People have remained faithful to the ideals of our forebears and true to our founding documents.
So it has been. So it must be with this generation of Americans. (ISp)

On the heels of his self-description as a raging storm, Obama unconsciously makes five appeals to uphold the Constitution: "We the People," "faithful to the ideals of our forebears," "true to our founding documents," "So it has been," "So it must be...with this generation of Americans." Notice "it must be"—he does not say that it *is*. He suggests this generation—specifically, himself—has trouble with such loyalty, making the strongest of confessions he has violated the Constitution, stormed against it as an illegal alien.

Four references to America/Americans in the first two sentences, including "We the People," further point to his guilt-ridden preoccupation with our nation and his need to confess. Extremely early into his speech Obama unconsciously screams, "American—American—American—faithful and true to Constitution—must be—must be—oath—oath." His desperation is palpable, his instruction plain: "Make sure I'm an American citizen—it must be." His deeper moral compass will not be silent—secretly revealing his other story, his other side.

By insisting so easily that he's an American, Obama embodies the title of his second book, *The Audacity of Hope,* which can be reinterpreted unconsciously as the inverse: *The Hope of Audacity.* Unequivocally he demonstrates incredible audacity by illegally assuming citizenship so easily. He also implies, "America has carried on not...because of...those in high office." He's urging the people to carry on in spite of his illegal presidency.

The Constitutional Crisis—War and Attack

That we are in the midst of crisis is now well understood. Our nation is at war, against a far-reaching network of violence and hatred. Our

---

1 Stephen Silverman, "Obama Repeats Oath of Office—This Time, Faithfully," January 22, 2009. People TV Archives, http://people.com/people/article/0,,20254160,00.html accessed May 20, 2012.

economy is badly weakened, a consequence of greed and irresponsibility on the part of some, but also our collective failure to make hard choices and prepare the nation for a new age. Homes have been lost; jobs shed; businesses shuttered. Our health care is too costly; our schools fail too many; and each day brings further evidence that the ways we use energy strengthen our adversaries and threaten our planet. These are the indicators of crisis, subject to data and statistics. (ISp)

From the powerful confession of a raging storm tossing the Constitution into the wind, Obama links this to an even more disturbing image: America at war with a deceptive foreign enemy.

With the key message marker "well understood," Obama highlights the message: "America, understand at this moment—'now'—I have just created a constitutional crisis." Next describing a far-reaching—implying foreign—network of violence and hatred, Obama makes an unconscious pronouncement: "As an illegal foreign-born president, I have just declared war on America, The Constitution, the forefathers, and current citizens." His image of a covert network of violence and hatred suggests Obama is not consciously aware of such anger although he's obviously aware of his deceit. Yet he confesses just how violent his super intelligence views his actions—what he has done by being unfaithful and untrue to our founding documents. Clearly he understands deep down that such an attack on our most basic foundation reflects "hatred"—his own word. Later in his speech, he predicts "the old hatreds shall someday pass." But remember, his hate stems directly from the hateful wounds caused by his father; they will not easily go away without the deep insight he lacks.

Alluding to a "network" of people in on the plan, he suggests that others in his campaign (his wife for sure) know the truth. His super intelligence/unconscious mind—honest to the core—never holds back. Repeatedly, his unconscious will underscore in this speech, "America is indeed in a crisis—with an illegal, secretly anti-American president—and our nation must take action if it is to survive." He has pointed out the first step of a decidedly subversive Saul Alinsky-type plan to penetrate America's command structure with the goal of destruction.

We find other vital aspects to his hidden confession. "Strengthen adversaries" refers to his foreign-born status automatically making him the constitutional adversary we have strengthened. He underscores "failure to...prepare the nation for a new age" pointing again to our leaders who by failing to investigate him have left America totally unprepared for the Obama Age with his covert plans. Unconsciously Obama announces what the media and Congress missed. In "indicators of crisis, subject to data and statistics," Obama's super-intel then points to exactly what should have been examined. He suggests data exists which proves his illegal status. Unmistakably he points toward the available data—the birth certificate or COLB such as it is. Later in Chapter 15 we will take the matter up.

And for the record he emphasizes his "irresponsibility...failure to make hard choices"—the clear message is that he recognizes he never should've run for president; he should have told Sen. Harry Reid "No" when his presidential run was first proposed to him as early as July 2006 in a surprise one-on-one meeting with the Senate Minority Leader on Capitol Hill.[2] Later he makes the identical confession, noting "our time...of protecting narrow interests and putting off unpleasant decisions—that time has surely passed." Obama unconsciously, but repeatedly, expresses thoughts about resigning as president.

He points out that his attack on America is far broader, far more threatening than "simply" breaking the law to become president. Obama refers here to a deceptive, violent, foreign force—reminiscent of the stealth attacks by Muslim extremists of 9/11—making plain his attacks will be disguised, as deceptive as he can possibly make them, again Alinsky-style. One of the continual myths surrounding Obama by many who greatly oppose his policies and have experienced first-hand his attack on America is that he's still a likeable man, 'just misguided.' Yet Obama establishes that his likeability is part and parcel of the deceptive front which Alinsky prescribed in his definitive revolutionary tome, *Rules for Radicals: a Practical Primer for Realistic Radicals.* Of all critics no one describes the real Obama with more brutal honesty than his own super intelligence labeling him a "raging storm...a far reaching network of violence." Unconsciously he emphasizes what our leaders and the media will not: the question of his eligibility is central to our democracy and an illegal presidency would announce that he fully well operates in the Alinsky-style in which he was trained—completely invested in it.

Link Key Ideas to Tell Story

A quick review of Obama's sequence of ideas and images reveals how he tells one continuous story, a narrative that corroborates his confession. Immediately Obama introduces the question of where he stands, that he is humbled, then introduces the birth question, linking it to sacrifices of ancestors. Next we find his oath taken under conditions of a raging storm—followed by desperate appeals to live by the Constitution—then America is in a constitutional crisis and at war with violent foreigner(s) who hate America. He follows with images of attacks on America's basic foundations with warnings of a global threat and predictions of America's inevitable decline. Finally he mentions someone who protects narrow interests and puts off unpleasant decisions.

When we explore the highlights of his speech, we find that he provides a historical never-before-seen view inside the mind of a powerful man carrying out an unimaginable plan.

---

2 John Heilemann and Mark Halperin, *Game Change: Obama and the Clintons, McCain and Palin, and the Race of a Lifetime* (New York: HarperCollins, 2010), 32-33.

Effect on America

> Less measurable but no less profound is a sapping of confidence across our land—a nagging fear that America's decline is inevitable, and that the next generation must lower its sights. Today I say to you that the challenges we face are real. They are serious and they are many. They will not be met easily or in a short span of time. But know this, America: They will be met. (ISp)

Obama paints vivid pictures of an electorate that unwittingly ushered in his illegal presidency: America had just declined, lowered its sights, and lost confidence in its great character while paying scant attention to the Constitution. Obama also describes in detail the intent of his attack: to sap America's confidence and great character, to make certain of our nation's inevitable decline so that the next generation must lower its sights. His unconscious mind makes known his motive: deep and bitter envy. He will bring America down just as his missing father lowered young Obama's sights.

He emphasizes that his attack began "today," that the "challenges [are] real...serious...and many." Yet his deeper moral compass assures us with a vivid message marker, "know"—"know this, America: they will be met." He's secretly telling us in this very speech that he will unconsciously show us how to meet his challenge. We see the two sides of Obama: the false hero filled with rage, and the true hero who confesses and points the way out for America

Motives Described—Childhood Issues

> On this day, we gather because we have chosen hope over fear, unity of purpose over conflict and discord. On this day, we come to proclaim an end to the petty grievances and false promises, the recriminations and worn-out dogmas, that for far too long have strangled our politics.
>
> We remain a young nation, but in the words of Scripture, the time has come to set aside childish things. (ISp)

After beginning his story with the strongest of confessions, Obama takes us to his major motive for the misguided anger he aims at America. He introduces his unresolved childhood pain—and how he transferred that pain onto America as we have discussed in Chapter 10. There we explored parts of his inaugural address. Now we review the same preeminent speech in more detail chronologically.

First he reveals that his need to become president grew out of his desperate denial of the deep "fear... conflict and discord" which controlled him. He attempted to simply proclaim his family pain away, by proclaiming himself president. Likewise he attempted to "proclaim an end to...petty grievances and false promises, the recriminations and worn-out dogmas, that for far too long have strangled" him. His severe abuse leaps off the pages at us, particularly "strangled"—pointing unmistakably toward his near abortion to which he will return several times. You simply don't wish away such excruciating pain.

To confirm he's unconsciously referring to his childhood, he continues, "We remain a young nation," as if to say, "I remain forever young fixated, entrapped in my frozen development." Even so, Obama's super intelligence refuses to excuse him: "in the words of Scripture [one of the strongest message markers], the time has come to set aside childish things." Deep down he knows he can't misuse the presidency in such a childish way, and we have yet another implied instruction to himself: "Step aside, step down as president." "Give up your childish presidency"—a familiar self-description.

Moral Compass Reminder: The Constitution—the Time Has Come

The time has come to reaffirm our enduring spirit; to choose our better history; to carry forward that precious gift, that noble idea, passed on from generation to generation: the God-given promise that all are equal, all are free, and all deserve a chance to pursue their full measure of happiness. (Isp)

We note references to: "enduring spirit... better history... precious gift...noble idea, passed on...God-given promise...all equal, free, deserve chance to pursue...happiness." Both the Constitution and the Declaration of Independence echo in his words. He emphasizes "choice"—that Americans can *choose* whether or not to be guided by our better history and founding documents or to suffer the consequences of a fraudulent leader.

In the 2008 election, millions of voters and most of the media were unconcerned about the issue of Obama's eligibility. Their apathy will have grave consequence, he warns. His prescience illustrates how his deeper observations remain far superior to those routinely made in the media. We can see his deepest longing to bring about a return to the time-honored moral compass we have lost—God's compass, the natural law which the Declaration so unmistakably espoused.

Entitled Obama Took Shortcut to the Presidency

In reaffirming the greatness of our nation, we understand that greatness is never a given. It must be earned. Our journey has never been one of shortcuts or settling for less. It has not been the path for the fainthearted—for those who prefer leisure over work, or seek only the pleasures of riches and fame. Rather, it has been the risk-takers... (ISp)

Obama's unconscious organizes his story in an amazingly logical way. He transitions smoothly from the Constitution to our nation's "greatness" to the ideas of "shortcuts" and "risk."

Clearly his main message here is: *he was given the greatness of the presidency, he didn't earn it, he took a shortcut—and he settled for less.* Remember, his code word for the presidency is "journey." When he says, "Our journey has never been one of shortcuts or settling for less," we read straight through his denial to see that it was, in fact, exactly that. He took the easy way—leisure over work—and sought the office for the riches and the fame as a desperate attempt to fill that deep hole of pain that has remained with him since childhood.

And a mesmerized electorate "settled for less" in choosing an illegal president. Mistakenly, they were in on all the fame and acclaim, the false excitement of the moment with the media 'slobbering all over themselves,' as Bernard Goldberg described.[3] Most of all they were focused in on the charity, the entitlement, while ignoring the requirements for the job. The super intelligence, as I have said, does not fool around. At crucial points it cuts no one any slack. It tells it like it is.

Obama's super intelligence lays out for all to see just how much denial we live with in our culture, and how destructive it can be. He continues to contrast the innate God-given wisdom of our super intelligence—the "other 90 percent of our brains"—with our amazingly limited conscious (10%) mind. This is his message from start to finish. *Nobody had a clue that Obama the professor had given the greatest single public lecture ever on modern psychology.* He demonstrated that when the unconscious mind goes unheard, it becomes more and more obvious. We see this in such thinly disguised messages *of not earning the presidency* presented through classic denial, "nation... greatness is never...given" set off by the important message marker, "we understand." His presidency was a gift. Jumping ahead in his speech, he repeatedly confirms the same message.

> *...that a nation cannot prosper long when it favors only the prosperous.* The success of our [country] economy has always depended...on the reach of our prosperity; on our ability to extend opportunity to every willing heart—*not out of charity*, but because it is the surest route to our common good. (ISp)

Here Obama tells us such charity is the surest route to our failure—that under such conditions our "nation cannot prosper long when it favors" any one person or any single group. But he was the one prospering in a largely unchallenged campaign favored by the media and the manic euphoria surrounding his candidacy. He immediately follows with "extend opportunity...not out of charity"—confessing through yet another denial to "his presidency, The Act of Charity."

He also tells us, in "the reach of our prosperity," that his presidency is unquestionably a "reach," outside the boundaries—that he simply took it.

Obama's Great Risk—and America's

> ...Greatness is never a given...must be earned. Our journey...never...one of shortcuts or settling for less...for those who prefer leisure over work, or seek only the pleasures of riches and fame... risk-takers... (Isp)

---

3 Bernard Goldberg, *A Slobbering Love Affair: The True (And Pathetic) Story of the Torrid Romance Between Barack Obama and the Mainstream Media* (Washington DC: Regnery, 2009).

We must appreciate his unconsciously linking "risk-takers" to his scathing description of his behavior—that his took shortcuts to his unearned presidency, settling for less, seeking fame and riches. Introducing the idea of risk-takers implies the question, "How big of a risk did Obama take becoming an illegal president?" And "How big of a risk did America take in electing one?" As we have noted, he provided the answers by pointing out that his presidency represented a harmful charity—a selfish reach on his part—a risk which threatened America's very survival.

The Risk Persists

Risking media and congressional disdain and condemnation, some brave Americans across the country continue to call for a full investigation of Obama's alleged long-form birth certificate, the one he reluctantly released in April 2011. In his statements, books and letters he has repeatedly confessed unconsciously that he was born in Africa. Somewhat more subtly his super intelligence has also admitted that both his short-form birth certificate released in 2008 and his long-form birth certificate are phony (which Chapter 15 will address).

Deep down, Obama anticipates an independent document examination of his (original, paper) birth certificate, while on the surface he continues to insist that the online version is authentic. If exposed as an illegal alien, he imagines race riots would break out, necessitating his having to activate the National Guard. As we have seen, in his pre-inauguration letter to his daughters he mentioned having "to send our young men and women into war and *other dangerous situations* to protect our country."

What if independent document examiners did determine that Obama's online birth certificate is indeed a complete fraud? We can envision the 24/7 headline news anchors saying:

> After being submitted to document analysis two weeks ago, President Obama's long-form birth certificate was unanimously judged fraudulent by the independent team of forensic examiners, the U.S. Justice Department announced today. The experts concluded that the document was created by computer graphics specialists, likely located in Honolulu. The investigation is continuing under the direction of the FBI.

> The announcement has prompted a resurgence of race riots across the country. Republicans led by the speaker of the house are calling for impeachment proceedings to begin. On Wall Street, financial markets continue spiraling downward.

Such a crisis would immediately call into question all of Obama's legislation, including Obamacare. All his U.S. Supreme Court appointees could be invalidated. All his administrative czars would likely face quick dismissal, and cabinet appointees would be likewise voided.

Given the economic instability in foreign markets, the possibility of a world-wide depression would grow even more likely than it is today. Vice

President Joe Biden would take over as president. National security and the military would be shaken. Our enemies certainly would attempt to exploit Biden's surprise presidency. Already, America's very foundations all have been shaken, but if the birth certificate proves inauthentic, those foundations will be tested from top to bottom.

For his part, Obama would stand by his birth certificate, insisting his citizenship is legal. Left-leaning journalists and the mainstream media would echo cries of "racism," fueling the flames of chaos. Meanwhile the National Guard would be called out to quell riots in cities around the nation. Dozens— perhaps hundreds—would die from the violence. The nation would sit on pins and needles.

It's a frightening possibility and stranger things have happened. Encouraged by Sheriff Joe Arpaio, the people now push for official examination of his birth certificate and the nation is only one short step away from that kind of violence. One person who has told us so is Barack Obama himself. No wonder he linked his presidency with a threat to the entire world. And the ominous ramifications of the risk Obama took by illegally assuming the presidency explain why the media, the Congress, and the courts could never entertain the real possibility of his foreign birth. It is altogether too overwhelming, too hard a truth, for a biased, fearful media to face. The media, like much of America, simply can't handle the truth. And because of that they exposed America to great risk—indeed they have been huge "risk-takers." The risk they took in not investigating Obama created a far greater risk.

In his book, *The Amateur: Barack Obama in the White House*, Edward Klein reveals much of Obama's presidential ineptness but overlooked the risk Obama took. Truth be told, Obama had a far more malevolent plan for the nation, a plan in which he has succeeded beyond his wildest imagination—so far. He has successfully sabotaged the major foundations of America, most of all our Constitution. His confession to that plan continues in the next chapter.

13

Inauguration Speech, Part II

Foolish Risk-Taking

> Rather, it has been the risk-takers, the doers, the makers of things—some celebrated, but more often men and women obscure in their labor—who have carried us up the long, rugged path toward prosperity and freedom.
>
> For us, they packed up their few worldly possessions and traveled across oceans in search of a new life. For us, they toiled in sweatshops and settled the West; endured the lash of the whip and plowed the hard earth. For us, they fought and died, in places like Concord and Gettysburg; Normandy and Khe Sahn.
>
> Time and again, these men and women struggled and sacrificed and worked till their hands were raw so that we might live a better life. They saw America as bigger than the sum of our individual ambitions; greater than all the differences of birth or wealth or faction. This is the journey we continue today. (ISp)

Amidst the crucial confession of his huge risk, Obama's brilliant unconscious picks this precise moment to confess that he was born in Africa and does so with several embedded but distinct references to that continent and several convincing 'birth markers.' First we follow the major ideas, "Risk-taker...celebrated...more often men and women obscure." Read: "I appear celebrated, but really I am an obscure person along with my equally celebrated, equally obscure wife. In fact, I am foreign-born and actually from Africa as my clues reveal."

Notice how the risk-takers are all foreigners who "traveled across oceans," "settled the West." "endured the lash of the whip"—suggesting slaves, African foreigners. Next, he makes several references to foreign enemies America had to fight in battles at Concord (on American soil), Normandy and Khe Sahn (Viet Nam). The unconscious message: "America, draw on your patriot heritage and fight the foreign usurper who is now your president." His other battle reference was to Gettysburg, the turning point of the American Civil War, unconsciously implying he had come to divide Americans, over his illegal presidency.

After describing foreigners coming across oceans to America he underscores, "This is the journey *we* continue today"—unconsciously identifying the journey from Africa as his trip. Again Obama tells the same story—how the illegal presidency represents his fruitless but utterly desperate attempt to claim a new life. Obama also implies he traveled a great distance on his path to his presidency, the result of a long-running plan. And he implies that America has a "long, rugged path toward" reclaiming its "prosperity and freedom." Once he assumed his unlawful presidency he realized how difficult it would be for anyone to remove him—America's first black president—from the highest office in the land.

In the end, however, Obama suggests that our nation will rise up to defeat him after Americans realize that his unconscious confession of his illicit presidency makes his foreign-born status clear. Meanwhile, he sweats it out daily as Americans attempt to ferret out the truth about him—a task which our leaders and our mainstream media have callously ignored. Millions of Americans now oppose Obama because of his attack on the economy but also because they believe he's foreign-born as his own words confirm.

Co-risk Takers: Michelle and Barack

Time and again, these men and women struggled and sacrificed and worked till their hands were raw so that we might live a better life. They saw America as bigger than the sum of our individual ambitions; greater than all the differences of birth or wealth or faction. (ISp)

We find a perfect match with "risk-takers"—the striking confession of Barack's and Michelle's intentions hidden in his sequence of ideas, "Time and again these men and women struggled... raw." Obama's administration has certainly been a "raw" deal for our country.

Why did the two of them so conspire? He answers, "so that we might live a better life." He then tells us, "They [We] saw America as...the sum of our individual ambitions; greater than all the differences of birth...wealth." Read it this way: "Michelle and I both saw America—the presidency—as the ultimate in our ambition." And that extreme ambition greater than Obama's vastly different foreign birth which would keep him—and them—out of office and away from all the wealth and prestige of the presidency. Notice another key birth marker, "differences of birth," implying "different birth"—foreign birth—yet keeping the "birth" idea front and center.

In the same imagery Obama also reveals that his and his wife's efforts amount to a hands-on raw grab for power ("their hands were raw")—that America was not only getting a "raw" president, a rookie, but also a "raw" deal because his presidency is in essence imaginary.[1] In the phrase, "sum of our individual ambitions...factions" his super intelligence admits the couple's wish to divide America, one other aspect to America's raw deal.

---

1 Obama already knew deep down that he would be a rank amateur when it came to the presidency. How accurate his observation was, as Ed Klein underscored three years later in his 2012 book on Obama, *The Amateur.*

Obama concludes this section, "This is the *journey* we continue *today*" reflecting "this is the presidency we continue today—remember, the word "journey" is Obama's code for "presidency," the ride on which they've taken America particularly "today," the day of deception finally enacted.

In effect Obama says, "I present to you our presidency, mine and Michelle's," summing up three straight times the first couple's byword, *"for us."* A joint version of *"all about me"*(Obama's earlier self-description). Indeed they have behaved like it, spending freely on themselves and their family.

We find another vital message in his depiction of women who worked hard to give someone a better life: the picture of his mother (and grandmother) working behind the scenes getting her hands bloody to obtain an illegal— "raw"—birth certificate in Hawaii to give him a better life. This would fit with getting her son "settled in the West"—as though he belonged there all along. Exactly like *"search for a new life"* in America suggests obtaining a new identity, a new birth certificate but simultaneously the instruction to search the matter out to establish his false identity. In short that evidence exists (see Chapter 15).

More Danger in Africa

In reaffirming the greatness of our nation, we understand that greatness is never a given. It must be earned. Our journey has never been one of shortcuts or settling for less. It has not been the path for the fainthearted -- for those who prefer leisure over work, or seek only the pleasures of riches and fame. Rather, it has been the risk-takers, the doers, the makers of things -- some celebrated, but more often men and women obscure in their labor -- who have carried us up the long, rugged path toward prosperity and freedom.

For us, they packed up their few worldly possessions and traveled across oceans in search of a new life. **For us,** they toiled in sweatshops and settled the West; endured the lash of the whip and plowed the hard earth. **For us,** they fought and died, in places like Concord and Gettysburg; Normandy and Khe Sahn. (ISp)

Yet there's another aspect to his story upon which he unconsciously appears to have shed major light—the time right after his birth when he crossed the ocean with this mother to escape from this father. In the context of "reaffirming the greatness of our nation" Obama implies "reaffirming the greatness of life"—namely his precarious life. He suggests that his life was not a given, that it was earned by this mother's hard work, a mother not at all fainthearted, Instead, she stood up to the shortcut of an abortion and "settling for less" the way Obama Sr. wanted. Her son called her "a risk-taker, a doer, a maker of things." Above all a mother is a people-maker, reflecting The Maker, The Creator in whose image we all are made. Again Obama notes that not only was his life at risk but that his mother took a huge risk standing up to his father. He next speaks of *"women obscure in their labor who have carried us"*—two commanding maternal images of childbirth and pregnancy with the personal emphasis on "us" suggesting "me." And his mother, he suggests, carried him "up the long, rugged path toward prosperity and freedom." This, of course, is not really a reference to the clichéd ideals of American achievement. It actually suggests a pitched battle with his father that continued until Obama experienced the prosperity and freedom of his own birth.

His images also continue to tell a sequential story. Beginning with three references to "for us" he tells us my mother did this "for me." She packed up, *traveled across the ocean* for a new life in America (the West) with her son, preserving his new life. Another life-threatening event took place in Africa shortly after his birth, he suggests. There, amidst Obama Sr.'s African family, Ann Dunham sweated things out, "endured the lash of the whip" from his father. Essentially she fought a war in a foreign country so that they might have a better life in America—so that Obama might live. "Time and again, these...women struggled and sacrificed and worked till their hands were raw so that we might live" suggests his mother (after the near abortion) fought another battle with his father there in Kenya, perhaps an encounter in which she had to defend herself with her own hands.

Is it possible that Obama Sr.—in one of his characteristic fits of uncontrolled rage—threatened his white wife's life? Or threatened the defenseless newborn boy? The feisty, ultraliberal new mother would have fought back, saving herself and her baby just as she had done when she refused to undergo an abortion. Obama knows that he owes his very existence to his mother, likely twice. The phrase "freedom and prosperity" indicates that she kept him alive twice, once by rejecting abortion and again when Obama Sr. attacked her/them. All in all, Obama unconsciously points to precisely why his mother immediately took him far away from his father to Seattle after she returned to America.

Super Intelligence 'Work To Be Done.'

We remain the most prosperous, powerful nation on Earth. Our workers are no less productive than when this crisis began. Our minds are no less inventive, our goods and services no less needed than they were last week or last month or last year. Our capacity remains undiminished. But our time of standing pat, of protecting narrow interests and putting off unpleasant decisions—that time has surely passed. Starting today, we must pick ourselves up, dust ourselves off, and begin again the work of remaking America.

For everywhere we look, there is work to be done. The state of the economy calls for action, bold and swift, and we will act—not only to create new jobs, but to lay a new foundation for growth. We will build the roads and bridges, the electric grids and digital lines that feed our commerce and bind us together. We will restore science to its rightful place, and wield technology's wonders to raise health care's quality and lower its cost. We will harness the sun and the winds and the soil to fuel our cars and run our factories. And we will transform our schools and college and universities to meet the demands of a new age. All this we can do. And all this we will do.(ISp)

After continually confessing that he is an African-born illegal president, at this crucial juncture Obama stops to repeatedly showcase the super intelligence which conveys the confession. In his inauguration speech, delivered on the day he assumes power, he most vehemently emphasizes the pivotal role of his unconscious mind.

We find multiple references to the super intelligence here—starting with a subtle one.

1. He informs us, "We remain the most prosperous, powerful nation on earth. Our workers are no less productive than when this crisis began." He's saying America can remain the most prosperous powerful nation on earth only if it uses the most powerful and productive part of the mind—the other 90 percent, the super intelligence. Only then can we can hear Obama truly speaking from his heart, again announcing he has just created a constitutional "crisis"—and a continual crisis along the way.

2. His next reference: "Our capacity remains undiminished" informs that the super intelligence remains in the mind at full capacity.

3. "Restoring science to its rightful place" means: give the new unconscious mind its rightful place—it communicates scientifically accurate messages and represents a true communication science of the mind.

4. "Wield technology's wonders to raise health care's quality and lower its cost," points out that unconscious intelligence is a "new technology" here aiming to protect our nation from Obama's costly presidential assault.

The super intelligence seeks students who understand the marked limitations of their conscious mind and demonstrate open-mindedness.[2] In short, it seeks people who can handle the truth that the conscious mind can easily fool you.

'Look At Who I Am'

> Our time of standing pat, of protecting narrow interests and putting off unpleasant decisions—that time has surely passed.

> For everywhere we look, there is work to be done. The state of the economy calls for action, bold and swift, and we will act—not only to create new jobs, but to lay a new foundation for growth. (ISp)

Yet again Obama describes precisely what he has done: stood pat, protected his narrow interests, put off the unpleasant decision to decline to run for re-election because he knows he was ineligible and his opportunity to come clean has passed. Instead he has conspired to create fraudulent birth certificates.

---

2 In another speech at Notre Dame University in 2009 Obama insisted that our abortion crisis could be solved by "open-mindedness," hinting strongly that new knowledge may well emerge—as we will see is the case with the super intelligence.

Simultaneously his super intelligence continues to urge Americans *not* to put off their unpleasant task of confronting him. Substitute "presidency" for "economy"—the one word synonymous with Obama and his plans. Read it this way: "Look everywhere [message marker], there is work to be done, the state of the presidency [including devastating economic plans] calls for bold swift action—act, lay a new foundation for growth." Obama's illegal presidency demands bold action to bring in a new, legal president to give America a true "foundation." How well the secret sequential story fits. It transforms Obama's narrative into the truth of narrow interests and deception. His unconscious brilliantly selects keywords such as "transform" to completely revamp his image.

My Ambition, My Government Work, My Bad Habits'—Breaking Trust

Now, there are some who question the scale of our ambitions—who suggest that our system cannot tolerate too many big plans. Their memories are short. For they have forgotten what this country has already done; what free men and women can achieve when imagination is joined to common purpose, and necessity to courage.

What the cynics fail to understand is that the ground has shifted beneath them—that the stale political arguments that have consumed us for so long no longer apply. The question we ask today is not whether our government is too big or too small, but whether it works—whether it helps families find jobs at a decent wage, care they can afford, a retirement that is dignified. Where the answer is yes, we intend to move forward. Where the answer is no, programs will end. And those of us who manage the public's dollars will be held to account—to spend wisely, reform bad habits, and do our business in the light of day—because only then can we restore the vital trust between a people and their government. (ISp)

First Obama instructs us to "question the scale of [his] ambition"—confessing that our government cannot tolerate such big plans of living outside the foundation provided by our founding documents. *He reminds us of the enormous risk he took.* His memory is also short. He has forgotten what this country has done in its common purpose of declaring men free during the Civil War.

At the same time Obama presents a scathing indictment of those who would ignore a potential illegal president failing to remain true to founding documents: "What the cynics fail to understand is that the ground has shifted beneath them—that the stale political arguments that have consumed us for so long no longer apply." (Isp) "Understand," he shouts, "the ground has shifted beneath" this country "when...stale political arguments [principles] no longer apply." Cynically, Obama confesses he has dissed the 'stale' Constitution without another thought. Understand his byword, *rules,* as in rules *"no longer apply"* to him.

189

The Question

The major question on his Inauguration Day is "whether our government works—whether it helps families." At that exact moment, is he helping or hurting the American family?

Does an illegal presidency really work for America? Does it help America to shake our very foundations? Does it help when the rules of our political life no longer apply to a president? Are we paying a decent price for a decent president, or are we paying too high a price for an illegal presidency which degrades our country's character? Can an illegal president truly provide the care America needs?

Obama tells us, "the answer is no...those of us who manage the public...will be held to account to...reform bad habits...do our business in the light of day...only then can we restore the vital trust between a people and their government." He comes back to the most important issue for a president—integrity and trust. The very principle he underscored in his opening sentence ("humbled by...the trust you have bestowed"), now he secretly informs us again that he has violated America's sacred trust, violated our founders who "pledged their lives, their fortunes and their sacred honor" to form our country by constructing a perpetual 'living Constitution.'

Obama confesses that he has dishonored America, himself and his family. Later he will tell us he has dishonored his own race. Deep down he demands to be held accountable: "to reform bad habits" of deceit. Obama knows the way to greatness for him—"restore the trust of the people" with "dignity," as in "retire with dignity" (which he links to "yes"). As in "find a job" and "we intend to move"—leave office. And he's not through yet. Desperately, he longs to come into the "light of day" as a person.

'A Watchful Eye'

> Nor is the question before us whether the market is a force for good or ill. Its power to generate wealth and expand freedom is unmatched, but this crisis has reminded us that without a watchful eye, the market can spin out of control—and that a nation cannot prosper long when it favors only the prosperous. (ISp)

After his core confession about breaking our trust, Obama picks up the pace, becoming more and more confrontational of his egregious ways with increasingly powerful imagery. Simply following his ideas, "the question before us...force for good or ill." Remember a favorite Obama code word for his "presidency" is the "economy" or here "the market [force]." Through denial, he again introduces "the question before us"—"whether the market [aka his presidency] is a force for good or ill," good or evil (as "ill" suggests). He notes that "its power...is unmatched." Indeed the president is the single-most powerful person in the world—and Obama implies he has forced his presidency on us. Introducing the idea of good or evil, Obama deep down identifies his deception as evil.

190

Then he answers his question with a (constitutional) crisis warning about this powerful force underscoring it with the message marker "watchful eye." Read *without* a watchful eye, our president "can spin out of control." He confesses again vividly that as an illegitimate president he has already spun out of control, presenting a crisis of the first order. The cause: America lacked a watchful eye with no thorough investigation of his presidential qualifications. Again he implies an investigation should take place immediately. In fact the phrase "watchful eye" reflects a powerful image of the all-seeing deeper mind.

Charter Upholds Rule of Law

As for our common defense, we reject as false the choice between our safety and our ideals. Our Founding Fathers, faced with perils we can scarcely imagine, drafted a charter to assure the rule of law and the rights of man, a charter expanded by the blood of generations. Those ideals still light the world, and we will not give them up for expedience' sake. (ISp)

Obama shouts at us his most obvious confession: *"we reject...false choice"*—his presidency is not authentic. Then he warns us to "reject the false choice between our safety and our ideals." He implies that his false presidency threatens our safety, but that we must not give up our ideals. Taking it a step further he links "our safety" with violent images-- "perils we can scarcely imagine" and "(spilled) blood of generations."

Unconsciously he suggests an ominous warning: that if truly challenged as an illegal president he would enable race riots, creating unimaginable perils for America. We note that in the autumn of 2011 Obama publicly supported the Wall Street protestors who threaten riots to accomplish their goals.

But his overriding hidden message remains, "Don't be intimidated by me"—"Don't give up your ideals out of fear." Obama's moral compass insists: we must face the peril he has created with "our common defense"—the Constitution, the rule of law, our charter which carries ideals that light the world. Later, he will refer to himself as our "common enemy." He admonishes, "do not give them up for expedience' sake"—describing his exact behavior as an ineligible president. He has chosen this key moment in his speech for another powerful repetitious shout-out, "Constitution, Constitution, Constitution." Next he explains precisely why.

Specific African Birth References

And so to all other peoples and governments who are watching today, from the grandest capitals to the small village where my father was born: Know that America is a friend of each nation and every man, woman and child who seeks a future of peace and dignity, and that we are ready to lead once more. (ISp)

Obama now speaks to the whole world including all American citizens, to himself and to foreign governments "who are watching today"—a vital message marker. He predicts that his next comment will be stupendous and will explain why he has so passionately highlighted the Constitution and his violation of it. Now, in the message, "from the grandest capitals to the small village where my father was born," Obama spotlights the small village in Kenya—where *he* was born. This is a striking *birth marker* of the highest order—as thinly disguised as possible by his unconscious—pointing unmistakably to his African nativity exactly as his step-grandmother claimed. For good measure he unconsciously confirms the image of his long journey from the small village in Africa to the "grandest capital," Washington, D.C.—on this very day. (Furthermore, he suggests that his father was with him when he was born in Kenya.)

Unconsciously Obama has built idea bridges—linking seemingly different roads of thought together—to get to one central destination. We can see how scientific his super intelligence is, how he confirms the same message over and over: that he came to America across the ocean from the east, the same journey made by slave ships from Africa.

How logical his deeper mind? How verifiable? This explains why Obama's superior unconscious recognized his communications as messages that could be understood using the new science of the mind. His confession represents the only scientific evidence we have of his Kenyan birth.

Next we see Obama logically unfolding his story to bring us back to his most basic motive—his deepest childhood pain. His super intelligence appeals for understanding from us and from himself: "Know that America is a friend of each nation and every man, woman and child who seeks a future of peace and dignity." Read: America is a friend of a child from each nation who seeks peace with it, implying America is at war with a foreign child that attacks America.

Confessing to Other Nations

Between the lines, Obama apologizes to foreign nations for misleading them as well—for failing to be a friend of dignity and peace. His foreign policies will increase world turmoil and make peace more precarious. Now his "apology tour" comes into focus. One commentator in the *Wall Street Journal* noted:

> President Barack Obama has finished the second leg of his international confession tour. In less than 100 days, he has apologized on three continents for what he views as the sins of America and his predecessors. Mr. Obama told the French (the French!) that America "has shown arrogance and been dismissive, even derisive" toward Europe. In Prague, he said America has "a moral responsibility to act" on arms control because only the U.S. had "used a nuclear weapon." ...And in Latin America, he said the U.S. had not "pursued and sustained engagement with our neighbors" because we "failed to see that our own progress is tied directly to progress throughout the Americas."

By confessing our nation's sins, White House Press Secretary Robert Gibbs said that Mr. Obama has "changed the image of America around the world" and made the U.S. "safer and stronger."[3]

Take note of that last sentence, and the level of denial when Obama's press secretary delivers the ludicrous conclusion that weakness will yield greater national security. By "confessing our nation's sins," we know that Obama was secretly apologizing for his own deceitful behavior. He was the one who "has shown arrogance and been dismissive, even derisive" toward the United States. He was the one who had turned the weapon of an illegal presidency on America and therefore was "unable to sustain an engagement with" our country. Obama reveals how his super intelligence continues to confess in multiple settings.

Fascism, Communism, and Entitled Behavior

Recall that earlier generations faced down fascism and communism not just with missiles and tanks, but with sturdy alliances and enduring convictions. They understood that our power alone cannot protect us, nor does it entitle us to do as we please. Instead, they knew that our power grows through its prudent use; our security emanates from the justness of our cause, the force of our example, the tempering qualities of humility and restraint. (ISp)

Obama confesses that his aggressive grab for power was demonstrably fascistic, like a communist who simply runs over people taking, by brute strength, whatever he wants. He hints at his philosophy of government along the subversive lines of Saul Alinsky who sought power for power's sake. In these strong self-accusations Obama indirectly admits just how egregiously he has attacked America, how overpowering is his inner rage. He then strongly appeals again to our Constitution, urging citizens "to face him down," to confront him.

Even more plainly, he then emphasizes a central problem, the notion that he's "entitled to do as he pleases"—entitled to the presidency because of all he has suffered. Obama represents a textbook case in which personal trauma distorts the mind, telling someone he is owed something. In fact Obama underscores a significant underlying influence as to how he was elected president—because many Americans thought a black man was *entitled* to be president.

Peace Possible if Warring Foreigner Leaves

We are the keepers of this legacy. Guided by these principles once more, we can meet those new threats that demand even greater effort—even greater cooperation and understanding between nations. We will begin to responsibly leave Iraq to its people, and forge a hard-earned peace in Afghanistan. With old friends and former foes, we will work tirelessly to lessen the nuclear threat, and roll back the specter of a warming planet. We will not apologize for our way of life, nor will we waver in its defense, and for those who

---

3 Karl Rove, "The President's Apology Tour: Great Leaders Aren't Defined by Consensus," http://online.wsj.com/article/SB124044156269345357.html accessed April 29, 2012.

seek to advance their aims by inducing terror and slaughtering innocents, we say to you now that our spirit is stronger and cannot be broken; you cannot outlast us, and we will defeat you. (ISp)

Obama insists that we need a greater understanding of foreign nations. What he's really saying is that Americans need a greater understanding that he is, in fact, a foreigner. He immediately alludes to two wars with foreigners (Iraq and Afghanistan, both of which harbored terrorists who infiltrated America). He speaks of "new threats that demand even greater effort" to ferret out, meaning himself.

Violent themes predominate. Unconsciously he points out how violently his illegal presidency tears at the fabric of our Constitution. He mentions again "those (foreigners) who...induce terror and slaughter innocents" reflecting how his dishonest presidency and radical government intentions will truly frighten and harm many innocent Americans. Indeed numerous citizens have been shaken to the core by Obama and his henchman Eric Holder playing fast and loose with the Constitution—shaking America to its core.

Obama insists that we must battle these foreign forces by upholding the Constitution. He emphasizes that we are "keepers of this legacy, guided by these principles," and so we can challenge this new threat. Single-mindedly he goes on, "We will not apologize for our way of life, nor will we waver in its defense." He continues confidently, "We say to you now"—Obama is here unconsciously addressing himself—America's "spirit is stronger [inspired by our great constitutional legacy] and cannot be broken; you cannot outlast us, we will defeat you." How strongly his unconscious insists on Constitution first, last and always.

Police detectives interrogating suspects talk about the signs guilty persons demonstrate when they are on the verge of breaking—unconsciously they reach out and touch the interrogator or start admitting to possibilities such as being near the crime scene. Remember Obama has repeatedly confessed to his guilt, yet he continues to reach out and touch the Constitution, secretly appealing to citizens to do the right thing. His message: "You can defeat me, you can break me, stay the course." Like guilty people everywhere, Obama secretly wants to come clean.

Patchwork Citizenship, Patchwork Religion: Confession By A Muslim Foreigner

For we know that our patchwork heritage is a strength, not a weakness. We are a nation of Christians and Muslims, Jews and Hindus—and nonbelievers. We are shaped by every language and culture, drawn from every end of this earth; and because we have tasted the bitter swill of civil war and segregation, and emerged from that dark chapter stronger and more united, we cannot help but believe that the old hatreds shall someday pass; that the lines of tribe shall soon dissolve; that as the world grows smaller, our common humanity shall reveal itself; and that America must play its role in ushering in a new era of peace.

194

To the Muslim world, we seek a new way forward, based on mutual interest and mutual respect. To those leaders around the globe who seek to sow conflict, or blame their society's ills on the West: Know that your people will judge you on what you can build, not what you destroy. To those who cling to power through corruption and deceit and the silencing of dissent, know that you are on the wrong side of history; but that we will extend a hand if you are willing to unclench your fist. (ISp)

If you read "our patchwork heritage" as "my patchwork heritage," Obama suggests he has experienced a major patch job regarding his citizenship, that it was patched up by his mother. She hid the truth of his Kenyan birthplace by covering it up with fraudulent Hawaiian paperwork. Reading through his denial he confesses, *"My patchwork heritage is a...weakness"* as president.

"We are a nation of...nonbelievers" is yet another blatant confession that "I am a nonbeliever in the American way of citizenship—in obeying the Constitution." Never before have "nonbelievers" ever been praised by an American president in anyway. Faith is a basic American value; disbelief is not.

Obama confesses even more blatantly to lacking citizenship highlighted by the message marker, "know"—"Know that your people will judge you on what you can build, not what you destroy." Again he suggests millions of Americans secretly know that he has scorned the Constitution. He continues his unconscious self-criticism—"Those who cling to power through corruption and deceit and the silencing of dissent," matches his longtime efforts to delay the release of an original paper birth certificate (if one even exists). These confessions reflect how badly he is rubbing America's face in the mud.

Again he suggests that citizens must take action against him—"must play its role" (again "must")—if they are to usher in a new era of peace, versus "the next civil war"[4] his behavior may be inspiring. Again Obama suggests all true Americans who put the Constitution above all else must lead a direct challenge to his presidency, demanding a complete and accurate original birth certificate.

Obama the Muslim?

If Obama were to secretly confess to his true faith, this would be the place and time. He has just placed his hand on a Christian Bible, the same bible Lincoln used. If he were secretly a Muslim, his unconscious would tell us. Interestingly, he speaks often about Islam.

His misplaced word order "we are a nation of Christians and Muslims, Jews and Hindus" forces America's actual "Judeo-Christian" identity into the background. The word "Muslim" has displaced the word "Jew," which normally, paired with "Christian," describes the religious orientation of the

---

4 A no less august source as 'Catholic Online' (Catholic.org) published "Troubling: Will Nov. 8 Be the Start of the Next Civil War in the USA?" on March 12, 2012, a mere seven months before Obama's chance to be reelected. http://www.catholic.org/national/national_story.php?id=45107 accessed April 29, 2012.

Founders' generation ('the Judeo-Christian tradition'). By choosing this phrasing, his super intelligence is putting forth another hint that Obama is a "Muslim" in his heart.

Further, in "we are a nation of Christians and Muslims," he suggests "I am a Christian *and* a Muslim." He inappropriately joins the two religions together, bypassing the Jews who were here long before the Muslims. Certainly Obama needed the imprimatur of Christian religion to be elected to major office—not Islam. The fact that Obama could never be elected to prominent political office as a Muslim could easily be a major factor in his reported Christian 'conversion' in Chicago, the anteroom to Obama's presidential run.

As a secret Muslim, Obama could claim, as Muslims do, that they also 'believe' in Jesus—which would match with Obama clinging to power by deceit. In linking "patchwork heritage" to "Christians and Muslims" (underscored with "we know") Obama further implies his Muslim "patchwork" religion. Obama's further unusual declaration that we're a nation of nonbelievers suggests that he is a nonbeliever in Christianity.

Recall that Jeremiah Wright, Obama's minister of 20 years, openly endorsed Louis Farrakhan's Nation of Islam. Wright invited Farrakhan to speak in Wright's church and has appeared on the church magazine's cover; Wright selected Farrakhan as recipient of his "Trumpeter Award, saying Farrakhan "truly epitomized greatness."[5] Wright obviously fails to clearly distinguish the two religions, so Obama's co-mingling of the two makes sense.

Obama's blatant declaration "to the Muslim world" suggests he is talking about himself—particularly since his messages describe perfectly his own behavior: (1) sowing conflict, blaming America for his problems, (2) clinging deceitfully to power and silencing dissent, and (3) being on "the wrong side" of history, a destroyer not a builder. He has consistently behaved as a secret Muslim—putting down Israel and favoring Muslims.

Secretly forcing a secret Muslim president on America would be the epitome in Alinsky-style subversiveness, and reflects maximum misguided rage and "untrammeled fury." Recall also Obama's slip during his ABC television interview with George Stephanopholus when Obama referred to "my Muslim faith" with George quickly coming to his rescue, correcting him: "...my Christian faith." In conclusion Obama's own words—and behavior—suggest an unconscious confession that he is a secret Muslim.

Crisis and Whispering a Secret

As we consider the road that unfolds before us, we remember with humble gratitude those brave Americans who, at this very hour, patrol far-off deserts and distant mountains. They have something to tell us today, just as the fallen heroes who lie in Arlington whisper through the ages. We honor them not only because they are

---

5 Richard Cohen, "Obama's Farrakhan Test," Jan. 15, 2008, http://www.washingtonpost.com/wp-dyn/content/article/2008/01/14/AR2008011402083.html accessed June 10, 2012.

guardians of our liberty, but because they embody the spirit of service; a willingness to find meaning in something greater than themselves. And yet, at this moment—a moment that will define a generation—it is precisely this spirit that must inhabit us all.

For as much as government can do and must do, it is ultimately the faith and determination of the American people upon which this nation relies. It is the kindness to take in a stranger when the levees break, the selflessness of workers who would rather cut their hours than see a friend lose their job which sees us through our darkest hours. It is the firefighter's courage to storm a stairway filled with smoke, but also a parent's willingness to nurture a child, that finally decides our fate. (ISp)

"As we consider the road that unfolds before us" Obama suggests his deeper unfolding story— filled with more violence. Obama builds to a crescendo. He first speaks of brave American soldiers who battle foreigners in far-off places—increasingly emphasizing the need for us to battle him, the foreign-born president.

His image of soldiers patrolling far-off deserts and distant mountains "at this very moment"–suggest soldiers with heightened attention. These images also suggest Obama's super intelligence as it speaks from his vast unconscious ("distant" and "far-off" territory). Patrolling, exploring dry "deserts" and high mountains reflects Obama's confession that he has *deserted* America in his *high* office.

Next we find two crucial special message markers. "They (these brave soldiers) have something to tell us today," followed by "whisper" implying Obama will reveal a major secret at this very moment. We read, "They have something to tell us today…just as the *fallen heroes who lie in Washington [Arlington] whisper*." Translation: "I, Barack Obama, am whispering the secret of fallen imperfect heroes who lie and live in Washington. I am that fallen hero lying to you about being an authentic president—in effect I am an ineffective powerless leader, just as powerless as a dead man."

Obama surrounds this secret revelation/confession with multiple references to the Constitution. The good Obama with his moral compass now urges these soldiers—American citizens—as guardians of liberty, in the spirit of service, to fight for something greater than themselves. Again his super intelligence is shouting "Constitution always." He repeats: America ultimately relies on the determination of the people, not the government.

Obama then shifts to three brief stories, three powerful images all continuing to illustrate his illegal presidency. The first and most powerful image points to the heart of his increasingly clear confession. He notes, "the kindness [of American citizens] to take in a stranger when the levees break"—*a vivid unconscious confession that we now have a stranger, an outsider from another country, as president who has caused the levee of the Constitution to break,* shortly linked to "our darkest hours." Indeed he is the "stranger" president from afar. Again he represents the ferocious storm which rages relentlessly against America.

His next images, "the selflessness of workers who would rather cut their hours...sees us through our darkest hours" represents Obama's distinct awareness that selfishly he will ask the American worker to cut his hours with reckless economic plans certain to cause joblessness. Indeed he will bring about one of America's darkest hours with an attack from within by an illegal president who has in essence cut his own hours because he can't fill the job. In that light, he suggests a course of action. He should unselfishly step down, cut his hours, and retire.

Yet Obama whispers another secret, his most painful. The phrase, "than see a friend lose their job which sees us through our darkest hours," represents a confession that Obama's conscious mind cannot bear to lose his job, he just can't give up the presidency. If he lost his cover—the deceptive power of the president—he would immediately be exposed to his "darkest hours," feeling the raw humiliation and powerlessness in that tremendous hole inside of him. It's the last place on earth Obama wants to go. This crucial information matches perfectly his self-profile in his autobiography—the short step from powerlessness to rage.

New Era of Responsibility: Determine Obama's Citizenship

Our challenges may be new. The instruments with which we meet them may be new. But those values upon which our success depends—hard work and honesty, courage and fair play, tolerance and curiosity, loyalty and patriotism—these things are old. These things are true. They have been the quiet force of progress throughout our history. What is demanded then is a return to these truths. What is required of us now is a new era of responsibility—a recognition, on the part of every American, that we have duties to ourselves, our nation and the world; duties that we do not grudgingly accept but rather seize gladly, firm in the knowledge that there is nothing so satisfying to the spirit, so defining of our character, than giving our all to a difficult task.

This is **the price and the promise of citizenship**. This is the source of our confidence—the knowledge that God calls on us to shape an uncertain destiny.

This is the meaning of our liberty and our creed—why men and women and children of every race and every faith can join in celebration across this magnificent Mall, and why a man whose father less than 60 years ago might not have been served at a local restaurant can now stand before you to take a most sacred oath. (ISp)

Now Obama informs us we have new challenges—his illegal presidency—but we can meet these challenges with new instruments, that is the super intelligence--"the quiet force of progress." Indeed quite a force for truth. He's reminding us to listen closely to the 'new way' his unconscious speaks so we can fully grasp the subversive nature of his presidency. Obama's unconscious repeats the same verse over and over hoping we catch on. A challenge to the truth—mentioned twice—of the "old" values of hard work and honesty (two values he most violated), tolerance and curiosity, courage and fair play and patriotism. All those values validated by the Constitution, all those notions of legal and ethical integrity, these he deeply violates as an illegal president. Why else would he have been going on and on about values and the Constitution?

So he demands "a return to these truths" as his moral compass shifts into high gear as he nears the finale of his speech. Every American citizen has a new duty and responsibility "to ourselves, our nation and the world" to recognize the breadth of his presidential deception. He calls on *every citizen* to willingly, not grudgingly, accept this duty—indirectly addressing sym-pathetic followers, especially blacks. It's an idea he'll quickly repeat.

Ardently he instructs us to "seize gladly" this duty to take back the presidency which he illegally seized. He holds up one word—"duty"—like a soldier who, feelings aside, is constantly 'glad' to do his duty for America.[6] Obama's super-intel understands the unpleasant duty of confronting a president gone wrong.

The words "firm knowledge" represent an important message marker. And he repeats it again in "the source of our confidence—the *knowledge* that God calls on us to shape an uncertain destiny." At this peak moment he unsurprisingly connects his appeal for just action to God. In Obama's deeper mind the deity Himself has instructed American citizens to take charge of this uncertain destiny Obama has created and return to the values on which this country was founded. *In the name of God,* Obama advises us to stop him. He does so by emphasizing the truth of natural law reflected in the Declaration of Independence that indeed there are clearly defined rules of God—"unalienable rights"—which at the time the British were violating in their treatment of colonial America in the 18th century and which he's now violating in the 21st century. Very presidentially, his deeper moral compass reassures America that our forefathers possessed sure knowledge about a fixed morality deep inside every man. This truth he personally demonstrates while speaking before a world witnessing his hidden confession. You simply cannot—while carrying out a great deception—place your hand on the Bible in front of millions of people and swear to God you're telling the truth. Your unconscious mind won't let you get away with it.

Citizenship Linked to Creed
"This is **the price and the promise of citizenship**....This is the meaning of our liberty and our creed" (Isp)

---

6 The U.S. Military Academy's motto "Duty, Honor, Country" precisely reflects this message and has guided West Point graduates as our military leaders since 1802. I learned this as a cadet at West Point for more than a year until I left to become a physician.

He instinctively links citizenship to "our creed" to make sure everyone understand the seriousness of the issue. Obama cannot stress the Constitution enough, and he reminds blacks, in particular ("every race"), that our "creed" trumps all other values.

Second Father Story
> ...and why a man whose father less than 60 years ago might not have been served at a local restaurant can now stand before you to take a most sacred oath. (ISp)

Obama now poses another stark contrast. He compares himself, a "man standing before you taking a sacred oath," to his father who might not have been served at a Washington restaurant because it was then "illegal" to serve an African-American or a black African. We have the image of his African father who cannot be served nor seated in Washington, D.C. Obama implies he should not be seated as president, as the father of our nation because legally he cannot serve (suggested in "not... serve").

Now simply connect his earlier father story as Obama directs by telling us two father stories close together in his speech. He suggests the message: "As I take this sacred oath of president I swear I cannot legally serve America now in this office—because, like my father, I was born in Africa." Once again brilliantly, Obama weaves his compelling imagery together to tell a deeper story. These two father stories are phenomenally important. To review Obama links "can't be served/can't serve" with "can't be seated" [specifically in Washington, D.C.] with "African father" and "an African birth in a small village" suggesting: "I am the African-born father of America, the foreign president who cannot legally be seated." At the very core of his story is the implied message: I do not have a legal American birth certificate.

In addition he further discloses his confession at a key place, right after mentioning the price of citizenship. The price he has not paid. Impeccable timing—and on top of this he makes this crucial confession in his inaugural address building to his dramatic close. In essence unconsciously he further announces "My illegal presidency is the central issue I have been talking about between the lines--go back and review everything I have said but first listen to just how much is at stake for America over this issue."

The New Patriots: Fight the Foreign Enemy
> So let us mark this day with remembrance, of who we are and how far we have traveled. In the year of America's birth, in the coldest of months, a small band of patriots huddled by dying campfires on the shores of an icy river. The capital was abandoned. The enemy was advancing. The snow was stained with blood. At a moment when the outcome of our revolution was most in doubt, the father of our nation ordered these words be read to the people:
>
> "Let it be told to the future world ... that in the depth of winter, when nothing but hope and virtue could survive... that the city and the

country, alarmed at one common danger, came forth to meet [it]."

America, in the face of our common dangers, in this winter of our hardship, let us remember these timeless words. With hope and virtue, let us brave once more the icy currents, and endure what storms may come. Let it be said by our children's children that when we were tested, we refused to let this journey end, that we did not turn back, nor did we falter; and with eyes fixed on the horizon and God's grace upon us, we carried forth that great gift of freedom and delivered it safely to future generations. (ISp)

Obama closes his speech with the same patriotic narrative with which he began. Opening with a major message marker: "*Mark this day* with remembrance"—he predicts an especially important forthcoming message dovetailing with "this moment," his repeat emphasis on "today." Obama clearly implies he has marked, scarred and sullied this day with his false oath.

In the first sentence we find a striking *birth marker* and another unique unconscious confession as Obama secretly continues talking about himself. Read: "Mark this day with remembrance of who I am and how far I have traveled. In the year of my birth ...the capital was abandoned." We have another thinly disguised sentence translated, "Remember how far I travelled to America from Africa right after I was born making me an outsider: I cannot be president and the capital is now effectively abandoned." "Abandoned capital" is another rich Obama image in a sequence of confessions such as "false choice" or "taking in a stranger." Notice the dire consequences of an abandoned capital—there's no legal president in the White House.

In the coldest of months, a small band of patriots huddled by dying campfires on the shores of an icy river. The capital was abandoned. The enemy was advancing. The snow was stained with blood. (ISp)

He has frozen out democracy, tried to drive the true patriots out (think of his accusations against The Tea Party—that they are motivated by racism, when in reality they are fervent patriots who love America way more than Obama ever will), and tried to distinguish the flame (campfire) of liberty. The Potomac has become an icy river, his presidency cold to America's needs. Continually he has advanced as an enemy against the nation's best interests. He indeed has done great violence to millions of citizens, having stained the pure blood of liberty that runs through their veins. Surely these patriots have spilled their emotional blood in sleepless nights and frightful days.

He alludes to those few patriots left—few as portrayed by the media but actually in the millions—who still question his presidential qualifications on the shores of an "icy river." Indeed, the matter has been frozen over, kept on ice.

At a moment when the outcome of our revolution was most in doubt, the father of our nation ordered these words be read to the people: (ISp)

He cannot overstate how desperate the situation is—deadly serious because the most crucial question of his presidency has never been fully addressed. Unconsciously, Obama continues to put America on higher and higher alert.

As always, we can count on Obama's unconscious to the rescue. He continues, "At a moment the outcome of the revolution [for liberty] was most in doubt," meaning at *this precise moment.*

Magnificently, the good Obama recalls the words of George Washington who ordered these words to be read "to the people." Letting Washington speak suggests letting a *real* president speak because of Obama's ineligibility, a subtle confession in itself.

> Let it be told to the future world...that in the depth of winter, when nothing but hope and virtue could survive...that the city and the country, alarmed at one common danger, came forth to meet [it].

The prominent message marker, "Let it be told to the future world," heralds Obama's confession to the world.

Read Obama's first instruction delivered via President Washington that nothing will see us through but our virtue, our values.

Then Obama via Washington secretly calls on Americans, "Come forth and meet my challenge—my danger threatening America's future—be alarmed!"

Obama Closes

> America, in the face of our common dangers, in this winter of our hardship, let us remember these timeless words. With hope and virtue, let us brave once more the icy currents, and endure what storms may come. (ISp)

Again Obama instructs us to face his attack with "hope and virtue." Alluding to the Constitution's "timeless words," he challenges us to brave the icy currents of "his current" presidency—and endure the Obama storm. The way he harps on "virtue" reiterates how deeply Obama truly desires to confess his lack of same.

> Let it be said by our children's children that when we were tested, we refused to let this journey end, that we did not turn back, nor did we falter...

> ...and with eyes fixed on the horizon and God's grace upon us, we carried forth that great gift of freedom and delivered it safely to future generations. (ISp)

And on what basis will we deliver our nation from the clutches of a dishonest, ineligible president? He focuses on the one idea that drives America, an ideal that lights the world, "freedom." In that light he continues, "We must not turn back, we must not falter as we carry forth that great gift of freedom"— again directing our attention to the Declaration of Independence and the U.S. Constitution." We must deliver "it *safely* to future generations," to "our children's children."

And now he has come full circle, tying his confession back to the opening of his 2008 Fathers' Day speech in which he referred to the parable of the vicious storm that ate away at the foundation of a home—a presidential candidate unconsciously warning the nation as that he was going to attack our country's very foundation, freedom and the rule of law. Now on this, his Inauguration Day, he confesses he has done exactly that. He removed America's foundation of safety and security. He has boldly defied the rule of law. Alas, Obama ends his speech quite unlike any in history.

He will add one more basic message to America in the form of another personal letter—allegedly to his children on Fathers' Day, five months hence. In it he will remind us of the egregious wrong he has perpetuated on America and on his own two daughters. Again he will instruct America and himself on the way to proceed. But for pure raw passion and heartfelt beliefs we will never see anything from him quite like his inaugural address.

In fact, it was his Inaugural Confession.

Our Response to His Confession?

If George Washington were asked, "What would you think of an unqualified person claiming falsely to be a U. S. citizen taking the office of president and of thousands of citizens taking the possibility lightly?" he would reply in exactly the same way as Obama's unconscious does.

In light of the dire implications of an illegal presidency, does such a high risk not deserve a completely thorough investigation of Barack Obama's citizenship, especially before he is allowed to run for office again? If our forefathers shed literal blood that we might have our freedom, do we not have enough courage to make sure a president is really a president?

Doesn't our mass media—regardless of political persuasion—have the same responsibility? The answer is yes, but we must remember George Washington's own instructions—in the end the citizens and not the media are the ones who must hold all leaders accountable.

So what's your response, America? In a most unexpected and unpredictable way, our time has come. To stand up for who we are, to be tested, to have our day in the sun as courageous patriots. Will we pass the test? Will we falter? What will our children's children say about what we did—or did not—do at this crucial juncture in history? Did we fight for the freedom to defend our Constitution, or to ignore it? Are we going to be citizens or not? Are we going to follow George Washington's teachings as suggested by Obama's own super intelligence? Or are we going to tuck tail and run—and leave it up to the old gang who couldn't shoot straight—the Congress, the courts, the media—none of which are capable of holding the president accountable to the degree he demands.

It's time to take a stand.

14

Fathers' Day Confession— a Year Later

As he settles into the White House, Barack Obama reflects on his unlikely path to the presidency in another letter to his daughters on Fathers' Day, June 21, 2009. This missive, actually directed to all America, comes five months after his inaugural address and pre-inauguration letter. In it he continues his confession of ineligibility. I recommend you stop reading at this point and turn to Appendix E to read this letter in its entirety; then come back.

Importantly, *Obama himself* requested that *Parade* magazine publish this letter for its 42 million monthly readers. A year prior, the magazine's editors had approached *him* regarding his pre-inauguration letter "to his daughters." As his guilt continues to mount, now that he has been falsely sworn into office, Obama unconsciously, but strongly, needs to continue his confession. He still hopes the people will take action. Marking his first Fathers' Day in the White House as the current father of our nation has had an unsettling effect on him.

> As the father of two young girls who have shown such poise, humor, and patience in the unconventional life into which they have been thrust, I mark this Father's Day—our first in the White House—with a deep sense of gratitude. One of the greatest benefits of being president is that I now live right above the office. I see my girls off to school nearly every morning and have dinner with them nearly every night. It is a welcome change after so many years out on the campaign trail and commuting between Chicago and Capitol Hill. (FD2)

In hallmark fashion, Obama's unconscious mind starts with a brief story, "Above the office of president." First Obama comes back to his daughters who have shown "patience"—implying patience with his great deception. We can still hear his heart longing to make things right for their sakes if not for the nation's.

His early reference to the "unconventional life into which they [we] have been thrust...first in the White House" suggests that he has thrust an unconventional president on America, a president not qualified for office, not a Constitutional-type president. The word "convention" itself alludes to our original Constitutional Convention of 1787, which Obama has indifferently dismissed.

Obama continues with a key message marker, the word "mark"—"I mark this Father's Day, our first in the White House." He suggests, "I mark this father [this president]…our first in the White House," confessing that he attacks—marks—the presidency with his illegality. And he suggests, "I mark this…White House"—translated "I have damaged" this nation and its foundation which is symbolized by the White House (white is the color of purity). Immediately, he reminds us of his thinly disguised foreign birth confession at the close of his inaugural address and how he marked his Inauguration Day in similarly disrespectful fashion ("mark this day with remembrance…, of who we are and how far we have traveled. In the year of [my] birth"). Obama tells us in his secret fury he has marked the oath, Inauguration Day, the presidency, and the White House—reminding us on Fathers' Day just as he was marked by his absent father. Repeatedly he uses "marked" to underscore his identity as a damaged child.

By linking "humor" with his "unconventional" illegitimate presidency, Obama again informs us "the joke is on America." Sadly, however, the joke's on his daughters as well—just as his own childhood woundedness was a cruel joke on him.

His unconscious continues. First, the embedded blatant phrase, "…the greatest benefits of being president is that I now live…above the office" or "I now live…above the office," suggesting arrogance in the way he stands above the constitutional requirements of president. Also "above" implies not in the office, therefore not really president. In addition, "right above" suggests his plan can be easily discovered, and along with "I now live right" points to his super intelligence confession and deepest wish. Obama's reference to the second floor of the White House harkens back to his inauguration speech in which he alluded to freedom fighters storming an upstairs room to rescue a distressed child from a fire. In this case "child" refers to citizen(s). Again Obama instructs America, "Come rescue this presidency which I'm in the process of destroying." The more it's ignored, the louder our super intelligence speaks.

With his daughters leaving the White House for school, his reference to "school" is an educational message marker mirroring Obama's ongoing message: "Americans, educate yourselves, because I need to leave the White House." He follows with the virtually identical blatant message "welcome change…out" suggesting, "Leave office, a welcome change." Next he paints a picture of commuting from a geographical place—Chicago—to Washington subtly suggesting he's an outsider president not from America.

> But I observe this Fathers' Day not just as a father grateful to be present in my daughters' lives but also as a son who grew up without a father in my own life. My father left my family when I was 2 years old, and I knew him mainly from the letters he wrote and the stories my family told…I still felt the weight of his absence throughout my childhood. (FD2)

Fathers' Day provides Obama another opportunity to elaborate on the enormous trauma he experienced at his father's hands which he's reenacting on America through his illegal presidency. The phrase "observe this Father's Day...without a father" describes both the way he personally experienced every Fathers' Day and how as a result today our country truly lacks a father of our nation, an authentic president.

And "I still felt the weight of his absence throughout my childhood" informs America that we indeed will feel his pain. But Obama also feels the heavy weight of his deception which continues to drive his confession.

Again Letter Contains Key

Once more in repeating the identical message from his Fathers' Day speech the year before, *"My father left...I knew him mainly from the letters he wrote,"* Obama confirms that we should "know me from the letters—including this very letter--and speeches I personally wrote to America." They contain the super intelligence key. He emphasizes this message in both the first and last of the serial four-part communication enclosing his saga in matching bookends.

The Marked Legislator/President

Near the top of the letter he identifies his painful motives. Obama's secret story remains crystal clear as he yearns for citizens to take charge.

> As an adult, working as a community organizer and later as a legislator, I would often walk through the streets of Chicago's South Side and see boys marked by that same absence—boys without supervision or direction or anyone to help them as they struggled to grow into men. I identified with their frustration and disengagement—with their sense of having been let down. (FD2)

Once more Obama tells us in a brief story, "The Damaged Abandoned Inner-City Kid" that he is "marked"—scarred. In, "a legislator...see boy[s] marked by that same absence," he implies clearly that we can see his emotional abuse reflected in the abusive way he governs. See the marked boy in Obama the president. Specifically the reckless way he has refused to submit to the "supervision or direction" of the Constitution as an illegal president. He also unconsciously alludes to his enabling supporters who left him "without supervision or direction." That lack of legitimacy stunts his growth as a man, which of course is the deepest need of a fatherless boy. Additionally, he predicts his exact behavior as president—constantly refusing to submit to rules, always skating around regulations. For example, late in 2011, during the unofficial Christmas break in Congress, Obama indulged himself in what he called 'recess appointments' of three radical officials who were sure to draw fire from the GOP and moderate Democrats alike. Yet Congress was not in recess, since the Senate had purposefully *not* declared a recess. Obama's appointments were thus illegal.[1] Obama arrogantly bet that GOP leaders would not call his bluff, and he won that bet.

In, "I identified... frustration... disengagement," Obama confesses to his anger prompting his illegal, disengaged presidency in which he will fail to lead America in a healthy direction.

> ...I came to understand the importance of fatherhood through its absence—both in my life and in the lives of others...understand that the hole a man leaves when he abandons his responsibility to his children is one that no government can fill. (FD2)

His confession continues, "hole a man leaves when he abandons his responsibility...no government can fill." Obama has abandoned his responsibility—an illegal president leaves a huge hole in the government which cannot be filled during his term. Again he makes the case for his need to leave office: you cannot assume responsibility with irresponsibility. You cannot fill a legal office with an illegal person.

> ...why we need fathers to step up, to realize that their job does not end at conception... what makes you a man is not the ability to have a child but the courage to raise one. As fathers we need to be involved in our children's lives not just when it's convenient or easy...but when it's difficult and thankless, and they're struggling. That is when they need us most.

> ...not enough to just be physically present. Too often, especially during tough economic times like these, we are emotionally absent: distracted, consumed by what's happening in our own lives, worried about keeping our jobs and paying our bills, unsure if we'll be able to give our kids the same opportunities we had. (FD2)

Obama confesses that his White House job ended the day he took it—at the conception, the beginning of his presidency because he really hadn't been a man and owned up to his lack of credentials. He simply took the easy, politically convenient way. He could not fill the job when America was struggling and most needed a bona fide president. Deep down Obama knows full well he's taking America down further and denying millions of Americans opportunities. He kicked the country in the face when it was already down.

He describes himself as an angry unlawful president: physically present, but emotionally absent even in the face of tough economic times; distracted and selfishly worried only about his own job—his narcissistic need to be president. His super intelligence continues to cut him no slack—and gives us good reason:

---

1 Edwin Meese III and Todd Gaziano, "Obama's Recess Appointments Are Unconstitutional," http://www.washingtonpost.com/opinions/obamas-recess-appointments-are-unconstitutional/2012/01/05/gIQAnWRfdP_story.html Accessed April 30, 2012. At press time for this book, there was a lawsuit challenging the appointments, but its outcome was unknown. An earlier court challenge to the same appointments to the NLRB was struck down by a judge.

Our children can tell. They know when we're not fully there. And that disengagement sends a clear message —whether we mean it or not— about where among our priorities they fall.

So we need to step out of our own heads and tune in. We need to turn off the television and start talking with our kids, and listening to them, and understanding what's going on in their lives.

We need to set limits and expectations. We need to replace that video game with a book and make sure that homework gets done. We need to say to our daughters, Don't ever let images on TV tell you what you are worth, because I expect you to dream without limit and reach for your goals. We need to tell our sons, Those songs on the radio may glorify violence, but in our house, we find glory in achievement, self-respect, and hard work. (FD2)

Every word, image, and phrase continues Obama's super intelligence confession. First children—citizens—can tell when president is not fully there, can't fully take office. His major message marker "tell" suggests his behavior is an obvious 'tell.' Unconsciously Obama knows his behavior since taking office has alarmed many citizens, here confirming their perceptions. In "priorities they fall" Obama richly pictures his low priority regarding his eligibility.

His reference to "whether we mean it or not" reflects Obama's two sides. One side of Obama that is indeed mean and destructive ("we mean") and his other side, which really didn't want to hurt America but was controlled by pain (even though he secretly wants to be a better man).

Guilt-ridden, Obama obsessively notes "we need to," (that is, "*I* need to") make multiple changes which he lists. He needs to "step out of his own head"— understand the citizens and then step out, as in, step away from the presidency and, for the hundredth time, *resign*. He specifically needs to forget about his television appearances and focus on America's true needs, and then he would turn off television himself: the image of no more President Obama, the message again—*resign*. In a striking matching image he needs to "replace the video game"—the Obama media-oriented phony game of president. All of this has been one big narcissistic game to Obama. On one level he sought power for power's sake to see if he could get away with it.

Next he returns obsessively to the idea of "work"—he needed to earn the presidency. He says it all with his vivid image, "in our house we find glory in achievement, self-respect, and hard work." Once again his deeper moral compass shouts at himself and America, "Don't you understand our basic value of achievement?" echoing his identical inaugural message of "no charity." He invokes this concept even as his shadow side continues to violate this basic natural law by authorizing more and more destructive entitlements for citizens.

And "one other thing, America" he tells us, "You needed and still need to do your homework on me"—alluding to his dishonest presidency. Then he notes that because he couldn't set limits and expectations on his illegal run for president, the people should. He implies that his enabling supporters really had low expectations of him—allowing him to operate outside of limits, in the end doing him no favors, in the end leading to disrespect.

> We need to realize that we are our children's first and best [or worst] teachers. When we are selfish or inconsiderate, when we mistreat our wives or girlfriends, when we cut corners or fail to control our tempers, our children learn from that—and it's no surprise when we see those behaviors in our schools or on our streets. (FD2)

The First Teacher/ The Worst Teacher

He profiles himself, specifically what his behavior says about him in becoming an absent father of our country: "selfish, inconsiderate, mistreat citizens when I cut corners, and fail to control my temper." "Cutting corners" reflects one of his clearest confessions and most specific images of being an ineligible presidential candidate. And most importantly he underscores that his behavior reflects a severe loss of his temper, of an extreme rage. He describes all the behaviors he should embody but doesn't—because he really can't, since good character wasn't built into him. Obama reminds us of from whence he came: he learned this behavior at his house at the hands of an impulsive, selfish, angry, absent father.

Yet deep down he yearns to be the best teacher—as a president should be. He continues to hold out to himself the one way he really can be that special teacher just for a moment, but a powerful moment it would be.

> But it also works the other way around. When we work hard, treat others with respect, spend within our means, and contribute to our communities, those are the lessons our children learn. And that is what so many fathers are doing every day—coaching soccer and Little League, going to those school assemblies and parent-teacher conferences, scrimping and saving and working that extra shift so their kids can go to college. They are fulfilling their most fundamental duty as fathers: to show their children, by example, the kind of people they want them to become. (FD2)

Little League President

Obama's blatant unconscious confession reveals exactly what he wasn't. Being an illegal president means, "I didn't work hard and earn it. I didn't treat citizens with respect, and have failed to contribute to the American community. Most importantly of all, I've failed in my most fundamental duty to our citizens, to show by example how an American should behave. A president should be a role model for all Americans. Instead I have deceived my countrymen—I have attacked America with my absence and deception just as my father did the same towards me."

It's as though he's confessing to being a Little League president—lacking the inner strength for the real Major League job—not knowing how to be a man. Men lead by example and simply tell the truth to start with. In this light, in the face of three major educational message markers (coaches, teachers, and

209

college), he's saying, "I'm informing both myself and you that I have only one choice: get another job. I don't deserve to remain in office. Only upon resigning would I finally achieve manhood by becoming the role model of integrity America needs."

> It is rarely easy. There are plenty of days of struggle and heartache when, despite our best efforts, we fail to live up to our responsibilities. I know I have been an imperfect father. I know I have made mistakes. I have lost count of all the times, over the years, when the demands of work have taken me from the duties of fatherhood. There were many days out on the campaign trail when I felt like my family was a million miles away, and I knew I was missing moments of my daughters' lives that I'd never get back. It is a loss I will never fully accept. (FD2)

My Family a Million Miles Away

Obama's secret confession continues with repeated references to his attainment of a false presidency. His off-the-charts self-criticism reflects the enormous burden of guilt which weighs heavily upon him: his presidency hard on America, his behavior irresponsible, "I know I have been imperfect," "I know I have made mistakes," "lost count of all the times" his selfish demands have taken him away from the fatherhood of this nation. That image itself suggests he was born far away, as does the phrase "my family was a million miles away."

He links the key images with "trail," alerting us that he has left an embedded trail of matching thoughtprint images confessing to his foreign birth. Obama confirms the message with a blatant confession, "I knew I was missing"—as a president. Read: "I knew full well I was an illegal. And I cannot undo the damage which will be significant." And indeed it has been. One more crucial message, "imperfect...made mistakes...lost count" suggests his moral compass instruction to citizens: "America, please lose the counting of my votes because I am an illegal president."

Other confessions include the fact that his policies will make him a million miles away from the American family—particularly away from the black American family where unemployment among adult black males averaged 15.7 percent for the years 2011 and 2012.[2] "I lost count" also suggests that he really lost the presidential count or vote, since it was dangerous to him, should anyone discover his eligibility problem. No wonder Obama so eagerly defends illegal immigrants.

> But on this Father's Day, I think back to the day I drove Michelle and a newborn Malia home from the hospital nearly 11 years ago—crawling along, miles under the speed limit, feeling the weight of my daughter's future resting in my hands. I think about the pledge I made to her that day: that I would give her what I never had—that if I could

---

2 Black male unemployment rate in May 2011 was 17. 2 percent; in May 2012 it was 14.2 percent. U.S. Department of Labor, Bureau of Labor Statistics, June 1, 2012, http://bls.gov/news.release/empsit.t02.htm.

be anything in life, I would be a good father. I knew that day that my own life wouldn't count for much unless she had every opportunity in hers. And I knew I had an obligation, as we all do, to help create those opportunities and leave a better world for her and all our children. (FD2)

Father Also Crawling

At precisely the most prominent place in a letter to make his point—at the end, like a lawyer in a closing argument—Obama makes a crucial link. This is typical of confessions from the super intelligence both in location and purpose, telling us a key story at a key time. He links his failures to the image of birth, the most important question hanging over his administration: "Where, Mr. President, were you born?"

He first draws our attention again to "this Fathers' Day" and his role as the father of our nation. Then in a striking message marker/highlighter, "think back," he introduces the image of childbirth and a newborn coming home from the hospital. We find the blatant suggestion, "I think back to the day...I...a newborn"—consciously a story of his daughter Malia, unconsciously a story about his own birth (and his newborn presidency). In the surface story, his daughter is not home but in a car, subtly suggesting "outside the home," an outsider president. More importantly, while he is in charge driving the car, the family (the nation) is "crawling along, miles under the speed limit." Because his birthplace was in Africa, he seems to say, he simply cannot drive America's car as president. He can't even walk but only crawl as president—another image of an incapable childish president.

In "pledge I made" (similar to "oath I took") we have another vital message marker followed by "that day wouldn't count" suggesting that the votes he drew on election day shouldn't count, didn't count. Obama's super intelligence again has ended this fourth of his key communications just as he did the other three--- with another birth story and message of his disruptive foreign birth.

In perhaps the strangest turn of all, Obama self-protectively reaches out for validation past his illegitimate presidency to make a confession. When all is said and done it's an unconscious attempt at authenticating himself—when no one else would. In a way, his super-intel declares, "See I really can count after all." A message to his father: "You built me all wrong but I can *potentially* make it right."

What a confession it would be—*if* he would act on his own inner guidance! Rarely has one man with so much power made such an admission of guilt, albeit unconsciously. And in the end he could inspire millions of other people who need to confess to their own shadow sides and misdeeds. In the ultimate scheme of things, it would be Obama's greatest gift to all of humankind. In the process he'd restore America's adherence to natural law. Obama unconsciously senses this monumental opportunity, "And I knew I had...to help create those opportunities and leave a better world...for...all our children."

He had been offered a low-count life, and he might find a way in the end to make it count. But as he said, "It is rarely easy," and such a confession would be rare beyond belief. Obama reveals just how hard the human heart can become. It's a confession he has fought at every turn, a confession that would be impossible without God's help, as he tells us next.

> On this Fathers' Day, I am recommitting myself to that work, to those duties that all parents share: to build a foundation for our children's dreams, to give them the love and support they need to fulfill them, and to stick with them the whole way through, no matter what doubts we may feel or difficulties we may face. That is my prayer for all of us on this Fathers' Day, and that is my hope for this nation in the months and years ahead. (FD2)

His moral compass now in high gear, Obama indirectly alludes to all his failures as an unlawful president. First he mentions "this Fathers' Day" three times here and once at the beginning of letter, stressing "this father, this president" and the unconscious message, "I am acutely aware of what it means to be the father of our nation and how I have particularly failed on this day, most symbolic of fathers/leaders."

He vows to "recommit myself" to the work of being a good father, strongly suggesting his commitment to America was previously lacking. He vows "to build a foundation for our children [citizens]....difficulties we may face," confessing that *he* is the difficulty which actually undermines our nation. Repeating the keyword "foundation," he takes us back to his first Fathers' Day speech and America's foundation forged by its patriots and founding documents. He has secretly confessed that he would storm against that foundation and do it great violence while unable to give the people the love and support of a president/father. In "fulfill" he takes us again to the presidential oath, realizing that he simply cannot fulfill the qualifications of president.

But then Obama offers to restore America's foundation by confessing what he has done to it so that he can be stopped, now, once and for all. He admonishes citizens to stick with the plan to secure America's basic tenets for the future-- no matter how difficult it may be to confront him ("to build a foundation for our [citizens'] dreams... to stick with them the whole way through, no matter what... difficulties we may face"). In his secret prayer for America—his "hope for this nation"—he advises us, at all costs, to face his illegitimate presidency. Insist he leave office, even if he refuses to do it himself.

And he still holds out hope that he could someday "stick with" his unconscious plan to resign from office "the whole way through, no matter what doubts" he "may feel or difficulties" he "may face." This is his secret prayer for himself—his hope for the future.

Deeper still, he reveals what he really needs from the people, "and to stick with [him] the whole way through, no matter what ... difficulties we may face"—if and a *big* if, he would confess. Obama owes himself and the country an apology on an equivalent level to his attack. He tells us, "That is my prayer for all of us [for him especially] on this Fathers' Day... my hope for this nation

212

[and me]." Obama is thus looking for God to be the father he never had, the one who will authenticate him, tell him he counted. We can only hope that, if by apologizing, by confessing his sins, Obama would tell God that He counted, and that America, which God blessed abundantly, counted more than his selfish ambition.

In recommitting himself to parental duties, to build his daughters' foundation, Obama reveals how badly he wants to make things right with his daughters, to be the pillar of integrity he longs to be. He knows deep down they're aware of his illegal presidency; the bitter truth is, unconsciously there are no family secrets.

15

"Birth Certificate" Release: The Sideshows

On April 27, 2011, at a surprise White House briefing Barack Obama dramatically released what he referred to as his long-form birth certificate online.[1] As usual, Obama commented on the matter publicly on several occasions. His super intelligence once more will be unconsciously reading and describing him at such a powerful moment—delving much deeper than his conscious mind could do.

With the citizenship matter increasingly pressuring him, Obama made perhaps the only move he felt he could make. But for the first time he clearly put "evidence" on the table either authentic or artificial. We now have a fresh opportunity to hear Obama's brilliant unconscious comment on a new matter. Previously, his super intelligence communicated its findings about Obama's citizenship. Now we can see what it has to say about his birth certificate and to demonstrate its ability to tell the truth and to advise Americans how to handle the matter.

Since his unconscious has already repeatedly informed us that he is an illegal, foreign-born president, we can predict with certainty he will confess to a fraudulent birth certificate. However, we must let his super intelligence speak— and hear the evidence.

Obama Links National Security to Issue

Prior to his official statement Obama makes a telltale spontaneous comment, "Now, let me just comment, first of all, on the fact that I can't get the networks to break in on all kinds of other discussions – (laughter). I was just back there listening to Chuck -- he was saying, 'it's amazing that he's not going to be talking about national security.' I would not have the networks breaking in if I was talking about that, Chuck, and you know it."[2] Obama immediately

---

1 For the record, Obama released an electronically-produced birth certificate on the Internet. He claimed it was from a certified copy of a Certificate of Life Birth (Long Form) on green security paper from the Hawaii Department of Health. However, a paper copy was never seen nor examined by any neutral trustworthy party. Strictly speaking his online birth certificate was a PDF image—an electronic 'picture' someone creates on a computer, and as such, it is open to examination by computer and imaging experts. There are several problems with the PDF's veracity.
2 Remarks by the President, April 27, 2011, James S. Brady Press Briefing Room, http://whitehouse.gov/the-press-office/2011/04/27/remarks-president accessed May 1, 2012.

suggests that he in fact unconsciously links the question of his birth certificate to national security. His message marker "know" along with his classic denial that he will not be talking about national security implies that is precisely what he is addressing. The issue is that crucial. Right off Obama's super intelligence warns America about the gravity of his deception. He further suggests that his sudden announcement represents the highest warning to America—that citizens must consider it an unconscious presidential break in on national television to confess to his true intentions. At the same time he teaches us, via the image of a media not delivering a national security message, that very simply the national media remains blind to his severe threat to America. In a nutshell Obama implies a confession beyond belief right off the bat.

Obama continues, "As many of you have been briefed, we provided additional information today about the site of my birth." Unconsciously Obama continues to strongly imply that at this moment with his deeper alarming confession that he continues to brief America himself with additional information about the "site of my birth"—specifically that he is covering up his foreign birthplace. He goes on, "We've had every official in Hawaii, Democrat and Republican, every news outlet that has investigated this, confirm that, yes, in fact, I was born in Hawaii, August 4, 1961, in Kapiolani Hospital." Here we have another complete untruth. He cannot name one popular news outlet that has done an unbiased investigation, or any politician. No hospital has verified his birth in their facility. But we see Obama's super intelligence wisdom calling for just such an open broad inquiry—distinctly holding up the solution to the issue for all Americans.

Tim Adams, Honolulu's former senior elections clerk during the 2008 presidential campaign stated no authentic Obama birth certificate exists. He signed an affidavit swearing that his supervisors informed him that there is no long-form, hospital-generated birth certificate for Obama in their records. Also, he declared that neither Queens Medical Center nor Kapiolani Medical Center in Honolulu had any Obama birth records.[3]

Obama Releases "Birth Certificate"—Confession of Sideshow

President Obama's comments regarding the surprise release of his birth certificate are revealing. He dismissively reports, "We're not going to be able to solve our problems if we get distracted by sideshows and carnival barkers…We do not have time for this silliness. We've got better stuff to do. I've got better stuff to do."[4]

Obama impetuously insists his birth certificate is authentic. He assumes no responsibility for dragging America through this major conflict for three years, creating unnecessary turmoil and dividing the country, encouraging name-

3 Jerome Corsi, "Hawaii official now swears: No Obama birth certificate," WorldNetDaily, June 24, 2011. http://www.wnd.com/2011/01/254401 accessed May 1, 2012.
4 Remarks by the President, April 27, 2011, James S. Brady Press Briefing Room, http://whitehouse.gov/the-press-office/2011/04/27/remarks-president accessed May 1, 2012.

calling and racial divides by playing a mean-spirited game of "keep away." This appears to be the height of "silliness" and "a carnival barking circus"—an unconscious confession on Obama's part—that he is describing himself. He also insists that people should believe him 'because he said so,' which is the specific strategy carnival barkers use, enticing you to follow their instructions to "step right in!"

He further suggests that his "birth certificate" release was just a bunch of "stuff" (a decidedly non-presidential word), and that now citizens truly have a bigger, better job—which his super intelligence says is to investigate the certificate.

Obama Warns Against Pretending—Another Hidden Confession

Insisting consciously that America should forget the birth certificate issue because we have "enormous challenges" and "very difficult decisions," he adds three more warnings: "We're not going to be able to do it if we're distracted...if we spend time vilifying each other...if we just make stuff up and pretend that facts are not facts."[5]

Obama reminds us in vivid images that America now has enormous challenges involving its illegal president who has just "made stuff up" by pretending that a phony birth certificate is a legitimate document. He's pretending that the facts of his foreign birth and lack of citizenship (which he previously revealed) and his avoidance of the matter are not facts. Hear his unconscious confession: this is a pretend birth certificate. *That* is the fact.

How perfectly his unconscious describes his behavior—lying and pretending—and how quickly he has provided a striking picture of deceit. He also unconsciously reveals his sideshow plan: distract citizens and cause increased animosity between Americans. That tactic quickly worked as his media supporters immediately labeled all "birthers" as racists and flat-earthers. Yet his super intelligence implicitly underscores one admonition, "Find out the facts. Don't pretend. Separate the real facts from the false claims." He suggests the obvious: submit the birth certificate to the best fact-finders—expert document analysts.

America Now Faces Monumental Choice Linked to Birth Certificate

Now operating in overdrive, his deeper moral compass continues, "We've got some big problems to solve...live in a **serious** time...have to get **serious**....," read: now America truly has "big—serious—problems to solve," beginning with his phony birth certificate.

Obama also noted, "(the week before) the dominant news story *wasn't about* these huge, monumental choices that we're going to have to make as a nation. It was about my birth certificate." Read through his denial—and understand he's continually talking about the present moment. The dominant

---

5 *Ibid.*

news story *now* indeed *is* his birth certificate and *the huge, monumental choices we must make as a nation.* Unconsciously he links the two ideas.

Now citizens must choose whether or not we are going to confront him about his ongoing deceit. This is the identical choice he underscored in his inaugural address. Indeed his phony birth certificate is the dominant news story of the decade. America now truly has *"big problems to solve"* —serious problems—as president he has doubled down on his deceit with a phony birth certificate. Notice that Obama never offered to submit his original, paper birth certificate to document-analysis for verification—which would have been a sign of true seriousness, especially after waiting for three years.

Obama Presents Wise Solution: Debates, Democracy

Again his deeper, unconscious moral compass shows the way out: "huge and serious debates, important debates...some fierce disagreements...how democracy is supposed to work...I am confident that the American people and America's political leaders can come together in a bipartisan way and solve these problems."

His wise counsel is hidden, but it's there: discuss and debate the matter of his birth certificate, the main issue at hand, in the name of democracy. This matches perfectly his previous super intelligence wisdom: quit pretending the facts are not the facts—examine the evidence.

Obama unconsciously acknowledges that fierce debate already surrounds around his birth certificate. Millions of Americans want his birth certificate officially examined by experts even though Congress and the media stubbornly ignore the matter. But Obama holds up a proposal for solving the problem—democracy, meaning the rule of law, the Constitution, justice, fair play to determine the truth of his certificate.

Obama's comment, "how democracy is supposed to work," suggests a confession that our nation is *not* working that way now, because Obama and his supporters still want to play "Pretend" when it comes to serious matters.

Obama Sideshow Number 2: White House Officials Suggest Cover-Up

Immediately following Obama's April 27 release of his long-form birth certificate, White House officials said they wanted to release the paperwork as quickly as possible to "pre-empt any further conspiracy theories about *whether it had been doctored.*"[6] In so doing they first revealed Obama's blatant strategy of surprise—suddenly and breathlessly releasing the birth certificate after delaying for two and a half years to produce it. Then they ridiculed further examination of the newly released document to assert that this would be the end of the matter. But in so doing, they've now introduced the key issue, a potentially "doctored"

---

6 Karen Tumulty and Anne E. Kornblut, "Obama, frustrated by 'this silliness,' produces detailed Hawaii birth certificate," *Washington Post*, April 27, 2011, http://washingtonpost.com/politics/obama-produces-his-birth-certificate/2011/04/27/AFFISyxE_story.html .

birth certificate. The same suggestion Obama made minutes earlier—that what appeared to be the facts could be nothing but fake facts. Implicitly, they suggested what is needed is a clear-cut document examination by unimpeachable experts.

And as the *Washington Post* reported, White House officials "were also aiming for an element of surprise."[7] Obama's blatant 'shock-and-awe' strategy employed after such a long delay was yet more evidence of a sideshow.

Sideshow Number 3: Unaccountability Journalism

Priding itself on "accountability journalism," the *Washington Post* continues to demonstrate the exact opposite.[8] Note the immediate bias, reporting that Obama "frustrated and annoyed" had released his birth certificate "after refusing for two years to indulge the most corrosive of conspiracy theories questioning his legitimacy…once the province of the political fringe…recently fanned by showman Donald Trump…"[9] After two years of refusing to obey the U.S. Constitution and spending millions of dollars refusing to release his birth certificate, Obama became frustrated—here is indulgence personified. The reporters' piece suggests Obama secretly confessed to the sideshow. Thus he avoided, for the moment, any possibility of being unmasked as an illegitimate president.

But the *Post* reporters' deeper moral compass finally emerged: "…several days of…secret maneuvering…culminated in an extraordinary moment Wednesday. The president appeared in the White House briefing room with evidence that he had been born in the United States as the Constitution requires."[10] The journalists unconsciously recognized the truly extraordinary moment: *that we now have evidence in the case as required by the Constitution* which can be analyzed by document examiners to check if it has been "doctored" (mentioning the exact word). Unconsciously the story clearly pointed to the solution while at the same time attacking it as extreme indulgence and a "corrosive…conspiracy," all the while implying they had no intention of examining the document.

The *Post* reporters also unconsciously further revealed the heart of the matter, "On April 19, Obama ordered White House counsel Robert Bauer to find out what it would take to retrieve a longer and more detailed version of his Hawaiian birth certificate, a document not routinely released by state authorities. That set into motion several days of intense, secret maneuvering that culminated in an extraordinary moment Wednesday."[11] Pay attention to the big idea. Because of the power of the presidency Obama obtained a special exception to

---

7 Tumulty and Kornblut, *op cit.*
8 Former *Washington Post* chief editor Leonard Downey made a major presentation entitled "Accountability Journalism" at Samford University (Birmingham, Alabama) in October 2006. I discussed the matter with him then.
9 Tumulty and Kornblut, *op cit.*
10*Ibid.*
11 *Ibid.*

the normal record keeping and reporting process of Hawaiian authorities. The *Post* also acknowledged intense secret maneuvering by Obama minions regarding the alleged birth certificate. These reporters had unconsciously picked up on Obama's manipulation of his birth certificate records now—and of course in the past. "Secret maneuvering" says it all.

In mentioning the surprise tactic of releasing the birth certificate, the *Post* reporters describe themselves: "...catching off-guard a White House press corps that had no hint that the administration might make the move."[12] The reporters here are suggesting yet another unconscious confession: they remain completely off-guard when it comes to protecting America, neglecting the press' duty to call for an objective examination of the evidence. They are blind to Obama's secret moves--the "off duty" media.

Post Suggests Another Obama Sideshow: A Visit to Oprah

The same reporters note that minutes after the president called for a return to serious business, he went off to tape an appearance on Oprah's television show—suggesting a true sideshow wherein he would have no fear of facing any questioning about a potentially doctored birth certificate. Unquestionably, the two *Post* reporters who wrote the article make plain they are complicit with Obama's sideshow of distraction.

Sideshow Number 4: Obama's Secret Message to Trump— 'You're On Right Track'

At the annual White House correspondents' dinner on April 30, 2011, just three days after releasing his purported long-form birth certificate, Obama made the birth certificate issue a central part of his speech. With Donald Trump in attendance, the president attempted to arrogantly dismiss the question—and Trump.

Surely some Obama advisor advised him to leave well enough alone, that unwisely attacking Trump could provoke further investigation and continue to draw attention to Trump's questions about Obama's presidential eligibility, but if that was true, Obama ignored it.

Things said in jest often unconsciously communicate hidden painful truths. Consciously Obama glibly expects America to believe him and not dare to investigate the birth certificate any further—yet, reading through his humor, his messages to Trump suggest the exact opposite.

At one point Obama shifted overtly to Trump with numerous wisecracks. Ridiculing the famous tycoon, Obama jokingly raised the question, "Did we fake the moon landing?"—the powerful image suggests a phony first-time-ever national event—pointing to the first-time black president. It also suggests a

---

12 *Ibid.*

phony hero and a phony mission to a foreign, faraway place.[13] It's as though Obama's saying, "I'm a fake American hero from a foreign land, and my presidency is a scam," matching Trump's claim that if Obama were an illegal president, "It would be one of the greatest scams in history."[14]

"All kidding aside," the president said to Trump, "we all know about your credentials and breadth of experience," suggesting, albeit with surface sarcasm, that Trump has indeed demonstrated authority and experience in his pursuit of Obama's real birth certificate. What makes this more impressive is that, while continuing to mock Trump, Obama again jokingly praised him: "job well-handled sir"—once more suggesting the message "you're on the right track." Preoccupied with Trump, Obama suggests he is unconsciously communicating with him.[15]

Jokingly also, "for the first time" Obama showed his birth video— a clip from the animated movie *The Lion King* set in Africa publicly linking his birth to Africa. He followed with more humor, "We're back at square one"—again suggesting an inauthentic president from the beginning.

In another self-deprecating video segment, Obama repeatedly stumbles after he loses his teleprompter, declaring "Let's start over." Once more the truth revealed in jest: America needs to start over because it has an inadequate, illegitimate president. He acknowledged actor Matt Damon and his latest movie *The Adjustment Bureau* about an ambitious politician longing for a Senate seat. In the movie just before the election unflattering photos are released due to the candidate's bad decision, and he fails miserably at the polls. Here Obama is admitting that if citizens fully understand his word pictures and secret confession, he will not be re-elected which is this narcissistic president's greatest fear.

He referred to Matt Damon as a popular actor "who can do no wrong in the eyes of his fans...[but] Enjoy it while it lasts." The idea of "doing wrong" weighs on Obama's mind. Unconsciously he alludes to his supporters who ignore his illegal presidency while many Americans—like Trump—see the wrong he has done. And again Obama predicts the truth will surface.

Immediately prior to addressing Trump directly, Obama jokingly asked, *"and where are The Biggie and Tupac?"*—making distinct references to violent black rappers who murdered and were murdered. And in fact they are both dead, that is "where they are." We might read this as an unconscious death threat to Trump and the message, "Don't mess with me."

---

13 Transcript of President Obama's speech at the White House Correspondents Association Dinner, April 30, 2011, http://articles.chicagotribune.com/2011-04-30/news/chi-obama-speech-transcript_1_laughter-applause-transcript accessed May 28, 2012.

14 Trump told Fox News host Bill O'Reilly,"If you are going to be the president of the United States you have to be born in the United States–and there is doubt [about Obama]," he said. "If he wasn't born in this country, it's one of the great scams," http://video.foxnews.com/v/4617078/donald-trump-in-no-spin-zone-part-2/.

15 While an Obama speechwriter was likely involved in structuring the president's dinner repartee, Obama was very personally involved in the program, appearing in several humorous video clips pre-taped for the occasion. We must consider this speech essentially verbatim communication from Obama—surely he sanctioned every word. And, by now, Obama's speechwriters at least unconsciously know the complete truth about his cover-up.

Obama Passionately Insists Reporters Investigate the Truth—The Obama Revolution

Seemingly changing the subject, Obama gets serious remembering "our neighbors across the South that have been devastated by terrible storms...from last week"—an unconscious reference to his conning of his countrymen with the newly released birth certificate. Remember, Obama unconsciously, and often, refers to his attacks on America as a severe storm.

Finally Obama's super intelligence moral compass delivered an impassioned speech specifically to the numerous reporters there—urging them to speak up for the people who have been devastated by his attacks (Hurricane Barack)— to "rush to the site of the storm." He then goes on about their courageous reporting on the revolutions in the Middle East ("Arab Spring"). He mentions, brave "danger to cover a revolution...give people a voice...and hold leaders accountable...we've seen daring men ...risk their lives for the simple idea that no one should be silenced...and everyone deserves to know the truth...that's the principle you uphold ...it's always important but especially important in times of challenge...like the moment America and the world is facing now."

He went on, "remember those reporters... lost [their lives]...consequence of the extraordinary reporting over recent weeks. They've helped... to defend our freedoms... help democracy flourish." It's yet another appeal to democracy—to understand the crucial decision facing America. The question is whether or not to stand up to his disguised Alinsky-style revolution as an illegal president. In his wildest dreams Alinsky could not imagine one of his own radical apprentices sitting in the White House. But there he is!

Obama also made plain that reporters have been killed for telling the truth, and that "it's gonna be a long road back" for those devastated by the storm. Obama confesses that he intends to fight efforts to professionally examine his birth certificate and *unconsciously* implies that race riots will bring loss of life if he's truly challenged and the truth comes out. It's the identical story Obama has told before—although this time he adds an *unconscious* veiled death threat to any reporter who would dare truly explore the matter, similar to his comments to Trump. He has just stated that reporters lose their lives for extraordinary reporting in defending "our freedoms and democracy."

Yet he insists that Americans will eventually prevail, that the truth will come out because they don't like being lied to about matters with such grave consequences. *His deeper moral compass continues to guide America to hear his confession and hold him accountable.* I suggest you watch Obama's performance on video online to get the full context on which my analysis is based.[16]

---

16 Do your own Internet search, or watch C-SPAN's coverage of this event on YouTube: http://youtu.be/n9mzJhvC-8E. Note below the video that you can see the entire program at C-SPAN's website. The opening video is practically shocking how it features, front-and-center, the phony birth certificate and claims, over and over, "I am a real American." Then when Obama

The sophisticated well planned program at the White House Correspondents' dinner filled with such ridicule of Trump and "birthers" in general matches Obama's put-off sarcastic style in his White House briefing comments perfectly. We can believe that the briefing/alleged birth certificate release and the dinner were two parts of an attempted crafty plan to distract and mock—again a classic Alinsky maneuver. When backed in a corner, come out with guns of ridicule blazing.

But once again three days after his stunning confession emerges as he releases a fraudulent birth certificate, Obama's unconscious continues with thinly disguised messages pointing to his guilt. His images of huge hoaxes such as fake moon landings perpetrated by a national hero, an African birth video ("in jest"), a devastating storm and reporters who must brave danger to cover a revolution are all images which point to a compelling secret confession.

Sideshow Number 5: Obama Unconsciously Confirms Trump Was Right

Three weeks later, while in England on May 24, 2011 Obama responded to a question from someone discussing the need for investors. "I know a good investor—Donald Trump," the president said. Yet another biting joke, the flippant comment also implied a positive message that people should "invest in Trump"—that Trump is not only good investor but also a good investigator. Obama's unconscious confirms Trump was right about his presidency. His extreme preoccupation with Trump points to major unresolved guilt around his birth issue.

Sideshow Number 6: Trump Retreats on Birth Certificate, Then Advances

On May 24, 2011, Trump called Jerome Corsi, inquiring about the author's plans to "reveal the truth about Obama." Trump expressed doubts about the veracity of the birth certificate, sharing his doubts that Trump had mentioned earlier to Corsi and WorldNetDaily editor Joseph Farah.[17] Yet Trump was in retreat about making further public comments challenging the birth certificate's authenticity. He wondered if Corsi was discouraged who quickly informed him he wasn't at all and that his new book, *Where's the Birth Certificate? The Case That Barack Obama is Not Eligible to be President,* was selling extremely well (soon to be number one on the New York Times best-seller list) and he was doing around the clock media interviews. In retrospect Trump appears the one discouraged, suggesting he had unconsciously picked up on Obama's implied threats to him at the White House Correspondents' Dinner. Unquestionably, Trump and Corsi were the twin forces which had pressured Obama to take the drastic step of releasing the long-form birth certificate. Corsi recommended that Trump publicly call for an independent examination of the birth certificate or he

---

begins his live remarks, he says with extreme sarcasm, "My FELLOW Americans..." to sickening applause from the complicit journalists in attendance. Opening remarks again are one of the most important positions in any speech or public communication.
17 Bob Unruh, "Trump pumps Corsi for latest on Obama," May 24. 2011
http://www.wnd.com/?pageId=303049#ixzz1NNlAyxVv .

could be perceived as working for Obama.

Two days later Trump released a written statement in the leftist *Mother Jones* magazine and to the media overtly denying that he had told Corsi he suspected a fraudulent birth certificate. Corsi, however, stood by his report. Trump's *Mother Jones* statement, however, suggests that unconsciously he was attempting to retract his denial: "Is [Obama's] birth certificate legitimate? I hope it is for the good of the country, but that's for experts to determine—not me. I have not read the book written by Jerry Corsi nor did we discuss whether or not the birth certificate was computer-generated or in any way fabricated."[18] Indirectly, but publicly, Trump challenged Obama to do exactly as Corsi advised—"for the good of the country," have the document investigated.

At this time I spoke to Corsi myself (informing him about my own work) and he was concerned that Trump would permanently retreat. We corresponded in several emails and I suggested that Trump unconsciously was still attempting to confront Obama. Corsi upon reflection agreed and that's how it turned out.

On June 4, 2011, at the Faith & Freedom Coalition's annual conference in Washington, D.C., Trump returned to overtly challenging Obama's birth certificate: "I don't know exactly what he [Obama] showed...but you know, someday somebody's gonna figure that one out."[19]

Parenthetically, I must mention how Jerome Corsi's vital book, *Where's The Birth Certificate?*, provides invaluable information on Obama's eligibility issue. Corsi's meticulous research establishes the blatant deception Obama and his powerful supporters (Hawaii state officials, at least one Hawaiian Congressman, and "neutral" verification websites [e.g., factcheck.com]) have resorted to in order to carry out his illegal presidency. Furthermore Corsi presents striking testimony from Obama's step-grandmother verified by Kenyan translators that he was born in Kenya. He also helped inspire Sheriff Joe Arpaio's investigation.

Sideshow Number 7: Obama's Slip—Mis-Dates Guestbook By Three Years
On May 24, 2011, while on a tour of Europe, Obama laid a wreath at the Grave of the Unknown Warrior at Westminster Abbey in London. He then signed the guestbook dating it "May 24, 2008," after first asking his wife the date—specifically the month. Several newspapers attributed his error to wishing he were back in 2008 as a popular presidential candidate rather than facing tough re-election conditions. Clearly the papers were referring to Obama's unconscious mind. So now let's go there with our advanced knowledge of the subject.

18 "Trump denies reading book he signed agreement to get: Issues statement distancing himself from suspicion about birth-certificate fraud," May 26, 2011, http://www.wnd.com/?pageId=303721#ixzz1NZMolnCp .
19 Jerome Corsi, "Trump's back! Casting doubt on birth certificate," June 06, 2011, http://www.wnd.com/?pageId=308041#ixzz1OcSlssPy .

His comment in the guestbook was, "it is a great privilege to commemorate our great heritage, and our common sacrifices" and suggests stronger unconscious motivations behind the slip. "Sacrifice"—"common sacrifice" —is heavy on Obama's mind.[20]

His immediate circumstance was the presidential tour of Europe—as an illegal, foreign-born president. All this glory, yet he knows deep down that he's a complete phony. Surely in the back of his mind he's thinking: "If they find out about this, they will 'hang me.' And most of all in Britain, America's greatest ally."

Obama has just doubled down on his deceit by releasing a fraudulent birth certificate—after a severe challenge to his presidency led by Donald Trump and author Jerome Corsi whose book *(Where's The Birth Certificate?)* had skyrocketed to the top of the best-seller list. In utter desperation Obama produced the fake birth certificate—a clear change in strategy—after three long years of stonewalling.

Now his slip regarding the date and his comments in the British guestbook provided powerful unconscious clues as to the real sources of his slip. Certainly, Obama had recently been on the precipice of "sacrificing" his presidency. Obviously, he didn't think he could stand up to the tidal wave of pressure regarding his birth certificate. Even liberal Chris Matthews said, "Produce the birth certificate and be done with it!" [21]

Obama demonstrates a strong urge to bond with Britain, claiming a common heritage and common sacrifices, a desperate self-protective urge. But note, "our great heritage"—that is his own concealed heritage and birthplace—is what's really on his mind. He also underscores "great privilege" suggesting an unconscious confession that he has deceitfully assumed the privileged office. Surely that would make him a ripe target for phenomenal scorn. Parading through Europe as The President—The Most Powerful Man in the World—including his visit to the grandest, most privileged place of all, his State Visit to Her Majesty, The Queen. All this pseudo-glory when in fact he is a charlatan—an emperor with no clothes. His vulnerability must be off the charts.

And he has just laid a wreath at the foot of the *unknown warrior*. Now recall his secret identification with the enemy British soldier (of 1783) in his inaugural address—he himself is the foreign enemy that he urged us to defeat in the name of George Washington, in a war no less. And what happens in war? You destroy the enemy before they destroy you. He is the dead soldier whose grave he has just honored. He knows that if the truth comes out his administration will be destroyed. He lives every moment of his life silently

20 Fiona Roberts, "Doesn't Obama know what year it is? President signs Westminster Abbey guestbook 2008!," Nov. 30, 2011, http://www.dailymail.co.uk/news/article-1390535/Obama-London-visit-2011-President-signs-Westminster-Abbey-guestbook-2008.html#ixzz1fEIg3T6k.
21 Jim Meyers, "Chris Matthews: Obama Should Release Birth Certificate," Newsmax, December 29, 2010. newsmax.com/InsideCover/Obama-birth-certificate-Matthews/2010/12/29/id/381362.

harboring that fear. No wonder Obama was so overwhelmed that day in the Abbey that he couldn't remember the day of the month and signed the wrong year, off by exactly three years.

Once again we can understand another reason why, on his earlier world-wide tour as a newly elected president, he apologized so profusely for the United States. In reality (his unconscious reality) he was apologizing for his illegal presidency and for thereby insulting every country he visited. This visit to England in May 2011 represented one giant flashback of his previous intentionally misleading international tour.

We have to ask again—why the misdate of three years? He takes us to the exact date of May 24, 2008, when he was a presidential candidate and in the midst of pulling the wool over America's eyes. Two strong unconscious messages emerge from his slip. First, "I want to retreat and undo the harm I've done." Secondly, "I am an illegal president just as I was on May 24, 2008. This is my way of resigning—of 're-signing,' of 're-dating' the entire matter—of confessing here in the guestbook."

Graphology of Obama's Signature

For the record we note Obama's unique signature with a huge capital "B" and "O" with small indiscernible letters for the remainder.[22] The B reflects a huge phallic symbol, befitting his grandiosity. The equally large "O" has a line through it—a zero that has been crossed out—suggesting his true identity as a phony, a 'zero' who doesn't count. Immediately he takes us back to the circumstances of his birth—when he didn't count for anything at all. And now, as an illegal president, he still doesn't.

An "O" with a line through it also suggests the universal message, "Stop, go no further"—similar to the huge marker at the Brandenburg Gate in Germany that formerly separated East and West Berlin. In context, he suggests, "Stop! I am an illegal president." And prior to that he suggests, "Stop what you are doing to me"—a reference to how he was nearly eliminated before he was born. His very signature is subtly sending his pro-life message to the world.

Sideshow Number 8: Sheriff Arapio's Investigation

In November of 2011 Sheriff Joe Arpaio began a three-month investigation of Obama's birth certificate with a team of over 200 forensic specialists including law enforcement, computer experts, and profilers. The major preliminary finding of Sheriff Joe's 'Cold Case Posse' volunteer law enforcement investigation pointed to fraud. "My investigators believe that the long-form birth certificate was manufactured electronically and that it did not originate in paper format as claimed by the White House," Arpaio told reporters

---

22 I suggest readers do their own Internet search for Obama's signature (there are various versions). For convenience' sake, here is a link that shows you his signature on the Obamacare bill: http://en.wikipedia.org/wiki/File:Obama_healthcare_signature.jpg accessed June 13, 2012.

on March 1, 2012. His citizen sleuths suspected the long-form document was a computer-generated forgery.[23]

To illustrate how the Obama long-form birth certificate may have been counterfeited via computer, Arpaio showed a series of five videos. The videos demonstrate that the Hawaii Department of Health Registrar's name stamp and the registrar's date stamp were computer-generated images imported into an electronic document. They were *not* rubber-stamp imprints inked by hand or machine onto a paper document, the posse maintained.[24]

Head investigator Mark Zullo found it "especially disturbing" that the probe pointed to an intentional falsification of the registrar stamps. "These stamp imprints are designed to provide government authentication to the document itself," Zullo said. If the registrar stamps are forgeries, he added, the document itself is likely a forgery.

Arpaio repeatedly insisted that the president himself could clear up the controversy by demanding that the Hawaii Department of Health release all of its 1961 birth records including those on paper, microfilm and/or stored on computers.

Another indication of deliberate deception regarding Obama's birth was a series of missing immigration records of international flight arrivals during 1961. The missing INS records could corroborate eyewitness testimony that Obama's mother was visiting her husband's family in Kenya shortly before the birth.[25]

Arpaio and his posse also questioned the authenticity of President Obama's U.S. Selective Service registration card from 1980. Investigators said that U.S. Postal indicia on the form was forged, a fraud that should be prosecuted as a federal felony. In addition, Sheriff Joe's Cold Case Posse is probing the mystery of Obama's multiple Social Security numbers.[26]

Sideshow Number 9: Document Analysts Declare Birth Certificate "Forgery"

Various document analysts released extensive reports declaring the purported long-form birth certificate fraudulent. We mention just a few.

1. An international expert on scanners and document-imaging software filed a 22-page criminal complaint the week of May 24, 2011 with the FBI, charging that the long-form birth certificate released by the White House is

23 Stephen Dinan, "Sheriff Arpaio: Obama birth certificate a 'forgery,'" March 1, 2012, http://washingtontimes.com/news/2012/mar/1/sheriff-arpaio-obama-birth-certificate-forgery/.
24 "Arpaio: 'Probable cause' Obama certificate a fraud," March 1, 2012, http://wnd.com/2012/03/sheriff-joes-posse-probable-cause-obama-certificate-a-fraud/.
25 "Arpaio investigation: Obama might be Kenyan - Records that could document status mysteriously missing," March 8, 2012, http://wnd.com/2012/03/arpaio-investigation-obama-might-be-kenyan/
26 ABC15 staff, "Arpaio requests Obama's Selective Service card," KNXV-TV, Phoenix, Ariz., March 21, 2012, http://abc15.com/dpp/news/region_phoenix_metro/central_phoenix/arpaio-requests-obamas-selective-service-card.

criminally fraudulent. "What the Obama administration released is a PDF image that they are trying to pass off as a Certificate of Live Birth Long Form printed on green security paper by the Hawaiian Health Department," Doug Vogt wrote, "but this form is a created forgery."[27]

2. Similarly, a typography expert points the flaws in the typefaces of the alleged long-form document. Paul Irey, a retired professional typographer with 50 years' experience, said, "My analysis proves beyond a doubt that it would be impossible for the different letters that appear in the Obama birth certificate to have been typed by one typewriter. This document is definitely a phony." [28]

3. Noted researcher Ronald J. Polland PhD. created from scratch a forged duplicate of the Obama long-form birth certificate demonstrating how it could be done. Previously he had demonstrated how the earlier 2008 short-form birth certificate could have been forged. Pollard spent months reviewing how the multiple anomalies in the alleged long-form birth certificate were created. He concludes emphatically the 2011 document Obama released was forged—as was the earlier COLB.[29]

4. For the record two days after the release of the birth certificate on April 27 Fox News reported computer graphic expert Jean Claude Tremblay had declared the birth certificate authentic. Quickly, Tremblay issued a statement that he had been misquoted and that he had reached no such conclusion on the document further declaring that he was not professionally qualified to reach such a conclusion.[30]

5. Ivan Zatkovich, of Tampa-based eComp Consultants, analyzed the various layers in the PDF file released by the White House, and concluded: "The content clearly indicates that the document was knowingly and explicitly edited and modified before it was placed on the Web." Zatkovich has 28 years of experience in computer science, computer networks and software engineering.[31]

6. Gary Poyssick, a longstanding expert on Adobe software (and early employee of the giant San Jose-based tech company) who has written more than 50 professional titles about Adobe software and related coding and programming asserts that the long-form birth certificate is highly unusual. He continues to maintain there is something "fishy" about Obama's birth certificate released by the White House. His opinion is that this was a

27 Jerome R. Corsi, "Criminal complaint charges Obama birth record 'forged,'" May 31, 2011, http://www.wnd.com/?pageId=305705#ixzz1O2QdV3MY.
28 Jerome R. Corsi "'Irrefutable' proof of Obama forgery, "July 17, 2011 'Irrefutable' proof of Obama forgery http://www.wnd.com/?pageId=322389#ixzz1SthyLlX0 accessed May 20, 2012.
29 Jerome Corsi, "Forged creation matches Obama's birth certificate," October 17, 2011, http://www.wnd.com/2011/10/356005/ accessed May 10, 2012.
30 Jerome Corsi, "Fox News expert denies he claimed birth certificate legit," June 21, 2011, http://www.wnd.com/?pageId=314041#ixzz1Q1HHRrBa
http://www.wnd.com/2011/06/314041/#ixzz1Q1HHRrBa
31 Corsi, "'Irrefutable' proof," *op cit.*

merged document from several original documents—implying it was inauthentic. [32]

Media's Weak Investigation—Final Comments

A few additional matters underscore the media's reluctance to investigate Obama's birth and other personal records. Observers such as California attorney Orly Taitz–who has litigated many legal challenges to Obama's eligibility– estimate that the president has paid lawyers more than $800,000 to keep his birth certificate from being properly investigated. Because he has fought more than three dozen legal actions over the issue of his nativity, Obama's legal bills may be in the millions. [33]

In May 2012 new evidence emerged pointing to Obama's birth in Kenya. His first literary agent back in 1991 had listed Obama in print as "born in Kenya and raised in Indonesia and Hawaii." [34] Naturally the media ignored it or laughingly explained it away as just another freak circumstance. Glenn Beck called it a simple typo. Unusual though how these circumstances keep surfacing. To his credit Lou Dobbs spoke up again saying he saw no reason at all to not at least ask questions about the controversial birth issue.

We review briefly the standard party line the media has adopted in its almost universal "reverse investigation" regarding Barack Obama's citizenship. Upon review their exceedingly simplistic approach stands out. They will also highlight a long known media weakness to insiders, "Birds of a feather flock together." [35] As *Washington Post* reporters Tumulty and Kornblut described in their April 27, 2011 article regarding the birth certificate release, "During the 2008 campaign, he [Obama] had produced the standard version of his birth record, and newspaper birth announcements at the time corroborated it." [36] They imply, "and he just provided the standard version of his long-form birth certificate." These two basic "proofs"—his short-form COLB/corresponding internet long-form birth certificate and the matching newspaper birth announcement in two Honolulu newspapers—are the core of their case. Both "proofs" are open to massive manipulation and prove nothing as established by numerous investigators, logical thinking and common sense.

The next level of the media's proof is "because somebody important said so"—those 'important' authorities being Obama, the Democrat Party, various congressmen and women, the media, so-called "neutral" investigative Internet

32 Jerome Corsi, "Adobe expert doubts Obama birth certificate," June 24, 2011, http://www.wnd.com/?pageId=314717#ixzz1QLbrdZ76 accessed May 15, 2012.
33 Bob Unruh, "Litigation over Sen. Obama's Citizenship: What did president tell Supreme Court?" February 4, 2009, http://usjf.net/2009/02/litigation-over-sen-obamas-citizenship-what-did-president-tell-supreme-court/ .
34 "The Vetting - Exclusive - Obama's Literary Agent in 1991 Booklet: 'Born in Kenya and raised in Indonesia and Hawaii'" http://www.breitbart.com/Big-Government/2012/05/17/The-Vetting-Barack-Obama-Literary-Agent-1991-Born-in-Kenya-Raised-Indonesia-Hawaii .
35 I was told this by a television news reporter and anchor in several major cities. Also this reporter was extensively familiar with the print media and too often had the identical opinion of them.
36 Tumulty and Kornblut, *op cit.*

sites, and Obama supporters. At that point the courts have joined in the party line. Finally, the media shifts tactics in the face of continued questioning by citizens: ridicule those who question legitimacy; call them 'birthers' and ignorant—and if need be question their motives as political, racist or whatever else. My personal favorite was the National Review (normally a fine publication) who in 2012 called Obama birth questions "tacky." And one other tactic—assure 'birthers' that their questions are harmful to the Republican Party goals of winning the 2012 election.

Notice we still have no verification of Obama's birth certificate—if one indeed exists—to this point. Two lightweight reasons for believing it does not an investigation make. You are looking at a sideshow--at a media investigation gone bad.

16

Obama, the Secret Pro-Life President

National pollsters often assess what Americans see as our nation's most troubling problems. The economy, of course, tops the list—high unemployment, sluggish commerce, home sales at a standstill, and our enormous, ever-increasing national debt. In turn, Obama's primary political strategy for 2012 seems to be blaming the rich for the recession and pushing for tax code regulations that will force them to share their wealth. Beyond the crumbling economy, Americans are concerned about constitutional government, foreign policy and—somewhere further down the list—millions express their pointed disapproval of abortion. Although Obama is on record as a pro-choice president, when his super intelligence weighs in on the matter, we find that it voices the *exact opposite opinion* of that expressed by his conscious mind.

As we dissect his confession we find it, filled with surprises, but now we witness the most surprising super-intel moment in his life. Having unconsciously confessed to numerous violations of America and its rule of law, Obama's wise, visionary super intelligence reveals itself as his true moral compass. It makes this revelation as he addresses America's most significant social problem. His answer will shock many who will be further surprised by his unconscious effort to heal the bitter division between pro-life and pro-choice forces. Amazingly, his super-intel dutifully marshals its most convincing powers of persuasion in order to ultimately unify us.

First Obama told us the story of the tremendous abuse he suffered— the near-abortion— which drives his raging re-enactment payback. Then he unconsciously spoke up against his abuse; now he takes the next step: to directly decry abortion. Naturally we're surprised because his surface stance remains pro-choice, but the realization of his own near-abortion gave him a deeply personal perspective on the ongoing harm that abortion-on-demand brings to our country. He has repeatedly clarified that he has a deeper moral compass, the one upon which our nation was founded, the one that has recently been replaced by making up our own rules as we go along.

But Obama is Pro-Choice

It's difficult enough to grasp that Obama believes two things at the same time. Abortion in particular remains such an emotionally charged matter, and Obama has taken such a brutal pro-choice stance—publicly supporting partial-birth abortions—that it becomes difficult to consider him in another light. Yet that's precisely what we've seen—while his conscious mind covers up, his unconscious mind confesses. We must constantly remind ourselves that Obama's conscious mind and his unconscious mind are worlds apart on abortion. Two different minds, two different views.

Ronald Reagan's glib comment, "I have noticed that all the pro-choice people have already been born," cleverly points out that all pro-choice people—including Obama—know deep down they're not treating the unborn as they were treated.

In fact, if protecting life is a natural law of human nature, we should actually *expect* Barack Obama to secretly confess that he's secretly pro-life. In a day and age when it's fashionable to make up our own rules, our brilliant super intelligence brings us back to our true moral compass—true to ourselves and true to God who placed the compass within each of us.

Obama will take us back to the day he nearly died—revealing how that experience made him a blood brother to the unborn child.

Psychologically, people experience a severe near-death trauma as frighteningly as a death experience itself. For example, Michel Navratil survived the sinking of the Titanic on April 15, 1912 as a four-year-old along with his two-year-old brother. They were put into a rescue boat by their father, who remained on the ship and perished. Years later Navratil, who died in 2001 at age 92, was asked about his Titanic experience. "I died when I was four," he said. "Since then I've been a fare-dodger of life."[1] To Obama, his near-abortion was, in his mind, a *completed* abortion. And that experience gave him a unique voice to use to speak up for all unborn children.

Obama has guided us at other moments to seek out his deeper mind's true view of abortion. In May 2009, in a highly controversial commencement address at the University of Notre Dame, Obama spoke about abortion. Surely many supporters advised him against taking his liberal platform to such a stronghold of pro-life activism. Nevertheless, Obama pressed on and told his audience that we must "work together to reduce the number of women seeking abortions [and] let's reduce unintended pregnancies."[2] He suggested that the Roman Catholic graduates keep an "open mind" about the issue of abortion.

In actuality Obama's super-intel was pointing us back to his four-part saga in which he had *already* opened his own unconscious mind on the matter and, in the process, attempted to open the minds of millions of Americans. In his four-

---

1 Andrew Wilson, "Shadow of the Titanic," *Smithsonian*, March 2012, p. 84.
2 Barack Obama, commencement address, University of Notre Dame, South Bend, Indiana, May 17, 2009, http://www.nytimes.com/2009/05/17/us/politics/17text-obama.html?pagewanted=all accessed June 1, 2012.

part narrative, Obama unconsciously speaks as a father who knows what a father should be. And if America ever needed a real father of our nation to step up, it's now. Surprisingly, the deeper Obama *is* that man. It's no accident that Obama's super-intel selected two successive Fathers' Days to begin dealing with this issue. It's no accident that he did so by writing two personal letters to his daughters. These occasions enabled Obama to frequently reference the treasure of children, and to spotlight a father's and mother's crucial roles as parents.

In essence these four sources present a "State of The American Family"— the deepest State of the Union address imaginable. We must trust his images. It's much like listening to poetry or parables. We must stay with Obama's mind, knowing that his light will never be brighter. His entire message tells America what it most needs to know now.

As you read this chapter, step back and really listen. Is Obama really pro-choice or is he in actuality pro-life?[3]

Fathers' Day 2008
> Good morning. It's good to be home on this Father's Day with my girls, and it's an honor to spend some time with all of you today in the house of our Lord. (FD1)

'My Girls'
"Good," pronounces Obama—"good to be home...Father." God meets with his children in a house where parents raise children in a secure, nurturing setting. The very opposite of abortion. Next Obama alludes to "my girls" communicating to parents that "my children" are his own flesh and blood.

People-Building—Creating Life
He then quotes Jesus' parable on wise home builders who build on solid rock foundations to withstand the storms of life.

> At the end of the Sermon on the Mount, Jesus closes by saying, "Whoever hears these words of mine, and does them, shall be likened to a wise man who built his house upon a rock: and the rain descended, and the floods came, and the winds blew, and beat upon that house, and it fell not, for it was founded upon a rock" (Matthew 7: 24-25). (FD1)

By analogy he depicts fathers and mothers as builders of their children's lives. People-builders, creators. Obama starts his story with the importance of a home *built to protect the people inside.*

Again we see Obama's denial of his near-abortion trauma by his omission of the rest of the story in which Jesus compared the wise builder with the foolish

---

3 Although we've covered many of these passages in previous chapters, now we take a slightly different lens to examine them. Obama is secretly showing us he has at the core of his being a pro-life lens, as passionately committed to protecting the unborn as any ardent pro-life activist! Partisanship aside, Obama's all-truthful super-intel demands to be heard.

builder whose home was destroyed by a violent storm.[4] He implies sudden, total destruction of the people inside the weak house in the catastrophic storm. Connecting his story to real-life people (fathers/parents), Obama suggests his foolish father (and mother) wanted to destroy his first home inside his mother's womb. Additionally, they wanted to destroy *him*. His images strongly point to a foolish parent who built an unborn child's temporary home on sand—and then turns on the child, becoming the vicious storm which beat on the house until it fell, and the child existed no more. Early on, Obama's images compellingly parallel the horror of an abortion.

He has begun by hinting strongly at life-or-death issues. Soon he will present more striking images—pointing even more specifically to abortion.

But upon reflection Obama's choice of Jesus' parable unforgettably illustrates how abortion represents a frontal attack on the very nature of a family home. By quoting Scripture, in the house of God no less, Obama in effect swears on the Bible how fully abortion violates God's most fundamental laws.

Increasing Violence
> Here at Apostolic, you are blessed to worship in a house that has been founded on the rock of Jesus Christ, our Lord and Savior. But it is also built on another rock, another foundation—and that rock is Bishop Arthur Brazier...he has built this congregation...to...20,000 strong—a congregation that...has braved the fierce winds and heavy rains of violence and poverty; joblessness and hopelessness. Because of his work...there are more graduates and fewer gang members in the neighborhoods surrounding this church... more homes and fewer homeless. There is more community and less chaos because Bishop Brazier continued the march for justice that he began by Dr. King's side all those years ago...And on this Father's Day, it must make him proud to know that the man now charged with keeping its foundation strong is his son and your new pastor, Reverend Byron Brazier." (FD1)

Obama establishes the importance of the home and the nurturing of children with the message, "you are blessed to worship in a house." In continued rich imagery, Obama tells us a second story of "fierce winds and heavy rains of violence" about gangsters attacking a neighborhood and a home—this time God's house, a church. But led by a rock of a pastor, the church has fought back and cleaned up the neighborhood creating "fewer gang members...more homes and fewer homeless." Less violence resulted in more people living in secure homes—a distinctly pro-life picture.

His reference to the pastor's son suggests son of God, child of God and, along with Obama's earlier "my girls," points to children being created by God.

Then Obama underscores how proud the pastor must be "that the man now

---

4 "Now everyone who hears these sayings of mine and does not do them will be like a foolish man who built his house on sand: and the rains came, and the winds blew and beat upon the house, and it fell. And great was its fall." Matthew 7:26-27, NKJV.

charged with keeping its foundation strong is his son and your new pastor."[5] By also reminding us the minister marched for justice with Dr. King, Obama's super-intel instructs Americans to march on Washington today demanding justice for the unborn, to keep their home intact.

Even further, Obama implies that we are looking at the new Obama, America's pastor/leader—a new Rev. Martin Luther King Jr. figure—who intends to lead America in a bold new direction and restore our nation's rock-solid foundation of the 'Laws of Nature.'[6]

Missing Lives

> But if we are honest with ourselves, we'll admit that what too many fathers also are missing—missing from too many lives and too many homes. They have abandoned their responsibilities, acting like boys instead of men. And the foundations of our families are weaker because of it. (FD1)

Once he has established a child's fundamental need for a family, Obama introduces, "The Problem"—"too many...fathers [and mothers] missing," means we're missing too many lives; our society is worse off because of these 'missing children.'

Obama's images grow more life-threatening. Specifically linking a death reference to the home, he suggests that abortion means the taking of a life, a missing life—and he insists we've been dishonest with ourselves about it. America is in denial and the result is too many homes missing—we are losing the family's foundation which weakens our entire country.

How Many Children Must We Lose?

> How many times in the last year has this city lost a child at the hands of another child? How many times have our hearts stopped in the middle of the night with the sound of a gunshot or a siren? How many teenagers have we seen hanging around on street corners when they should be sitting in a classroom? How many are sitting in prison when they should be working, or at least looking for a job? How many in this generation are we willing to lose to poverty or violence or addiction? How many?
>
> Yes, we need more cops on the street. Yes, we need fewer guns in the hands of people who shouldn't have them. Yes, we need more money for our schools, and more outstanding teachers in the classroom, and more after school programs for our children... need more opportunity in our communities. (FD1)

Now Obama's super-intel points even more directly at abortion. In a stunningly violent death image he establishes that we're accurately reading his

---

5 Obama's sentence can also be read, "The man charged with keeping foundation...strong...son"—alluding to his father, charged with keeping him a strong son with a strong foundation, who utterly failed him. Obama equates "foundation" with life.
6 Again Jefferson in the Declaration of Independence described "The Laws of Nature...and Nature's God."

deeper message. In a back-to-back picture he unconsciously defines abortion as a "lost child" destroyed at the hands of a childish parent—a child shot through the heart with a gun. He almost chants, *"How many [unborn children] in this generation are we willing to lose...to violence—how many, how many?"*

His voice becomes louder as he shouts out that America must learn about the devastation of abortion with three back-to-back educational markers: more schools, more teachers, and "more [pro-life] programs for our children." America must study abortion, its rising statistics, and its ruinous social effect, to fully understand its crippling impact on our nation.

Life Begins at Conception

> But we also need families to raise our children. We need fathers to realize that responsibility does not end at conception. We need them to realize that what makes you a man is not the ability to have a child—it's the courage to raise one. (FD1)

Obama plays his trump card—conception—the central issue in this speech and in his life, the moment when his major conflict began. Conception represents the most basic "life-or-death" issue of all: either you exist or you don't.

The central question secretly confronting him daily and with which he confronts America: does "responsibility [for a child]... end at conception?" His phrase "end at conception" suggests "end life—death at conception." This secretly confirms that his life essentially ended shortly after conception with his near-abortion.

No More Dropping

> We need to help all the mothers out there who are raising these kids by themselves; the mothers who drop them off at school, go to work, pick up them up in the afternoon, work another shift, get dinner, make lunches, pay the bills, fix the house, and all the other things it takes both parents to do. So many of these women are doing a heroic job, but they need support. They need another parent. Their children need another parent. That's what keeps their foundation strong. It's what keeps the foundation of our country strong. (FD1)

With stunning images, Obama continues issuing instructions to mothers by pleading, "We need to help mothers...raising kids...mothers who drop them." He encourages unmarried women who want to abort their unborn children— "drop them"—to instead "pick them up," i.e., raise these kids. Then, with perfect timing, he emphasizes the importance of marriage: "takes both parents...women need another parent...children need another parent." He confronts another violation of natural law plaguing our nation—the casual devaluation of marriage, as witnessed by the epidemic of single motherhood so common in our society today.

Unequivocally Obama warns us that how we treat conception and marriage will determine our future—"It's what keeps the foundation of our country strong." His actions as a committed husband and father certainly match his super-intelligence wisdom.

His Personal Story

> I know what it means to have an absent father, although my circumstances weren't as tough as they are for many young people today. Even though my father left us when I was two years old, and I only knew him from the letters he wrote and the stories that my family told, I was luckier than most. I grew up in Hawaii, and had two wonderful grandparents from Kansas who poured everything they had into helping my mother raise my sister and me—who worked with her to teach us about love and respect and the obligations we have to one another. I screwed up more often than I should've, but I got plenty of second chances. (FD1)

Deep down Obama believes that his "two wonderful grandparents from Kansas poured everything they had into helping my mother raise…me." In other words, they talked his mother out of aborting him. They "worked with her to teach [her] about love and respect and the obligations we have to one another"— that is they taught her how to act toward him, her unborn child. Obama was "lucky," implying he was lucky to stay alive in the womb. *His super-intel carefully chooses each word, each image, each story.*

Obama thus says to expectant mothers considering abortion, "Your love for your unwanted child can grow—as millions of mothers who kept their 'unwanted' child would testify. As one of those children, I can tell you."

Premier School on Abortion

> And even though we didn't have a lot of money, scholarships gave me the opportunity to go to some of the best schools in the country. A lot of kids don't get these chances today. There is no margin for error in their lives. So my own story is different in that way. (FD1)

In sequence, Obama persuasively tells a far deeper story. His super-intel— grasping the crucial messages—informs us that it's providing "the best school in the country" on what abortion means for America. Abortion means "a lot of kids don't get these chances today"—as Obama acknowledges the destructive shift in our culture in which the unborn is no longer a child. His super-intel argues that pro-life is our only sane choice.

Promise to Break Cycle

> Still, I know the toll that being a single parent took on my mother— how she struggled at times to pay the bills; to give us the things that other kids had; to play all the roles that both parents are supposed to play. And I know the toll it took on me.
>
> So I resolved many years ago that it was my obligation to break the cycle—that if I could be anything in life, I would be a good father to my girls; that if I could give them anything, I would give them that rock—that foundation—on which to build their lives. And that would be the greatest gift I could offer. (FD1)

236

Obama sees the toll his near-abortion took on him. He sees the missing father who tried to destroy him. He understands above all a father's primary goal: *"if I could be anything...life...be a good father"* meaning, give life to your unborn child, protect that child. You'll never do anything greater than giving and protecting life.

Speaking to his daughters but actually to all the unborn, he vows to break the cycle of abuse—abortion. He insists, "if I could give them anything, I would give them...that rock on which to build—their lives...would be the greatest gift I can offer." He cannot say it any plainer: "Life is the greatest gift a parent can give a child."

Failing the Unborn

> I say this knowing that I have been an imperfect father—knowing that I have made mistakes and will continue to make more; wishing that I could be home for my girls and my wife more than I am right now. (FD1)

In perfect step with his secret narrative, Obama's super-intel confesses not only to his illegal presidency, "I have been an imperfect father [to America as president] I have made mistakes," but it also simultaneously confesses to the great guilt he suffers for his public pro-abortion stance. Read, "I have been an absent imperfect father *to the unborn*, I've made the mistake of failing to preserve their natural home in *their womb*—and continue making the same mistake." His images even speak for that unborn child who never saw the light of day, "wishing I could be home," wishing he could live.[7]

> I say this knowing all of these things because even as we are imperfect, even as we face difficult circumstances, there are still certain lessons we must strive to live and learn as fathers—whether we are black or white; rich or poor; from the South Side or the wealthiest suburb. (FD1)

Obama reminds us with a vivid message marker, "I say this knowing—all of these things," knowing about abortion firsthand. Promptly he tells pro-choice America—"know we are imperfect as we face difficult circumstances" of unexpected pregnancies ending in abortion. Then he speaks for the unborn. To them, "We...strive to live." That is, we must strive for knowledge, to learn to let our unborn live.

Responsibility Extends to Washington

> Our young boys and girls see...when you are ignoring or mistreating your wife. They see when you are inconsiderate at home; or when you are distant; or when you are thinking only of yourself. And so it's no surprise when we see that behavior in our schools or on our streets. That's why we pass on the values of empathy and kindness to

---

7 A mother, father, and child will all refer to the family dwelling as "my home." Any parent worth his or her salt, however, would tell you that children come first—they can't provide their own home—even though the parents legally own the house.

The Obama Confession

our children by living them. We need to show our kids that you're not strong by putting other people down—you're strong by lifting them up. That's our responsibility as fathers.

And by the way—it's a responsibility that also extends to Washington. Because if fathers are doing their part; if they're taking our responsibilities seriously to be there for their children, and set high expectations for them, and instill in them a sense of excellence and empathy, then our government should meet them halfway. (FD1)

First Obama reminds us how he knew all about his near-abortion: children "see" the family secrets. In the same way, he now sees America's dark family secret.

Obama cannot stop talking about children. He speaks again of parents mistreating children "thinking only of" themselves. Instead we are "to pass on kindness to our children"—"pass on...our children...living"—let them live. And he declares we are weak for "putting other people down"—a clear abortion reference. Abortion, his super-intel insists, greatly weakens America.

Obama's Pro-Life Platform—The Real Choice
We should be making it easier for fathers who make responsible choices and harder for those who avoid them. We should get rid of the financial penalties we impose on married couples right now, and start making sure that every dime of child support goes directly to helping children instead of some bureaucrat. We should reward fathers who pay that child support with job training and job opportunities and a larger Earned Income Tax Credit that can help them pay the bills. We should expand programs where registered nurses visit expectant and new mothers and help them learn how to care for themselves before the baby is born and what to do after—programs that have helped increase father involvement, women's employment, and children's readiness for school. We should help these new families care for their children by expanding maternity and paternity leave, and we should guarantee every worker more paid sick leave so they can stay home to take care of their child without losing their income. (FD1)

Obama unconsciously elaborates on his massive pro-life education program and the government's role. He wants to make it "easier for fathers [parents] who make *responsible choices*" and harder on those parents who make irresponsible choices. With the magic word "choice" Obama labels "pro-choice" as the irresponsible choice it is, and how it avoids the truth, matching his central declaration that parental responsibility begins at conception.

His unconscious mind sees "that every dime of [government] child support goes directly to helping [all unborn] children" live—implying again that we should end government support for abortion in the monies we spend on child services.

Most strikingly as he alludes to "choice," Obama speaks of expanding government programs "where registered nurses visit expectant and new mothers to help them learn how to care...before *the baby is born*." Obama's super

238

intelligence as the nurturing medical person again underscores an expectant mother carries a baby in her womb—and that the government should be involved declaring that fact. Such programs would "increase father involvement, women's employment, and children's readiness for school." Read eliminating abortion as an option would make father's more responsible, help pregnant mother's assume their true job of a caretaker and allow for the unborn child to one day go to school. The message marker "school" points clearly to the Supreme Court implying go to school on the rules of parenthood which includes conception.

Indeed the world has rarely had a better pro-life spokesman, a man who came within a hair's breadth of being an unborn child himself. Image by image, Obama reveals where his passion for life originated. Image by image, he warns us that this is our "final lesson." Obama's deeper consciousness begs America to pay attention: It's now or never.

Nurture the Small Part of You

> I was answering questions at a town hall meeting in Wisconsin the other day and a young man raised his hand, and I figured he'd ask about college tuition or energy or maybe the war in Iraq. But instead he looked at me very seriously and he asked, 'What does life mean to you?' Now, I have to admit that I wasn't quite prepared for that one. I think I stammered for a little bit, but then I stopped and gave it some thought, and I said this: When I was a young man, I thought life was all about me—how do I make my way in the world, and how do I become successful and how do I get the things that I want.
>
> But now, my life revolves around my two little girls. And what I think about is what kind of world I'm leaving them. Are they living in a country where there's a huge gap between a few who are wealthy and a whole bunch of people who are struggling every day? Are they living in a county that is still divided by race? A country where, because they're girls, they don't have as much opportunity as boys do? Are they living in a country where we are hated around the world because we don't cooperate effectively with other nations? Are they living in a world that is in grave danger because of what we've done to its climate? (FD1)

Obama poses the central question for America, "What does life [implying life of the unborn] mean to you?" Then he becomes America's answer man, "When I was a young man, I thought *life* was all about me. But now, my *life* revolves around my two little girls." Obama's message: like too many, he thought life was one thing when it's really another. Aborting a child is totally selfish, the denial of life. But real life—for a parent or a nation—revolves around how it treats children, including unborn children. The power to create life and protect it carries phenomenal responsibility.

He then introduces his concern about what kind of world are we leaving our children. His super-intel asks four tough questions for parents, all beginning with the key phrase, *"Are they living?"* In a country divided by economics, race, and opportunity—a country hated around the world—the major question is: are unborn children allowed to live? Our entire future is at stake over this. Obama's great unconscious could not be any more adamant.

Obama's super-intel has an ominous vision of what America would look like if we don't address our most crushing problem—the routine slaughter of the unborn, implied by children who are "hated" and in "grave danger." Obama deep down sees that abortion of pre-natal babies trashes a basic American tenet, and this will eventually poison the entire nation. Obama's super-intel cuts him (and us) no slack on this urgent matter: "And what I've realized is that life doesn't count for much unless you're willing to do your small part to leave our children—all of our children—a better world. Even if it's difficult. Even if the work seems too great. Even if we don't get very far in our lifetime." (FD1)

Our lives don't count, our country doesn't count unless you take care of "your small part." Obama tells a woman (and a nation) that an unborn baby is a part of you. He continues, "leave all our children a better world"—meaning, leave the unborn child in the world. Even if it's difficult on us and we have to stand up to our own superficial "pro-choice" impulses and those of others—to guarantee the life of the unborn counts. He makes plain the unborn child is a person, contrary to what the NARAL[8] lobby states.

But now he turns to his plan for our nation, a society strewn with the tiny bodies of unborn children.

Natural Law Will Prevail

> That is our ultimate responsibility as fathers and parents. We try. We hope. We do what we can to build our house upon the sturdiest rock. And when the winds come, and the rains fall, and they beat upon that house, we keep faith that our Father will be there to guide us, and watch over us, and protect us, and lead His children through the darkest of storms into light of a better day. That is my prayer for all of us on this Father's Day, and that is my hope for this country in the years ahead. May God Bless you and your children. Thank you. (FD1)

His final comments on this Father's Day paint another dramatic picture defending life. He repeats the ultimate responsibility for parents: build your children, be their rock foundation and do not abort them. And he assures us that "the Father"—God—"will be there...to guide...watch over and protect," again referring to God's natural law by which He protects and guides. This law will "lead 'His' [unborn] children through the darkest storms" of abortion "into the light of a better day." America will someday celebrate "Pro-Life Day" every day.

Obama's final words, "my prayer for all of us...Fathers [and mothers]...my hope for this country in the years ahead. May God Bless *you and your children*"—especially the unborn who need deliverance from destruction.

---

8 National Abortion Rights Action League.

The Pre-Inauguration Letter—A Father Leads the Way

> I know that you've both had a lot of fun these last two years on the campaign trail, going to picnics and parades and state fairs, eating all sorts of junk food your mother and I probably shouldn't have let you have. But I also know that it hasn't always been easy for you and Mom, and that as excited as you both are about that new puppy, it doesn't make up for all the time we've been apart. I know how much I've missed these past two years, and today I want to tell you a little more about why I decided to take our family on this journey.

> But then the two of you came into my world with all your curiosity and mischief and those smiles that never fail to fill my heart and light up my day. And suddenly, all my big plans for myself didn't seem so important anymore. I soon found that the greatest joy in my life was the joy I saw in yours. And I realized that my own life wouldn't count for much unless I was able to ensure that you had every opportunity for happiness and fulfillment in yours. (ILtr)

Obama continues speaking up for the unborn. It's his secret campaign. He immediately depicts a mother and father failing to nurture their children by carelessly feeding them junk food. He introduces a birth image, "a new puppy," but links it to an irreparable separation between a parent and a child: "all the time we've been apart," how a parent has missed years with a child. He points toward the permanent loss of children—abortion. Yet he wants to keep the American family together—as he takes them on a [joyous] journey of discovery about the unborn—saying, "I want to tell you."

Immediately Obama describes the birth of children ("came into...world") and their magical effect on parents: their curiosity, their mischief, their smiles that fill your heart and light up your day. Not only do children provide a parent's greatest joy, he says, they teach parents their true importance as co-creators of a human being. Indeed, "children are magic personified." But selfish parents neglecting unborn children don't "count." We hear Obama's warning, 'If you lose the magic of children, you lose the magic of America.'

He wants to "ensure every opportunity for happiness"—for every unborn child in this nation. And we can read his words another way: Obama's own life "wouldn't count" unless he speaks up for the unborn.

> In the end, girls, that's why I ran for President: because of what I want for you and for every child in this nation.

> I want all our children [citizens] to go to schools worthy of their potential schools that challenge them, inspire them, and instill in them a sense of wonder about the world around them. I want them to have the chance to go to college—even if their parents aren't rich. And I want them to get good jobs: jobs that pay well and give them benefits like health care, jobs that let them spend time with their own kids and retire with dignity. (ILtr)

Plainly Obama underscores for the first of many times, "I want... *every* child in this nation." Read, "including every unborn child." And he links this

241

uncompromising pledge to *"why I ran for president*...for every child in this nation." Again he wants to "give them [the unborn] benefits like health-care." Despite his deceptive presidency, Obama deeply desired a presidential platform to protest against the abortion pain that led him astray.

Sonograms to Save Lives—"So That You'll Live"

> I want us to push the boundaries of discovery so that you'll live to see new technologies and inventions that improve our lives and make our planet cleaner and safer. And I want us to push our own human boundaries to reach beyond... (ILtr)

Obama speaks so plainly for the unborn "I want us to push the boundaries of discovery *so that you'll live... lives... make... safer.*" First, he pushes us to discover natural law and deeper values in the unconscious, the new technology of the mind which desperately wants to protect the unborn.

Then he urges us "to see the new technologies" that make the lives of the unborn safer. He alludes to the new technology that sees the unborn child in the womb—suggesting a sonogram—for every parent desiring an abortion so they can see the hands, the feet, the head—a tiny human being! And this will make America cleaner and rid us of our hidden and burdensome guilt. He wants us to reject abortion as a routine social convenience and reset the boundaries of our country that allow us to take an unborn's life. He unwittingly suggests his pro-life campaign slogan: 'A sonogram for every woman before she considers abortion.'[9] Can you imagine the blessing if the federal government, instead of funding the wholesale slaughter of babies, would create a nationwide series of Crisis Pregnancy Centers, the way churches have been doing for decades? To help women who have a surprise pregnancy regain their emotional footing and put their unselfish focus on their unborn child?

The War Against the Unborn

> Sometimes we have to send our young men and women into war and other dangerous situations to protect our country—but when we do, I want to make sure that it is only for a very good reason, that we try our best to settle our differences with others peacefully, and that we do everything possible to keep our servicemen and women safe.

> And I want every child to understand that the blessings these brave Americans fight for are not free—that with the great privilege of being a citizen of this nation comes great responsibility. (ILtr)

Obama's story continues, *"sometimes we...send our young men and women... into... dangerous situations...protect."* He's saying we must stop sending our young unborn boys and girls into dangerous situations at abortion clinics. Obama reveals the so-called 'war on women' they accuse the GOP of waging is too often a woman's war on their own unborn child—and he declares

---

9 Very few parents who abort ever view a sonogram—to maintain their inordinate denial their unborn is a child.

a truce. To pro-choice women he says "settle…differences with others [the unborn child] peacefully"—no more abortion war.

Above all "we do everything possible to keep these young servicemen and women safe"—reminding us to "keep them," not discard them. After all, our boys and girls also serve us.

In "I want every child to understand that [they are] the blessings these brave Americans fight for," Obama unconsciously insists we fight for every unborn child. He implies citizenship rights of the unborn begin at conception.

Equal Rights for the Unborn
> That was the lesson your grandmother tried to teach me when I was your age, reading me the opening lines of the Declaration of Independence and telling me about the men and women who marched for equality because they believed those words put to paper two centuries ago should mean something. (ILtr)

Obama follows by unconsciously asserting that the Declaration itself guarantees the unborn the unalienable right to life. He speaks for the unborn by recalling "when I was your age" and nearly aborted.[10] His super-intel passionately instructs Americans to march—this time demanding equality of life for the unborn, equal rights for future citizens.[11] Unconsciously Obama levels his concerned stare directly upon the Supreme Court Justices. His message: America needs a new policy against abortion, based on the nation's founding documents.

Improve America or 'Our Union Falls'
> She helped me understand that America is great not because it is perfect but because it can always be made better—and that the unfinished work of perfecting our union falls to each of us. It's a charge we pass on to our children, coming closer with each new generation to what we know America should be. (ILtr)

Continuing his references to childbirth ("each new generation"), Obama charges America to specifically stand up in favor of passing life on to its children. His super-intel underscores America's glaring imperfection of abortion and issues an ominous warning: "Our union falls" if we fail to protect the unborn. If we fail to protect the most vulnerable and under-privileged in our society, we will ultimately fail to protect our nation.

Daughters Instructed—To Work for Pro-Life
> I hope both of you will take up that work, righting the wrongs that you see and working to give others the chances you've had. Not just because you have an obligation to give something back to this country that has given our family so much—although you do have that obligation. But because you have an obligation to yourself. Because it is only when you hitch your wagon to something larger than yourself

10 He reminds us again that his grandmother saved him from abortion appealing to the Declaration.
11 Many women who pushed for the ERA failed to push for equal rights for unborn girls.

that you will realize your true potential...
These are the things I want for you—to grow up in a world with no
limits on your dreams and no achievements beyond your [my] reach,
and to grow into compassionate, committed women who will help
build that world. (ILtr)

Obama now has distinct instructions for his daughters. First he wants his
children to "take up that [pro-life] work of righting the wrongs" to "give others
the chances you've had"—to live. His super-intel clearly labels abortion as
wrong, informing us "we all see it" unconsciously. As recipients of life, his
children have an obligation to this nation to speak up to give all unborn children
a chance.

Higher Values

"And I want every child to have the same chances to learn and dream
and grow and thrive that you girls have. That's why I've taken our
family on this great adventure." (ILtr)

Speaking non-stop for the unborn he informs us, "[I want] every child...the
same chances to... grow and thrive," which says it all. "Every child" points to
Obama's relentless secret push for a reversal of *Roe v. Wade*. Presidentially he's
taking the American family on "this great adventure" of standing up for the
unborn. A large, successful nation has a generous heart for the life of the
unborn. Take that heart away and a nation loses its soul.

New Life in the White House

I am so proud of both of you. I love you more than you can ever know.
And I am grateful every day for your patience, poise, grace, and
humor as we prepare to start our new life together in the White
House. Love, Dad. (ILtr)

Obama takes us back to abortion, to "new life"—when life began,
specifically his. "I am grateful every day for...grace...for new life." Once more
he speaks out for the Christian God of grace that saw him through his near-
abortion death, the same grace that saw America through its own near-death
experience at our founding.[12]

Obama closes this letter speaking those very words to the unborn child, to
new life—that so many neglect. "I love you, unborn children, more than you
will ever know. Prepare, America, you have a president in the White House who
represents 'new life'—pro-life—because I once was a new-life kid on the edge.
Love, Dad."

Revealing the extent of his passion, Obama still has more to say on this
matter, in two more personal communications. Unabatedly he will continue his
same message on behalf of the pre-natal child, the unborn one who lives in the
womb.

---

12 Islam's core beliefs reflect a performance-based religion, whereas the grace of God is at the center of
Christianity.

17

Obama: More Passion for Pro-Life

Fathers' Day Reminders—The Second Open Letter

The second of Obama's open letters to his daughters appeared on Fathers' Day 2009. *Each of his four key communications has its own characteristics regarding his deep down pro-life stance.* In this letter we find Obama presenting less violent images of abortion. Remember, he has already confessed to committing violence on America, a transference of the severe violence he received as a child. At the time of the three prior communications, he was either not yet president or had just been inaugurated—and all were written prior to his formally assuming the office.

Now he sits back and attempts to reason with America about its misguided ways regarding the unborn—speaking presidentially. In this brief letter, Obama uses "lives" and "life" five times each. He refers to "my own life" three times, demonstrating just how seriously his life had been threatened. Obama carries on speaking in code, but his super intelligence—ever the teacher—allows for a clear and concise decoding.

Father of the Young

> As the father of two young girls who have shown such poise, humor, and patience in the unconventional life into which they have been thrust, I mark this Father's Day—our first in the White House—with a deep sense of gratitude. One of the greatest benefits of being president is that I now live right above the office. I see my girls off to school nearly every morning and have dinner with them nearly every night. It is a welcome change after so many years out on the campaign trail and commuting between Chicago and Capitol Hill. (FD2)

Obama's opening imagery says it all, "the father of...[the] young"—of the very young, the unborn. No doubt he continues speaking especially for one group in America. Again he tells us why.

"I mark this Fathers' Day...with a deep sense of gratitude"—he was thrust into the "most unconventional life" early on, nearly thrust out of his mother's womb. And now he becomes "the most unconventional" president to stand up for the unborn. We would never think it possible, but deep down he tells us, "I now live right." He has become spokesman for the forgotten unborn because "I now live...I see" the value of life.

He confesses "I see my children"—the unborn—but he does it by telling us surface stories about seeing his daughters off to school or having dinner with them, of missing them when he's away. His unconscious message: "Go to school on what abortion really means. It means not feeding your kids, not wanting to be with them, missing out on family, missing out on taking them to school."

Marked Unborn Children

As an adult, working as a community organizer and later as a legislator, I would often walk through the streets of Chicago's South Side and see boys marked by that same absence—boys without supervision or direction or anyone to help them as they struggled to grow into men. I identified with their frustration and disengagement—with their sense of having been let down. (FD2)

Not missing a beat, Obama unconsciously tells another brief story about abortion. On Chicago's South Side he sees unborn boys marked—unwanted—by absent parents as "they struggled to grow." That boy was once him and now he sees untold millions just like him.

He depicts an unborn child who struggled to grow against a parent's wishes—not an ounce of supervision or direction, headed nowhere but down and out—totally alone "without anyone to help" him. Obama cries for the unborn, "*I want to grow.*" How many times must he use the word?

Obama wants us to feel the pain of every unborn child who loses out on life. He speaks to mothers and fathers on the edge of abortion. He wants them to hear their unborn child calling out, "Can't anyone help me? Can't you show me the way home? I need supervision, I need my parents. I'm struggling to make it."

Abortion Leaves a Huge Hole

In many ways, I came to understand the importance of fatherhood through its absence—both in my life and in the lives of others. I came to understand that the hole a man leaves when he abandons his responsibility to his children is one that no government can fill. We can do everything possible to provide good jobs and good schools and safe streets for our kids, but it will never be enough to fully make up the difference. (FD2)

Next Obama tells us, "Understand the importance of [parenthood] through its absence in my life and in the lives of others." He adds, "Understand the hole a [parent] leaves" who "abandons his responsibility to his [unborn] children" cannot be filled, neither in the child nor the parent.

For the child, abortion is an empty hole. Suddenly you are nothing. Suddenly you cease to exist in this world. For the mother, a physical and emotional hole occurs in the womb of her heart. A mother's heart. Obama unconsciously grasps that such are the laws of nature which God placed within us. His super-intel pointedly warns parents, "You cannot cheat human nature.

246

It's who you are."

Then he informs us that "we...do everything possible to provide...safe streets for our kids," meaning we must provide safe delivery into the world for the unborn.

Conception—Take Courage

> That is why we need fathers to step up, to realize that their job does not end at conception; that what makes you a man is not the ability to have a child but the courage to raise one.
>
> As fathers, we need to be involved in our children's lives not just when it's convenient or easy, and not just when they're doing well—but when it's difficult and thankless, and they're struggling. That is when they need us most. (FD2)

Obama comes to the centerpiece of this letter—repeating his previous Fathers' Day message that a parent's job *"does not end at conception"* implying "nor does life end at conception." He persists in establishing the legal definition of when life begins—his super intelligence a lawyer unconsciously making his case.

He teaches parents of unwanted pregnancies, "Take courage, raise your child." To the irresponsible pro-choice folks he declares, "You have no courage." He calls them cowards. His super intelligence simply does not mince words. The hour is late. The time is dire.

Unwanted Pregnancies

> And it's not enough to just be physically present...during tough economic times like these... emotionally absent...consumed by what's happening in our own lives...unsure if we'll be able to give our kids the same opportunities we had.
>
> Our children can tell. They know when we're not fully there. And that disengagement sends a clear message—whether we mean it or not—about where among our priorities they fall.
>
> So we need to step out of our own heads and tune in. We need to turn off the television and start talking with our kids, and listening to them, and understanding what's going on in their lives. (FD2)

He identifies a parent's predicament with an unwanted unborn child: "During tough...times like these...consumed by what's happening in our own lives." His counsel remains steady, "Give our kids [the unborn *is* a child] the same opportunities we had"—life.

He asks a question of parents intent on an abortion: "Where among our priorities" are these unborn children? He answers, "they fall"—the kid no longer lives and the parents fall too. Abortion is guaranteed to bring them all down in more ways than one.

Again he tells us to "tune in," to talk, listen and understand "what's going on in their lives." Subtly he suggests parents on the verge should stop and listen to their child's heartbeat at the doctor's office—a beating heart. It's the only way an unborn child can tell you, "Hear me, I have a heart. Don't rip my heart out—or yours."

Media Glorifies Abortion

> We need to set limits and expectations. We need to replace that video game with a book and make sure that homework gets done. We need to say to our daughters, Don't ever let images on TV tell you what you are worth, because I expect you to dream without limit and reach for your goals. We need to tell our sons, Those songs on the radio may glorify violence, but in our house we find glory in achievement, self-respect, and hard work. (FD2)

Compellingly, Obama admonishes parents, "make sure that homework gets done," meaning work to give your unborn child a home. Appreciate the true worth of kids—keep your unborn child.

He counsels that parents should stop letting "the media glorify [the] violence" of abortion. Just as he said above, "cut off the television." In the home, parents find their glory in self-respect, achievement and hard work. Keep your unborn child, give her a home and indeed you will have that glory. And build the same thing into her. Abortion, on the other hand, means no self-respect, no achievement and no work—which is why abortion drags America down.

The Abortion Nation

> We need to realize that we are our children's first and best teachers. When we are selfish or inconsiderate, when we mistreat our wives or girlfriends, when we cut corners or fail to control our tempers, our children learn from that—and it's no surprise when we see those behaviors in our schools or on our streets. (FD2)

As a near victim of abortion, Obama sees the effects of abortion on the unborn and on America. Abortion means parents fail to control their tempers. Terminating a pregnancy is, after all, an expression of extreme anger toward an unborn child. Obama speaks for the child who surely experiences abortion as an angry attack. Anger directed at the most helpless, defenseless, vulnerable victim in the entire world—in the ICU of the mother's womb no less. Such anger spawns unbelievable guilt no mother or father can escape.

No wonder pro-choice (who are really pro-death) people become so vicious in their attacks on anyone who challenges them. They must turn their internal volcano of guilt-induced rage on others, lest they implode. Obama reveals another dark secret. Parents who abort are America's "best"—read, most powerful—teachers. Secretly they espouse violence. The visionary Obama understands deep down that the violence of abortion is directly linked to increasing violence in our society.

America has cut corners by ignoring its true moral compass—lost its way, headed in the wrong direction. It pays a costly price that will morally bankrupt our nation.

Parent-Teacher Conference

> But it also works the other way around. When we work hard, treat others with respect, spend within our means, and contribute to our communities, those are the lessons our children learn. And that is what so many fathers are doing every day—coaching soccer and Little League, going to those school assemblies and parent-teacher conferences, scrimping and saving and working that extra shift so their kids can go to college. They are fulfilling their most fundamental duty as fathers: to show their children, by example, the kind of people they want them to become. (FD2)

On the other hand Obama's deeper moral compass now shows America the way home. He is having a parent-teacher conference with the parents of the unborn child. These are the lessons: treat the unborn child with respect. Parents should go to school on what real parents do—protect the unborn and raise them, work extra hard so their kids can live and learn. That is what big-league parents do. *That is what a great country does.*

Parents Who Aborted

> It is rarely easy. There are plenty of days of struggle and heartache when, despite our best efforts, we fail to live up to our responsibilities. I know I have been an imperfect father. I know I have made mistakes. I have lost count of all the times, over the years, when the demands of work have taken me from the duties of fatherhood. There were many days out on the campaign trail when I felt like my family was a million miles away, and I knew I was missing moments of my daughters' lives that I'd never get back. It is a loss I will never fully accept. (FD2)

Obama now unconsciously confesses for failing the unborn as president with his longstanding mistaken pro-choice stance. Simultaneously he confesses for millions of parents who aborted their unborn children.

First he acknowledges the children who lost their lives, "days of struggle and heartache when we [the unborn], despite our best efforts, fail to live." Then Obama explains why—because "we [those of us in control] fail to live up to our responsibilities."

He asserts, "I have been an imperfect father" to the unborn. "I have made mistakes. I have lost count of all the times, over the years, when [my] demands...have taken me from the duties of fatherhood" to the unborn in America. He lost count of how many lives have been lost on his watch.

Obama continues, "There were many days when my family [of unborn children] were a million miles away...I knew I was missing...lives that I'd never get back." We can then hear his resolve which drives his secret campaign on their behalf, "It is a loss I will never fully accept." Presidents feel responsible for all citizens—deep down they know it is their job to protect them.

And Obama counsels America—you can't get back those lives of aborted children, but you can refuse to accept any more losses.

Consider Abraham Lincoln as he confronted the injustice of slavery. He knew that the practice violated natural law, and now Obama—as his super-intel confronts abortion—points us toward an identical misdirection of our God-given moral compass. Just as Negro slaves were human beings who were wrongly deprived their freedom to pursue life as they saw fit, so are unborn babies deprived of life itself. Our founders believed a Creator assigned every human soul unalienable rights and that this Creator allowed us to be created in the womb. Just as Lincoln's Emancipation Proclamation began to right the wrongs of decades, so too Obama's super-intel here proposes the emancipation of the unborn. "Let them live free," his super-intel pleads! "Let them live free or our nation will wither."

But maybe God is giving America a second chance. It's possible that God has selected a near-abortion victim who can speak persuasively and powerfully, a man with nationwide and worldwide influence. Who can issue an internal warning to America like Lincoln or King did? Obama the prophet?

A Closing Pledge

> But on this Father's Day, I think back to the day I drove Michelle and a newborn Malia home from the hospital nearly 11 years ago—crawling along, miles under the speed limit, feeling the weight of my daughter's future resting in my hands. I think about the pledge I made to her that day: that I would give her what I never had—that if I could be anything in life, I would be a good father. I knew that day that my own life wouldn't count for much unless she had every opportunity in hers. And I knew I had an obligation, as we all do, to help create those opportunities and leave a better world for her and all our children. (FD2)

Unconsciously he describes his burden now as president, "On this Fathers' Day...feeling the weight of [America's] future in my hands." He reasserts that our nation's future depends on how well we care for the unborn, the nearly-newborn. For now, he notes, America is just barely crawling along, slowed down by the weight of hidden guilt.

Then he makes a striking pledge to the unborn child, "I would give her what I never had...life—that...I could be..." He's guaranteeing that every unborn child would be allowed to exist. He goes on, "If I could be anything in life, I would be a good father" [of our nation, a father to the unborn]. I knew that day that my own life wouldn't count for much unless she [the unborn] had every opportunity [for life] in hers."

His daughters thus become a symbol for the unborn who strive for enriching lives. "And I knew I had an obligation, as we all do, to help create those opportunities and leave a better world for her and all our [unborn] children." Hear Obama: we must leave *all our unborn children* in the world—it makes a better world for America. He has just taken a pledge to America's unborn on our behalf. Obama reminds us once more that how we treat the most vulnerable among us is a central part of who we are.[1] How well Obama knows this—he who nearly left the world before he'd ever entered it.

Recommitment and Prayer

> On this Father's Day, I am recommitting myself to that work, to those duties that all parents share: to build a foundation for our children's dreams, to give them the love and support they need to fulfill them, and to stick with them the whole way through, no matter what doubts we may feel or difficulties we may face. That is my prayer for all of us on this Father's Day, and that is my hope for this nation in the months and years ahead. (FD2)

Continuing Obama's story, we read "children" as "unborn children" and see how clearly his super-intel speaks. Beyond his pledge Obama adds a recommitment: "I am recommitting myself to that work, to those duties that all parents share: to build a foundation for our [unborn] children's dreams, to give them the love and support they need...to stick with them the whole way through [the pregnancy], no matter what doubts...or difficulties we may face."

Obama concludes, "That is my prayer for all of us...this Father [of our nation included]...my hope for this nation in the months and years ahead." Unconsciously he wants America to stick with their unborn children despite whatever difficulties arise in reversing that atrocity called *Roe v. Wade*. He can see that day—indeed that's his deepest hope for America—but he knows the work it will take in the months and years ahead.

Story by story, Obama has made his case for the unborn child to the American people—ending on a crescendo of a pledge and a prayer. He's talking to all parents in all of America about all of the children —reflecting the law of the home. And with the phrase "my prayer," his super intelligence points us to God, the originator of natural law which promises the unborn the unalienable right to life, liberty and the pursuit of happiness.

Obama's Greatest Speech—Part II

Fittingly, Obama's deepest self chooses his life's most triumphant moment—his Inauguration Day—to passionately make the case that the smoldering crisis of abortion is America's greatest threat. Obama's super intelligence expertly employs the language of story and images to loudly decry the violence of abortion as never before.

This time, however, *his unconscious message is more symbolic, making fewer overt references to children than in his other three key communications*. Nevertheless, he builds his case slowly but surely to a shocking and undeniable conclusion—and his symbolic images enable him to speak even more powerfully about what abortion truly means.

---

[1] This is reminiscent of Jesus' idea, "...inasmuch as ye have done it unto the least of these my brethren, ye have done it unto Me" (Matt. 25:40) KJV.

Born Sacrifice

"I stand here today humbled by the task before us, grateful for the trust you have bestowed, mindful of the sacrifices borne by our ancestors. I thank President Bush for his service to our nation, as well as the generosity and cooperation he has shown throughout this transition." (ISp)

"I stand here humbled" immediately reveals the life-long stamp of humiliation he bears brought on by "sacrifices borne," a phrase which vividly suggests he was nearly sacrificed before he was born—"a born sacrifice." Obama links birth to sacrifices of human life. The key words "…mindful of… sacrifices…by our ancestors" suggest his ancestors, his parents, considered aborting him. His mind is overwhelmed by that trauma, unconsciously obsessed with it. Right off we see the power of his images—abortion sacrifices the life of the nearly born. Obama's super-intel declares that abortion violates the "trust bestowed" by the child.

Crisis of Cultural Values

That we are in the midst of crisis is now well understood. Our nation is at war, against a far-reaching network of violence and hatred. Our economy is badly weakened, a consequence of greed and irresponsibility on the part of some, but also our collective failure to make hard choices and prepare the nation for a new age. Homes have been lost; jobs shed; businesses shuttered. Our health care is too costly; our schools fail too many; and each day brings further evidence that the ways we use energy strengthen our adversaries and threaten our planet. These are the indicators of crisis, subject to data and statistics. (ISp)

Immediately Obama gets to the core of America's abortion problem. He declares, "We are in the midst of a crisis"—of cultural values. Echoing the words of Franklin Roosevelt after the surprise attack on Pearl Harbor, Obama proclaims, "our nation is at war"—against "a far-reaching network of violence and hatred"—an exact description of the taking of life advocated by the pro-choice movement. He continues to issue severe warnings about abortion's inherent destructiveness.

His poignant images of abortion continue: (1) "homes have been lost"—the now homeless unborn (2) "our [lack of] healthcare is too costly"—for neglecting the unborn. A striking number of women suffer overt post-abortion trauma reflected in depression, suicide attempts, psychiatric hospitalizations, substance abuse, and medical illnesses.[2]

Obama's deeper wisdom connects America's economic problems caused by

---

[2] Coleman PK, "Abortion and mental health: quantitative synthesis and analysis of research published 1995–2009," The British Journal of Psychiatry (2011) 199, 180–186, http://bjp.rcpsych.org/content/199/3/180.full accessed June 1, 2012. Reardon DC, Ney PG, Scheuren FJ, Cougle JR, Coleman, PK, Strahan T., "Deaths associated with pregnancy outcome: a record linkage study of low income women," *Southern Medical Journal*, August 2002, 95(8):834-841, article quoted with permission.
http://www.afterabortion.org/pdf/DeathsAssociatedWithAbortion.pdf accessed June 1, 2012.

bad judgment to our careless destruction of life—"Our economy is badly weakened...a consequence of... irresponsibility." Chuck Colson, the late prison-reformer, made the same connection, "If the nation's current economic crisis has taught us anything," Colson wrote, "it's that a healthy economy cannot thrive in the midst of moral breakdown."[3]

But what about all those women who claim abortion didn't hurt them? Ladies, Obama is speaking about *your unconscious*, the other 90 percent of your mind, those secret motivations about which you live in total denial. His super intelligence is speaking for *your* super intelligence because deep down we all know the rules of life: you reap what you sow. End the life of your unborn and you reap the whirlwind even if unconscious.

Next Generation at Risk

> Less measurable but no less profound is a sapping of confidence across our land—a nagging fear that America's decline is inevitable, and that the next generation must lower its sights. Today I say to you that the challenges we face are real. They are serious and they are many. They will not be met easily or in a short span of time. But know this, America: They will be met. (ISp)

Obama's images continue to subtly depict abortion: "decline [of unborn] inevitable...next generation must lower its sights"—in fact the next generation of the aborted unborn no longer see or exist. He tells us the abortion crisis has "less measurable but no less profound" effects—that as we persist in this behavior "America's decline [is]...inevitable." The challenge which abortion presents to America, he warns, "are... real...serious...and many" as in "many abortions." Obama's super-intel understands that the battle to defeat pro-abortion forces will require a monumental effort. Yet he speaks with the confidence and certainty of someone who nearly suffered a sudden end: "Know this, America, we will meet that challenge."

The Only True Choice

> On this day, we gather because we have <u>chosen</u> hope over fear, unity of purpose over conflict and discord. On this day, we come to proclaim an end to the petty grievances and false promises, the recriminations and worn-out dogmas, that for far too long have strangled our politics. "We remain a young nation, but in the words of Scripture, the time has come to set aside childish things. (ISp)

Spot on, Obama next moves to the issue of "choice." His passionate story leaps from his speech. He has come today to alert Americans to *a new choice*—to choose the hope and purpose of motherhood over the conflict and fear of abortion. His super-intel beseeches, "Mothers, get over your 'petty

---

[3] Charles Colson, "Morality and the Economy," Breakpoint Daily, January 9, 2012, http://www.breakpoint.org/about-bp. Breakpoint, established by the late Charles Colson, provides a Christian perspective on the news via radio, interactive media, and print. Colson, based on his decades of ministering to prisoners and their families, noted that fatherless homes produce sons twice as likely to be incarcerated. These homes also produce 70% of institutionalized juveniles and high-school dropouts.

grievances...that for far too long have strangled'—grievances which caused you to take the breath out of your unborn child.

Obama vividly informs us "abortion strangles America with discord." Unconsciously, he proclaims an end to such behavior "today" and "worn out" pro-choice dogmas. Thus he proclaims his Inauguration Day as National Pro-Life Day.

He concludes with references to the "young." He harkens back to "words of Scripture" which inspired the Declaration of Independence, informing expectant mothers, "This is ultimately an independent individual in your womb. Abortion deprives a child the benefits promised by the Declaration. Unconsciously Obama tells these mothers, "For the sake of your baby, it's time to set aside your childish, selfish wishes. And for America, it's time to set aside childish things that set aside children. It's time to end abortion."

Pass On the Gift of Life

> The time has come to reaffirm our enduring spirit; to choose our better history; to carry forward that precious gift, that noble idea, passed on from generation to generation: the God-given promise that all are equal, all are free, and all deserve a chance to pursue their full measure of happiness. (ISp)

Relentlessly Obama focuses on a different "choice." He insists that we must choose life, reaffirm "life" that endures. We must "choose our better history"—the decision we made long ago in American history to protect life. And why? "...To carry forward that precious gift, that noble idea, passed on from generation to generation"—that precious gift we call a child.

He then calls the unborn child "noble"—further restoring her dignity—and adds to it "God-given." Could he describe children any more beautifully? Surrounded by maternal images—pregnant mothers must "carry forward" their unborn children, let them live passing on life "from generation to generation." Implicitly he knows unborn children choose life.[4]

Obama insists America stands at a turning point. We must not wait to end abortion, his super-intel says. No, "The time has come"—now. It's time for a new policy to end the national self-sabotage.

Challenging the Shortcut of Abortion

> In reaffirming the greatness of our nation, we understand that greatness is never a given. It must be earned. Our journey has never been one of shortcuts or settling for less. It has not been the path for the fainthearted—for those who prefer leisure over work, or seek only the pleasures of riches and fame. (ISp)

Between the lines we follow the clear thread of Obama teaching America

---

[4] Obama identifies the biggest blind spot of the pro-choice movement which has forgotten that the unborn child also has a choice, and he and she *always* chooses to live. The child's actions speak volumes as it pursues its own happiness by eating, growing, playing, and dancing in the womb.

all about abortion and all about the unborn. He emphasizes, "understand…that greatness is never a given… [and] must [constantly] be earned." In a nutshell, he implies that mothers earn their greatness by doing the hard work of raising children. And mothers who abort take "shortcuts—settle "for less"— faintheartedly prefer leisure.

New Foundation For Unborn

> This is the journey we continue today. We remain the most prosperous, powerful nation on Earth. Our workers are no less productive than when this crisis began. Our minds are no less inventive, our goods and services no less needed than they were last week or last month or last year. Our capacity remains undiminished. But our time of standing pat, of protecting narrow interests and putting off unpleasant decisions—that time has surely passed. Starting today, we must pick ourselves up, dust ourselves off, and begin again the work of remaking America.
>
> For everywhere we look, there is work to be done. The state of the economy calls for action, bold and swift, and we will act—not only to create new jobs, but to lay a new foundation for growth. We will build the roads and bridges, the electric grids and digital lines that feed our commerce and bind us together. We will restore science to its rightful place, and wield technology's wonders to raise health care's quality and lower its cost. We will harness the sun and the winds and the soil to fuel our cars and run our factories. And we will transform our schools and colleges and universities to meet the demands of a new age. All this we can do. And all this we will do. (ISp)

His story continues unabated. He will not be silent.

Obama's symbolic imagery remains strongly maternal as his phrases and images encourage allowing all our unborn children to live. He compares productive factories to productive mothers, but also points out that the mother and her aborted child have been put out of a job. They have been stymied by "narrow interests" of pro-choice. And we have been "standing pat," putting off the unpleasant decision—*the choice*—of confronting their destruction. But he insists "that time has passed." The time of ending life must end.

In another violent image Obama portrays mothers—and their unborn child—having been knocked to the ground, degraded by the abortion movement. These mothers must now pick up themselves along with their unborn child and dust them both off. Dust suggests "shake off the dust of death."

And "we will act" as he guides us with a variety of maternal images: "we will…*create* [new babies]…lay a new foundation for *growth* [of the unborn]. We will build the [bridges]… lines *that feed*…and bind us together"—no more cutting off an unborn child's sustenance by aborting it, but instead sustain the maternal bond. Rebuild the bridge between mother and child. We will *"restore [the unborn] to its rightful place"* in the womb. "We will *"raise[s] health care's quality"* [for the unborn]* and lower the enormous cost we are secretly paying over our abortion guilt.

We will do so with "technology's wonders"—suggesting a mandatory high-resolution sonogram to persuade parents of the wonders of a child they can now see.

To hear these deeper messages we must grasp that we are in a new day and age, the age of the super intelligence. If not, we will be left behind in the old days of Obama's cover-up and propaganda. His "take action now" theme persists, "Starting today."

Obama assures us confidently—passion unabated, "All this we can do. And all this we will do."

If this seems "too symbolic," hang on—he will remove all doubts to anyone who wants to think, who chooses to get a new education about the mind and the amazing super intelligence. Soon he will present shocking images of the unborn child in a womb.

The Grand Vision

> Now, there are some who question the scale of our ambitions—who suggest that our system cannot tolerate too many big plans. Their memories are short. For they have forgotten what this country has already done; what free men and women can achieve when imagination is joined to common purpose, and necessity to courage.
>
> What the cynics fail to understand is that the ground has shifted beneath them—that the stale political arguments that have consumed us for so long no longer apply. The question we ask today is not whether our government is too big or too small, but whether it works—whether it helps families find jobs at a decent wage, care they can afford, a retirement that is dignified. Where the answer is yes, we intend to move forward. Where the answer is no, programs will end. And those of us who manage the public's dollars will be held to account—to spend wisely, reform bad habits, and do our business in the light of day—because only then can we restore the vital trust between a people and their government. (ISp)

Unconsciously Obama bitterly critiques the pro-choice movement. He speaks indirectly about children, but his ideas fit abortion precisely.

Immediately he identifies the pro-choice people who would question his ambition to end abortion. Such people have short memories, he implies. They have "forgotten what this country has done" to "free men and women"—alluding to our need to free unborn little boys and girls from the slavery of destruction. Strong words for mothers who impose their wills on the unborn.

Yet we must free these women from the prison of mistaken choice and self-punishment to once more achieve their dignity via their high calling, motherhood. We must understand our deeper mind—our brilliant super intelligence which possesses enormous vision and imagination—which sees the common purpose, the universal laws of freedom, and which demands we end abortion.

Can you hear him, Supreme Court justices? He addresses them—"you who have broken the vital trust between a people and their government." Vital trust

256

as in vital signs—a medical term indicating life. They have signed off on the unborn who now have no vital signs. All zeros. Obama wants these justices to restore the rights of the unborn to live.

Reject False Choice

> Nor is the question before us whether the market is a force for good or ill. Its power to generate wealth and expand freedom is unmatched, but this crisis has reminded us that without a watchful eye, the market can spin out of control—and that a nation cannot prosper long when it favors only the prosperous. The success of our economy has always depended not just on the size of our gross domestic product, but on the reach of our prosperity; on our ability to extend opportunity to every willing heart—not out of charity, but because it is the surest route to our common good.

> As for our common defense, we reject as false the choice between our safety and our ideals. Our Founding Fathers, faced with perils we can scarcely imagine, drafted a charter to assure the rule of law and the rights of man, a charter expanded by the blood of generations. Those ideals still light the world, and we will not give them up for expediency's sake. (ISp)

His super-intel continues its quick read on abortion: "Force for ill...power to generate wealth...crisis causing America to spin out of control."[5] America "cannot prosper long" when it favors "only the prosperous"—those adults who already have life. Obama alludes to the market of aborting children—a market generating millions of dollars—which has spun America out of control. A nation cannot prosper long when it enables [favors] those who prosper monetarily on unborn children.

Our success does not depend on our GDP but "on our ability to extend opportunity to every willing heart." And every unborn child wills to live.

Most strikingly, Obama implores us to reject as false the pro-choice view of choosing between the life of the child and "reproductive rights." He reminds us that America has already made another choice. We have a charter, a Constitution, "that assures the rule of law and the rights of man" including rights of the unborn child. The guarantees in that charter declare 'pro-choice' to be a false choice. In fact we have falsely expanded that charter claiming rights that are not there resulting in "the blood of generations" of unborn children, little ones who have "faced perils we can scarcely imagine."[6]

America's Future

> And so to all other peoples and governments who are watching today, from the grandest capitals to the small village where my father was

---

[5] Planned Parenthood made $164,154,000 from abortion in 2009. Andy Newbold, "Laura Ingraham Grossly Misrepresents Planned Parenthood's Budget," Media Matters to America, February 18, 2011, http://www.mediamatters.org/research/201102180003 accessed June 1, 2012. Nationwide the abortion industry generates more than one-half billion dollars annually. http://www.abort73.com/abortion_facts/us_abortion_statistics/ accessed June 1, 2012.
[6] As demonstrated in the well-known anti-abortion film *Silent Scream.*

born: Know that America is a friend of each nation and every man,
woman and child who seeks a future of peace and dignity, and that
we are ready to lead once more. (ISp)

Now Obama gets personal. Having established the phony claims of pro-choice and his vision for protecting the unborn, in sequence he speaks about the birth of a newborn. Without a doubt he speaks unconsciously on behalf of the unborn. Specifically he speaks of his father's birth in a small Kenyan village—really his own birth there. Obama speaks from the experience of nearly being an aborted unborn child and he addresses the entire world, "all other peoples and governments."

He informs them that "because of our abiding charter and the rights of man...know that America is a friend of ...every...child who seeks a future of peace and dignity." Unconsciously Obama underscores the blatant reality: "every child seeks a future"—every unborn child wants to live, live in peace. He declares, "that we are ready to lead" the world as a beacon of liberty for all those children. Obama's vision for rights of the unborn extends across continents because natural law's moral compass rules every human heart.

Obama needed to say it as plainly as possible for the Supreme Court and the whole world to hear: "Every unborn child seeks a future."

'Slaughtering Innocents'

We are the keepers of this legacy. Guided by these principles once more, we can meet those new threats that demand even greater effort—even greater cooperation and understanding between nations. We will begin to responsibly leave Iraq to its people, and forge a hard-earned peace in Afghanistan. With old friends and former foes, we will work tirelessly to lessen the nuclear threat, and roll back the specter of a warming planet. We will not apologize for our way of life, nor will we waver in its defense, and for those who seek to advance their aims by inducing terror and slaughtering innocents, we say to you now that our spirit is stronger and cannot be broken; you cannot outlast us, and we will defeat you. (ISp)

He comes to his crescendo. Buckle up because only a super intelligence would speak so forthrightly, so certain of the continued violation of natural law in America, a violation that deeply offends our collective soul.

He reminds us that "we are the keepers of this legacy" of freedom and justice—for the unborn. Holding true to natural law principles, we will meet the new threat from pro-choice activists. He urges greater understanding of the protective laws of human nature that live deep within each of us. This will spur us to greater cooperation, and we will stop waging a war on children and enjoy the fruits of peace.

To do that, we must work tirelessly to lessen the nuclear threat called abortion. While this is an unpopular stance among the intelligentsia and others, Obama assures us, "We will not apologize for our way of life, nor waver in our self-defense." And he does not apologize for his violent images—or for his

258

totally honest super intelligence.

To those who support abortion, Obama shares the hardest truth he has yet spoken —that you *"induce terror and slaughter innocents."* Instead of "inducing delivery" of a newborn, they induce terror in the innocent child they slaughter, he says. In the name of those unborn he tells them, "We say to you that our spirit is stronger and cannot be broken" as his near-abortion tried to do to him—"and we will defeat you." We will defend to the end the unborn child and "roll back the specter of a warming"—hell-bound—"planet."

For the third time Obama has emphatically declared that America will end abortion. Unconsciously he articulates his vision, his dream for America as passionately as Martin Luther King, Jr. did in this same city four decades before to inspire our nation to action. To make his point even more clearly he mentions the very issues Dr. King addressed.

Slavery, Segregation, and Abortion

> For we know that our patchwork heritage is a strength, not a weakness. We are a nation of Christians... shaped by every language and culture...and because we have tasted the bitter swill of civil war and segregation, and emerged from that dark chapter stronger and more united, we cannot help but believe that the old hatreds shall someday pass...that as the world grows smaller, our common humanity shall reveal itself; and that America must play its role in ushering in a new era of peace.

> "To the Muslim world, we seek a new way forward, based on mutual interest and mutual respect. To those leaders around the globe who seek to sow conflict, or blame their society's ills on the West, know that your people will judge you on what you can build, not what you destroy. To those who cling to power through corruption and deceit and the silencing of dissent, know that you are on the wrong side of history; but that we will extend a hand if you are willing to unclench your fist. (ISp)

Obama's depiction of abortion's raw destructiveness continues unabated. He speaks in the present—that "we have tasted the bitter swill of civil war and segregation"—warred against the unborn for rights to enslave them and segregate them, separate them unto death. Obama tells America that we are now in the midst of another dark chapter in our history where the unborn never sees the light of day, knowing only darkness. He implies even King and Lincoln would be appalled at abortion because it brutally takes an innocent life.

He continues to confront the abortionists trying to bring about a permanent peace. First he tells them, "We seek a new way forward based on mutual respect"—respect for the life of an unborn as much as your own. He adds, "To those who seek to sow conflict or blame, know that your people will judge you on [lives of the unborn] you can build, not destroy." With barely a pause, he continues, "To those who cling to power through deceit [including self-deceit] and the silencing of dissent, know that you are on the wrong side of history,"

which testifies to the deeper moral law. Vividly Obama counsels "pro-choice" people: you can "extend your hand" to the unborn if you will unclench your fist toward them. Finally, he identifies our deterioration into the "patchwork heritage" weakness offered the unborn. Patchwork mothers first offer the unborn life in the womb before ripping a hole in his heritage with "my freedom to take it away."

Pledge to the Unborn

> To the people of poor nations, we pledge to work alongside you to make your farms flourish and let clean waters flow; to nourish starved bodies and feed hungry minds. And to those nations like ours that enjoy relative plenty, we say we can no longer afford indifference to suffering outside our borders; nor can we consume the world's resources without regard to effect. For the world has changed, and we must change with it. (ISp)

Obama maintains the pace of his encoded message with intense imagery. Now his super intelligence makes a welcome pledge to the unborn: "To those poor unborn whose bodies have been starved by refusing to feed them, refusing to let their hungry minds grow, we pledge to now let the unborn flourish and help our nation be cleansed of its haunting abortion guilt. We can no longer afford 'indifference to suffering outside the' boundaries of life."

We cannot "consume the [unborn's] resources without regard to effect." Yes, the unborn possesses phenomenal resources for America—life. Understand "the world has changed" with the discovery of a deeper moral law that protects the unborn, and now "we must change" in response to that realization.

The Unborn Whisper

> As we consider the road that unfolds before us, we remember with humble gratitude those brave Americans who, at this very hour, patrol far-off deserts and distant mountains. They have something to tell us today, just as the fallen heroes who lie in Arlington whisper through the ages. We honor them not only because they are guardians of our liberty, but because they embody the spirit of service; a willingness to find meaning in something greater than themselves. And yet, at this moment—a moment that will define a generation—it is precisely this spirit that must inhabit us all.
>
> For as much as government can do and must do, it is ultimately the faith and determination of the American people upon which this nation relies. It is the kindness to take in a stranger when the levees break, the selflessness of workers who would rather cut their hours than see a friend lose their job which sees us through our darkest hours. It is the firefighter's courage to storm a stairway filled with smoke, but also a parent's willingness to nurture a child, that finally decides our fate. (ISp)

Obama looks at the road ahead for America and abortion—his super-intel on patrol whispering secrets, doing "intel" work on behalf of America.

Unconsciously he continues on the same road of freeing those among us who are not free, those who at this hour remain at war—unborn yet very much alive citizens. He looks back at their silent history informing us their deceased brethren "have something to tell us today...the fallen ...who lie [in the grave] whisper through the ages."

At this moment—a moment that will define a generation—they ask all Americans to keep the unborn alive. Whether we turn our backs on them or serve them—whichever the case—that choice will define our generation. And how we define the unborn will determine our choice. Is it a child or a mother's little plaything? We must redefine "pro-choice" more positively as "pro-child," the only healthy choice.

Obama knows that deep down we all agree. We simply must discover that eternal truth, that secret our deeper mind has been "whispering through the ages," that an unborn child in the womb is a human being. We stand on the precipice of enormous failure or success.

He understands that our government has failed the unborn by sanctioning legalized abortion. Our future then rests—not on government—but squarely on the determination of the American people. "The kindness to take in the stranger" of an adopted child rather than see them aborted unto death. The selflessness of mothers who would sacrifice their own freedom rather than see their friend, their child, lose their life and their job (of chasing away the darkest hours with the natural joy children represent). It is the freedom fighter's courage to storm America's stairway filled with the haziness of millions of self-indulgent women blowing smoke about their rights while completely forgetting the rights of the unborn.

As a nearly unborn child himself, Obama understands. Pro-choice women and men must change, they must find meaning "in something greater than themselves"—in their unborn children. These women must understand they have a deeper will, a deeper choice they truly want to make. America must find a new will to fight for the unborn.

Vividly Obama declares, "It is a 'parent's willingness to nurture a child" that will ultimately decide America's fate. Can you hear him, *'a parent's willingness?'* At first it appears to be a rhetorical sort of question—who wouldn't nurture a child? But then again "pro-choice"—"pro-me"—wouldn't. *Unmistakably Obama unconsciously links our future with how we treat a child— an unborn child.* Ironically, this tiny human being growing in the womb will determine the fate of the greatest, most powerful nation in the world. Obama asks us, "So what is your choice America? Nurture or destruction?"

God Calls America

Our challenges may be new. The instruments with which we meet them may be new. But those values upon which our success depends—hard work and honesty, courage and fair play, tolerance and curiosity, loyalty and patriotism—these things are old. These things are true. They have been the quiet force of progress throughout our history. What is demanded then is a return to these

> truths. What is required of us now is a new era of responsibility—a recognition, on the part of every American, that we have duties to ourselves, our nation and the world; duties that we do not grudgingly accept but rather seize gladly, firm in the knowledge that there is nothing so satisfying to the spirit, so defining of our character, than giving our all to a difficult task.
>
> This is the price and the promise of citizenship. This is the source of our confidence—the knowledge that God calls on us to shape an uncertain destiny.
>
> This is the meaning of our liberty and our creed—why men and women and children of every race and every faith can join in celebration across this magnificent Mall, and why a man whose father less than 60 years ago might not have been served at a local restaurant can now stand before you to take a most sacred oath. (ISp)

Obama emphasizes that the key to his entire "intel operation" is the super intelligence. We meet the new challenge of abortion with our deeper moral compass which "demands"—guides us—to return to our tried-and-true values. The hard work and honesty of a mother—not the dishonesty and leisure of abortion; the fair play and courage to raise a child when all around you resound the incessant voices of selfishness.

Indeed we are in a "new era of responsibility." Obama addresses all American citizens who now have a duty, an obligation to give themselves to the difficult task of making certain the unborn receive the citizenship they deserve. He declares that *"God calls on us to shape an uncertain destiny"* of the unborn into a certain destiny: a safe delivery unharmed into the world.

"This is the meaning of our liberty and our creed"—a unifying force among blacks and whites and all Americans. Obama confesses that, as a pro-choice advocate, he failed to serve America, but now unconsciously he is standing up for the most helpless because he knows helplessness. Obama knows powerlessness like no president we have ever had.

'Mark This Day'

> So let us mark this day with remembrance, of who we are and how far we have traveled. In the year of America's birth, in the coldest of months, a small band of patriots huddled by dying campfires on the shores of an icy river. The capital was abandoned. The enemy was advancing. The snow was stained with blood. At a moment when the outcome of our revolution was most in doubt, the father of our nation ordered these words be read to the people:
>
> "Let it be told to the future world ... that in the depth of winter, when nothing but hope and virtue could survive... that the city and the country, alarmed at one common danger, came forth to meet [it]." (ISp)

Obama's super-intel ends this speech in compelling fashion. We decode his message between the lines: "Let us mark this day remembering who we are as pro-life people, how far we have come in opposing the destruction of life of the unborn. In the year of America's birth problem—when abortion was legalized—a small, determined group of patriots came together amidst the flickering campfires of the dying children. Leaders in our nation's capital had abandoned them and still do. The enemy within America, misguided by a short-sighted pro-choice ideology continues to advance. Abortion advocates are aided by an equally destructive media and a permissive society blind to the deeper moral law within them. The blood of our lost unborn children stains our hands. When the revolution to end this hideous policy was most in doubt—today—I order these words read, words with which George Washington would agree, words which speak out against abortion and for freedom.

"Let it be told that in the depth of winter for the unborn only our virtue, from which springs hope, will ensure America's survival. I remind you our deeper virtue will determine America's future, not the superficial conscious virtues so easily manipulated by our selfishness. Having capitulated to the notion that life for the unborn is simply a relative individual conscious choice—disregarding our unconscious mind which has a different wiser choice—one thing will restore our virtue. We must come to the conviction based on a new science of the mind that the same deeper virtues for protecting and honoring life exist in all of us.[7] Such a scientific breakthrough brings new life to our abiding, eternal, deeper moral compass."

> America, in the face of our common dangers, in this winter of our hardship, let us remember these timeless words. With hope and virtue, let us brave once more the icy currents, and endure what storms may come. Let it be said by our children's children that when we were tested, we refused to let this journey end, that we did not turn back, nor did we falter; and with eyes fixed on the horizon and God's grace upon us, we carried forth that great gift of freedom and delivered it safely to future generations. (ISp)

Continuing on its heart-felt anti-abortion theme, the president's super-intel reflects on George Washington's words and applies them to the current crisis: "Now in the face of our common danger of abortion in this winter of our loss of virtue, let us remember these timeless words. Virtue—our deeper moral compass—alone serves as our guide to brave the icy currents and the storms of limited conscious concerns about 'reproductive rights' which insist that our minds and hearts lack deeper character.

"Let it be said by our children's unborn children that when we were tested, we refused to give into the permissiveness that ruled the day. We refused to relinquish our support for the unborn. We refused to turn our backs on them. But with eyes fixed on God, a mother now carried forth that great gift in her womb, the unborn child with his God-given right to freedom, and delivered that child

---

[7] Obama's earlier reference to restoring science to its proper place reflected his super-intel understanding that unconscious communication is scientifically accurate.

safely to future generations.

"The grace of God stands ready to forgive those millions of American women who have been brain-washed into having an abortion. Rights come not from themselves but from one source alone, our Creator, a righteous God who pursues life and freedom for all unborn children."

18

Obama the Potential Hero Unconsciously Rescues America

Barack Obama has just told us his secret story. His super intelligence has covered all the major points from his troubled childhood up through his second major effort to deceive America with the release of a phony birth certificate. We have before us a great confession—but against all odds, an impossible confession for him to own consciously, personally. One thing is for sure—America can profit from his confession even if Obama never chooses to—if we listen. And if one day—miraculously—he follows through on his confession, it would be the kind of turnabout that changes everything for the better. But that is not today's reality.

This means *we* must see the matter through immediately, as Sheriff Joe Arpaio's team currently is doing through judicial means—challenging Obama's constitutional eligibility to appear on state ballots as a 2012 presidential candidate meeting the 'natural-born citizen' criteria. Citizens should demand Obama either provide bona fide proof he is legitimate or step down—or be impeached. Unmistakably these were Obama's unconscious instructions to America.

Yet, given the lateness of the hour and the 2012 presidential election around the corner, the likelihood of American citizens mustering enough group strength now to demand an investigation of Obama is not great. Sheriff Joe's praiseworthy attempt to utilize legal routes to enforce the eligibility requirements—and expose Obama's phony birth certificate, probably will not be enough now. Efforts should still continue full force—but success in the judicial branch has repeatedly been denied. There are overwhelming judicial, political and media forces opposing a true and vigorous investigation of Obama's eligibility which must be overcome. Imagine the turmoil and protests if Obama were denied access to a single state ballot. Will any judge risk doing that? Surely it would be best for America to face once and for all the cover up. Whatever the immediate outcome—including Obama's potential defeat or victory in 2012—we must not miss the bigger picture. We must fully appreciate Obama's phenomenal unconscious confession. His super intelligence provides America significant guidance about where we go from here.

Obama's Deepest Longings

Already Obama has revealed how he was driven by his overwhelming emotional trauma into becoming an angry, deceitful leader. On one hand he had a choice, on the other he didn't. He was built, built on a foundation of sand. *Once again his unconscious confession was his way deep down of standing up to his abuse.* Specifically he was responding to his abusive father who had struck Obama's foundation like a hurricane.

In an amazing twist, Obama secretly wants to be a hero to the America he so deeply dislikes. *With his hidden confession Obama reveals just how great the divide can be between our conscious selves and unconscious selves.* On one hand if by now your blood is not boiling over what Barack Obama has done to America something is wrong. He has behaved in the most horrific fashion imaginable—and a large part of him wants to push us to the brink of destruction. He has many Americans frightened to death.

But on the other hand he—his super intelligence—has confessed to his great misdeeds, which is the first step toward redemption. He talks about great leaders—George Washington and Martin Luther King Jr.—reflecting his deep desire to be one. He continues to seek a better role model than his destructive father, just as he seeks to break the pattern of destructiveness he has inherited.

Obama Establishes Natural Law Exists

Exploring the "accomplishments" of Obama's super intelligence confession, we can see that he has shined the light on his sterling deeper—unconscious—moral compass. In that sense he can be viewed in a strange way as an American 'hero'—unconsciously. All his heroic efforts start and end here. For many readers it will be difficult to see him in this light but we must, for the future of America. Let his deeper moral compass have its say.

He underscores two major principles—one for individuals, the other for our nation, for our lives as citizens together. They serve as an overriding guiding light, a template to which we will return time and again.

First he insists upon individual achievement and character—and accountability to those rules. "It's up to us as fathers... to instill this ethic of excellence in our children [citizens]...in my house we give glory to achievement, self-respect, and hard work...set high expectations...examples of excellence in our own lives." (FD1)

Then he insists America must live by the rule of law—specifically the Constitution. "At these [difficult] moments, America has carried on...because We the People have remained faithful to the ideals of our forebears, and true to our founding documents. So it has been. So it must be with this generation of Americans.

"Our Founding Fathers...drafted a charter to assure the rule of law and the rights of man, a charter expanded by the blood of generations. Those ideals still light the world." (Isp) Obama has pointed us to basic laws of human behavior—of parental responsibility and of community values. Above all Obama's super intelligence makes plain a deeper moral compass exists within everyone.

In one fell swoop he brushes aside the ridiculous notion of moral relativism—of political correctness—the huge cultural shift which has our nation in a choke hold. Moral relativism—the myth that says absolute moral rules don't really exist—has divided our culture via a civil war of values. Mind you, he unconsciously tells us this. Consciously he doesn't really believe fully his own words and remains a dyed-in-the-wool 'go with whichever the way the wind blows' political relativist.

Amidst this horrific battle inside of him (which he is losing and) which threatens to destroy our nation he has highlighted the rule of law, specifically the Constitution and the Declaration which went hand-in-hand establishing that "unalienable rights" (consistent laws of human behavior) truly exist in the mind of man.

And his words have called America back to its old moral compass. The Constitution, his super intelligence insists, is not a document in flux that we can adjust according to popularity polls or political pressure. Nor is it a document simply constructed in a biased fashion by fifty white men, No, it reflects the active, immediate, moral law deep in our hearts and minds. In this light we see all the various aspects of his confession; it addresses the human mind and human choices, moral and immoral behavior.

The 'Hero President' Awakens America

In February 2010, real estate broker Gary Hubbell wrote a popular article in the *Aspen Weekly Times* entitled "Barack Obama has Awakened a Sleeping Giant" about how the president's election was actually good for America, because it awoke slumbering giants who became involved citizens and constituted themselves for example into the Tea Party Movement which scored big gains for the GOP in the 2010 congressional mid-term elections. Hubbell's piece struck a nerve and was quickly circulated on the Internet. He observed:

> Barack Obama is the best thing that has happened to America in the last 100 years. Truly, he is the savior of America's future...

> Barack Obama plunged the country into...debt not previously imagined...entitlement programs ballooned to unsustainable levels...Obama is the symbol of a creeping liberalism that has infected our society like a cancer for the last 100 years...

> We slowly learned to tolerate these outrages...But Barack Obama has ripped the lid off a seething cauldron of dissatisfaction and unrest. Average Americans...have woken up. There is a level of political activism in this country that we haven't seen since the American Revolution... Obama has been the catalyst that has sparked a restructuring of American political and social consciousness."

> Americans have had enough. They're organizing, they're studying the Constitution...they're showing up at rallies...a keen awareness that

> our priorities...must be radically re-structured...Just as the pendulum swung to embrace political correctness and liberalism...A hundred years from now, history will perceive the year 2010 as the time when America got back on the right track. And for that, we can thank Barack Obama.

Yes, with his egregious behavior, Obama has awakened a sleeping America—but, understand, this was a major part of his *unconscious* plan. His super intelligence tried to help the America he has harmed. Crediting the president for inspiring citizens—again unconsciously—to reconnect with the Constitution, Hubbell was right on target. But Hubbell himself made the familiar mistake of many conservatives—he failed to confront Obama's most egregious constitutional violation and never addressed the birth issue which is the most basic way Obama can be legally confronted. He failed to use the power of the Constitution. Again as the two reporters reminded us (in Chapter 15) we now have hard evidence Obama has put on the table with his birth certificate, and we had it earlier in his COLB posted on line. Hubbell with his great heart for America demonstrates in the end a failure to use the maximum strength given to the people by our ancestors who paid the maximum price to give it to us. (We will come back to the problem of handling success shortly.)

In the back of his mind Obama spotted the weakness in liberalism (as Hubbell did) which violated the law of achievement, hard work, high expectations and excellence—though his surface side carried it out self-destructively. Repeatedly Obama reveals how desperately he needs strong rules and boundaries. In essence Obama shows our culture of diversity what it is not providing. Obama's super intelligence calls the American family out of complacency and back to the deeper, truer rules of life. His *deeper* moral compass repeatedly leads America in the exact opposite direction than what Obama consciously espouses. *Yet we will see Obama observed a fatal flaw in our nation which he tried to correct.*

Obama Protectively Warns: 'Expect Presidential Misbehavior'

From the beginning of his presidency Obama was unconsciously protective of America warning us of his anticipated attacks first on the economy. Seeing through his denials, he prophetically describes his reckless spending—public officials who don't spend wisely, health care plan too expensive, and the result: America's decline is "inevitable."

Recall how Obama specifically warned us in similar ways about how his foreign-policy mistakes would weaken America. He confessed he would strengthen our enemies and increase the nuclear threat in the world.

> ...too many fathers also are missing—missing from too many lives and too many homes [such as the White House]...children who grow up without a father are five times more likely to commit crime...twenty times more likely to end up in prison. They are more likely to have behavioral problems. (FD1)

268

Continuing to be guided by his moral compass like a sentinel on the alert, Obama's super-intel warned us about his behavior problem. He tells us how he learned this behavior from his father who taught him to attack the foundations of society—the legal and moral laws. His message: "I will be like my absent father—keep an eye on me." Yet, amidst his negligent leadership Obama unconsciously attempts to protect America. That is the purpose of his secret confession—a hidden 'heads-up'—which he cannot stop.

Obama the Educator Explains the Mind Behind the Confession

Then Obama, via his super intelligence the great educator, explains the mind with its deeper moral compass which prompts his confession. He has taught us about one of the great breakthroughs in history—the discovery of the super intelligence—and underscored that it was "pushing the boundaries of discovery." He's telling us how to hear an intelligence so bright we can scarcely believe it is possible. And of course trying to get his own conscious attention.

He explained the deeper method of communication upon which everything rests so that not only could we hear his confession but also how he was guiding us to make major corrections to attitudes which were destroying our society.

He first confirmed that a brilliant unconscious existed by describing it in further picturesque terms and informing us how crucial it was to America's future. In one example he referred to the super intelligence as a "cutting-edge technology" with the power to affect our planet: "I want us to push the boundaries of discovery... see new technologies... that... make our planet cleaner and safer." (ISp)

He also called it a new instrument for meeting the unspeakable challenge he presented to America: "Our challenges may be new. The instruments with which we meet them may be new." (ISp)

How was this new technology of super intelligence going to meet his challenge and make our lives better and our planet safer? It was going to educate us—to a new language, to deeper messages *specifically moral-compass messages of confession and guidance*: how to proceed from here.

He even challenged people to "get their butts back to school," go to graduate school—to learn about "higher education"—the super intelligence.

Obama made plain the super intelligence transformed us to a whole new day and age of education: of the deeper mind—but only if we heard it, learned its language. "And we will transform our schools and colleges and universities to meet the demands of a new age." (ISp)

He informed us that the super intelligence—the new wondrous technology—communicated with scientific accuracy. Indeed we are in a whole new day and age of the mind.

Obama Spots America's Great Flaw

Americans until very recently consciously believed in natural law—fixed rules, absolutes. But with the huge shift in public consciousness to political correctness and diversity—'anything goes' has become society's new slogan. Above all we must not judge others—"judge" being the terrifying word. America is now deeply divided about our moral compass. Conservatives cling to their old fixed values, but "progressives" insist the moral compass was flexible. Into that turmoil, Obama presents a solution.

While he consciously believed in a relative standard, politically correct to be sure, his super intelligence has presented the "New Hi-Tech Natural Law Moral Compass" in all its glory. *Obama's super intelligence gave America back its moral compass that made it great.* He unwittingly showed us it was even more fantastic than we could imagine. And he told us how this new morality will solve America's war over cultural values.

> Guided by these principles once more, we can meet those new threats that demand even greater effort—even greater cooperation and un-derstanding... Our challenges may be new...But those values upon which our success depends—hard work and honesty, courage and fair play...loyalty and patriotism—these things are old. These things are true. They have been the quiet force of progress throughout our history. What is demanded then is a return to these truths. (ISp)

Unconsciously Obama shouts at us (and his conscious self) "natural law compass"—guiding principles, old values that are true. He insists that we return to them—the success of America depends upon it. Step by step Obama shows us how this deeper moral compass works. Then he told us what it would take to truly hear it—humility—which retrains our natural tendency to listen only to our conscious minds. "Our security emanates from the justness of our cause, the force of our example, the tempering qualities of humility and restraint." (ISp)

And he demonstrated how this old but new high-tech moral compass worked—revealing its power with one moral confession after another.

The Unconsciously Humble Leader Confesses Illegality

Obama's highly attuned unconscious—after challenging us to investigate him—has confessed to his illegal presidency, a truly humbling act. As we saw, he particularly underscored his attacks on the Constitution and the rule of law at the exact moment of overt deception—his inauguration. He emphasized that he really hadn't adhered to his own high standard of achievement and excellence, that he had not earned the job.

His high-tech moral compass points America toward healing other wounds. Obama wisely confronted the racial divides that his shadow side had helped greatly exacerbate. First he violated the rules then used a show-and-tell to instruct America how to deal with it. He insists that blacks and whites can celebrate around the rule of law and justice: the same natural law that freed blacks from slavery and segregation. "This is the meaning of our liberty and our creed—why men and women and children of every race and every faith can join in celebration across this magnificent mall." (ISp)

In so doing he follows in the steps of Martin Luther King Jr.—who based his entire case on natural law when he wrote his famous letter from a Birmingham jail establishing that segregation was a major injustice. Deep down Obama's super-intel reflects Dr. King's vision of a colorblind society—despite his contradictory conscious messages.

Potentially Resolves 'Birther' Issue

Without realizing it Obama has "solved" America's "birther issue" which he consciously used to divide us racially. With his super intelligence confession that he is indeed an illegal president, he completely undercuts the rampant charges of racism directed at birthers. He reinforces the birthers' concern of his constitutional eligibility. Additionally, his insistence on achievement, self-respect and the highest ethics implies that citizens shouldn't be afraid to ask the questions: did Obama earn the presidency? Has he behaved with the highest ethics? Did he abide by the Constitution? Do you want a black president—ever, but particularly the first—held to such low standards, in turn losing his self-respect?

If we can hear his super intelligence, Obama has challenged anti-birthers to apologize as he unconsciously does, to recognize racism is not around every difference of opinion. That a black man, a person of color, should be held to equal standards with the white man—again "in my house we give glory to achievement, self-respect, and hard work...set high expectations...examples of excellence in our own lives." If not, it lowers him, requires no excellence and ushers him to the back of the achievement bus. In a nutshell Obama has put achievement and character above any race—the ultimate in fair play and justice.

Test For America: 'Heroic' Obama Points To Plan B On Ineligibility

Assuming Obama continues to escape the full consequences of his illegal presidency and his double-down deception of a bogus birth certificate, he has left America a huge test to go along with his instructions about restoring our moral compass.

All along he establishes that you reap what you sow; you work for what you get. You live in a strong house if you build one. You build strong kids if you build strength into them with your presence and discipline. And you build a strong nation if you build it right—living laws of human nature, living boundaries, true relationships—morality/moral compass has a name.

He has made clear that to this point he has not only committed a heinous act as an illegal president (and more), his all-wise moral compass tells us that America should do something about it because there are always consequences, 'reaping what you sow.' That means he helped create—aided by many supporters—a huge flaw that exists in our framework. Indeed an organic framework where the rules of life never change—they continue in all their power for good or bad. His bottom line is that his violation of America has not gone away even if he has gotten away with it. In short, he asks, "Will I still

271

deserve to be called President my entire life—after I told you I never deserved it in the first place?"

> And those of us who manage the public's dollars will be held to account -- to spend wisely, reform bad habits, and do our business in the light of day -- because only then can we restore the vital trust between a people and their government. (Isp)

To be even plainer Obama emphasizes accountability—always. He instructs us for the good of America to bring everything about his ineligibility including his co-conspirators, *into the light of day*. Only then can we restore vital—life giving—trust in America. Or we will live in a broken country and continue down the path of self-deception when all too much already exists in D.C. ("Deception City").

Heroically, if you will, Obama's great super intelligence continues to come to America's aid about what we do about an illegal presidency—present or past. Perhaps the reality is that America can only deal with his violations in retrospect. Whenever we find our courage as citizens regarding this serious constitutional crisis we will still be in, Obama says we must find it: "They have forgotten... what free men and women can achieve when imagination is joined to common purpose, and *necessity to courage*." (Isp) He reminds us again: "...those values upon which our success depends -- hard work and honesty, *courage* and fair play...loyalty and patriotism." (Isp)

Still we see how strongly he urges himself to confess. And he takes us deeper into why he must confess and how America must likewise confess in a new way. 'Reap what you sow' never changes; Obama asserts that an overt confession is a different way of reaping. Sow humility with confession and we reap grace; and not a cheap grace—not by a long shot. True grace restores.

Obama Confronts Atheism

The grand sweep of Obama's deeper moral compass to get America back on track is utterly amazing. Indirectly he has confronted the atheistic scientific community, stood them on their heels demonstrating that all people live by natural law. Obama has revealed that absolute right or wrong truly exists in the unconscious mind of every person—even if the conscious mind has rationalized it away in the false spirit of political correctness.

The late Harvard paleontologist Stephen Jay Gould, a leading public spokesman for what amounts to atheistic evolutionists, once said, "There is no natural law out there waiting to be discovered."[1] Gould understood that if natural law were ever discovered in the human psyche that meant a law giver—God—existed. Obama's super-intel has basically trumped Gould's thinking and informed the scientific community: you too get your butts back to school—super

---

1 There are two types of evolutionists—atheists and theists—although the atheists manipulatively try to claim science as exclusively their discipline. Stephen Jay Gould, "Impeaching a Self-Appointed Judge," *Scientific American*, July 1992, p. 118.

intelligence school—so you can see God.

As simple as that might appear, this single issue—natural law—proves the existence of God. To have laws of human nature we must have a law-giver or Creator who also gave each of us life. Modern atheistic science stands aghast. In so doing, Obama shouts out, "See? The founders of America and Martin Luther King Jr. had it right—there *is* justice because all men must answer to God's laws: fair play and equal opportunity." The super intelligence clearly establishes that a universal moral code exists.

Obama Establishes True Religion—Points to America's Great Need

Now having provided a basis for God's existence, Barack Obama makes the case that true religion undergirds America with its moral compass just as George Washington once commented, "It is impossible to rightly govern a nation without God and the Bible."

Could it be that our founders were also right about religion in that they understood morals had to come from a higher source? Yes, some like Jefferson were only deists, but they all believed in a God, the giver of natural law.

While people have questioned Obama's liberal version of Christianity and have, for good reason, suspected he is secretly a Muslim, his unconscious view of religion and natural law points strongly toward the Christian faith. Having confessed to egregious destructive acts toward Americans, Obama well knows imperfection and the need for forgiveness. Deep down he understands all people ultimately face God's judgment and that he himself must account for his actions. This is why he makes repeated references to destructive leaders who do wrong.

> To those leaders around the globe who seek to sow conflict, or blame their society's ills on the West: Know...your people will judge you on what you can build, not what you destroy. To those who cling to power through corruption and deceit...you are on the wrong side of history; but...we will extend a hand if you are willing to unclench your fist. (ISp)

Obama suggests that God urges him to unclench his fist. He unconsciously seeks grace as he tells us in his powerful close to his inaugural address, quoting George Washington.

> America...in this winter of our hardship, let us remember these timeless words. With hope and virtue, let us brave once more the icy currents, and endure what storms may come. Let it be said by our children's children that when we were tested, we refused to let this journey end, that we did not turn back, nor did we falter; and with eyes fixed on the horizon and God's grace upon us, we carried forth that great gift of freedom and delivered it safely to future generations.

Again Obama suggests he wants to be delivered safely—this time in God's presence, by God's grace. In yet another twist, Obama the conscious Muslim becomes the unconscious Obama in need of Christ and his forgiveness. Only

273

grace will meet his need, not the performance-oriented Muslim faith.

Obama suggested the same thing in his revealing 2008 Fathers' Day speech at the Apostolic Church: "It's an honor to spend some time with all of you today in the *house of our Lord*...Here at Apostolic, you are blessed to worship in *a house* that has been founded on the rock of Jesus Christ, our Lord and Savior." Twice Obama connects his need for a "house"—a home—to Jesus, to salvation and forgiveness.

In a similar way he chose Washington's image of "eyes fixed on the horizon and God's grace," suggesting his own eyes were unconsciously fixed on his need for that grace. Very presidentially, Obama takes us back to our founders who knew that in the end it was God who blessed America—God who was ultimately responsible for America becoming the shining city on a hill. It's the identical belief shared by George Washington and all the rest, carried on by Abraham Lincoln and Ronald Reagan. Obama continues to tell America's Christian-based story—that God blessed us with natural law, and our faith in that moral compass was responsible for the founding of America.

In so doing his deeper, wiser, moral compass points us toward America's great need today—restoration of reliance on natural law. He makes the case that it has to start with honoring God, the originator of all law. He counsels America to realize our dependence upon God—in his own way calling for a renewed spirituality. Unconsciously Obama agrees with Pat Buchanan's recent book, *Suicide of a Superpower*, in which Buchanan declares that our religious, cultural and ethical foundations are falling apart because of the cult of multiculturalism and diversity. He quoted the great jurist John Jay on America, "one united people...professing the same religion, attached to the same principles of government." From start to finish, Obama establishes that our deeper moral compass is not multicultural but reflects one universal culture of natural law, the same abiding principles for all.

Some will be offended by the idea of Obama's heroic side in light of all the havoc he has wreaked. Certainly Obama has truly hurt millions of Americans. Yet we remember that the zealot Paul was on his way to kill believers when he was chosen by God to take the Christian message of forgiveness around the world. And we can't forget the slave trader John Newton who, in his confessional agony, wrote "Amazing Grace," for decades the most popular Christian song in America. Without doubt, Obama's moral compass urges him over and over to confess.

Pushing Past His Muslim Faith

Obama unconsciously implies he wants to push past his Muslim performance-based faith which keeps him from seeing what could be the best in him: forgiveness and grace from the best kind of God—a forgiving God. He wants to push the boundaries of religion—which we can read two ways. "And I want us to push our own human boundaries to reach beyond the divides of race

and region, gender and religion that keep us from seeing the best in each other."
(PLtr)

Obama Prays for America

Even more shockingly perhaps—but also reflecting the greatness of the moral compass God built into us—we discover that Obama unconsciously confessed praying that God would overcome his negative effect on America. He wants God to lead the citizens through the darkest of storms—that would be him—into the light of a better day. Deep down Obama wants citizens to identify exactly who he is—and guides them to do something about it.

> And when the winds come, and the rains fall, and they beat upon that house, we keep faith that our Father will be there to guide us, and watch over us, and protect us, and lead His children through the darkest of storms into light of a better day. That is my prayer for all of us on this Fathers' Day, and that is my hope for this country in the years ahead. May God bless you and your children. Thank you. (FD1)

Benefits of Unconscious Confession

Obama has first and foremost unconsciously reframed the very Constitution he has confessed to violating. Reframed it not in a sleek modern frame but in a rich, heavily gilded new frame befitting its glorious history—supported by a fuller understanding of its moral base. Obama cannot stop pointing to the very moral compass that shines the light on his misdeeds—provided the evidence of his imperfections. This deeper, far more accurate natural law guides everyone toward accountability.

On top of that, Obama once again has challenged the major social dilemmas of our times starting with the curse of abortion which destroys "that great gift of freedom"—life. No one has ever made a stronger case against it than the near-abortion victim himself. He has also pointed the way toward more racial healing. With all the controversy surrounding our first black president Obama emphasizes that the real issue involves our moral compass: (1) that the Constitution and rule of law is our unifying force; (2) he has put achievement and character above any race—the ultimate in fair play and justice. He eliminates such distractions as the birther issue and holds up Dr. King's model of non-racial voting—lacking skin-color favoritism.

Not playing any favorites, we will see in the next chapter how Obama's super-intel confronts the media over their own failures to adhere to America's true moral compass. Secretly, Obama has observed all the media biases they would prefer not to see—and above all he will address how they handled his great constitutional violation.

With his confession he has shown the nation many things a leader must not do—and challenged America to learn from it and correct it. He has been a living demonstration of the great lesson from history for successful nations: they decline because of bad leadership decisions, so pay especially close attention to your leaders. In fact, *expect* leaders to start trashing America's success. Spot them, hold them responsible and stop them.

Recalling Jesus' famous words, "You should not be surprised at my saying, 'You must be born again.' The wind blows wherever it pleases. You hear its sound but you cannot tell where it comes from or where it is going. So it is with everyone born of the Spirit."[2] Is it possible that God has chosen Obama in all his human fallibility to reveal to the world major discoveries about the need to confess, how we secretly long to confess? Has the Spirit begun to blow on Barack Obama in unexpected ways? The very man who described himself repeatedly as a violent storm is now the recipient of the warm, kind breeze of his real Father, hopefully drawing him to confession of sin (that dreaded word) and repentance, and to receive the blessings of forgiveness in Jesus Christ, whom he publicly has called Savior. Obama suggests his super intelligence was trying to tell him something.

Final Issue for Obama

Finally, Obama's super intelligence has issued him the greatest challenge. In the images borrowed from Jesus, will Obama continue to see the speck in his neighbor's eye—the fault in others? Or is it the log in his own eye that must go? The question remains: Will Obama eventually make his unconscious confession overt, follow the lead of his true moral compass and confess to his misdeeds? Will he truly become heroic and "retire with dignity?" The American people are very forgiving of sincere confession. Surely he's trying to tell himself that he needs God's help to confess. As C.S. Lewis said: It takes a good man to repent, and we're all bad men.

Obama ultimately stands on the threshold of greatness or continual self-sabotage, engulfed in his pain and anger--trying to take America with him. His story has taken yet another twist. He has shown the world its deeper moral compass in the most intelligent way possible—a truly world-changing event. While the Obama confession seems on the surface the story of an illegal president who has broken the rules, and is begging for someone to stop him, it is far more than that. It's the story of mankind's potential maturation to become adept at communicating at unimaginable levels, to delve deeply within ourselves to reconnect with natural law, to thoroughly self-actualize, guided by the grace of God.

In the end Obama's story in its own way represents every man's story—as Jesus boldly told us when He said, "No one is good--except God alone."[3] For those in our day and age who presume mankind's innate goodness, Obama confronts this most basic of lies we tell ourselves.

In his overwhelming fury wanting to destroy America, as he was destroyed, Obama shines the light of truth on mankind. Put it plain and simple: we need an

---

2 Gospel of John 3: 7-8, NIV.
3 Luke 18:19 (NIV)

atonement forgiveness of our sins, the equivalent of our destructiveness—our personal destructiveness, each of us. We cannot atone for our own sins nor 'be our own best' friend and just forgive ourselves willy-nilly; the human mind does not work that way, as Obama spells out in detail with his secret confession pouring out of him. When modern schools of Christian theology and secular society agree that we have altogether as people not really gone that bad, Obama answers, "Oh yes we have."

In so doing he matches our Founders who insisted that sacrifice was the name of the game. Sacrifice as we were sacrificed for—as by far the vast majority of them pointed to Christ and drew their strength from Him.[4] They produced quite a nation with such a mindset, and Obama with all his wanderings and misguided rage urges us back to where our nation began. Our Founders were in need of the Son of God's atonement forgiveness, and most were certain they had it; they were then free to become people of courage and conviction. Is there a message here for us today?

We could do worse than merely correcting the illegal presidency of Barack Obama. We could as T.S. Eliot said, "have the experience and miss the meaning."[5] We could fail to learn the lesson of this propitious moment in history and miss who we are as God's human beings. In our pride Obama's opponents can insist there is no lesson to learn, just as his blind supporters do. But Obama drives us back to one plain and pure simple fact: we are the people of the moral compass that is true and straight. Will it guide America once again as it guided our great nation to success unsurpassed in history? Our answer awaits.

---

4 David Barton, *America's Godly Heritage,* (Aledo, Texas: Wall Builder Press, 1993).
5 T.S. Eliot, *Four Quartets.*

19

Obama the Reporter v. the Modern Media

When all is said and done, I am a detective first…and then a reporter. I am a detective of the human mind, a completely new kind of detective who uses the instincts and intelligence of the very person I'm investigating. Specifically, I listen to the person's own "inner detective." In this case I listen first to what Barack Obama is confessing between the lines as he speaks and then to the media. I become a reporter telling the story Obama secretly asks to be told—I speak for him, for his super intelligence. The existence of the super intelligence brings us to an entirely new day and age of reporting.

What if the Media Missed the Story?

Donald Trump observed that if Barack Obama had actually attained the presidency illegally, "it would be the greatest scam in American history?" His suspicions propelled Trump to undertake a serious investigation of Obama's birth. Trump was roundly ridiculed by the media for pursuing the issue especially after Obama suddenly produced a supposed long-form birth certificate on April 27, 2011, partially in response to Trump's pressure. The media followed up by ignoring any efforts to validate Obama's birth certificate.

In light of Obama's secret confession, here's the question of the century: Could the press have failed to cover the biggest scam in American history? And, since the phony birth certificate has also been virtually ignored, who can believe our 24-7 camera-ready media could miss the big story *twice*—the one they're all allegedly dying to get? Now we know not only that the media egregiously overlooked the story but we also know why they went into such denial. Once more they missed the far more important deeper story of Obama's unresolved fury directed at America, putting our nation at great risk in all too many ways. The birth certificate matter was hugely symbolic of his much greater deception.

Obama Teaches the Media

Barack Obama knows how badly the media failed to uncover his subterfuge—and has told them why. In a fascinating twist to his secret narrative, his super-intel turns its lens on the media revealing an entirely separate level of analysis. The mind accurately observes each of the crucial players simultaneously. Never has the media been confronted with such mental acumen.

The media—one of Obama's loyalist constituencies—feels it has the president in its back pocket, and now he informs them that is not the case. His unconscious is its own man, a man with a superior moral compass, a man not about to be tucked into anybody's back pocket.

The media overlooked his real narrative because they don't speak the language of the super intelligence. They didn't know it existed, and Obama unconsciously tried to teach them about it. Here we see a truly gifted teacher at work.

Obama's Super-Intel Analyzes Media—Fathers' Day 2008

> The first is setting an example of excellence for our children—because if we want to set high expectations for them, we've got to set high expectations for ourselves. It's great if you have a job; it's even better if you have a college degree. It's a wonderful thing if you are married and living in a home with your children, but don't just sit in the house and watch *Sports Center* all weekend long. That's why so many children are growing up in front of the television. As fathers and parents, we've got to spend more time with them, and help them with their homework, and replace the video game or the remote control with a book once in a while. That's how we build that foundation.
>
> We know that education is everything to our children's future. We know that they will no longer just compete for good jobs with children from Indiana, but children from India and China and all over the world. We know the work and the studying and the level of education that requires.
>
> You know, sometimes I'll go to an eighth-grade graduation and there's all that pomp and circumstance and gowns and flowers. And I think to myself, it's just eighth grade. To really compete, they need to graduate high school, and then they need to graduate college, and they probably need a graduate degree too. An eighth-grade education doesn't cut it today. Let's give them a handshake and tell them to get their butts back in the library!
>
> It's up to us—as fathers and parents—to instill this ethic of excellence in our children. It's up to us to say to our daughters, don't ever let images on TV tell you what you are worth, because I expect you to dream without limit and reach for those goals. It's up to us to tell our sons, those songs on the radio may glorify violence, but in my house we give glory to achievement, self-respect, and hard work. It's up to us to set these high expectations. And that means meeting those expectations ourselves. That means setting examples of excellence in our own lives. (FD1)

Starting with his Fathers' Day communication in 2008, we find a fascinating sequence involving the media.

Obama underscores the crucial role of fathers "first is setting an example of excellence for our children...set high expectations for them...for ourselves." He implies that no less is expected of the media—excellence and high expectations—and he portrays the media negatively as a direct result of its oversight.

He then elaborates on *excellence in education.* But in code he puts down the media for its lack of education about super-intel communication. He elaborates, "even…if you have a college degree…don't just sit in the house and watch *Sports Center* all weekend…so many children are growing up in front of the television. As fathers…we've got to…help them with their homework, and replace the video game or the remote control with a book." Obama's message to the media: "I'm trying to help you grow, help you with your homework to learn something new about communication—specifically about how you can read me like a book."

To get their attention, Obama issues the most severe warning, "We know [note the Message Marker here] that education is everything to our children's future"—in code, "Understand me, the future of America depends on hearing the new symbolic language I am speaking to you." He continues speaking unconsciously to the media which highly values education but remains ignorant of the new knowledge about the unconscious, "to really compete…need to graduate high school…graduate college, and…need a graduate degree too. An eighth-grade education doesn't cut it today…[Here is] a handshake…now get [your] butts back in the library!" The message: "I'm taking you by the hand and showing you that *the opportunity to read me like a book* is staring you in the face. Go learn how."

He goes on, "It's up to us—as fathers and parents—to instill this ethic of excellence in our children. It's up to us to say to our daughters, 'Don't ever let *images on TV* tell you what you are worth'…up to us to tell our sons, 'Those *songs on the radio may glorify violence*, but in my house we give glory to achievement, self-respect, and hard work.'" Again he leaves no doubt he's speaking to the media, unconsciously critiquing it for its extreme bias: "You have falsely portrayed my worth, my authenticity, to America and have glorified the violence I have inflicted on our nation. You have fawned over me and completely failed to demonstrate the 'ethic of excellence' in investigative journalism, failed to demonstrate ethics in the whole matter of my citizenship. You have allowed an unlawful president to take office."

Obama has brought the matter of ethics and excellence—education, achievement and hard work—front and center. He points to the dreaded "A" word—accountability. He accuses the media of failing to be accountable, and he is not finished.

Father's Day 2009—Déjà Vu

In his second Fathers' Day message in 2009, Obama repeats the same basic message with crucial additions. After noting that children—that is, citizens—can tell "when we're not fully there," indirectly referring to the media, he comments,

We need to step out of our own heads...We need to turn off the television...start talking with our kids [citizens] and listening to them, and understanding what's going on ...We need to set limits and expectations...replace that video game with a book and make sure that homework gets done.

We need to say to our daughters, "Don't ever let images on TV tell you what you are worth." We need to tell our sons, "Those songs on the radio may glorify violence, but in our house, we find glory in achievement, self-respect, and hard work." (FD2)

In four negative images, Obama unconsciously emphasizes how the media has painted a false picture of what he means to America and glorified his disregard of the rule of law a disregard which amounts to an act of violence.

His perceptive unconscious persists in admonishing the media, "Get out of your own heads and start listening to my deeper messages so that you can 'start understanding what's going on' with me. You need 'to set limits' with yourselves, understand the significant limitations on your knowledge, then you 'can set expectations' of better education, more advanced learning. Then you could grasp the violence you've done by enabling my destructive and illegal presidency which is not good for America.

"Notice I am telling you about this when I am describing my human development here again on Fathers' Day—showing you all the pain that was built into me that resulted in my attacks on America. Here's one place to start your education—human development—and you need to stop neglecting it."

Here Obama's unconscious adds crucial advice to show the media how to listen, how to truly understand motives so that it can accurately report the story. Here he underscores the significant limitations of the media's traditional direct-questioning interview style. They cannot get to the whole truth that way. No matter what penetrating questions are posed, it comes down to listening—in this case listening to Obama's super intelligence, that part of his mind that sees 50 miles further down the road than they do.

Once more he reminds us, "in our house"—the White House—that achievement and hard work should be the standard. Not only does he imply his presidency was really unearned, but between the lines his super-intel attempts to undo the media's participation in his charade. The super-intel is ever-faithful to moral fortitude, no matter how duplicitous the conscious mind.

Obama Still Addressing Media—Pre-Inauguration Letter

Dear Malia and Sasha,

I know that you've both had a lot of fun these last two years on the campaign trail, going to picnics and parades and state fairs, eating all sorts of junk food your mother and I probably shouldn't have let you have...I know how much I've missed these past two years, and today I want to tell you a little more about why I decided to take our family on this journey.

When I was a young man, I thought life was all about me...But then the two of you came into my world with all your curiosity and mischief and those smiles that never fail to fill my heart and light up my day. And suddenly, all my big plans for myself didn't seem so important anymore. I soon found that the greatest joy in my life was the joy I saw in yours. And I realized that my own life wouldn't count for much unless I was able to ensure that you had every opportunity for happiness and fulfillment in yours. In the end, girls, that's why I ran for President: because of what I want for you and for every child in this nation. (ILtr)

Junk Food and Investigation

Reviewing Obama's pre-inauguration letter, we find he's still unconsciously speaking to the media in code.

It's as though he's saying, "I know the campaign trail was fun for you reporters, but I want to tell you about the junk information I fed you, and why I decided to take the presidency illegally. After announcing how self-centered— "all about me"—that choice was, I instructed you to investigate me, to come into my world with curiosity and a journalist's investigative eye, not as a supporter, to see that I ran as an ineligible candidate. Then you would see my votes didn't really count—and then you'd stop feeding the citizens 'junk' information as well."

I want all our children to go to schools worthy of their potential— schools that challenge them, inspire them, and instill in them a sense of wonder about the world around them. I want them to have the chance to go to college—even if their parents aren't rich. And I want them to get good jobs: jobs that pay well and give them benefits like health care, jobs that let them spend time with their own kids and retire with dignity.

I want us to push the boundaries of discovery so that you'll live to see new technologies and inventions that improve our lives and make our planet cleaner and safer. And I want us to push our own human boundaries to reach beyond the divides of race and region, gender and religion that keep us from seeing the best in each other. (ILtr)

New Mind School for Media

Obama unconsciously harps on "education" and "dis-covery." His super-intel message: "All journalists need to go to a school worthy of the other 90 percent of your intelligence, no longer ignoring it. You are in that school now if you pay attention to my teaching and you see my confession. Only then can you fulfill your government-watchdog purpose. Here's your chance to score the scoop of the century. Here's your chance to gather information like never before, information direct from the deepest recesses of our brilliant unconscious minds."

Sometimes we have to send our young men and women into war and other dangerous situations to protect our country—but when we do, I want to make sure that it is only for a very good reason, that we try our best to settle our differences with others peacefully, and that we do everything possible to keep our servicemen and women safe. And I want every child to understand that the blessings these brave Americans fight for are not free—that with the great privilege of being a citizen of this nation comes great responsibility.

That was the lesson your grandmother tried to teach me when I was your age, reading me the opening lines of the Declaration of Independence and telling me about the men and women who marched for equality because they believed those words put to paper two centuries ago should mean something.

She helped me understand that America is great not because it is perfect but because it can always be made better—and that the unfinished work of perfecting our union falls to each of us. It's a charge we pass on to our children, coming closer with each new generation to what we know America should be. (ILtr)

His message continues, "I want to remind you that with the privilege of being an American citizen and a reporter in this great nation comes great responsibility. Why am I telling you citizenship isn't free? You need to figure out all the violence I have done as an unlawful president—the reason I keep telling you our country is in danger. Then you can report it to the people. Do your job."

I hope both of you will take up that work, righting the wrongs that you see and working to give others the chances you've had. Not just because you have an obligation to give something back to this country that has given our family so much—although you do have that obligation. But because you have an obligation to yourself. Because it is only when you hitch your wagon to something larger than yourself that you will realize your true potential.

These are the things I want for you—to grow up in a world with no limits on your dreams and no achievements beyond your reach, and to grow into compassionate, committed women who will help build that world. (ILtr)

His voice continues, "You, of all people, have an obligation to do the hard work of understanding the truth spoken by my super-intel. That work will help you right my wrongs. Hitch your wagon to a cause greater than yourselves—namely to natural law which prompted my confession and can guide America back to greatness. Only then will you realize your true potential as an investigative reporter."

More Messages to Media

Our challenges may be new. The instruments with which we meet them may be new. But those values upon which our success depends—hard work and honesty, courage and fair play, tolerance and curiosity, loyalty and patriotism—these things are old. These things are true. They have been the quiet force of progress throughout our history. What is demanded then is a return to these truths. What is required of us now is a new era of responsibility—a recognition, on the part of every

> American, that we have duties to ourselves, our nation and the world; duties that we do not grudgingly accept but rather seize gladly, firm in the knowledge that there is nothing so satisfying to the spirit, so defining of our character, than giving our all to a difficult task. (Isp)

Truth

At his inauguration, Obama emphasizes values again and recalls the journalist's goal to expose the truth. Using another vivid super-intel image he tells the media, "I represent a new challenge as an unlawful president, and you need *a new 'instrument,' a new translator* who knows my unconscious language and can hear my confession.

"Above all you must examine my life for truth, specifically for honesty, fair play, courage, curiosity, loyalty and patriotism—the true values that made America great. Ask hard questions of me on that basis.

"I demand 'a return to these truths' because you have abandoned your own journalistic curiosity, your duty to scrutinize me: my honesty, my patriotism and loyalty to the Constitution. Isn't it strange that I have never straightforwardly acknowledged natural questions about my birthplace except in a condescending, degrading fashion? Now you have a duty to uncover that reality—a difficult task—but when you do it, you'll return America to its most cherished values."

Humility

> They understood that our power alone cannot protect us, nor does it entitle us to do as we please. Instead, they knew that our power grows through its prudent use; our security emanates from the justness of our cause, the force of our example, the tempering qualities of humility and restraint. We are the keepers of this legacy. Guided by these principles once more, we can meet those new threats that demand even greater effort. We are the keepers of this legacy. (Isp)

Continuing to guide the media, between the lines Obama underscores a journalist's most basic trait, "Recall the power of enduring convictions and the prudent use of power—that journalists are not entitled to do as they please according to their biases. Your power grows from just causes and is tempered by humility and restraint. You are still the keeper of this legacy, and to meet my threat to America you must learn how to hear my deeper messages instead of being guided by your biases."

We could pick any number of journalists—who, failing to restrain the power of the press—have imprudently forced their limited conscious opinion upon us about the crucial matter of Obama's unlawful citizenship. The usually clever conservative columnist Ann Coulter provides a striking example--with her own super intelligence consistently correcting her. Back on July 25, 2009 during an interview she criticized citizens focused on Obama's birth certificate as irresponsible "cranks" who fail to realize that the certificate "is not an issue."[1]

---

1 "Ann Coulter says Obama's Birth Certificate 'Not an Issue,'" July 26, 2009. http://freerepublic.com/focus/f-news/2301488/posts. This was based on an interview on the Geraldo Rivera Show of July 25, 2009, the video of which was pulled by Fox News Channel after this post hit the Internet.

She blamed the *media's lack of in-depth reporting* for causing the misguided belief that the truth of Obama's birth was being kept from the people—a perfect description of her own lack of in-depth research and reporting. Shortly, she followed that with her own column declaring that "every major conservative news outlet -- including Fox News, The American Spectator, Human Events, National Review and Sweetness & Light" had discredited the idea of Obama's foreign birth.[2] Again we have the "birds of a feather" approach to research—"we all agree"—along with her classic tongue-in-check style.[3]

Then in 2012 she described 'birthers' as irresponsible trouble-makers who fail to "spend five minutes of calm confrontation to see that he [Obama] had already produced it."[4] Again we see her own super intelligence at work suggesting that she had immediately accepted Obama's alleged birth certificate released in April 2011 at face value. Instead unconsciously she recommends that she calmly spend five minutes showing respect to document examiners who spent hours determining the birth certificate was fabricated.

That might lead her to see that there were a thousand holes and two tons of avoidance in Obama's story and that he reluctantly released the long-form under serious pressure. Then she might be open to the fact that Obama's unconscious has already produced an extensive confession of his dishonest presidency. That in effect his four key communications examined in this book represent forensic documents open to a new type of forensic examination—specifically the technique of 'thoughtprint decoding' previously mentioned which I developed by listening for unconscious communication, not just surface messages.

Media Violence: Bias

That we are in the midst of crisis is now well understood. Our nation is at war, against a far-reaching network of violence and hatred. Our economy is badly weakened, a consequence of greed and irresponsibility on the part of some, but also our collective failure to make hard choices and prepare the nation for a new age. Homes have been lost; jobs shed; businesses shuttered. Our health care is too costly; our schools fail too many; and each day brings further evidence that the ways we use energy strengthen our adversaries and threaten our planet.

At these moments, America has carried on not simply because of the skill or vision of those in high office, but because We the People have remained faithful to the ideals of our forebears, and true to our founding documents. So it has been. So it must be with this generation of Americans. (ISp)

When faced with the violence media bias has done to the truth—about

---

2 Ann Coulter, "Obama Birth Certificate Spotted in Bogus Moon Landing," August 5, 2009, http://www.anncoulter.com/columns/2009-08-05.html accessed May 10, 2012.
3 Once more in 2009 I had not even begun my own investigation into Obama's birthplace—nor had Corsi extensively, Trump, or Arpaio.
4 Ann Coulter, *Human Events, 2012*

him—Obama confronts the press even more directly. In his inaugural address his super intelligence powerfully confronts them with more striking images—crisis, dangerous network, preparations for a new age.

Unconsciously, he says, "When I referred to our nation 'at war against a *far-reaching network* of violence and hatred' I was referring to my dishonest presidency, the story you refused to pursue, Instead of digging into me, you've torn down those who would uphold the Constitution. You dismissively label them as 'birthers.' You may as well call them 'ignorant racists' or some other baseless charge. In fact, these 'birthers' are the true defenders of our Constitution.

"But notice in the next breath I linked this to 'irresponsibility on the part of some...*our collective failure* to make hard choices and prepare the nation for a new age.' I wasn't just talking about me but about your collective failure to prepare the people for the age of a deceptive president. You were the educational institutions, 'the schools that failed too many.'

"Again you have strayed from our old values to reinterpret them as you see fit outside the Constitution and any rules of natural law. You were so hell-bent on my election that you didn't make the hard choice to investigate me. You ignored my constitutional corrections, my multiple references that we "must live by Constitution." Indeed we have a media crisis—which weakens America and strengthens our enemies—because you have undermined our strength, our moral high ground, our enduring convictions which as I said enabled us to defeat enemies like communism.

"You simply don't believe that natural laws of human nature—the abiding values of the Declaration—truly exist for all people in all places. While attempting to destroy America's historical moral compass, you have offered us moral relativism, political correctness. This was your central mindset behind your choosing me. My illegal presidency reflects how you have poisoned the minds of Americans, allowing them to think the rules weren't important, just as you've done for abortion. 'Network of violence' and 'far-reaching' perfectly characterize the modern mainstream media which attempts to bring down America with its ongoing violation of natural law."

A New Age of Truth

On this day, we come to proclaim an end to the petty grievances and false promises, the recriminations and worn-out dogmas, that for far too long have strangled our politics....

What the cynics fail to understand is that the ground has shifted beneath them—that the stale political arguments that have consumed us for so long no longer apply. The question we ask today is not whether our government is too big or too small, but whether it works —whether it helps families find jobs at a decent wage, care they can afford, a retirement that is dignified. Where the answer is yes, we intend to move forward. Where the answer is no, programs will end. And those of us who manage the public's dollars will be held

> to account—to spend wisely, reform bad habits, and do our business in the light of day—because only then can we restore the vital trust between a people and their government. (ISp)

Obama's unconscious continues, "All this time ironically another new age, a better age of truth—the age of the super intelligence—was staring you in the face. That's why I can proclaim 'an end to [your] petty grievances and false promises, the...worn-out dogmas that for too long have strangled our politics'— strangled the political environment as you report it. The worn-out dogmas of moral relativism you display without realizing they're dogmas. Indeed they reflect petty grievances in light of the realization that a sterling natural law truly guides us all deep down even as it guides my confession.

"Remember 'those of us who manage the public' will be held to account by nature's laws, those maxims you so freely violate, as did I. You must re-embrace integrity and reform your haphazard creation of societal boundaries. Only then can you restore the vital trust between the people and the media which you have lost."

Media Crisis of Misguided Charity

> But this crisis has reminded us that without a watchful eye, the market can spin out of control and that a nation cannot prosper long when it favors only the prosperous. The success of our economy has always depended not just on the size of our gross domestic product, but on the reach of our prosperity; on our ability to extend opportunity to every willing heart—not out of charity—but because it is the surest route to our common good...

> Let it be told to the future world ...that in the depth of winter, when nothing but hope and virtue could survive...that the city and the country, alarmed at one common danger, came forth to meet [it]. (ISp)

Referencing the media's role with compelling images such as "watchful eye" and "let it be told," Obama continues speaking in code to the media: "Then maybe you can comprehend how this media crisis played into my unwise election and a crisis of misguided charity. You continued to favor those people you agreed with, who likewise believed they could make up their own laws of life. By favoring me, you ignored the rule of equal opportunity, equal accountability and equal justice for all.

"You also lost your watchful eye and didn't pay attention to the discovery of a far wiser part of the mind which confirmed your blindness and favoritism. And you entirely overlooked my admission that my presidency represents a dangerous charity.

"In so doing, *you failed to tell the truth that in the end our country can survive only as long as our virtue does—our natural law-based virtue is our only hope.* That this moral compass alone registers 'danger' whenever justice and freedom are violated—as my illegal presidency did. You not only failed to warn Americans of the 'common danger' any such presidency presents but because of that, now you embody 'the common danger' to America."

Did the Media Follow Obama's Instructions?

From his extensive public databank of ideas, Obama invites a series of questions regarding the media. Did they hold him to the highest ethic of excellence? Did they give glory to the nation's house, The White House, and make sure that he measured up to the highest standards in his words "of achievement, self-respect, and hard work?"

Did they make sure he remained "faithful to the ideals of our forebears, true to our founding documents," true to "We the People?" In Obama's words, the Constitution is "a charter to assure the rule of law and the rights of man, a charter expanded by the blood of generations." Did they show this document the respect it is due by establishing that he fully met all presidential requirements?

Did they take seriously his warning of how misguided charity is dangerous—the surest route to our decline? Or did the media at every turn give Obama a pass, accept the flimsiest of evidence of his citizenship?

The media considered the racial implications of verifying his birth certificate and quickly swept it under the rug. A black journalist claimed that to thoroughly vet Obama was like asking a brother driving through a white neighborhood to see his driver's license as though Obama were a common law-breaker. The journalist completely avoided the fact that "Obama had no tag on his car," no verifiable birth certificate. Instead, he insisted that he was above the law. The journalist went on to insist all 'birthers' were unconscious racists—even if they didn't realize it.[5] Yet not surprisingly by introducing the very subject of unconscious motivation *this journalist's own super intelligence was guiding him* to examine his own unconscious—and Obama's—to get the real story. Then he could grasp the fact that he was unconsciously picking up that Obama had indeed violated the Constitution.

Obama Challenges Media

When Obama's unconscious remains unheard, it becomes more and more blatant. After he released his "official" birth certificate in April 2011, he unconsciously confessed to deception with references to pretending. He implied that, in the name of democracy, reporters should investigate and report the facts (i.e. have the birth certificate examined). Three days later at the White House Correspondents' Dinner he challenged the media to focus on the truth: go to the site of the storm and unconsciously instructed them that, if they could find the courage, to report on his revolution against America.

Could anyone in the media who has failed to confront Obama's eligibility issue stand up to the scrutiny of Obama's all-seeing unconscious? Could any

---

5 Leonard Pitts, "Commentary: 'Presidenting while black' is birthers' biggest issue with Obama," *Miami Herald*, May 5, 2011. http://mcclatchydc.com/2011/05/05/113738/commentary-presidenting-while.html.

reporter accept his super-intel's evaluation of them? No wonder the super intelligence becomes the very last thing an inquiring journalist would naturally embrace.

Should The Media Have Known?

Should the media have known about the discovery of the super intelligence? Obama's unconscious has already answered the question. The media should have been paying attention and gotten out of their own heads, their own limited paradigm, and tuned in to what was going on in the world of psychology with its new understanding of people. They should have been attuned to cutting-edge innovators in psychology presenting new ideas. But he reflects on the human tendency to fixate on one way of thinking. To inspire the media he used vivid images depicting the new super unconscious such as new digital information, new translator, new technology, a new foundation for growth, transform education to a new age, and harness the light.

> For everywhere we look, there is work to be done. The state of the economy calls for action, bold and swift, and we will act—not only to create new jobs, but to lay a new foundation for growth. We will build the roads and bridges, the electric grids and digital lines that feed our commerce and bind us together. We will restore science to its rightful place, and wield technology's wonders to raise health care's quality and lower its cost. We will harness the sun and the winds and the soil to fuel our cars and run our factories. And we will transform our schools and colleges and universities to meet the demands of a new age. All this we can do. And all this we will do. (ISp)

The media ignored information in its midst about the existence of the super intelligent mind. Malcolm Gladwell provided the press with a major clue in his 2003 bestseller, *Blink,* popularizing the unconscious with the sub-title: *How to Think without Thinking.* Although he was late to the game himself, as an investigative reporter he established how the unconscious mind is thinking when you don't know it—and thinking hard. Calling what we know as the super-intel "the dazzling adaptive unconscious," Gladwell demonstrated how the unconscious quick-reads situations in the blink of an eye and is vastly more perceptive than the conscious mind.

Despite its status as a bestseller, *Blink* was largely overlooked by the news media. Surely it might occur to the media that the quick-read subliminal mind had to work in everyday life. You would expect investigative journalists to be seeking out those who used the new unconscious in creative ways. Dr. Robert Langs, veteran psychoanalyst and discoverer of the super intelligence, has written some 43 books on the subject of our brilliant instinctive unconscious that speaks uniquely in its own symbolic language.[6]

The discovery of the super intelligence was further trumpeted in four books of my own (three on using the unconscious in forensic profiling) along with

---

6 See Appendix A.

multiple media appearances. On Leeza Gibbon's national television show, I profiled Bill Clinton by decoding his self-written speech apologizing for the Lewinsky scandal. A Washington, D.C. journalist on the show was moved by Clinton's poignant unconscious explanations of his motives.

Nevertheless, this ground-breaking discovery of the new unconscious has gone almost entirely unnoticed by the mainstream media. The media's only efforts to address our phenomenal unconscious intelligence occur occasionally on Bill O'Reilly's cable television newscasts with his focus on body language, but even that falls woefully short.

Despite communication breakthroughs in numerous other fields, the media ignores the full potential of the human mind. Recent years have produced revolutionary breakthroughs in information technology which has changed the world. In science, molecular biologists have discovered how extensive communication occurs in a single human cell which carries a database larger than the *Encyclopedia Britannica*.[7] Yet when it comes to the most complex and fascinating part of nature, the human mind, the media has shown no curiosity about improving its listening abilities. In a nutshell, the press failed to get the story about one of the greatest breakthroughs in human knowledge. Because of that, the media missed Obama's super intelligence unfolding a candid confession.

Challenge of Breakthroughs

Obama's super-intel understands—and I understand—what I'm asking of the media and readers. We have a new way of listening, listening to deeper symbolic messages delivered between the lines, and it challenges us because we've grown so used to listening only to the conscious mind. All previous efforts, initially led by Freud, to explore the unconscious became quickly clouded for laymen by mumbo-jumbo professional jargon.

Any scientific breakthrough requires a new learning step—and never have we had one like this: people saying one thing but also saying another; that other being a far more important message. Obama's super intelligence emphasized the hard learning required to recognize the deeper intelligence. But he assured us it could be done and must be done because America's future rides on truly understanding him.

Criteria of Expertise

That brings us to another matter—expertise—and why Obama repeatedly referred to excellence and achievement, and educational breakthroughs. In Gladwell's book, *Outliers of Success*—the follow-up to *Blink*—this perceptive observer describes an expert as someone who has spent 10,000 hours in a particular endeavor. For the past three decades as both as a therapist and a

---

7 Lennox, John, "God's Undertaker (Has Science Buried God?)," (Oxford, England: Wilkinson House, 2007), p. 128.

forensic profiler, I've logged more than 80,000 hours listening to the unconscious mind.

The media has not been trained in super-intel communication —nary one hour. Most readers haven't been trained either. This is where trust comes in—and it came in for me too. I had to learn to trust the super intelligence, and indeed it was shocking to hear about its existence first from therapy cases where it can be most closely studied. Over the years my trust has grown enormously. As I learned that it had a striking moral compass, based on natural law, and operated on life-giving principles, I saw how wise and visionary it truly was. My faith in the learning process paid off.

Faith

New learning begins with faith that you have something to learn. This was implicit in Obama's unconscious instructions to the media to get more education. He understood that new learning is blocked by faith in your current knowledge, clinging to the idea that you already know what you need to know, to continue to look at new information through the same old conscious-mind lens.

Many will object to Obama's unconscious communication, concluding that I have simply forced my own ideas on him. Those are the people who stay exclusively in their conscious mind. They'll take the easy, natural, comfortable way to go, particularly if Obama's confession makes them uncomfortable.

Personal Experiences with Media, Avoidance of Super-Intel

For better or worse, I've had personal experience with some of the big names in journalism—broadcast and print. I understand their limits. My experiences with the media represent a microcosm of the larger problem.

I've appeared on national news programs discussing high-profile criminal cases in which suspects unconsciously confessed. I've also been interviewed extensively by both print and broadcast journalists about my books, including *The Deeper Intelligence*, my 1994 book which reveals the existence of the super-intel.

In one forensic case a reporter said he didn't like my method of "reading people's minds"—when in fact the suspect was quick-reading his own motives and telling all about it. I was just reporting the messages. The real issue was the reporter, who had his own personal issues which prevented him from dealing in any way, shape, or form with his unconscious. A natural resistance.

In another case, when approached with research on the super intelligence, a prominent science writer for a major news magazine turned a deaf ear to the language of the unconscious. Instead the writer focused on the biology of the mind—the "exciting new work on brain research" completely missing the "dazzling new adaptive unconscious *mind*." The writer preferred to deal with the technical biology of the brain rather than the less-obvious and more challenging communicative workings of the mind.

Lastly, I recall my encounter with Len Downie, Jr., then the editor of the *Washington Post,* when I attended a speech he gave at a local university on "Accountability Journalism." At a private reception, I informed him about the scientific breakthrough to the super intelligence and its vast implications. He expressed interest, and we later had cordial contact by email. He quickly dismissed the existence of the super-intel, however, because he wanted "accountability journalism" on his terms only—in the realm of the surface mind.

How the Media Could Have Reacted

There were some people who appreciated the crucial discovery of this special new intelligence especially as applied to our culture. As the late Dr. Richard Halverson, then chaplain of the U.S. Senate, described in his endorsement of my seminal 1994 book *The Deeper Intelligence*—"It is as if God planned this book for this crucial moment in time...[it] brings us face to face with reality—transcendent and profoundly temporal...addresses us with a healing message which is reconciling, restorative, and renewing." Dr. Halverson thought the information important enough to send the book to then President and Mrs. Clinton and several congressmen, some of whom sent me personal letters. He understood we had now "re-discovered" natural law in the unconscious mind, a discovery which could solve our cultural dilemmas.

Intuitively, Dr. Halverson was also trying to guide me to look more closely at presidents and demonstrate how their own super intelligence could help them lead. My career path took me first to psychotherapy and then to forensic profiling where I learned the value of listening to verbatim communication from a person's own mind—because the super-intel was constantly speaking, and always told the truth. As a therapist I learned my patient's unconscious was constantly communicating which invariably involved confessions of a better way. Circumstances then led me into forensic profiling where again I learned the value of verbatim communication (interrogations, letters, etc.) whereby guilty suspects could not stop their super intelligence from confessing.

How the Media Could Have Started to Listen

Our new knowledge about the mind reveals the media has much to learn about listening. An open-minded media might have heard some of Obama's deeper messages. What if the media had really listened to Obama's speeches and his personal communications surrounding Fathers' Day and his inauguration? We can ask the same questions of Congress and the courts, but for now we'll focus on the media, the supposed watchdog of our nation.

An unwritten media rule advises never speculate about a person's motives because you can't speak for them. "Don't question motives"—"Just the facts ma'am," like Joe Friday. But what if the mind spelled out its motives in a discernible language? Wouldn't it be an investigative journalist's job to at least consider that possibility?

Setting all this aside, reporters might have wondered what crisis Obama kept alluding to in his inaugural address. Why the story about George Washington and the desperate straits America finds itself in 'when nothing but hope and virtue will prevail?'

And with the enormous constitutional eligibility question looming in the background, his obsessive references to the Constitution might have caused them to wonder if he were 'protesting too much' about his devotion to it, particularly given his prior anti-Constitution comments.

Perhaps they might have noticed Obama's frequent references to the destructiveness of entitlement and charity and how Americans must live by natural law stressing achievement and hard work. But they didn't know how to listen at all. This was well demonstrated three years later when African-American journalist Leonard Pitts noted that no one could remember anything Obama said in his inauguration speech. But this was also Pitts' super-intel urging him to review the speech to hear Obama's secret confession.

News Report of the Future

Paradigm shifts in knowledge affect every field, and breakthroughs in knowledge determine the future. Since decision-making about the human mind and human motivations will forever remain at the heart of news-gathering, the discovery of a super intelligence should dramatically change investigative journalism. In that light we can envision this telecast after Obama's Inauguration Day speech.

Good evening, I am Ralph Johnson reporting on the deeper news of the day. Today President Barack Obama delivered his inaugural address to a watching world—thousands of people in the nation's capital and millions more watching around the world.

First, I will tell you about my interview with our expert on 'mind language' and the super intelligence, Dr. Gene O'Leary, who looked at Obama's speech not only for what he told us directly but more importantly—given the existence of his unconscious super intelligence—what he told us between the lines. Dr. O'Leary stated that Obama unconsciously warned us about his misguided plans for America. Obama suggested first that his economic plans will seriously disrupt America, worsen the existing financial crisis leading to a rise in unemployment and create a difficult climate for small business. He alluded to a radical environmentalism and hinted that a new health-care proposal will be far too expensive. Unconsciously, by protesting too much he predicted that he will cause the next generation to lower its economic expectations.

What particularly struck O'Leary was Obama's underlying prediction that he would operate his government largely in secret and predicted that he'd be a one-term president who will eventually be held accountable for a strikingly poor economic performance. Furthermore, Obama's excessive emphasis on the dangers of entitlement and charity and his reference to the importance of achievement suggests that Obama will significantly increase entitlement spending, further draining the economy.

The president's super intelligence has been significantly affected by his abandonment by his birth father who left him when he was an infant. His emphasis on his absent, abusive father would provide a powerful motive for his misguided anger directed at America.

On another issue, Dr. O'Leary wondered why Obama made so many references to the Constitution. Was he possibly confessing his own unconstitutionality? Why did he link blacks and whites uniting around the Constitution? And why did Obama repeatedly insist America had a huge crisis on its hands, a crisis far more threatening than an economic downturn?

O'Leary reassures Americans that evidence exists one way or the other as to whether Obama is secretly confessing. For the good of America, the doctor said, citizens should keep their cool and carefully examine the evidence. As Obama's moral compass declared, the rule of law must prevail.

The Heavy Price for the Media's Failure

There are huge consequences for America resulting from the media's ignorance of Obama's super-intel communication—especially for ignoring his instructions to confront him.

If the media had known about the super intelligence, they could have picked up on Obama's hidden confession. After his 2008 Fathers' Day speech, journalists could have questioned his citizenship and certainly his character. Then—based of his own emphasis on the Constitution and rule of law—they could have pushed for a real investigation of Obama's birth documents.

With such an approach, the media would've taken a step toward modern journalism—truly accountable journalism based on vital new knowledge about the mind.

Instead of coming to America's rescue, the silent media allowed our nation to pay a tremendous price with Obama carrying out his destructive, divisive plan. Along the way, the world has become a far more dangerous place. Millions of Americans have paid and continue to pay extraordinary costs, suffering economically and emotionally. So instead of securing our nation, the media allowed fear and uncertainty to prevail. This explains Obama's repeated unconscious message to the media that they were doing great violence to America by enabling his ill-advised presidency.

Recall Obama confessed that he was taking a huge risk by becoming an illegal president, in effect sabotaging our Constitution. Understand by not investigating him the media took the same risk. By now having painted themselves into a corner, the media still refuses to examine the subject. Instead of facing the turmoil earlier of confronting a possibly illegal president despite his being the first black presidential candidate who had come this far, the media allowed the risk to continue. Now imagine the turmoil if his illegality was established and came front-and-center. The risk has grown and grown. This is always the case. I see it all the time as a therapist when a family allows a kid to be out of control—things get worse until the rules, the boundaries are finally set. America as a nation really is no different. Natural laws of human behavior apply to our nation.

Why Media Missed the Story

Obama's dazzling unconscious makes him a mainstream media expert. His deeper look at the media reveals a tough assessment. Speaking of the media's craving for scoops, Obama provides the scoop on what secretly rules the nation-sabotaging media. All along, step by step, he has brought us to "accountability journalism." Speaking for the media, he tells us unconsciously, "We don't hold ourselves accountable to achievement—least of all accountable to the achievement of others whose knowledge would threaten us because we are lacking in it." Additionally Obama points to a major media secret—behind the closed doors of editorial boards, atheism covertly rules. This anti-religious bias has become increasingly obvious according to media critic and former CBS News reporter Bernard Goldberg [8]

Above all, Obama unconsciously declares, "Most fundamentally we the media are not accountable to America's 'old moral compass' based on the outdated idea of fixed rules of behavior. Instead we have offered the world the new moral compass of political correctness, moral relativism—tolerance above all." In their new media world, truth doesn't exist, only tolerance (and intolerance for conservatives' views).

In repeat references to crisis, Obama's deeper mind identifies the "Media P.C. (political correctness) Crisis"—a crisis attacking the truth. As Obama spoke of ethics of excellence—implying excellence in ethics—his super intelligence insists the media has failed to instill ethics in America.

Media Reluctant to Investigate Obama

The mainstream media has long refused to investigate Obama. Journalists have let him slide on his refusal to release records—medical, academic, and of course, an authentic birth certificate.

As a result, the mainstream media has remained mired in denial about Obama. No subject has been more off-limits than the question of his birthplace and the legality of his presidency. More than anything else, the issue of his birthplace and birth certificate puts his presidency in serious jeopardy, but the media refuses to even acknowledge it. Instead, the press insists there has been adequate investigation. Even prominent conservative columnists and commentators have acquiesced. The media allowed Obama to go unchallenged regarding his birthplace. When the president finally produced a supposed long-form birth certificate, *the media simply rubber-stamped it.* No effort was made to examine a paper original at all.

Even when the putative long-form birth certificate was declared a fraud by respectable document examiners, the media ignored their findings. The press also ignored Jerome Corsi's excellent body of research on the topic and declared the investigative website WorldNewsDaily as radioactive. Many dubbed it "WorldNutDaily," which reflects another media supper-intel moment. Attempting to cover over their deficiency with sarcasm, we have the media's unconscious admission they failed to use their mental capacity to investigate, and that Obama's birth certificate touches on powerful chaotic issues of near-madness.

The media actually *fought* efforts to authenticate Obama's birth certificate because such an effort would shine a light on their slipshod, supposedly investigative journalism. We're left gazing in disbelief at a media quaking in its boots, fearful of facing the truth about a deceptive president.

Without question, investigating Obama is a major media taboo. Why the taboo? Because he's a liberal Democrat, as are the vast majority of reporters, editors and news directors in the mainstream media. But when even prominent conservatives join their liberal colleagues in refusing to investigate crucial citizenship requirements, powerful unconscious reasons can certainly explain the avoidance.

Obama's confession has given us important insight into the deepest fears of the human psyche. These fears, surrounded by emotional powder kegs, come alive around the loaded issue of Obama's presidency. We consider the following.

- **Denial of Powerful Emotions:** In this politically correct society, "See no evil" is the media's conscious byword. Who can consciously take in that a president wishes to inflict "unimaginable perils," including Constitutional violations?

- **Deep-seated guilt:** The fact that the media tolerates such deception points to an underlying emotion: deep-seated guilt which says we deserve such treatment. Guilt is a deeply feared emotion, *often buried deep in our unconscious*. Unresolved deep-seated "white guilt" which says, "I now need to be punished just as black slaves were punished." Cutting-edge knowledge of the super-intel reveals "borrowed guilt" or "inherited guilt" can linger unconsciously for generations when cultural violations have occurred.[9] It is a phenomenon best understood by the super-intel. It runs long and deep. We do not quickly recover from cultural abuses such as slavery and segregation. Indulging Obama is, simply put, a guilt-relieving mechanism. And again it is totally unconscious

- **More Unconscious Guilt** There is more guilt over confronting Obama. (1) The guilt over possibly removing a president from office—for whatever reason, and despite his hidden admission to an illegal presidency; (2) guilt

---

9 Robert Langs, M.D. currently is writing a book revealing crucial cultural patterns around deeply embedded guilt being played out in cultural self-sabotage.

over destroying the dream of electing a black president.

- **Unconscious Fear** There is another terrifying emotion which explains the constant pass Obama received from the media: overwhelming fear. The possibility of race riots repeatedly predicted by Obama's super-intel, haunts professional observers such as the press and the police.

Even the great Rush Limbaugh unconsciously confesses to this fear. On his radio broadcast on September 8, 2011, following yet another Obama jobs speech, he observed how a Democrat congressman opposed the employment initiative but feared being the first one to publicly criticize Obama and avoided speaking up. Limbaugh has long vacillated over confronting Obama's illegal presidency but finally warned people "this was a dead end." Almost certainly "dead" is what Limbaugh unconsciously fears over raising the issue—deaths caused by turmoil and riots.

Obama continues to point toward life-or-death issues as his unconscious advises the country to bravely face his illegal presidency.

- **Lack of Courage:** We've failed to stand up for the Constitution, which Obama insists "we must do." Our success as a nation, his super-intel says, depends on a return to "courage and patriotism," joining "purpose and necessity to courage"…all of which he links to the price of citizenship. Who in the media can face Obama's confrontation, "You lack courage?"
- **Birth certificate release:** At the 2011 White House Correspondents' dinner—three days after the alleged birth certificate release—Obama passionately challenged reporters to explore the truth in all matters—even *instructing them to risk their lives.* Unconsciously he pointed to the media's failure to examine his birth credentials. He implied that the threat of riots must not thwart the pursuit of the truth.
- **Racism is not the issue:** Obama repeatedly appeals to us to hold him to standards of excellence and ethics. He repeatedly warns that favoritism leads inexorably to decline. He has made several appeals to defend the Constitution and the rule of law. How did the media miss all this?

Squashing Sheriff Joe

Following Sheriff Joe Arpaio's extensive three-month investigation, where his findings in March 2012 pointed to a fraudulent Obama birth certificate and the media took things to a new low. Not only did major news outlets—including conservative sources—refuse to report the story, recognized online conservative news websites withdrew popular articles about Arpaio's findings on their sites. This included Forbes online[10] and Townhall.com (which describes itself as the "leading conservative and political opinion website") spiking *not one but three*

---

10 John Mariotti, "Is There An Imposter In The White House?," *Forbes*, March 24, 2012 (originally). http://obamareleaseyourrecords.blogspot.com/2012/03/forbes-scrubs-article-questioning.html accessed May 20, 2012.

such articles. Two of the articles were by regular Townhall columnist, Diana West, whose second article "Why the Silence About Obama's Historic Scam?" was eventually published elsewhere online.

Her words issue a sober warning regarding the media, "Clearly, something has us all on lockdown. That's much, much scarier than even the amazing possibility that some con artist might be pulling off the biggest scam in history."[11] Frighteningly, she warns us America faces not one but two historic scams—an illegal president and a totally silent media.

Earlier in her article, West confirmed the enormous fear controlling the media, "One editor told me the problem is the evidence of fraud might prove to be true! A very famous conservative figure told me that if the president were proved to be an identity thief, 'that would alienate too many people' from the Republican Party!" The stakes get higher and higher—now the Republican Party joins with the press in unconscious collusion governed by intolerable fear. Surely any serious investigator understands how Congress on both sides of the aisle has avoided the issue. If the dam ever broke all the enablers would pay a price. Ironically in the end, all the major players—the press, Congress, the political parties and the courts—like Obama are controlled by secret fear.

This brings us back to all that's left—the citizens—just as George Washington told us it would be, and we must realize that not one of the three branches of government can do the people's job of enforcing accountability. Presciently, our first President saw this day coming.

America again faces another major test. Who would ever have imagined such a test [of our deepest core values no less, the values which made us great] complicated by a free press now enslaved to fear? But we have been here before, when nobody thought we would make it. And it's always good to turn the lights on so we can see where we are and who we must overcome—one more unique twist in our ever-unfolding challenge of maintaining the greatest nation in the history of the world.

With our backs to the wall, now we will truly see what we the citizens are made of. Denial or truth—which will it be, ladies and gentlemen? And if we choose truth, how hard are we willing to fight for it?

---

11 Diana West, "Why the silence about Obama's historic scam?, March 22. 2012, http://www.wnd.com/2012/03/why-the-silence-about-obamas-historic-scam accessed May 20, 2012.

Afterword: Chief Justice Roberts' Confession Confirms Obama's

The day before this book was supposed to go to press, the crucial matter of Obama's illegal presidency surfaced in yet another disguised but persuasive way; the stunning news of the U.S. Supreme Court upholding Obamacare broke upon the national stage.

Just when it appeared that Obama might skate all the way to the 2012 election untouched, he received a confrontation from a surprising source. The blow was delivered in the most discrete way conceivable—so slick, nobody saw the punch land.

It all has to do with the exquisite below-the-surface interaction between Chief Justice John Roberts and Barack Obama, which can be traced directly back to his Inauguration Day. Keep in mind Roberts' memorable fumbling the words of the presidential oath, a stumbling so severe that the Chief Justice found it necessary to return to the White House later in the day to correctly administer the oath for legality's sake. We know that such slips at key moments reflect major unconscious, super intelligence issues.

We all know that the real behind-the-scenes action in Washington D.C. often remains hidden in back-room deals which never see the light of day. The same thing is true about the human mind when it comes to difficult decisions and being in unexpected binds, just the kind of bind in which Roberts found himself in January 2009. But the super intelligence—this time Roberts', not Obama's—is a master at disclosing the truest and deepest story. It does so only after tremendous guilt prompts him to confess his complicity in Obama's grand deception.

The Surface Story

As with Obama, we must first identify the telling words, phrases and images in Roberts' own writing to analyze, which we find, naturally, in his written opinion on the case. We start with the surface narrative, which is strange indeed. On June 28, 2012, Chief Justice Roberts joined with the four most liberal justices to refuse to overturn Obamacare—the president's signature legislative "achievement." Both conservatives and liberals were caught completely off guard. Conservatives felt betrayed, and believed Roberts decided *against* the Constitution as he voted in favor of the president.

Obamacare

How could John Roberts—a man who boasts about being 'a good constitutional umpire calling balls and strikes'—miss this call so badly that it permanently damaged his stellar career (and more importantly, damaged the Constitution)? He saw strike three come hurtling right down the middle of the plate. All he needed to do was throw up his right hand and signal "Strike three!" and the Obamacare bill is out! But instead he called it a ball, thus throwing the game to Obama's revisionist team.

So out of bounds was his decision that prominent colleagues called for his resignation.[1] Prominent constitutionalist and radio commentator Mark Levin called it "a lawless decision" and presented his analysis as an extension of his book, *Men in Black: How the Supreme Court is Destroying America*, published seven years before. Even liberals had been preparing for a decision against Obamacare: just two weeks prior, *Time* magazine had published a cover story on Justice Anthony Kennedy entitled "The Great Decider." Everyone thought Kennedy, not Roberts, might cast a swing vote to support Obamacare. For the record, Kennedy struck down all provisions revealing just how bad a bill he thought it was. The image we saw on the news was of Justice Roberts, bigger than life, repeatedly pictured with the four left-leaning justices with whom he had voted. An indelible image, a picture truly worth a thousand words. As the saying goes, "The company you keep says a lot about you." Roberts, who had started running as the lead dog no less, now ignobly stood with four ultra-left justices; a sorry picture indeed for American jurisprudence.

When making remarks at the end of the session, Roberts even declared the verdict himself in those unforgettable words, "We disagree"—that Obamacare is unconstitutional. He spoke for 14 minutes without revealing a clue of the majority opinion and the Court's verdict. Yet as awareness dawned, both conservatives and liberals were aghast, sitting in the courtroom stunned with their mouths agape. As the constitutionalists saw it, Roberts had pulled defeat from the jaws of victory—again.

Roberts Confesses

The explanation of Roberts' pro-Obama decision cannot be found on the surface. His motivations lurk deep in his own unconscious. Deep down Roberts knew just how bad a call he made. In a classic confession, his denials tell the whole story. First we have the recognition that all his words reflect his unconscious take on himself, that his brilliant super intelligence quick-reads the log in his eye to see past his denial. At other moments we will read straight through *his overt denials* and continue to see the log in his eye.

Roberts' behavior displays two hallmarks of hidden confessions: self-

---

1 Josh Feldman, "On *O'Reilly Factor*, Law Professor Says John Roberts Should Resign Over Obamacare Ruling," June 29, 2012, http://www.mediaite.com/tv/on-oreilly-factor-law-professor-says-john-roberts-should-resign-over-obamacare-ruling/ accessed July 1, 2012.

sabotage and self-punishment, both reflecting deep-seated guilt. We are looking into the Chief Justice's unconscious, the 90 percent of reality outside his surface awareness. In his denials, Roberts demonstrated how he drifted away from his usual protective framework. It was reported from trustworthy sources that the four conservative justices including Justice Kennedy doggedly tried to dissuade Roberts of his misjudgment for more than a month, but all to no avail.

The apparent fact that Roberts changed his vote from his normal constitutional stance also represents a red flag. Such self-destructive reasoning occurs when decision-makers abandon the law and the Constitution in favor of indulging fanciful personal inclinations. In the end, Roberts's super intelligence will admit he was dealing with an unresolved personal matter between himself and Obama.

Roberts' First Denial

Let's start with Roberts' three main denials. His written opinion stated that the Court could not rule on the constitutionality of forcing people to buy health insurance. He wrote, *"We do not consider whether the Act embodies sound policies. That judgment is entrusted to the Nation's elected leaders."* Here we see his denial that he was responsible to embody a sound judicial decision.

Applying every word to himself, we have the message, "I did not consider/demonstrate sound judicial policy in refusing to rule on the soundness of the Obamacare law. I did not utilize the judgment entrusted to me as the Nation's leading judge." Unconsciously Roberts introduces the question of whether a decision is sound or unsound and confesses that he failed to make a sound decision—and failed to lead.

But we must not miss that he implies that Congress also failed to make a sound judgment. Keep that in mind for the deeper story that will emerge.

Roberts' Second Denial

Just as Obama's super intelligence trumps his endless denials, Roberts' unconscious also reveals his true motivations. The Chief Justice stated, *"We possess neither the expertise nor the prerogative to make policy judgments."*

Reading through that blatant denial, staying with the main ideas, we find another set of images and confession: he failed to demonstrate the expertise he possessed, and indeed he did make a "policy judgment"—Obamacare stands. His specific super-intel images need to be seen this way, "As a judge I just made a policy statement but I do not want to own that consciously. I do not want to see what I really did."

By not ruling in his normal fashion—through the eyes of the Constitution—he allowed a political decision to prevail. Think of Roberts' self-criticism by his all-seeing unconscious: he failed to judge, he backed off, he lacked courage. His super intelligence secretly informs him just how self-punishing his foolish decision was—reflecting that deep guilt controlled him *before his ruling* and led to such an aberrant assessment of Obamacare. Understand deep-seated unconscious guilt exerts powerful influence over anyone's choices. But what exactly is John Roberts guilty about? He will tell us.

Roberts' Third Denial

In Roberts' third prominent denial he demonstrates once more his sudden lack of expertise, the loss of his ability to judge. His statement was,

> We ask only whether Congress has the power under the Constitution to enact the challenged provisions ... Because the Constitution permits such a tax, it is not our role to forbid it, or to pass upon its wisdom or fairness.

We will examine this comment step-by-step.

First we can see his moment of judicial chaos when he established that the liberals' beloved commerce clause—the banner under which they hope to control matters—cannot support the bill. End of case. Game, set, match—or so it seems.

But then it is as if Roberts suddenly proclaims, "Don't cut off what's left of the lights because court is not over. I need to add something." Add what? He continues implying, "The bill's supporters really made a weak secondary argument so I must make it more strongly for them. I insist that you call this bill a tax."

Yet a tax is a tax is a tax, and Obama and his minions in Congress told us this was not a tax when they were promoting the bill. They knew it would never gain enough votes as a tax plan. To have Roberts participate in Obama's "bait and switch" trickery is morally repulsive and intellectually dishonest.

Now Justice Roberts' denial comes into full focus. Right off he unconsciously confesses to poor judgment in even considering the Obamacare law as a tax. He cannot tell us that enough, stating, "We ask only whether Congress has the power under the Constitution to enact the challenged provisions." Read his super intelligence saying: "I ask only did *I have the power* under the Constitution as a judge to challenge the way the Obamacare bill was presented—as a law, not as a tax."

The obvious answer was, "Why, of course you did, your honor."

Roberts adds, "Because the Constitution permits such a tax, it is not our role to forbid it, or to pass upon its wisdom or fairness." We note his overt denial, "it is not our role" and simply read right through it. Read his unconscious message "it was my role" to forbid Obamacare if necessary, to rule on it in a wise and fair fashion. Yet he abdicated his role. He also was in denial about the Constitution which really did not permit such a tax but Roberts' dishonest spin did.

The Chief Justice had unconsciously confessed. Roberts' super intelligence again describes a man in major retreat from his expertise and from his judicial role. Deep down his self-criticism echoes loudly and picks up more steam. His own ideas reflect that he had been unwise and unfair, ultimately burdening the people, not serving them by protecting their individual liberty. He showed himself to be an unconstitutional judicial activist. He had created an all-permitting Constitution out of whole cloth.

Again we ask what could have prompted such self-sabotage? It must be a powerful reason, and indeed it was, as he later tells us. Mistakenly he renounced his true role—and tried to blame Congress for his cowardice. Later we will get to a much deeper reason he did so.

Colleagues Spot Roberts' Destructiveness

Justice Kennedy in his dissent specifically addressed Roberts' blindness and neurotic need to change reality: *"What Congress calls a penalty, we [Roberts] call a tax ... Congress went to great lengths to say it was a penalty ... In short, the court [Roberts] imposes a tax when Congress deliberately rejected a tax."*

Columnist Thomas Sowell echoed the bitter sentiment declaring that 313 million Americans were the people whom "Chief Justice Roberts betrayed when he declared constitutional something that is nowhere authorized in the Constitution." Sowell also observed that "Chief Justice Roberts admitted that (his interpretation) might not be the most 'natural' reading of the law,"[2] an understatement of biblical proportions.

His conservative colleagues' stringent criticism reveals how Roberts would normally have seen things and how far he had departed from his normal judgment. They fully understood how bad Roberts' decision was. Justice Antonin Scalia called it "trying to force on the nation a new law." Justice Kennedy accused Roberts of "judicial legislation" and "vast judicial overreaching." These assessments, harsh words spoken by colleagues whose views he generally shares, certainly wounded him deeply. Roberts surely heard the criticism and unconsciously agreed with it. But as Roberts will later unfold, not one of them had walked his lonely road, the path which he hinted had brought him to his aberrant decision.

Roberts' Blind Spot

The story of Roberts' enormous blind spot emerges between the lines. Do not overlook his central motivation. As all good investigators know, *we must first understand the context of someone's behavior.* Roberts points to an event which took place on the world's stage, the biggest moment ever in Roberts' public life. We will get to that story shortly, which he will unfold for us. First we must look past the various speculative motivations others have put forth for what all agree was his puzzling decision.

We consider these possible rationalizations: a (weak) judicial tendency to not declare an act of Congress unconstitutional, his open-mindedness (a trait liberals treasure), his cleverness as the brightest Justice, his desire to appear

---

2 Thomas Sowell, "Chief Justice betrays Americans," *Birmingham News,* July 4, 2012.

more balanced, and even the possibility that he was manipulated by the media and Obama wishing to avoid a barrage of criticism. Each of these possibilities may contain a grain of truth, but the real key is how they all link to his deepest motivations. Again we return to context and now we remember "The Slip" at Obama's inauguration when Roberts fumbled the presidential oath and Obama fumbled it again. Think about it.

Remember Roberts is supposed to be the Guardian-in-Chief of the U.S. Constitution—the ultimate Rule Book which guides the fundamental rule of law. He swears in the president of the United States, making sure the president-elect puts his hand on the Bible, attesting to his intentions. Roberts carries a grave responsibility.

Now suppose he suspected the president-elect lacked documentation sufficient to prove he was a legal citizen. That's what Roberts' verbal slips suggested (see Chapter 12). As the Chief Stickler for the Law, Roberts would certainly have raised the question in his own gifted legal mind—even if for only a moment, a possibility lurking in the back of that mind—especially with legal challenges to Obama's eligibility already being argued in various lower courts, as he was no doubt aware. He surely knew about former Reagan ambassador Alan Keyes' lawsuit filed November 14, 2008, requiring Obama to document natural-born citizenship. Of course he also knew about Obama's opponent, John McCain, having been challenged as an eligible presidential candidate in 2008 because of his foreign birth on a military base where his father was stationed (both McCain's parents were natural-born American citizens).

But then, like everyone else, Roberts runs head-on into the prevailing winds of political correctness and the special rule of compassion that America must elect an African-American president—regardless of complications. And of course he saw Obama's oratory gifts and the media's unceasing praise of the man.

However, deep down Roberts knows he's shirking his duties—he knows the law of the land regarding presidential eligibility. It was his responsibility before this nation and before God as he also raised his right hand to swear that this impending president was the real deal. Symbolically Roberts' palm alighted upon that very same Bible just as the president's hand did. Like everyone else, however, the Chief Justice had gone into massive denial and tried not to think about it. He pushed aside his fears of the constitutional crisis that would arise if an illegal candidate slipped past his watch. It was Roberts' chief nightmare. So now he had to repress it.

But his quick-read unconscious mind that picks up on reality quicker than you can say "Barack Obama" understood that this president really had not been *legally* vetted by Congress, the DNC or the media. He knows there is not even a good strictly adhered-to process in place to truly carry out such constitutional certification. This would explain the many petitions filed in the courts. In his shrewdness, Roberts would understand the DNC's lack of constitutional concern over Obama's eligibility and intuit that they had not thoroughly investigated his qualifications—Obama was all too popular. He also knows that Obama's father was a foreign-born Kenyan and that there were questions about whether Obama was actually born in Hawaii. The Chief Justice surely recalls Obama's blatant refusal to release his records.

Roberts also knows full well that an alleged online copy of a short-form birth certificate posted on the Internet is no proof at all. He also understands that two Hawaiian newspaper announcements prove absolutely nothing. And these are the two central "proofs" for Obama's legality. Forget about the ridiculous claim that Hillary Clinton would have used the phony birth proofs against him in the primaries if it were true—Obama's past was hands-off to her as well. She never brought it up publicly, and John McCain followed suit in mute obedience to political correctness. Roberts' brilliant, see-all super intelligence knows this in half a heartbeat—and he cannot escape that his moral compass insists he tell the truth to America.

Deep in his core, Roberts—the meticulous lawyer—knows it is ultimately his job to validate an authentic president. Or to disqualify an imposter.

Obama's Inaugural Confession

Immediately after delivering, in effect, his legal testimony on behalf of Obama the president, Roberts then sat down and listened to Obama's inauguration speech. As we have seen, that speech was really Barack Obama's inaugural confession in which he admitted between the lines that, like a far-reaching foreign network of violence, he had just created a constitutional crisis as an illegal president. (See Chapter 12) Roberts' super intelligence heard every word.

In fact the Chief Justice would have heard Obama's super intelligence shout "constitutional crisis" repeatedly between the lines, with Obama referring to "crisis" a half-dozen times in his speech. It must have put a knife through John Roberts' heart to hear those words. And then to hear Obama insist we must all live by the Constitution and repeatedly hold up the rule of law would have completely overwhelmed Roberts deep down. Roberts spotted the hypocrisy in Obama in a millisecond—but then he also spotted it in himself.

That's when Roberts knew for sure just how bad it was. Deep down Roberts could do the constitutional math. America sat on a potential powder keg—and he, Chief Justice John Roberts, had done this to his country. He had poured gasoline upon a smoldering constitutional crisis.

Think of the potential implications if Obama were an ineligible president. Every action he took would be unconstitutional. Obama's two Supreme Court nominees—Sotomayor and Kagan—would be invalid. *Every* bill that passed Congress during the four years of Obama's term would now be invalid, since no valid president signed them. The overwhelming possibility would strike terror deep inside of Roberts.

Roberts would have been chewing on his mistake deep down ever since. His conscience would have been chewing on him. Secretly Roberts was consumed by guilt which caused him to continue telling us what a bad judge he was. Now we see why.

Thomas Sowell well describes such deep-seated guilt in Roberts for his deficient Obamacare decision but the same phenomenon applies 20 times more to his poor inauguration judgment: "Chief Justice John Roberts need fear [losing his job]...because he has lifetime tenure on the Supreme Court. *But conscience can be a more implacable and inescapable punisher—and should be.*"

To underscore Roberts' guilt over Obamacare alone Sowell commented once more, "What he [Roberts] did was betray his oath to be faithful to the Constitution of the United States." And Roberts knew that he had betrayed "We the people" in a far greater way.

To appreciate the full extent of Roberts' growing internal pressure, however, we must look back at what took place between the inauguration and the Obamacare hearing. Ever since Obama's January 20, 2009 inauguration, his birth certificate came increasingly under suspicion. In April 2011 Obama suddenly produced an alleged birth certificate—pressured by business magnate Donald Trump and Jerome Corsi's bestseller *Where's the Birth Certificate?* followed by Sheriff Joe Arpaio's fearless investigation confirming Obama's ineligibility. And Roberts knew that, after skilled document analysts proclaimed the birth certificate phony, Lou Dobbs stood up to his media colleagues both at CNN (formerly) and Fox News and bravely issued a reasonable call to examine the purported birth certificate. And Roberts would have known about polls showing more than half of all American citizens do not believe Obama is a legal president. He likely scoffed at all this, but Roberts' his super intelligence didn't.

What could Roberts have done back on Inauguration Day? The matter was never adjudicated by the Supreme Court, since lower courts had repeatedly thrown out eligibility suits, usually on technicalities or flimsy reasoning. Today a few lawsuits remain 'alive,' but are very slow to advance up the line. Roberts' only option on that day was to refuse to administer the oath, and if challenged to "do his job," to retire with honor. Imagine what would have happened then! For once, America would have been challenged to consult the Rule Book, and the Constitution may have prevailed—though probably not, given the weaknesses of all the parties in the drama. But John Roberts could have scored an immeasurable moral and legal victory nonetheless.

But who would have the nerve to do that when nobody else would? His reputation would be up in smoke. He would be labeled a "kook"—ridiculed by the press and the liberal establishment, including 99% of the law school professors in America.

So Roberts passed the time from inauguration until Obamacare came to a head. Now we can understand his bizarre decision. Unconsciously Roberts was screaming at himself over what he had done.

Roberts' 1st Denial Secretly Linked to Obama Inauguration

We know that the human psyche tends to employ an escape mechanism I call "pleading down," to confess to a more minor violation when in fact that confession covers a more heinous act. We see that Roberts' confession about his poor performance as Chief Justice in the Obamacare decision really covered and reflected secretly his far worse performance in Obama's illegal swearing-in.

Take his initial denial in the Obamacare ruling as a deeper confession. In his words, "We do not consider whether the Act embodies sound policies. That judgment is entrusted to the Nation's elected leaders." Regarding Obama's inauguration as an illegal president, Roberts confessed that he had not demonstrated sound judgment and had failed to live up to the judicial responsibility entrusted to him to properly assess our nation's elected leaders.

And Roberts points to Congress who neglected their duty in not verifying Obama was an authentic candidate and fully met constitutional criteria.

Roberts' 2nd Denial Secretly Linked to Obama Inauguration

In his second key denial he stated, "We possess neither the expertise nor the prerogative to make policy judgments." Reading through that denial, we see that his super intelligence makes plain that he had failed to utilize judicial expertise to assess the legality of Obama's presidency in 2009. He had not exercised his prerogative as judge to uphold the Constitution. Instead he made a "policy judgment"—bowed to the liberals' political will without any judicial will involved in the historic moment.

We can deny it (as he does) but reality is reality. There are always consequences and we are looking directly at Roberts' self-imposed consequences for backing off three and a half years earlier. He shames himself before us as a judge and rains self-punishment down upon his head by making a truly horrible decision on Obamacare, his behavior illegally favoring *once more* the illegal president.

Roberts' 3rd Denial Secretly Linked to Obama Inauguration

We ask only whether Congress has the power under the Constitution to enact the *challenged* provisions ... Because the Constitution permits such a tax, it is not our role to forbid it, or to pass upon its wisdom or fairness.

First Roberts even more strongly suggests his unconscious message to Congress, "We ask only whether Congress has the power under the Constitution to enact the challenge," implying a challenge to Obama's legal rights to the presidency. This barely disguised blatant message makes the case that Congress still reserves that right to repeal Obamacare at any point in time—even after Obama leaves office. Justice Roberts' unconscious message strikingly ties this part of his Obamacare commentary to the real issue of the inauguration. Naturally, he continues reminding us that deep down he rightly feels that Congress never should have left the matter up to him. His secret story keeps unfolding with key images.

As he continues unconsciously responding to his inauguration decision, he now asks himself whether he had the power under the Constitution to challenge Obama's presidency. Again his super intelligence surprises us with a new idea. If he had had the courage, Roberts would've looked the American public in the eye with the Constitution in hand and declared that Obama must be vetted as a legal candidate. But of course Roberts would have risked his life and reputation—and experienced tremendous ridicule. (He implies once more Congress could have done the same thing and still should—and of course stand up to the ridicule.)

Roberts tell us, "The Constitution permits such a tax, it is not our role to forbid it, or to pass upon its wisdom or fairness." Apply these words to his failure to question the flimsy documentation of Obama's eligibility. Read his words this way: "The political climate has permitted America to be burdened with an illegal president as heavy as a huge new tax, and indeed Obama taxes America's strength—and I permitted it. I have renounced my role to keep him from so burdening America, took a pass on my wisdom to stand up to such a president and abandoned my role to declare the complete unfairness of such an act to America. I have effectively resigned as the nation's Supreme Court Chief Justice."

In summary Roberts' Obamacare decision secretly spoke volumes about his inauguration decision: "I didn't use my expertise, I retreated from standing up for the Constitution, I failed to judge, I was a bad judge and failed America." Deep down Roberts was ruled by unimaginable guilt—doubt it not.

We still have one more comment from the Chief Justice's ruling which points to Roberts' inauguration decision as *the* most relevant underlying issue. It is apparent which of the two issues was the most crucial to America. The ongoing constitutional crisis caused by an illegal president clearly takes precedence over the ill-advised approval of an unconstitutional law being approved. Obamacare pales in comparison to the eligibility question, since all of the man Barack Hussein Obama's actions would never have been 'presidential.'

It's Payback Time

At his inauguration, Obama had left Roberts in an untenable position, unable and unwilling to speak up; likewise in June 2012 the Chief Justice returned the favor. In the positive aspects of his ruling, Roberts had ruled out the commerce clause as a constitutional basis for the tyrannical 'individual mandate,' and at the same bizarrely ruled Obamacare a tax.

For reelection purposes, the last thing Obama really wanted was to have his bill declared a tax. Roberts had also minimized the fighting spirit of Obama supporters by giving them the win that they wanted by allowing Obamacare. They now had no protest to organize and fire up their base of voters. At the same time he energized conservatives into a galvanized opposition movement for the 2012 election. Within four hours Mitt Romney had raised millions of dollars from people who said, "OK, we'll throw all the rule-breakers out in the next election."

Notice how Roberts secretly urged this in his Obamacare position, "...policy judgments...Those decisions are entrusted to our nation's elected leaders, *who can be thrown out of office if the people disagree with them.*" Here is *the most specific major clue* to Robert's secret confession in June 2012 which strikingly points back to his inauguration failure: he should have "thrown Obama the president-elect out of office" unless he produced an undeniable, fully validated, original paper U.S. birth certificate. Roberts adds that a citizen should take such action against a leader "if the people disagree with them," powerfully suggesting he did not believe that Obama could produce one and had violated the trust the people had shown in him.

Roberts couldn't express his own anger at Obama for placing him in such a bind as Chief Justice. Just like Obama, who hid his anger but purged it indirectly, here we have the passive-aggressive Chief Justice going 15 rounds with the passive-aggressive pretender president.

Exquisite Interaction

We have repeatedly seen that we are all infinitesimally complex creatures, but in the end we Americans are to be people of the law and of the moral code that unites us.

Step back and review the evidence. We have Roberts' illogical Obamacare decision which points to a deeper motive outside his conscious awareness—culminating in respected colleagues calling for his resignation. His repeated denials fit hand-in-glove with his underlying guilt and need for self-punishment. In condoning Obamacare, John Roberts was doing penance for his failure on January 20, 2009. *His confession takes us back three-and-a-half years to his prominent slip at the Obama inauguration, which brings the unconscious mind front and center.* It points to the longstanding secret interplay between the two men. All of this takes into account the ongoing existence of the super intelligence and how it reveals the deepest narrative.

In a nutshell, we find a powerful unconscious motive which explains Roberts' bizarre judicial change of mind at the last second, according to reports—and why he was immune to persuasive pleading arguments by his most trusted colleagues. He heard their arguments in his conscious mind, but his unconscious mind was speaking more loudly.

Roberts' Blind Spot: 'Constitutional Phobia'

Roberts reveals he was caught up in an ongoing cycle of "no law, no guilt" especially as it pertains to dealing with Obama. As Roberts' guilt mounts, he must deny it and continue outside the boundaries of the law. Roberts first failed to stand up for the Constitution at Obama's inauguration, which I will call a brief *constitutional phobia*—he avoided it. This constitutional violation prompted deep overwhelming guilt which of course he couldn't face either, exactly like he couldn't face his lack of courage for the judicial task three years later.

Now ruling on Obamacare he must once more find some way around the Constitution—to rationalize away its power over him, to judge him and hold him accountable. He must find some way that document also doesn't hold his partner in crime, Obama, accountable either. With Roberts' bizarre unconstitutional Obamacare decision, once more they are both free of guilt—temporarily, on the surface. Yet Roberts' reveals the typical law-breakers' pattern: More guilt, more reason to run from the law, more violations, more guilt, and the cycle repeats. Obama and other leaders who continually stretch the Constitution to suit their ends are caught in the identical cycle.

This pattern controls far too many leaders (and, sadly, ordinary citizens) today; they continue turning the rock-solid Constitution into a living, mushy, powerless, feel-good document. As a result, they are secretly ruled by fear and guilt.

In a final note along those lines, we understand Roberts' changing his mind regarding his Obamacare decision in an even deeper way. First, it was a confession that he changed his normal legal mind to stand up for the Constitution *at Obama's inauguration*—again secret guilt. Secondly, deep down he was ruled by fear---he could not bring himself to end a presidency. The great taboo—bringing down America's symbolic father. Whether the president-elect was legal or not, whether he was an African-American or not, had nothing to do with it on the deepest level of the psyche.

Understanding Motivation: Our Crucial Need

Understanding motivation is crucial—what we do not understand we are destined to repeat. Grasping the power of unconscious motivation reveals the devastation in its path, and brings psychology into the 21st century to help us tame such emotional hurricanes. Anything less means we will remain victims of buried fear, guilt and rage—the unholy trinity of buried emotions.

Roberts and Obama both teach us that failure to understand our deeper motivations can wreak havoc. Burying our heads in the sands of using only our conscious mind means powerful unknown forces will continue to have their way. Both of them rationalized their attacks on the Constitution. It's altogether too bad if we fail to utilize the super intelligence—one of the greatest scientific breakthroughs in history.

If America is the victim of poor decision making by a leader due to a lack of knowledge and acting on the wrong reason, and new knowledge and superior reasoning becomes available for vastly improved decision making—how foolish would leaders be not to acquire such knowledge? How foolish would citizens be not to push their leaders to acquire such knowledge—especially when history teaches us that successful nations fall because of leaders who make bad decisions?

This is precisely the case where America finds itself today, both with the leader of the executive branch, Barack Obama, and the leader of the judicial branch, John Roberts.

Wherever the cutting-edge of knowledge is, that will be the future—eventually. With the uncovering of the superior intelligence we can continue to run and hide from it and postpone the future advantages of such brilliance or we can take a giant step into the future by embracing it. The choice is ours; the future is there for the taking.

Does America Want to Win? Will *We* Play by the Rules?

The deeper interaction between Obama and Roberts reminds me of what the basketball great Bill Russell once said about his epic battles with Wilt Chamberlain back in the day when they battled for the NBA title in the 1950s and '60s. As Russell put it in his biography, nobody knew Chamberlain like he did because of their battles in the paint, that area of the court down close to the goal where players triumph as much with muscle as technique. He contended that in this man-to-man struggle he could sense something deep in Chamberlain, a massive athletic physical specimen—physically much stronger than the agile, more-determined Russell (who, in my opinion, remains the greatest pure winner the NBA has ever seen). Over time, Bill Russell emerged as the decisive winner when the two met in competition because he observed a weakness in Chamberlain. Russell sensed that deep down Wilt really didn't want to win—and Russell took advantage of this mismatch of willpower.

By analogy, John Roberts detected the same weakness in Obama—that he really doesn't want to win. If you don't play by the rules, deep inside you're a loser. And when it came time for the Chief Justice to play by the rules in this crucial situation he underscored how he was a loser, too. That's the real story from John Roberts, the formerly acclaimed judge, a man who proved that he is merely a man, and became just another activist lawyer on two momentous occasions because of his lack of courage Unfortunately, Roberts missed his chance to lead in the noblest sense, and in his blind spot lost sight of the Constitution.

Tragically John Roberts gave in to weakness and, like Wilt Chamberlin, he didn't even recognize the flaw. But America did and his colleagues did—and the Constitution does. When it came time for a real leader to stand up for America—when nobody else would—he just gave in with a wink and a nod and a photo-op grin.

The same lesson applies to America—if we don't play by the rules, laid down for us by the Founders, then we too are losers. Does America really want to win today in the grand experiment in nationhood that began in 1776?

Or will we just go along, shuffling in line with the Progressives who want to gut America by ignoring our nation's foundational documents?

'We the People' for example must decide to play by the rules by insisting that *only constitutionally qualified candidates* be allowed to run for president.

Think about it: if John Roberts had listened to his super intelligence way back in January 2009, he could have won and refused to swear in a man whom he believed was constitutionally unqualified to be elected president; today there would not have been two illegally-appointed Supreme Court justices to make up a 5-4 majority. Indeed, there would have been no Obamacare to have to strike down. Roberts so badly fumbled the words of the swearing-in ceremony because his super-intel was warring with his conscious mind regarding his reservations about Obama's lack of citizenship. If only Roberts had done the right thing at the outset, America wouldn't have been saddled with the constitutional crisis the nation faces today.

Still, we can take hope in the four Justices—Clarence Thomas, Anthony Kennedy, Samuel Alito and Antonin Scalia—who tried to hold the line for the Constitution in its important role of limiting the power of an intrusive federal government.[3] Sowell echoed this thought when he wrote about Roberts' decision in his Fourth-of-July column, "Chief Justice Betrays America,"

> But what does the Bill of Rights seek to protect the ordinary citizen from? The government! To defer to those who expand government power beyond its constitutional limits is to betray those whose freedom depends on the Bill of Rights.

America must battle on—and the battle lines have been drawn. Can we rise above it all and win again? Today, it seems, we are learning just how hard it was for our forefathers to throw off the tyranny of King George III.

Perhaps we will overcome the misplaced compassion and head-in-the-sand constitutional avoidance that elected an illegal president, and discover a greater compassion for each other and ourselves, and a greater joy.

Above all, we must make sure we are living beneath the wings of the protection provided by the deepest values of human nature, those given us by the Founders and "the laws of Nature, and of Nature's God." We must shelter under the wings of The American Eagle, which hovers over our Constitution and our land.

---

3 The Constitution clearly specifies in the 10th Amendment that all powers not clearly delegated to the federal government are reserved to the states and to the people.

Appendices A - E

Appendix A: The Super Intelligence

Robert J. Langs was the psychiatrist who first established in 1971 that our unconscious possesses a superior intelligence which functions far beyond anything we had previously believed. He was the genius who discovered the super intelligence in the practical, hands-on setting of therapy. Here he learned that his patients—using disguised unconscious communications—were secretly trying to guide him to new understandings of themselves. Deep down, his patients knew exactly what they needed to face to begin healing their wounds, and they dramatically improved when Dr. Langs listened and indicated he heard that guidance.

Langs is a psychoanalyst by training, based in New York City, who has now authored more than 40 books. He was the first clinician to *fully* tap into unconscious communication—the first man to truly understand how a patient's unconscious (or subconscious) mind structured its messages in patterns designed to reveal what it alone perceived, to thereby guide the therapist in his efforts to help.

As Dr. Langs' research unfolded, all the other clinical researchers working with him (including myself) were amazed and astounded by the remarkable abilities of the unconscious or what I call the super intelligence.

First he learned that the unconscious mind observes what's going on at a much deeper level, reading situations instantaneously-- which he termed "unconscious perception." This was identical to what Malcolm Gladwell years later in his book *Blink* called "quick-reading." Langs appreciated that the unconscious also accurately communicates its secret observations between the lines in its own unique language which he termed "unconscious communication." I refer to the same phenomenon as the super intelligence "quick-speaking."

Repeatedly, this brilliant subconscious mind demonstrated it was extremely honest, always insisting on the truth. The breakthrough research in which I participated has shown that the subconscious mind is truly a super intelligence far superior to the conscious mind. The unconscious is commonly known as "the other ninety percent" of our minds, and research reveals it more than lives up to the metaphor.

Obviously, then, the key to unlocking a whole new world of knowledge— the super intelligence-- lies in understanding how the subconscious mind communicates. Basically, Langs' research has demonstrated that the unconscious mind tells stories (and uses images) which are filled with disguised symbolic messages—the identical language of dreams. In a nutshell, the unconscious mind speaks in symbolic code. Therefore, a therapist's basic job is to read code, to decode otherwise "hidden" messages from the most fantastic computer imaginable, the human mind. (I applied the same process to forensic profiling.)

To put it another way, the unconscious mind communicates *symbolically* while the conscious mind communicates *literally*. The familiar idea that left-brain communication is literal ("just the facts") and right-brain communication is symbolic (think "images") will also help clarify the difference in conscious and unconscious communication. In my model, by analogy the conscious mind speaks "left brain" and the unconscious mind speaks "right brain," which further helps to explain how both can speak *simultaneously*.

Therapy Examples

A quick example from therapy demonstrates how the subconscious communicates. A patient announces he's ready to stop therapy, but his unconscious mind then guides him to "casually" tell several stories featuring unfinished business. To cite just two examples, he mentions that his daughter needs to continue her college education even though she wants to drop out. Then he talks about the addition onto his house, which he's been working on for months but hasn't yet finished.

What he's really saying in these two examples—and what he might even repeat in other stories, over and over again—is that he knows unconsciously that he needs to continue therapy, no matter how much his conscious mind wants him to stop. A therapist keyed into the unconscious can read the repetitive "unfinished business" code to help the person see what he has picked up on—guiding him to stay in therapy.

In such a secret "repeat-the-matching-story" pattern, the unconscious super intelligence can communicate virtually any message it wants to, in code. First, it quick-reads situations and then it "quick speaks" revealing its brilliant observations.

Let's take another common situation in therapy to again demonstrate the ability of the subconscious mind to guide. A person in therapy requests to change her regular appointment time, consciously a seemingly minor event. Invariably such a patient communicates unconsciously again through matching stories advising the exact opposite. She presents stories of people who lost their place and were destabilized: "my neighbor disrupts her kids by moving them from school to school," "my boss constantly changes the time of our team meetings which makes us inefficient," and "my favorite airline no longer assigns seats which creates chaos for me." Secretly her super intelligence reads her deeper needs realizing regular appointment times stabilize her. Between the lines she tells her therapist, "Don't let me move my appointment time--keep the stability." She underscores one of the key unconscious benefits of therapy—that people never outgrew their need for stability. Here we have an example of "keep the stability" code which the super intelligence spelled out in its infinite wisdom—once more revealing its astounding ability to comment on any important matter in a disguised story code.

(In more recent years Dr. Langs has revealed new techniques demonstrating

314

how to access the super intelligence immediately at will. Once again other clinical researchers confirmed this newer method.)

For further information see my website http://deeperintelligence.com

Profiling Method: Thoughtprint Decoding

In many ways the forensic profiling approach I developed is an identical process to what occurs in therapy. Largely, I have adapted the language for forensic purposes. However, there are unique features in forensic documents which allow for the super intelligence to communicate in remarkably creative ways: spacing, punctuation, cross-outs, vertical messages, lettering and a host of other ways.

In forensic work I have called the unconscious symbolic story-messages "thoughtprints," all of which tell the same story in different ways, further allowing the subconscious or super intelligence to present important details. A thoughtprint, then, is a *symbolic* idea as opposed to a *literal* idea.

Forensic documents which I examine in profiling in a nutshell tell secret stories. In that setting a person's unconscious mind strings together a number of secretly matching symbolic thoughts or "thoughtprints" to tell a consistent story. This was the basic approach I utilized to discover Barack Obama's thoughtprints and secret story.

For further information see my website http://forensicthoughtprints.com

Appendix B: Father's Day Speech, June 2008

Good morning. It's good to be home on this Father's Day with my girls, and it's an honor to spend some time with all of you today in the house of our Lord.

At the end of the Sermon on the Mount, Jesus closes by saying, "Whoever hears these words of mine, and does them, shall be likened to a wise man who built his house upon a rock: the rain descended, and the floods came, and the winds blew, and beat upon that house, and it fell not, for it was founded upon a rock." [Matthew 7: 24-25]

Here at Apostolic, you are blessed to worship in a house that has been founded on the rock of Jesus Christ, our Lord and Savior. But it is also built on another rock, another foundation – and that rock is Bishop Arthur Brazier. In forty-eight years, he has built this congregation from just a few hundred to more than 20,000 strong – a congregation that, because of his leadership, has braved the fierce winds and heavy rains of violence and poverty; joblessness and hopelessness. Because of his work and his ministry, there are more graduates and fewer gang members in the neighborhoods surrounding this church. There are more homes and fewer homeless. There is more community and less chaos because Bishop Brazier continued the march for justice that he began by Dr. King's side all those years ago. He is the reason this house has stood tall for half a century. And on this Father's Day, it must make him proud to know that the man now charged with keeping its foundation strong is his son and your new pastor, Reverend Byron Brazier.

Of all the rocks upon which we build our lives, we are reminded today that family is the most important. And we are called to recognize and honor how critical every father is to that foundation. They are teachers and coaches. They are mentors and role models. They are examples of success and the men who constantly push us toward it.

But if we are honest with ourselves, we'll admit that what too many fathers also are is missing – missing from too many lives and too many homes. They have abandoned their responsibilities, acting like boys instead of men. And the foundations of our families are weaker because of it.

You and I know how true this is in the African-American community. We know that more than half of all black children live in single-parent households, a number that has doubled – doubled – since we were children. We know the statistics – that children who grow up without a father are five times more likely to live in poverty and commit crime; nine times more likely to drop out of schools and twenty times more likely to end up in prison. They are more likely to have behavioral problems, or run away from home, or become teenage parents themselves. And the foundations of our community are weaker because of it.

How many times in the last year has this city lost a child at the hands of another child? How many times have our hearts stopped in the middle of the night with the sound of a gunshot or a siren? How many teenagers have we seen hanging around on street corners when they should be sitting in a classroom? How many are sitting in prison when they should be working, or at least looking for a job? How many in this generation are we willing to lose to poverty or violence or addiction? How many?

Yes, we need more cops on the street. Yes, we need fewer guns in the hands of people who shouldn't have them. Yes, we need more money for our schools, and more outstanding teachers in the classroom, and more after-school programs for our children. Yes, we need more jobs and more job training and more opportunity in our communities.

But we also need families to raise our children. We need fathers to realize that responsibility does not end at conception. We need them to realize that what makes you a man is not the ability to have a child – it's the courage to raise one.

We need to help all the mothers out there who are raising these kids by themselves; the mothers who drop them off at school, go to work, pick up them up in the afternoon, work another shift, get dinner, make lunches, pay the bills, fix the house, and all the other things it takes both parents to do. So many of these women are doing a heroic job, but they need support. They need another parent. Their children need another parent. That's what keeps their foundation strong. It's what keeps the foundation of our country strong.

I know what it means to have an absent father, although my circumstances weren't as tough as they are for many young people today. Even though my father left us when I was two years old, and I only knew him from the letters he wrote and the stories that my family told, I was luckier than most. I grew up in Hawaii, and had two wonderful grandparents from Kansas who poured everything they had into helping my mother raise my sister and me – who worked with her to teach us about love and respect and the obligations we have to one another. I screwed up more often than I should've, but I got plenty of second chances. And even though we didn't have a lot of money, scholarships gave me the opportunity to go to some of the best schools in the country. A lot of kids don't get these chances today. There is no margin for error in their lives. So my own story is different in that way.

Still, I know the toll that being a single parent took on my mother – how she struggled at times to the pay bills; to give us the things that other kids had; to play all the roles that both parents are supposed to play. And I know the toll it took on me. So I resolved many years ago that it was my obligation to break the cycle – that if I could be anything in life, I would be a good father to my girls; that if I could give them anything, I would give them that rock – that foundation – on which to build their lives. And that would be the greatest gift I could offer.

I say this knowing that I have been an imperfect father – knowing that I have made mistakes and will continue to make more; wishing that I could be home for my girls and my wife more than I am right now. I say this knowing all of these things because even as we are imperfect, even as we face difficult circumstances, there are still certain lessons we must strive to live and learn as fathers – whether we are black or white; rich or poor; from the South Side or the wealthiest suburb.

The first is setting an example of excellence for our children – because if we want to set high expectations for them, we've got to set high expectations for ourselves. It's great if you have a job; it's even better if you have a college degree. It's a wonderful thing if you are married and living in a home with your children, but don't just sit in the house and watch "SportsCenter" all weekend long. That's why so many children are growing up in front of the television. As fathers and parents, we've got to spend more time with them, and help them with their homework, and replace the video game or the remote control with a book once in awhile. That's how we build that foundation.

We know that education is everything to our children's future. We know that they will no longer just compete for good jobs with children from Indiana, but children from India and China and all over the world. We know the work and the studying and the level of education that requires.

You know, sometimes I'll go to an eighth-grade graduation and there's all that pomp and circumstance and gowns and flowers. And I think to myself, it's just eighth grade. To really compete, they need to graduate high school, and then they need to graduate college, and they probably need a graduate degree too. An eighth-grade education doesn't cut it today. Let's give them a handshake and tell them to get their butts back in the library!

It's up to us – as fathers and parents – to instill this ethic of excellence in our children. It's up to us to say to our daughters, don't ever let images on TV tell you what you are worth, because I expect you to dream without limit and reach for those goals. It's up to us to tell our sons, those songs on the radio may glorify violence, but in my house we live glory to achievement, self-respect, and hard work. It's up to us to set these high expectations. And that means meeting those expectations ourselves. That means setting examples of excellence in our own lives.

The second thing we need to do as fathers is pass along the value of empathy to our children. Not sympathy, but empathy – the ability to stand in somebody else's shoes; to look at the world through their eyes. Sometimes it's so easy to get caught up in "us," that we forget about our obligations to one another. There's a culture in our society that says remembering these obligations is somehow soft – that we can't show weakness, and so therefore we can't show kindness.

But our young boys and girls see that. They see when you are ignoring or mistreating your wife. They see when you are inconsiderate at home; or when you are distant; or when you are thinking only of yourself. And so it's no surprise when we see that behavior in our schools or on our streets. That's why we pass on the values of empathy and kindness to our children by living them. We need to show our kids that you're not strong by putting other people down – you're strong by lifting them up. That's our responsibility as fathers.

And by the way – it's a responsibility that also extends to Washington. Because if fathers are doing their part; if they're taking our responsibilities seriously to be there for their children, and set high expectations for them, and instill in them a sense of excellence and empathy, then our government should meet them halfway.

We should be making it easier for fathers who make responsible choices and harder for those who avoid them. We should get rid of the financial penalties we impose on married couples right now, and start making sure that every dime of child support goes directly to helping children instead of some bureaucrat. We should reward fathers who pay that child support with job training and job opportunities and a larger Earned Income Tax Credit that can help them pay the bills. We should expand programs where registered nurses visit expectant and new mothers and help them learn how to care for themselves before the baby is born and what to do after – programs that have helped increase father involvement, women's employment, and children's readiness for school. We should help these new families care for their children by expanding maternity and paternity leave, and we should guarantee every worker more paid sick leave so they can stay home to take care of their child without losing their income.

We should take all of these steps to build a strong foundation for our children. But we should also know that even if we do; even if we meet our obligations as fathers and parents; even if Washington does its part too, we will still face difficult challenges in our lives. There will still be days of struggle and heartache. The rains will still come and the winds will still blow.

And that is why the final lesson we must learn as fathers is also the greatest gift we can pass on to our children – and that is the gift of hope.

I'm not talking about an idle hope that's little more than blind optimism or willful ignorance of the problems we face. I'm talking about hope as that spirit inside us that insists, despite all evidence to the contrary, that something better is waiting for us if we're willing to work for it and fight for it. If we are willing to believe.

I was answering questions at a town hall meeting in Wisconsin the other day and a young man raised his hand, and I figured he'd ask about college tuition or energy or maybe the war in Iraq. But instead he looked at me very seriously and he asked, "What does life mean to you?"

Now, I have to admit that I wasn't quite prepared for that one. I think I stammered for a little bit, but then I stopped and gave it some thought, and I said this:

When I was a young man, I thought life was all about me – how do I make my way in the world, and how do I become successful and how do I get the things that I want.

But now, my life revolves around my two little girls. And what I think about is what kind of world I'm leaving them. Are they living in a county where there's a huge gap between a few who are wealthy and a whole bunch of people who are struggling every day? Are they living in a county that is still divided by race? A country where, because they're girls, they don't have as much opportunity as boys do? Are they living in a country where we are hated around the world because we don't cooperate effectively with other nations? Are they living a world that is in grave danger because of what we've done to its climate?

And what I've realized is that life doesn't count for much unless you're willing to do your small part to leave our children – all of our children – a better world. Even if it's difficult. Even if the work seems great. Even if we don't get very far in our lifetime.

That is our ultimate responsibility as fathers and parents. We try. We hope. We do what we can to build our house upon the sturdiest rock. And when the winds come, and the rains fall, and they beat upon that house, we keep faith that our Father will be there to guide us, and watch over us, and protect us, and lead His children through the darkest of storms into light of a better day. That is my prayer for all of us on this Father's Day, and that is my hope for this country in the years ahead. May God Bless you and your children. Thank you.[304]

---

[304]"Transcript, Obama's Father's Day Remarks," http://www.nytimes.com/2008/06/15/us/politics/15text-obama.html?pagewanted=all accessed April 23, 2012.

Appendix C: Letter from Obama to His Children on the Eve of His Inauguration.

During the months between his election in November 2008 and his inauguration in January 2009, Parade *magazine asked the President "to get personal and tell us what you want for your children." His letter was published on Jan. 18, 2009, two days before his swearing-in.*

Dear Malia and Sasha,

I know that you've both had a lot of fun these last two years on the campaign trail, going to picnics and parades and state fairs, eating all sorts of junk food your mother and I probably shouldn't have let you have. But I also know that it hasn't always been easy for you and Mom, and that as excited as you both are about that new puppy, it doesn't make up for all the time we've been apart. I know how much I've missed these past two years, and today I want to tell you a little more about why I decided to take our family on this journey.

When I was a young man, I thought life was all about me—about how I'd make my way in the world, become successful, and get the things I want. But then the two of you came into my world with all your curiosity and mischief and those smiles that never fail to fill my heart and light up my day. And suddenly, all my big plans for myself didn't seem so important anymore. I soon found that the greatest joy in my life was the joy I saw in yours. And I realized that my own life wouldn't count for much unless I was able to ensure that you had every opportunity for happiness and fulfillment in yours. In the end, girls, that's why I ran for President: because of what I want for you and for every child in this nation.

I want all our children to go to schools worthy of their potential—schools that challenge them, inspire them, and instill in them a sense of wonder about the world around them. I want them to have the chance to go to college—even if their parents aren't rich. And I want them to get good jobs: jobs that pay well and give them benefits like health care, jobs that let them spend time with their own kids and retire with dignity.

I want us to push the boundaries of discovery so that you'll live to see new technologies and inventions that improve our lives and make our planet cleaner and safer. And I want us to push our own human boundaries to reach beyond the divides of race and region, gender and religion that keep us from seeing the best in each other.

Sometimes we have to send our young men and women into war and other dangerous situations to protect our country—but when we do, I want to make sure that it is only for a very good reason, that we try our best to settle our differences with others peacefully, and that we do everything possible to keep our servicemen and women safe. And I want every child to understand that the blessings these brave Americans fight for are not free—that with the great privilege of being a citizen of this nation comes great responsibility.

That was the lesson your grandmother tried to teach me when I was your age, reading me the opening lines of the Declaration of Independence and telling me about the men and women who marched for equality because they believed those words put to paper two centuries ago should mean something.

She helped me understand that America is great not because it is perfect but because it can always be made better—and that the unfinished work of perfecting our union falls to each of us. It's a charge we pass on to our children, coming closer with each new generation to what we know America should be.

I hope both of you will take up that work, righting the wrongs that you see and working to give others the chances you've had. Not just because you have an obligation to give something back to this country that has given our family so much—although you do have that obligation. But because you have an obligation to yourself. Because it is only when you hitch your wagon to something larger than yourself that you will realize your true potential.

These are the things I want for you—to grow up in a world with no limits on your dreams and no achievements beyond your reach, and to grow into compassionate, committed women who will help build that world. And I want every child to have the same chances to learn and dream and grow and thrive that you girls have. That's why I've taken our family on this great adventure.

I am so proud of both of you. I love you more than you can ever know. And I am grateful every day for your patience, poise, grace, and humor as we prepare to start our new life together in the White House.

--Love, Dad

Appendix D: Inauguration Speech of Barack Hussein Obama January 20, 2009

My fellow citizens: I stand here today humbled by the task before us, grateful for the trust you have bestowed, mindful of the sacrifices borne by our ancestors.

I thank President Bush for his service to our nation...as well as the generosity and cooperation he has shown throughout this transition.

Forty-four Americans have now taken the presidential oath.

The words have been spoken during rising tides of prosperity and the still waters of peace. Yet, every so often the oath is taken amidst gathering clouds and raging storms. At these moments, America has carried on not simply because of the skill or vision of those in high office, but because We the People have remained faithful to the ideals of our forebears, and true to our founding documents.

So it has been. So it must be with this generation of Americans.

That we are in the midst of crisis is now well understood. Our nation is at war against a far-reaching network of violence and hatred. Our economy is badly weakened, a consequence of greed and irresponsibility on the part of some but also our collective failure to make hard choices and prepare the nation for a new age.

Homes have been lost, jobs shed, businesses shuttered. Our health care is too costly, our schools fail too many, and each day brings further evidence that the ways we use energy strengthen our adversaries and threaten our planet.

These are the indicators of crisis, subject to data and statistics. Less measurable, but no less profound, is a sapping of confidence across our land; a nagging fear that America's decline is inevitable, that the next generation must lower its sights.

Today I say to you that the challenges we face are real, they are serious and they are many. They will not be met easily or in a short span of time. But know this America: They will be met.

On this day, we gather because we have chosen hope over fear, unity of purpose over conflict and discord.

On this day, we come to proclaim an end to the petty grievances and false promises, the recriminations and worn-out dogmas that for far too long have strangled our politics.

We remain a young nation, but in the words of Scripture, the time has come to set aside childish things. The time has come to reaffirm our enduring spirit; to choose our better history; to carry forward that precious gift, that noble idea, passed on from generation to generation: the God-given promise that all are equal, all are free, and all deserve a chance to pursue their full measure of happiness.

In reaffirming the greatness of our nation, we understand that greatness is never a given. It must be earned. Our journey has never been one of shortcuts or settling for less.

It has not been the path for the faint-hearted, for those who prefer leisure over work, or seek only the pleasures of riches and fame.

Rather, it has been the risk-takers, the doers, the makers of things – some celebrated, but more often men and women obscure in their labor – who have carried us up the long, rugged path towards prosperity and freedom.

For us, they packed up their few worldly possessions and traveled across oceans in search of a new life. For us, they toiled in sweatshops and settled the West, endured the lash of the whip and plowed the hard earth.

For us, they fought and died in places Concord and Gettysburg; Normandy and Khe Sanh.

Time and again these men and women struggled and sacrificed and worked till their hands were raw so that we might live a better life. They saw America as bigger than the sum of our individual ambitions; greater than all the differences of birth or wealth or faction.

This is the journey we continue today. We remain the most prosperous, powerful nation on Earth. Our workers are no less productive than when this crisis began. Our minds are no less inventive, our goods and services no less needed than they were last week or last month or last year. Our capacity remains undiminished. But our time of standing pat, of protecting narrow interests and putting off unpleasant decisions -- that time has surely passed.

Starting today, we must pick ourselves up, dust ourselves off, and begin again the work of remaking America. For everywhere we look, there is work to be done.

The state of our economy· calls for action: bold and swift. And we will act not only to create new jobs but to lay a new foundation for growth.

We will build the roads and bridges, the electric grids and digital lines that feed our commerce and bind us together.

We will restore science to its rightful place and wield technology's wonders to raise health care's quality...and lower its costs.

We will harness the sun and the winds and the soil to fuel our cars and run our factories. And we will transform our schools and colleges and universities to meet the demands of a new age.

All this we can do. All this we will do.

Now, there are some who question the scale of our ambitions, who suggest that our system cannot tolerate too many big plans. Their memories are short, for they have forgotten what this country has already done, what free men and women can achieve when imagination is joined to common purpose and necessity to courage.

What the cynics fail to understand is that the ground has shifted beneath them, that the stale political arguments that have consumed us for so long, no longer apply.

The question we ask today is not whether our government is too big or too small, but whether it works, whether it helps families find jobs at a decent wage, care they can afford, a retirement that is dignified.

Where the answer is yes, we intend to move forward. Where the answer is no, programs will end.

And those of us who manage the public's dollars will be held to account, to spend wisely, reform bad habits, and do our business in the light of day, because only then can we restore the vital trust between a people and their government.

Nor is the question before us whether the market is a force for good or ill. Its power to generate wealth and expand freedom is unmatched.

But this crisis has reminded us that without a watchful eye, the market can spin out of control. The nation cannot prosper long when it favors only the prosperous.

The success of our economy has always depended not just on the size of our gross domestic product, but on the reach of our prosperity; on the ability to extend opportunity to every willing heart -- not out of charity, but because it is the surest route to our common good.

As for our common defense, we reject as false the choice between our safety and our ideals.

Our founding fathers faced with perils that we can scarcely imagine, drafted a charter to assure the rule of law and the rights of man, a charter expanded by the blood of generations.

Those ideals still light the world, and we will not give them up for expedience's sake.

And so, to all other peoples and governments who are watching today, from the grandest capitals to the small village where my father was born: know that America is a friend of each nation and every man, woman and child who seeks a future of peace and dignity, and we are ready to lead once more.

Recall that earlier generations faced down Fascism and Communism not just with missiles and tanks, but with the sturdy alliances and enduring convictions.

They understood that our power alone cannot protect us, nor does it entitle us to do as we please. Instead, they knew that our power grows through its prudent use. Our security emanates from the justness of our cause; the force of our example; the tempering qualities of humility and restraint.

We are the keepers of this legacy, guided by these principles once more, we can meet those new threats that demand even greater effort, even greater cooperation and understanding between nations. We'll begin to responsibly leave Iraq to its people and forge a hard- earned peace in Afghanistan.

With old friends and former foes, we'll work tirelessly to lessen the nuclear threat and roll back the specter of a warming planet.

We will not apologize for our way of life nor will we waver in its defense.

And for those who seek to advance their aims by inducing terror and slaughtering innocents, we say to you now that, "Our spirit is stronger and cannot be broken. You cannot outlast us, and we will defeat you."

For we know that our patchwork heritage is a strength, not a weakness.

We are a nation of Christians and Muslims, Jews and Hindus, and nonbelievers. We are shaped by every language and culture, drawn from every end of this Earth.

And because we have tasted the bitter swill of civil war and segregation and emerged from that dark chapter stronger and more united, we cannot help but believe that the old hatreds shall someday pass; that the lines of tribe shall soon dissolve; that as the world grows smaller, our common humanity shall reveal itself; and that America must play its role in ushering in a new era of peace.

To the Muslim world, we seek a new way forward, based on mutual interest and mutual respect.

To those leaders around the globe who seek to sow conflict or blame their society's ills on the West, know that your people will judge you on what you can build, not what you destroy.

To those who cling to power through corruption and deceit and the silencing of dissent, know that you are on the wrong side of history, but that we will extend a hand if you are willing to unclench your fist.

To the people of poor nations, we pledge to work alongside you to make your farms flourish and let clean waters flow; to nourish starved bodies and feed hungry minds.

And to those nations like ours that enjoy relative plenty, we say we can no longer afford indifference to the suffering outside our borders, nor can we consume the world's resources without regard to effect. For the world has changed, and we must change with it.

As we consider the road that unfolds before us, we remember with humble gratitude those brave Americans who, at this very hour, patrol far-off deserts and distant mountains. They have something to tell us, just as the fallen heroes who lie in Arlington whisper through the ages.

We honor them not only because they are guardians of our liberty, but because they embody the spirit of service: a willingness to find meaning in something greater than themselves.

And yet, at this moment, a moment that will define a generation, it is precisely this spirit that must inhabit us all.

For as much as government can do and must do, it is ultimately the faith and determination of the American people upon which this nation relies.

It is the kindness to take in a stranger when the levees break; the selflessness of workers who would rather cut their hours than see a friend lose their job which sees us through our darkest hours.

It is the firefighter's courage to storm a stairway filled with smoke, but also a parent's willingness to nurture a child, that finally decides our fate.

Our challenges may be new, the instruments with which we meet them may be new, but those values upon which our success depends, honesty and hard work, courage and fair play, tolerance and curiosity, loyalty and patriotism -- these things are old.

These things are true. They have been the quiet force of progress throughout our history.

What is demanded then is a return to these truths. What is required of us now is a new era of responsibility -- a recognition, on the part of every American, that we have duties to ourselves, our nation and the world, duties that we do not grudgingly accept but rather seize gladly, firm in the knowledge that there is nothing so satisfying to the spirit, so defining of our character than giving our all to a difficult task.

This is the price and the promise of citizenship.

This is the source of our confidence: the knowledge that God calls on us to shape an uncertain destiny.

This is the meaning of our liberty and our creed, why men and women and children of every race and every faith can join in celebration across this magnificent mall. And why a man whose father less than 60 years ago might not have been served at a local restaurant can now stand before you to take a most sacred oath.

325

So let us mark this day in remembrance of who we are and how far we have traveled.

In the year of America's birth, in the coldest of months, a small band of patriots huddled by dying campfires on the shores of an icy river.

The capital was abandoned. The enemy was advancing. The snow was stained with blood.

At a moment when the outcome of our revolution was most in doubt, the father of our nation ordered these words be read to the people:

"Let it be told to the future world that in the depth of winter, when nothing but hope and virtue could survive, that the city and the country, alarmed at one common danger, came forth to meet it."

America, in the face of our common dangers, in this winter of our hardship, let us remember these timeless words; with hope and virtue, let us brave once more the icy currents, and endure what storms may come; let it be said by our children's children that when we were tested we refused to let this journey end, that we did not turn back nor did we falter; and with eyes fixed on the horizon and God's grace upon us, we carried forth that great gift of freedom and delivered it safely to future generations.

Thank you. God bless you.

And God bless the United States of America.

Appendix E: Letter from Obama to his Children on Father's Day 2009

This letter was also published in Parade *magazine on Sunday June 21, 2009. The Editors introduced the letter thusly: "On this Father's Day, we asked the President to reflect on what fatherhood means to him."*

Dear Malia and Sasha,

As the father of two young girls who have shown such poise, humor, and patience in the unconventional life into which they have been thrust, I mark this Father's Day—our first in the White House—with a deep sense of gratitude. One of the greatest benefits of being president is that I now live right above the office. I see my girls off to school nearly every morning and have dinner with them nearly every night. It is a welcome change after so many years out on the campaign trail and commuting between Chicago and Capitol Hill.

But I observe this Father's Day not just as a father grateful to be present in my daughters' lives but also as a son who grew up without a father in my own life. My father left my family when I was 2 years old, and I knew him mainly from the letters he wrote and the stories my family told. And while I was lucky to have two wonderful grandparents who poured everything they had into helping my mother raise my sister and me, I still felt the weight of his absence throughout my childhood.

As an adult, working as a community organizer and later as a legislator, I would often walk through the streets of Chicago's South Side and see boys marked by that same absence—boys without supervision or direction or anyone to help them as they struggled to grow into men. I identified with their frustration and disengagement—with their sense of having been let down.

In many ways, I came to understand the importance of fatherhood through its absence—both in my life and in the lives of others. I came to understand that the hole a man leaves when he abandons his responsibility to his children is one that no government can fill. We can do everything possible to provide good jobs and good schools and safe streets for our kids, but it will never be enough to fully make up the difference.

That is why we need fathers to step up, to realize that their job does not end at conception; that what makes you a man is not the ability to have a child but the courage to raise one.

As fathers, we need to be involved in our children's lives not just when it's convenient or easy, and not just when they're doing well—but when it's difficult and thankless, and they're struggling. That is when they need us most.

And it's not enough to just be physically present. Too often, especially during tough economic times like these, we are emotionally absent: distracted, consumed by what's happening in our own lives, worried about keeping our jobs and paying our bills, unsure if we'll be able to give our kids the same opportunities we had.

Our children can tell. They know when we're not fully there. And that disengagement sends a clear message—whether we mean it or not—about where among our priorities they fall.

So we need to step out of our own heads and tune in. We need to turn off the television and start talking with our kids, and listening to them, and understanding what's going on in their lives.

We need to set limits and expectations. We need to replace that video game with a book and make sure that homework gets done. We need to say to our daughters, Don't ever let images on TV tell you what you are worth, because I expect you to dream without limit and reach for your goals. We need to tell our sons, Those songs on the radio may glorify violence, but in our house, we find glory in achievement, self-respect, and hard work.

We need to realize that we are our children's first and best teachers. When we are selfish or inconsiderate, when we mistreat our wives or girlfriends, when we cut corners or fail to control our tempers, our children learn from that—and it's no surprise when we see those behaviors in our schools or on our streets.

But it also works the other way around. When we work hard, treat others with respect, spend within our means, and contribute to our communities, those are the lessons our children learn. And that is what so many fathers are doing every day—coaching soccer and Little League, going to those school assemblies and parent-teacher conferences, scrimping and saving and working that extra shift so their kids can go to college. They are fulfilling their most fundamental duty as fathers: to show their children, by example, the kind of people they want them to become.

It is rarely easy. There are plenty of days of struggle and heartache when, despite our best efforts, we fail to live up to our responsibilities. I know I have been an imperfect father. I know I have made mistakes. I have lost count of all the times, over the years, when the demands of work have taken me from the duties of fatherhood. There were many days out on the campaign trail when I felt like my family was a million miles away, and I knew I was missing moments of my daughters' lives that I'd never get back. It is a loss I will never fully accept.

But on this Father's Day, I think back to the day I drove Michelle and a newborn Malia home from the hospital nearly 11 years ago—crawling along, miles under the speed limit, feeling the weight of my daughter's future resting in my hands. I think about the pledge I made to her that day: that I would give her what I never had—that if I could be anything in life, I would be a good father. I knew that day that my own life wouldn't count for much unless she had every opportunity in hers. And I knew I had an obligation, as we all do, to help create those opportunities and leave a better world for her and all our children.

On this Father's Day, I am recommitting myself to that work, to those duties that all parents share: to build a foundation for our children's dreams, to give them the love and support they need to fulfill them, and to stick with them the whole way through, no matter what doubts we may feel or difficulties we may face. That is my prayer for all of us on this Father's Day, and that is my hope for this nation in the months and years ahead.

--Love, Dad

About the Author

ANDREW G. HODGES, M.D., is a board-certified psychiatrist in private practice. Previously he was an assistant clinical professor of psychiatry at the University of Alabama at Birmingham School of Medicine.

Dr. Hodges has helped pioneer a breakthrough to the brilliant unconscious mind, which he explained in his 1994 groundbreaking book *The Deeper Intelligence* (which he now calls the "super intelligence"). A noted forensic profiler, he developed his technique, "ThoughtPrint Decoding," by accessing the unconscious super intelligence of suspects during criminal investigations, basing his analysis on *verbatim* testimony, transcripts of police interviews, letters and emails created by the suspects.

He discovered a deeper moral compass which prompts people to always tell the truth—between the lines—in the special symbolic language of the subconscious. His work added a whole new dimension to the forensic science of psycholinguistics.

Law enforcement authorities nationwide, including the FBI, have consulted him. Criminal investigators and journalists have sought Dr. Hodges' expertise in cases ranging from the high-profile disappearance of Natalee Holloway in 2005 to the murder of JonBenet Ramsey in 1996. In the Ramsey case he applied his technique to the infamous ransom note—the smoking gun--then wrote two highly acclaimed books on the case, *A Mother Gone Bad* and *Who Will Speak for JonBenét?* (Village House, 1998 & 2000). Along with two forensic colleagues he submitted an 80 page report with 14 conclusions to Boulder authorities.

He also collaborated with the former Police Chief of the Wichita, KS Police Department in 2005, just weeks before the apprehension of the "BTK killer." Dr. Hodges was the only expert to accurately predict from his recent letters that "BTK" would kill again after 20 years of dormancy, as he later confessed.

In the Natalee Holloway case Hodges described the exact scenario to which Joran Van der Sloot confessed in conversations secretly taped months after Hodges' prediction. Dr. Hodges was consulted by Aruban authorities who read his profile—and by the FBI at Aruba's request. His book, *Into the Deep: The Hidden Confession of Natalee's Killer*, (Village House, 2007) told the whole story.

In 2011 Hodges revealed how Casey Anthony secretly confessed to killing her daughter in 200 letters written to a jail mate. Once again he showed how key hidden messages from a suspect go overlooked.

Dr. Hodges has written for a major FBI publication and presented his cutting-edge technique at a law enforcement conference at the FBI training facility in Quantico, Virginia. In addition to assisting criminal investigators, Dr. Hodges also applies his super-intelligence technique in the analysis of leaders who confess unconsciously when they are violating their deeper moral compass. For example, he examined Bill Clinton's self-sabotaging behavior and secret confession of his deeper motives in the Monica Lewinsky affair on Leeza Gibbons' nationally syndicated television show. Hodges believes that the discovery of the super intelligence holds great promise for unifying our nation and solving the cultural values battle, because deep down, everyone has an identical built-in sense of right and wrong.

Dr. Hodges reveals how important spiritual issues are in the unconscious. He utilized decoding techniques to explore the human personality of Jesus Christ in his book, *Jesus: An Interview Across Time—A Psychiatrist Looks at His Humanity* (Bantam, 1988). Religion columnist Mike McManus called it "the most important book I've read besides the Bible."

Village House Publishers

Made in the USA
Lexington, KY
08 November 2012